Modernism in
the Magazines

Modernism in the Magazines

An Introduction

ROBERT SCHOLES
CLIFFORD WULFMAN

Yale
UNIVERSITY PRESS
New Haven and London

To the librarians and archivists who preserved the
magazines we discuss in this book.

Yale University Press books may be purchased in quantity
for educational, business, or promotional use. For
information, please e-mail sales.press@yale.edu (U.S. office)
or sales@yaleup.co.uk (U.K. office).

Set in Minion type by The Composing Room of Michigan, Inc.
Printed in the United States of America.

Library of Congress Cataloging-in-Publication Data

Scholes, Robert.
Modernism in the magazines : an introduction / Robert Scholes
and Clifford Wulfman.
p.   cm.
Includes bibliographical references and index.
ISBN 978-0-300-14204-4 (cloth : alk. paper)   1. Little
magazines—Publishing—United States—History—20th
century.   2. Little magazines—Publishing—Great Britain—
History—20th century.   3. Modernism (Literature)—United
States.   4. Modernism (Literature)—Great Britain.
5. Pound, Ezra, 1885–1972—Knowledge—Periodicals.
I. Wulfman, Clifford.   II. Title.
PN4878.3.S36   2010
051—dc22
2009046314

A catalogue record for this book is available from the
British Library.

This paper meets the requirements of ANSI/NISO
Z39.48-1992 (Permanence of Paper).

10   9   8   7   6   5   4   3   2   1

Contents

Preface   *vii*

ONE   Ezra Pound, Founder of Modern Periodical Studies   1

TWO   Modernity and the Rise of Modernism: A Review   26

THREE   Rethinking Modernist Magazines:
From Genres to Database   44

FOUR   Modernism in the Magazines: The Case of Visual Art   73

FIVE   Modernism's Other: The Art of Advertising   118

SIX   How to Study a Modern Magazine   143

SEVEN   "On or About December 1910"   168

EIGHT   The Hole in the Archive and the
Study of Modernist Magazines   196

Appendix: Studies in Contemporary Mentality, Ezra Pound 223

Works Cited and Consulted 327

Index 331

Color plates follow page 148

Preface

We have called this book an "introduction" because we intend it to be just that. It is aimed mainly at two distinct but connected audiences: (1) scholars of modernism who may wish to use periodicals as a way of helping their students enter the world of modern culture and the print media that shaped it, and (2) students and young scholars who are beginning to find their way around the world of modernity and modernism and are looking for projects that will lead them deeper into that world. With this in mind, we have tried to provide (in Chapter 2) a summary of the background of modernist studies that seasoned scholars may not need for themselves but may find useful for their students. (And such scholars can always correct what they believe we have gotten wrong.) We have also tried to open up the way into modernist periodical studies by doing several things:

- situating as a pioneer in this field Ezra Pound, who both helped to create many elite modernist magazines and also provided a model of one way to study and criticize modern periodical culture;
- considering modernism as a response to the social and cultural conditions of modernity and to previous modes of art and literature;

- examining the contents of modernist magazines, including the roles of visual art and advertising in those magazines;
- studying the ways in which these magazines have been classified and categorized in the past, and proposing other methods of organizing information about these periodicals;
- offering methods and examples of how to read and study individual journals and groups of related magazines;
- examining the archival situation of modernist periodicals, including "the hole in the archive," and looking closely at the role of digital technology in preserving and studying those periodicals;
- including as an appendix Ezra Pound's pioneering series of articles on the magazines of 1917 and 1918.

As you will see, Ezra Pound is a thread that runs through all of these efforts. This did not happen because we loved him. The anti-Semitism and support for fascism he displayed from 1936 on have not endeared him to many people. But the Pound of the first three decades of the twentieth century was a different figure: a brilliant and indefatigable supporter of other writers and artists, a talented and learned poet, and a literary and cultural critic of enormous energy and biting wit. He shaped modernism in two ways. First, he arranged for the publication of work by other writers in magazines and books, and he helped visual artists publicize and sell their work. Time has confirmed most of his judgments about which writers and artists were doing work of lasting value. Second, through his critical writings in magazines and books he shaped the perception of modernism that came to be accepted by several generations of teachers and their students. Quite simply, he had more to do with our present understanding of modernism than any other individual. He was a pioneer of comparative literary studies, of cultural studies, and of periodical studies in the academic world, though he often professed to despise that world, which had rejected him. However one may rank his creative achievement as a poet, one must put him at the very top as an impresario and propagandist for the view of modernism that prevailed in the English-speaking world.

The other thing we want to say in this brief preface is that our exemplary and technical studies are not meant to be definitive. We are trying to open the way for others rather than close it down by covering all the bases and solving all the puzzles. There is much to be done, by scholars, teachers, and students of modernism, using the periodical resources that are only now becoming available to us through digital technology. This book is meant to be an invitation and a help in getting started: in short, an introduction.

We would like to thank the people who helped us in our work. Our MJP colleagues Mark Gaipa and Sean Latham read early versions and made useful suggestions, and two anonymous readers for Yale University Press did the same. We are especially grateful to the one who said that our fourth chapter was the weakest, which led to a total rewriting of that chapter. And we want to thank Stephen Ferguson, Curator of Rare Books at Princeton, who helped when help was needed, and Jennifer Kinnear, for permission from the Perth and Kinross Council to use an image of J. D. Fergusson's *Rhythm* in this book. We also thank Alison MacKeen and Dan Heaton of Yale University Press for editorial assistance.

Modernism in
the Magazines

Fig. 1.1. Drawing of Ezra Pound by Wyndham Lewis, 1919.
The Apple (of Beauty and Discord), April 1920, 97

Ezra Pound, Founder of Modern Periodical Studies

I am doing a series of satires on English Magazines, and it is a fairly amusing
lark, I don't know whether the solemn quarterlies or the "popular" weeklies
are the more ludicrous.

Ezra Pound, Pound/Joyce

I had intended to provide the book derisively with an appendix, vermiform.
Papa Flaubert compiled a *sottisier,* I also compiled a *sottisier.* I do not yield a
jot in my belief that such compilations are useful, I concede that there may be
no need of reprinting mine at this moment. At any rate the snippets are there
on file. You can't know an era merely by knowing its best.

Ezra Pound, Make It New

Never yet got any attention to "Studies in Contemporary Mentality" (yu
prob/bombadeering at time) anyhow tellin the goddam Brits wot was pizin'em
via print on noose-stands. Even the O. M. [T. S. Eliot] cdnt see the utility,
when I tried for a reprint in volumette, and now lookat their goddam hempire.

Ezra Pound, Pound/Lewis

The three epigraphs to this chapter are from different moments in Ezra Pound's career, but they refer to the same text. In the source of the first, he was writing to James Joyce, in September 1917, about a series of twenty articles called "Studies in Contemporary Mentality" that appeared in *The New Age,* running through January 1918. In the second, he was writing about the same series, as Forrest Read noted years ago in connecting the two quotations (Pound, *Pound/Joyce,* 128n4). In this second epigraph, from the introductory section of *Make It New,* Pound was acknowledging, somewhat cryptically, that he had accepted advice to leave the series out of this book, where he had intended it to appear as an appendix. He was also, however, defending its usefulness. (The "snippets," clipped from pages of *The New Age,* must have been sent to Faber with the other materials for the book, which was mainly a collection of things previously published in various places.) This is confirmed by the third epigraph, from a letter to Wyndham Lewis, written in Pound's hypercolloquial style from St. Elizabeths hospital in 1950. In that letter to Lewis, Pound indicates that it was T. S. Eliot, at Faber and Faber, who was responsible for eliminating "Studies in Contemporary Mentality" from *Make It New* in 1934, perhaps repaying Pound for the cuts he had made in Eliot's *Waste Land* a decade or so earlier.

In any case, it is clear that even as late as 1950 Pound still was thinking of this series and regretting that it had not been republished. A *sottisier* is a collection of stupidities such as those in Flaubert's *Bouvard et Pécuchet,* or the "Current Cant" section of *The New Age,* which regularly quoted stupidities collected from various sources. But this was not just a collection of amusing banalities. In 1950 Pound told Lewis that back in 1917 he had attempted to explain to his British readers how they were being poisoned by the printed material they got from newsstands (or "noose-stands" as he later called them). These printed stupidities were making the whole nation stupid, in Pound's view. There were other magazines, of course, including the one he was writing for (*The New Age*), that Pound thought were not purveying cultural poison, and his elaborate involvement with them is part of the whole story of Pound and modernist magazines.

Forty years ago Richard Ellmann began his biography of James Joyce by observing that we were still learning to be Joyce's contemporaries. What he said of Joyce is also true—still true—of Ezra Pound. And one of the things we are still trying to learn is expressed in the last line of the second epigraph: "You can't know an era merely by knowing its best." These words have special weight because no one championed the best more fiercely than Pound. Moreover, in championing that best, as every student of modern culture knows, Pound had an enormous influence on the way modernism took shape in the English-speaking world. He gave help and advice to writers, artists, and editors, including William Butler Yeats, Ford Madox Ford, Harriet Monroe, Margaret Anderson, T. S. Eliot, James Joyce, Hilda Doolittle (H.D.), Henri Gaudier-Brzeska, Wyndham Lewis, Marianne Moore, Ernest Hemingway, and James Laughlin. What is less widely appreciated, however, is the nature and importance of his direct involvement with magazines in the crucial decade that culminated in 1922. His efforts on behalf of other writers and artists often took the form of placing their work in magazines and producing manifestos and critical essays in the magazines to support that work. He had direct editorial involvement with a number of those periodicals he called "the free magazine or the impractical or fugitive magazine" ("Small Magazines," 702), and he wrote extensively about them and about "commercial" magazines as well. We, who are belatedly following in his footsteps, may properly begin, then, by looking more closely at those very steps.

Any study of Pound's engagement with periodicals, whether undertaken by a beginning student or by a seasoned scholar, must follow a similar pattern and rely on similar tools. The student of Pound's magazine work will need a good biography, such as A. David Moody's *Ezra Pound: Poet,* and a good bibliography, such as Donald Gallup's *Ezra Pound: A Bibliography,* along with the various editions of Pound's letters, with special attention to his correspondence with people connected to the magazines, like Ford Madox Ford, Harriet Monroe, Alice Corbin Henderson, Margaret Anderson, Wyndham Lewis, James Joyce, and John Quinn. This researcher will also need access to the magazines themselves, either in libraries or through digital editions, such as those provided by the Modernist Journals Project. (Everything we have to say about his career in this chapter is based on our reading of those sources, which are listed in our bibliography, though we cite only specific borrowings and quotations below.) Moody and Gallup alone will teach us that Pound's interest in magazines goes back well before this crucial decade of 1910 to 1920. A photograph of him lounging in his tower studio or "den" as a boy (Moody, after 144), shows a number of interesting objects on the wall behind him, including some fencing foils and a poster for *Scribner's* magazine. Very early in his career, he sent his work to magazines, and he often fenced, intellectually, with their editors. As we shall see in Chapter 2, he was sending poems to *The Bibelot* as early as 1905, when he was twenty years old, and one of his first published poems appeared in the large-circulation monthly *Munsey's* in 1906.

But even before that he had been sending his work to magazines, publishing in the *Times Chronicle* of Jenkinstown, Pennsylvania, in 1902 and in the Hamilton College literary magazine in 1905. From 1906 onward he published frequently in Philadelphia's *Book News Monthly*. Then, in 1908, he mailed to his father stories and essays from Italy with instructions to send them out to a series of magazines, including some of the most popular monthlies in the country at that time. He published a poem in the *English Review* of Ford Madox Ford (still Hueffer then, actually) in 1909, and he made his first appearance in *The New Age* in 1911 with a series of articles called "I Gather the Limbs of Osiris," headed by a note from the editor, explaining that "Under this heading Mr. Pound will contribute expositions and translations in illustration of 'The New Method' in scholarship" (*New Age*, 10, no. 5, p. 107; hereafter cited *NA* 10.5:107).

Later on, his work appeared not only in the magazines he called "small" but in such places as *The Smart Set,* which had a circulation in the midrange (around seventy-five thousand copies). He wrote frequently for *The New Age,* a weekly that is never included among the little magazines in lists like those of Hoffman, Allen, and Ulrich or Sader and had a circulation ranging from four thousand to twenty thousand at different times. *The English Review,* on the other hand, though it looked like a large-scale magazine, never got much beyond one thousand copies in circulation per issue. Following a single writer through the magazines involves using the best biographical and bibliographical information available—or generating it, if it is not available—and it involves moving back and forth from the life, the letters, and the records of the work to the work itself in its original journalistic settings.

Table 1.1: Ezra Pound's Contributions
to Magazines, 1905–1926

Year	Number of Magazine Contributions
1905	1
1906	4
1907	0
1908	5
1909	6
1910	8
1911	7
1912	37
1913	53
1914	47
1915	46
1916	31
1917	71
1918	117
1919	89
1920	89
1921	23
1922	16
1923	6
1924	24
1925	11
1926	3

Students of modernism know something about Pound's involvement in what he called "small magazines," though few of us are aware of the full extent of his association with them and with the other magazines of modernism. Drawing on the information in Donald Gallup's *Bibliography*, we can find an interesting pattern in Pound's contributions to magazines, if we follow the number of contributions per year from the time he was twenty until just after he reached the age of forty (table 1.1).

What we find in these raw numbers is that his peak years of contributions to periodicals occurred when he was in London. He arrived there in 1910, but it took him a couple of years to make connections and establish himself. He left in 1920, and from 1912 through 1920 he averaged around one publication per week in the magazines. We can get a good idea of just what he was publishing—and where—if we look at the distribution of his work for the year in which his periodical contributions first jumped to well over one per week: 1917. Of his seventy-one contributions to magazines that year, he had ten in *Poetry*, fourteen in *The Egoist*, nineteen in *The Little Review*, and twenty-six in *The New Age*. Furthermore, almost none of these were works of poetry. They were mainly criticism—and not just of literature. In *The New Age* during this year, Pound wrote art criticism under the name of "B. H. Dias," music criticism as "William Atheling," and, most interesting of all for our purposes, a series of critiques of periodicals under his own name that extended into 1918 and ultimately ran to twenty articles—the *sottisier* or "series of satires on English Magazines" called "Studies in Contemporary Mentality."

This series is worth looking into because it tells us something about Pound as a student of magazines, and about Pound's evolving cultural attitudes and values. Later, in 1930, his essay "Small Magazines" appeared in an American journal published by the National Council of Teachers of English. This essay is well known to students of those magazines. It was one of the stimuli that led to Hoffman, Allen, and Ulrich's *Little Magazine*, and many later scholars have read and cited it. But few have attended to his earlier series of articles on the more popular magazines of Britain in 1917. David Moody is one of the few, and he makes some typically perceptive remarks about them in his biography (336–337), but we propose to go into them more deeply, since we must recognize Pound as a founder or progenitor of modernist periodical studies. We are catching up to him only now, after nearly a century—a period in which other media have replaced the magazine as the shapers of what Pound called "contemporary mentality." We can divide our study of Pound's magazine work, then, into two phases or aspects: (1) Pound's direct involvement with the editing of magazines and (2) his critical writings on magazines. Obviously, these two aspects of Pound's magazine work were closely related, but we shall understand them better if we examine them separately.

Table 1.2: Pound's Editorial Involvement with Magazines, 1909–1923

Years of Pound's Involvement	Editors	Journals
1909–1910	F. M. Hueffer (later Ford)	*The English Review*
1910–1920	A. R. Orage	*The New Age*
1912–1921	Harriet Monroe	*Poetry*
1912–1916	W. H. Wright, H. L. Mencken	*The Smart Set*
1913–1914	Dora Marsden	*The New Freewoman*
1914–1919	Marsden, H. S. Weaver	*The Egoist*
1914–1915	Wyndham Lewis	*Blast*
1916–1919	Margaret Anderson	*The Little Review*
1920–1920	J. Middleton Murry	*The Athenaeum*
1920–1923	Scofield Thayer	*The Dial*

Pound was directly involved with ten magazines in England and America during this period, in varying capacities, official and unofficial (table 1.2).

Pound's thinnest connection in the list is probably with *The Smart Set*. His name never appeared on its masthead, but he had some rapport with its editors—first W. H. Wright and then H. L. Mencken—and he described himself to James Joyce as an unofficial editor who could send things in for them to consider (*Pound/Joyce*, 18). He did indeed send in three of Joyce's *Dubliners* stories, and *The Smart Set* published two of them. His own work also appeared in the magazine on nine occasions from 1912 to 1916. We have also included *The English Review* in our list, though Pound's association with it was informal and very brief. Pound socialized with its first editor, Ford Madox Ford, who helped him modernize his poetry. They remained friends for quite a while, but he never was directly involved in the editorial work of *The English Review*, as he was with many other magazines. In the cases where his involvement was more direct, he often followed a pattern of withdrawing when he disagreed with the editor(s) and then returning less officially. This happened with *Poetry,* with *The Little Review,* and with *The New Age.* In the case of *The Athenaeum* he had no editorial connection, but he wrote as a paid drama critic under the name of "T. J. V." from March of 1920 until he was fired in July of that year (Moody, 389, 398).

With A. R. Orage, the editor of *The New Age,* Pound frequently disagreed, but he became one of the few paid contributors to the journal Orage sometimes called the "no wage." They split over Vorticism, but Pound returned to the magazine with a vengeance after his nemesis, Beatrice Hastings, left it, and he gradually moved closer to Orage's views on economic matters, though they never agreed about poetry. That did not stop Pound from covering both art and music for the magazine for several years. Over these years he published more frequently in *The New Age* than in any other periodical. But he never had an editorial say in the magazine. It is significant, as we shall see, that both Ford and Orage were men with strong views, who neither needed nor accepted outside help, though both socialized with Pound and enjoyed his company. Ford, of course, was a terrible businessman, and lost control of his journal shortly after its first year of operation. Orage, on the other hand, managed to keep *The New Age* going from 1907 until he resigned in 1922. Though none of these ten journals had a vast circulation, three of them do not quite fit the category of "little magazines." *The New Age* was a political weekly that took a serious interest in literature and the arts; *The English Review* was in the format of the big monthly reviews like *Blackwood's,* though it was far less conservative, and it was meant to pay its way over the years as those magazines did; and *The Smart Set,* as we have noted, had a circulation well beyond that of any magazine called "little"—which did not prevent Hoffman, Allen, and Ulrich from listing it in this problematic category. Pound interacted with all these editors, but he never had control over what they published.

What he wanted, however, was just that: control over what was published. And he achieved it—in varying ways and to varying degrees—with most of the other magazines on this list. In the case of *Poetry* he was one of a number of poets contacted in 1912 by the founding editor, Harriet Monroe, and invited to contribute. Monroe was herself a poet, living in Chicago, where she had social and economic connections. In 1911 she began collecting subscribers who would pledge fifty dollars a year for five years to help her start a magazine that would contribute to the cultural prestige of Chicago in the same way the Art Institute and the Symphony did. This funding would enable her to pay contributors decently. The first issue of her magazine appeared in October of 1912, and by November she was naming Pound "foreign correspondent." He was encouraged to submit work he found abroad, by himself and others, but he never had full control of even a section of the magazine. Monroe, who was twenty-five years older than Pound, valued his work and his advice, but she ran her own magazine, with the help, in particular, of Alice Corbin Henderson, a younger poet, who screened all the submissions and wrote shrewd critical essays as well as poems (with the poems appearing under her maiden name, Alice Corbin) until her health forced her out in 1916.

Pound and Monroe agreed about the value of poetry, but Monroe's impulses were more democratic. She put some words of Whitman's on her masthead and never wavered in her commitment to them: "To have great poets there must be great audiences too." She saw the creation of such an audience as the mission of her magazine. Pound, on the other hand, hated that motto and muttered against it for years—sometimes in print, in *Poetry* and other magazines, insisting that "the artist is *not* dependent upon his audience" (*Poetry* 5.1: 29). He was an elitist, and his deep immersion in the European Renaissance left him thinking that for the arts to flourish in the modern world they required the support of patrons like the Medici. Monroe's hundred wealthy Chicagoans were too many for him, and too undistinguished. But he discovered T. S. Eliot and sent "The Love Song of J. Alfred Prufrock" to Monroe, who found it depressing and hesitated for months before printing it. Pound considered Alice Corbin Henderson brighter than Monroe, so he directed more of his foreign correspondence through her, and included her poetry as well as Monroe's in his *Catholic Anthology* when he published it in 1915. Monroe and Henderson wanted the magazine to be American with international connections. Pound wanted the magazine to be international, with American poets included when they reached an international standard (*Letters,* 10–11).

He sent in the work of Robert Frost, whose first book had appeared in England, and of Ford Madox Ford and H.D., as well as poems by James

Joyce. He had a real eye for literary talent, but he also had his blind spots. He never noticed Emily Dickinson and he rarely mentioned Wallace Stevens in his whole career as a critic, being interested, mainly, in writers and artists he had discovered himself. He was ambivalent about William Carlos Williams, and his view of other writers often changed dramatically. He urged Monroe to publish only poetry of the highest quality, shrinking the pages devoted to verse and increasing the criticism if necessary. Monroe saw a continuum of poetry, extending from Native American chants and cowboy songs to the highest level of literary achievement, and she felt that an American audience could be created by means of that continuum. She resisted elements in Pound's work that she thought would insult or offend that audience, asking him to change some of his nastier poetic expressions and refusing to print some of his poems altogether. They were two strong people who were devoted to the cause of poetry but saw poetry in very different ways. Monroe was consistent and eloquent in her praise of Stevens, for example, and she found new poets like Glenway Wescott and Yvor Winters whom Pound barely noticed. (In the single mention of Wescott in his correspondence with Harriet Monroe, Pound misspelled his last name; *Letters,* 205.) As a result of these differences Pound's connection with the magazine fluctuated over the years from 1912 to 1920, but never quite ended. For a while, he saw *Poetry* and *The Egoist* as American and English branches of a literary enterprise over which he had some control, but this did not last, and his relationship with the British magazine is as complicated as that with the American.

With *The New Freewoman* he was invited by the assistant editor, Rebecca West, to help edit the literary section of the magazine. The editor, Dora Marsden, wrote the philosophical section but did not give her full attention to the literary section of the magazine, which began to grow when West started editing it. Pound had met West through Ford and Ford's companion, Violet Hunt. He had also found a financial backer in John Gould Fletcher, which allowed him to offer to pay contributors to the literary section, and he insisted on total control over that section of the paper—control that quickly grew from a few columns to a third of every issue. But Dora Marsden remained firmly in charge of the journal, as Bruce Clarke has demonstrated, provoking Pound into writing his important series of articles on "The Serious Artist."

What Pound wanted, as he explained eloquently to various people, was control over a place to publish work by himself and a few other
writers chosen by himself. By this time he had "discovered" Joyce, Eliot,
and Wyndham Lewis, whose works he sponsored in the magazine, as its
title changed from *The New Freewoman* to *The Egoist*. This change in title
suited both Pound and Marsden, who approved of the egoistic philosophy set forth in Max Stirner's *The Ego and His Own,* which had appeared
in Germany in 1845 but was first translated into English in 1907 by Steven
Byington, who was a regular contributor to *The New Freewoman*. The
date of this translation made it a part of the modernist movement in the
English-speaking world. And in 1909 James Huneker's *Egoists: A Book of
Supermen* linked Stirner and Nietzsche to writers like Stendhal, Baudelaire, and Flaubert, making explicit the connection between modernism
and egoism, which is implicit in all Pound's magazine work.

Pound himself had made it explicit enough in a letter of September 1913 to the American literary critic Milton Bronner, in which he suggested that male editors wanted to run things themselves but female editors might be more pliable (Moody, 219). As it happened, however, he
kept running into exceptions. Harriet Monroe resisted his attempts to
control *Poetry,* and Dora Marsden appointed Richard Aldington literary editor of *The New Freewoman* when Rebecca West left, which ended
Pound's dominance of the literary section of the magazine, though Joyce's
Portrait appeared in *The Egoist*. When Harriet Shaw Weaver (who had
been financing *The New Freewoman*) began editing *The Egoist,* she shared
Pound's admiration of Joyce's work and became for Joyce a patron along
the lines of Pound's beloved Sigismondo Malatesta. Pound had managed
to get Joyce, Eliot, and Lewis into the magazine, but he never got the control he wanted, and he attributed this in part to Marsden's editorship.
His tendency toward misogyny broke loose in some letters to John Quinn,
in which he proposed a "male review" which would not allow any contributions from females because "most of the ills of american magazines
(the rot of medieval literature before them for that matter) are (or were)
due to women." He allowed that there might be "six women writers
whose work I should regret losing but the ultimate gain . . . in vigor—
in everything—might be worth it" (*Pound/Quinn,* 54). The "male review" never happened, of course, and it is hard to say just how serious

Pound was in proposing it, but he finally found his pliable female editor in Margaret Anderson at *The Little Review* in 1916. Before that, however, he had a taste of full co-editorship with another man.

This man was the formidable Wyndham Lewis, whose visual and literary work Pound admired. Together they developed the theory of Vorticism in the arts, borrowing some ideas from T. E. Hulme, and in 1914 started the magazine *Blast*, which was full to the brim with manifestos and shocking literary and visual texts, including the first chapter of what became Ford Madox Ford's best novel and a clever story by Rebecca West. Vorticism was a name for the kinds of modernism that Pound and Lewis approved of, to the exclusion of those they considered passé, like Imagism, or wrong-headed, like Futurism and Cubism. The magazine was a shocker, but it was eclipsed by the larger shock of the First World War, which followed close on its heels. *Blast* managed a second issue but then disappeared in 1915, ending Pound's only experience of actual editorship until he edited *The Exile*, some years after the period we are considering. When Lewis returned from the war and started *The Tyro* as a successor to *Blast*, Pound was not interested in joining him, though T. S. Eliot helped out a bit. Pound, as it happened, had made another magazine connection in 1916, with another female editor.

Before that, however, he had made another serious attempt to get control of a magazine in London, hoping to enlist John Quinn as a financial supporter for this venture. He wrote Quinn in May 1915 that "there is the faint chance, the faint nuance of a chance that I may get an ancient weekly to edit" (*Pound/Quinn*, 27). That weekly, *The Academy*, did not fall into his hands, but Pound continued writing to Quinn about starting a new magazine or taking over an old one, debating the merits of weekly versus monthly publication, citing the Parisian *Mercure de France* as a model of what a modern magazine should be, and wondering whether, in his ideal magazine, it might be necessary to include the work of "the better, populace-drawing writers from time to time" (*Pound/Quinn*, 35) in order to gain enough circulation to make the magazine economically viable, citing Hilaire Belloc as an example of the sort of writer he had in mind for this function. In this extraordinary series of letters, which ran through most of 1915, Pound's plans became more and more specific and detailed as to costs, contributors, and numbers of subscribers—and more and more detached from the actual possibilities of magazine production, until they culminated in the bizarre plan for an all-male journal. These dreams never became a reality, and Pound had to settle for another role in an existing journal.

Margaret Anderson started *The Little Review* on a shoestring in Chicago in 1914. In its early years it looked much like its neighbor *Poetry,* and shared a number of contributors with it, but it was anarchistic in spirit and embodied, perhaps more than any other journal, the quintessence of the "little magazine"—as the word *little* in its title proclaimed. Pound himself referred to it as "the Small Review" in a letter to Harriet Monroe in 1914, leading one to believe that he was offended by the cuteness of the word he avoided in the title of his own article on such magazines. But he did not make a direct connection to Margaret Anderson's magazine until 1916, when the magazine moved to California briefly, back to Chicago, and then on to New York. In the same year Anderson met Jane Heap, who helped her edit the review for some years, and the editors left the first thirteen pages of an issue blank, complaining that they had not received enough work of quality. Pound, who began contributing that year, obviously found this gesture sympathetic, and in April 1917 he joined the magazine officially as its foreign editor, essentially deserting *Poetry* to do so, though he continued publishing in *Poetry* for some years. He explained his reasons for this move in a manifesto opening the May issue, taking the occasion to attack Monroe for what he considered her excessive deference to old fogies and the Christian religion. (The charge was unfair. Monroe thought of herself as "a quite untroubled heathen" [449], and she made her own editorial decisions.)

Pound's formal affiliation with *The Little Review* lasted only until 1920, when he shifted allegiance to *The Dial.* There he received a salary as Paris correspondent until the editor, Scofield Thayer, fired him in 1923, in a dispute over support for T. S. Eliot. He continued to publish in both *The Little Review* and *The Dial* for some years, but his major achievements for these two journals were the publication of *Ulysses* in one and *The Waste Land* in the other. He was also instrumental in giving *The Little Review* a motto in deliberate contrast to that of *Poetry:* "Making no compromise with the public taste." Orage mocked this motto in the pages of *The New Age* (23.6: 89), but Orage also mocked the first installment of

Ulysses. Still, there is no doubt about the pattern of Pound's involvement with these magazines. He had an elitist agenda and he wanted enough control to ensure that only work he valued appeared in the literary sections of these journals. But he seemed unable to function during these years without a periodical affiliation of some sort. From 1909 to 1923 he had formal affiliations with *Poetry, The New Freewoman/The Egoist, Blast, The Little Review, The Dial,* and *The Athenaeum,* though he published more pieces in *The New Age* than in any of the others. And he liked to find patrons to underwrite the sections of the journals he controlled: first Fletcher, with *The New Freewoman,* and later John Quinn, with both *The Egoist* and *The Little Review.* Scofield Thayer had plenty of money, paying Pound to edit and also paying contributors better than most of the elite journals.

Pound's attempts to control those journals constitute just one side of the story of his interest in periodical studies. The other side, as one might expect, is represented by his critical writing about those very journals and his "series of satires" or *sottisier* on the "solemn quarterlies" and "popular" magazines of the time. And this *sottisier* will tell us as much about Pound's views as his better-known involvement with what he called the "small magazines." As we have mentioned, it took the form of a series of twenty articles in *The New Age,* called "Studies in Contemporary Mentality," which we may properly see as inaugurating the serious study of periodicals as a way into modern culture (table 1.3). The articles are witty, sometimes biting, and thoroughly Poundian.

The titles alone give a fair idea of the range Pound covered in this series. But only a reading of the full set can convey just what he has done with them. Wyndham Lewis, writing to Pound from France, where he had read a couple of issues of *The New Age* containing articles from this series, told him, "They are certainly the best things the New Age has contained for many a day" (Pound, *Pound/Lewis,* 114), and Pound replied that "Orage hopes to get the Contemporary Mentality published as a book" (ibid., 115). But that did not happen, and years later, writing to Lewis in 1950, Pound had forgotten Lewis's earlier praise of the series. Now, following Orage's lead and Pound's wishes to see these pieces published in a book, we have included the entire series as the appendix of this volume, so that current scholars of modernism and periodical studies can consider

Table 1.3: "Studies in Contemporary Mentality" as It Appeared in *The New Age* from August 1917 Through January 1918

Date	Volume, Issue	Title	Notes
August 16, 1917	21, 16	I. "The Hibbert"	
August 23	21, 17	II. "Blackwoods"	
August 30	21, 18	III. On Quarterly Publications	*Quarterly Review; Church Review; Edinburgh Review*
September 6	21, 19	IV. "The Spectator"	
September 13	21, 20	V. "The Strand," or How the Thing May Be Done	
September 20	21, 21	VI. "The Sphere," and Reflections on Letter-Press	
September 27	21, 22	VII. Far from the Expensive Veal Cutlet	*The Quiver*
October 11	21, 24	VIII. The Beating Heart of the Magazine	*The Quiver*
October 18	21, 25	IX. Further Heart Throbs	*The Family Herald* and *Punch*
October 25	21, 26	X. The Backbone of the Empire	*Chambers' Journal*
November 1	22, 01	XI. Bright and Snappy	*Answers*
November 8	22, 02	XI. Hash and Rehash	Misnumbered from this point on; *Answers*
November 15	22, 03	XII. The Emblematic	*Old Moore's Almanac*
November 22	22, 04	XIII. The Celestial	*The Christian Herald*
November 29	22, 05	XIV. Progress, Social and Christian	*The British Weekly*
December 13	22, 07	XV. A Nice Paper	*Forget-Me-Not*
December 20	22, 08	XVI. Aphrodite Popularis	*Nash's Magazine*
December 27	22, 09	XVII. The Slightly Shop-worn	Sixpenny weeklies; *The Bookman; The English Review; The Church Times*
January 3, 1918	22, 10	XVIII. Nubians	*The Church Times*
January 10	22, 11	XIX. ? Versus Camouflage	Conclusions

what Pound accomplished in these articles, and we encourage our readers to do just that. The whole series must be read to appreciate the full flavor of Pound's attack on contemporary British mentality. The interpretation of this work that we offer here is meant to direct attention to the full text, not to substitute for it. Still, it is important to understand what Pound was trying to do in these articles and what he actually accomplished in them. (Note that the numbering in *The New Age* went awry at one point, with two articles numbered "XI." In the appendix we provide the numbers from the original pages, with the correction in brackets. In referring to them here, however, we shall use only the corrected numbers where they apply, and we shall use arabic numerals for all the essays, to avoid confusion.)

One of the problems Pound tackled was that of classification. As we shall see in Chapter 3, this is a complex matter indeed. Pound recognizes the complexity but insists that his work is not meant to be definitive. He begins his attempt at categorizing magazine genres (in no. 6) by saying that he will work not as a "theologian interpreting the Divine Will" but "as a simple-hearted anthropologist putting specimens into different large boxes—merely for present convenience tumbling things apparently similar into the same large box until a more scientific and accurate and mature arrangement is feasible." His criteria are a combination of goal and audience, as we shall see. Here are the five categories he generates, in his own words:

> First: . . . those designed to keep thought in safe channels; to prevent acrimonious discussion in old gentlemen's clubs. e.g., respectable quarterlies, "The Spectator," [and all that sort].
>
> Second: Periodicals designed to inculcate useful and mercantile virtues in the middle and lower middle classes or strata, e.g., "The Strand," and "Cocoa" in general.
>
> Third: Trade journals, such as "The Bookman," "The Tailor and Cutter," "Colour," etc.
>
> Fourth: Crank papers. Possibly one should include here as a sub-heading "religious periodicals," but I do not wish to press this classification; I do not feel the need of two categories, and my general term will cover a number of crank papers

which are not definitely religious, though often based on "superstition," i.e., left-overs of religions and taboos.

Fifth: Papers and parts of papers designed to stop thought altogether.

By "contemporary mentality" Pound means what we would now probably call ideology. In his introduction to *Make It New* he referred to his method as an examination of "symptoms which the visiting anthropologist or student of Kulturmorphologie would have noticed as 'customs of the tribus Britannicus.'" He is investigating the ways in which one medium, the magazine, regularly promotes a particular ideology—an ideology that hides, or, as he says, "camouflages" certain realities. This means that, when he looks at a magazine, he not only attends to the "content" but examines the advertising as well, and explores the relationship between the two. For example, he sees most Christian churches as corporations:

> "The Church Times" . . . but why go on with this camouflage? Christ Himself, His brilliant remarks, His attractive personality, His profound intuitions, being now scarcely more than a bit of camouflage draped over a corporate body, or, rather, several corporate bodies styling itself and themselves, "His Church." These corporations are useful to various people and participants; so effective is the camouflage that only now has someone in America let out the egregious cat that Lincoln once consorted with free thinkers, read Payne and Voltaire, wrote an essay in accord with their beliefs, *and that this did not ruin his character.* (no. 19, ellipsis Pound's)

And he connects the promises of advertisers (in this case, specifically those of corsets) to those made by certain Christian writers:

> As the paradisiacal promise, such as that concerning the corsets, has always been used as a lure, so this wheeze about the horror of nothingness, the end of the world, the day of judgment, etc., has been used as a shake-up, as an hysteria-

producer to weaken the will, and it has even masqueraded as
an argument for believing or accepting or tolerating all sorts
and conditions of doctrines. (no. 11)

He continues this discussion by noting that "to judge from our periodicals the vast majority of our neighbours do not know enough science to keep their bowels open. I think there is not one paper of all those
I have looked at which does not proclaim some cathartic." The point here
is that the advertisers and the marketers of religious nostrums share an
interest in concealing certain things from the people they are addressing. And Pound discusses both kinds of propaganda regularly. Some of
the magazines he considers are specifically religious, and others most definitely not, but they share, as Pound sees them, in the process of ideological distortion or camouflage.

Pound's treatment of the magazines is more anecdotal than sys-
tematic. He is witty, biting, and lively, as we, who plod along academically in his satirical footsteps, are only too aware. He is something like
contemporary bloggers, discussing what comes to hand, taking up a new
project each week. One of the more interesting of his finds is an article
he cites as "My Girls and the New Times, a frank talk, by a middle-aged
mother" from a magazine called *The Quiver*. Founded in Victorian times,
The Quiver was an illustrated eight-penny magazine with a religious bent
that had become known for publishing serial fiction. According to Pound,
it was popular with servants and especially women. He mentions this
article in his seventh piece and then begins the eighth by saying, "I return
with interest undiminished to the 'frank' and middle-aged mother—
my periscope for surveying the no-man's land of the unexplored popular heart." He begins with style, inventing a new term for a certain kind
of formulaic writing:

> "Those days of peace which now seem so remote were not al-
> together happy for parents." I take this sentence from near her
> beginning. For the word "peace" substitute almost any other
> temporal designation, for "parents" substitute any other noun
> indicating any other group of humanity, the sense of the state-
> ment will remain, I think, unimpaired. "Cliché," as generally

used, has meant a set phrase; we have here something slightly different; it may be called the "gapped linotype."

This is a syntactic formula, rather than a semantic one, and therefore a linotype with gaps rather than a phrase locked in type (cliché), but for Pound it signifies the substitution of formula for thought, and he returns to the concept a number of times in discussing this article, which he treats at exceptional length. The frank mother is concerned with daughters who have grown discontented and sought new lives of their own because of what the mother calls a "restless, wavering temperament that seeks escape from home." We have another name for this temperament—we call it "modernism" and see it as a response to the conditions of modernity. This is quite explicit in the mother's discourse: her girls "'would discuss Shaw and Nietzsche, but they would not discuss a leak in a gas-pipe, or the making of a simple soup.'"

Pound is a bit daunted by this. To reach the popular mind, his periscope needs to "go further. We must find some family where they did not read Shaw and Nietzsche. However, let us keep on with this stratum." The need to get beyond, or, more precisely, below the level at which Shaw and Nietzsche are read becomes a refrain in these articles, but there is plenty to study at this level, and he dissects the mother's discourse in considerable detail—too much for us to follow here. But his conclusions from this investigation resonate:

> Note the ground tone. The ground tone not only of this little "frank talk," but of all this sort of writing. Whether the talk is "frank" makes little difference; if it is not the talk of a mother, or of someone expressing her own personal and typical mentality, but merely the tour de force of someone writing for a given audience, it is at least a successful tour de force. It represents the mentality of the not innumerous readers who accept it. This sort of didacticism proceeds by general statement, it is specifically ignorant of individual differences, it takes no count of the divergence of personalities and of temperaments. Before its swish and sweep the individual has no existence. There are but two conclusions: 1. That these peo-

ple do not perceive individuality as existing; 2. That individual differences in this stratum are so faint as to be imperceptible.

The obliteration of the individual under the pressure to conform Pound finds to be one of the major effects of the kind of journalism he is investigating—and he finds it hateful. This is the face of modernity to which modernism in the arts is a response. Pound's future direction as a poet is one of the things we may find revealed in this extraordinary series of articles.

In the ninth article we find Pound noting that "in the hope of getting below the Shaw-Nietzsche zone I purchased the 'Family Herald.'" And he knew he had reached that level when he found in the magazine an advertisement for Rankin's Head Ointment (figure 1.2). In explaining this choice, he goes on to observe, "This paper I had often heard mentioned. Whenever a stylist wishes to damn a contemporary, especially a contemporary novelist, he suggests that said novelist is specifically fit to 'write for the "Family Herald."'" The *Family Herald* was a one-penny weekly, subheaded *The Household Magazine of Useful Information and Entertainment.* The Rankin's ad gave Pound a way of ranking the *Family Herald* in the order of popular magazines he was trying to generate:

> As an indication of stratum note that the "Family Herald" is the first paper in which I have found ads. relative to "nits and vermin in the hair," and the ad. beginning "IF YOUR CHILD has nits or head pests." It is arguable, by these portents, that the "Family Herald" reaches, or at least approaches, the verminous level, but still it is a cut above "Punch." The "family physician" is useful, and "Punch's" book reviews are of no use whatever, though they be camouflaged by Punch's "pleasantry."

Pound was certainly looking for stupidity in this series, but he was also looking for flashes of intelligence or sanity in unexpected places. This series was not just a *sottisier,* but something more complex and, finally, more interesting.

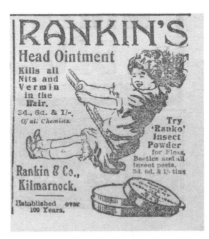

Fig. 1.2. Ad from *The Family Herald,*
August 18, 1917, 302

In addition to looking at the articles and the advertisements, Pound turns his attention to the more "literary" texts in the journals he is studying. With the verse, he is usually content with a mocking phrase or a quotation, but he gives the fiction more extended attention. Part of this attention involves noting who appears where—and with whom. He can hardly control his glee at the combination of authors he finds in the popular monthly *Nash's Magazine:*

In this life we find certain perfect adjustments.

Who, for example, could have dreamed of finding a poem by E. W. Wilcox, a serial by Miss Corelli, a poem by Chas. Hanson Towne, a tale by Gouverneur Morris, another by Robt. W. Chambers, another by Stephen Leacock, and "Beyond" by John Galsworthy, together with sundry actresses' limbs, *all, all* assembled in the one set of covers, all surrendered to one for 8d.?

Christian and Social Progress has found no more happy equation; for what, in Zeus' name, could be more Christian than Miss Marie Corelli, or more social than Mr. John Galsworthy? And how united the tone, how beautifully, how almost transcendentally all these people "belong"; what utter

and super-trinitarian unity thus binds them together in
Nash's! (no. 17)

Pound feels no need to discuss the "actual works of Corelli, Chambers,
Galsworthy and Co." because they are already familiar to himself and
his readers, but he enjoys situating them among the ads in the magazine:

> Your hair; Macassar Oil; Eyes Men Idolize; The Kind of beauty
> that men admire; Add a pleasure to life; Protective Knickers;
> Author's Manuscripts; Somebody's Darling; A sweet little set,
> beautifully hand-made and picot edged; Irresistible; What does
> your brain earn; Good Pianist; Asthma; Daisy; don't let pain
> spoil your good looks; Why People Marry; King of Hearts; Au-
> tumn Beauty; Neptune's Daughter; Beauty pictures; Soap;
> Safety-filler; the cure of self-consciousness; Lovely Eyelashes;
> Add to your income; Power: scientific concentration; Height
> increased; Healthy Women; Esperanto; Makes straight hair
> wavy and lustrous; YOU can PLAY the PIANO. (no. 17)

This mélange, then, is the background for the assemblage of writers already noted, whom Pound will not discuss. In another article, however,
on the enormously popular *Strand* magazine, he will give one writer seriously mocking attention: Arthur Conan Doyle.

He begins by noting, grudgingly, that Doyle has "done it," contributed something to the culture: "Caines and Corellis lie by the wayside. Sherlock has held us all spellbound." Pound sees this as a sort of
conjuring trick, which he proceeds to expose in the present instance, a
story in which Holmes defeats a German spy. After discussing the im-
probabilities in the story, Pound concludes:

> Sherlock is unique, but mankind remains amazingly unaltered
> and unalterable. He likes a relief from reality, he likes fairy sto-
> ries, he likes stories of giants, he likes genii from bottles. Sher-
> lock with his superhuman strength, his marvellous acumen,
> his deductive reasoning (which is certainly not shared with

the reader), has all the charms of the giant. He is also a moral
Titan: right is never too right. The logical end of these likes
is, or was, God. The first clever Semite who went out for monotheism made a corner in giantness. He got a giant "really" bigger than all other possible giants. Whenever art gets beyond
itself, and laps up too great a public, it at once degenerates into
religion. Sherlock is on the way to religion, a modern worship
of efficiency, acumen, inhumanity. Only a man on familiar
terms with his public as Sir Arthur, as habituated to writing
for that public, would dare "lay it on so thick." (no. 5)

As with advertising, Pound connects the Holmes stories to religion, and,
in this case, to a modern religion compounded of "efficiency, acumen,
inhumanity." He is much gentler with a serialized romance we might
expect him to despise, which he finds in *Forget-Me-Not*:

The paper is printed for people who prefer keeping their hands
clean. It is religious and moral, i.e., it is religious in providing a paradise, sic: a country house, a picture gallery, etc.; it
is moral in that virtue is rewarded. It has even some literary
merit, I mean solely that part of the complete novelette which
forms the number before me must be well told, even though
it is not well written. (no. 16)

Pound goes on to point out some ways in which the tale is not well
written, adding that to its audience this can make no difference at all: "I
feel about these dainty little romances very much as the landed class feel
about religion: 'Why destroy it, why attack it, what are you going to put
in its place? It keeps so many people contented.' This feeling is, of course,
in the present case, sheer sentimentality. The reader would be neither
more nor less happy if the flaws were removed." His main point here is
that improving the writing would not damage the reader's pleasure in the
fiction. What offends him most, however, is that the police are portrayed
so very favorably: "Religious feeling shown in depiction of police (cf.
guardians of the law, divine messengers, angels with flaming swords in
earlier and more cumbrous religions)." Aside from this and the other

flaws he points out, this tale does not offend him because it has no god-like hero. It is simply "fiction" as defined by Oscar Wilde's Miss Prism (in *The Importance of Being Earnest*), with the good ending happily and the bad unhappily.

These articles are lively, shrewd, opinionated, and unlike anything else being written at that time, because Pound was really an original—a critic like no other. But the common critical thread that holds these pieces together is Pound's view that a mentality of camouflage is being spread through this medium—in its religion, in its advertising, and in its fiction, resulting in the suppression of individual differences by the religiosity, nationalism, and corporate capitalism purveyed in these popular journals. It is a powerful indictment, fueled by Pound's belief that literature should tell the world the truth about itself and enable individuality to flourish. Thirteen years later, writing for *The English Journal* (the predecessor of *College English*), Pound examined the other side of the question, looking at the achievements of what he called "small magazines," reaching four conclusions:

1. "The last twenty years have seen the principle of the free magazine or the impractical or fugitive magazine definitely established. It has attained its recognized right to exist by reason of work performed."
2. "The commercial magazines have been content and are still more than content to take derivative products ten or twenty years after the germ has appeared in the free magazines. There is nothing new about this."
3. "Work is acceptable to the public when its underlying ideas have been accepted. The heavier the 'overhead' in a publishing business the less that business can afford to deal in experiment. This purely sordid and eminently practical consideration will obviously affect all magazines save those that are either subsidized (as chemical research is subsidized) or else very cheaply produced (as the penniless inventor produces in his barn or his attic)."
4. "Literature evolves via a mixture of these two methods."

Since the last of these conclusions is the crucial one, it is important to note that Pound stated it unequivocally and authoritatively. He knew enough about all kinds of magazines to know that the movement from "impractical or fugitive" journals to more established ones was inevitable and proper. And he knew that there was a middle ground between those he had considered in "Studies in Contemporary Mentality" and the "small" ones discussed in this later essay. The lesson he leaves with us, then, is that to understand modernism we must follow its workings in both the "free" magazines and those that are bound to the marketplace. In this book we have tried to follow that lesson. And we will start, in the next chapter, by reviewing the social and technological developments that we call "modernity" and the rise of the cultural response to those developments that we call "modernism," remembering, as we go, that we have already encountered Pound's modernist response to modernity as it was manifested in British magazines.

Modernity and the Rise of Modernism

A Review

Modernity is a social condition. Modernism was a response to that condition. We utter these simple propositions as a way of situating a discussion more concerned with clarity than with originality. Many different and even contradictory things have been said about modernism—and most of them are true, to some extent. We shall be seeking here not to add something new to this array of definitions but to extract from this critical discourse and to amplify a single strand of thought that seems to us to offer the most explanatory power as a description of the cultural event or process known as modernism. This strand of thought sees modernism as a textual response to the demographic, economic, and technological developments that produced the modern world. It was also a response to developments within the world of art itself, driven by a sense that the artist must go beyond any predecessors and achieve a new way of responding to the world, a view which Ezra Pound codified in the title of his book of 1934: *Make It New*. What we think of as modernist literary and visual art was not the only possible response to these conditions. There were others, and the study of modernism and modernity requires consideration of the full range of such responses, including those not thought to be quintessentially "modernist," as Pound himself would be the first to advise.

We begin, then, with modernity—a condition reached in certain parts of the world in the late nineteenth century. It is an urban condition. Cities were not merely the setting for modernity. Their growth during the nineteenth century was an essential ingredient of the modern world. Modernity is a mass phenomenon, a function of masses of people working and living in large cities. Another major force in the shaping of modernity was technological, led by discoveries and improvements in transportation and communication, including the railroads and trolleys that assisted urbanization, along with new methods for printing words and pictures. A third major force in this process was the spread of public education, which resulted in a reading public much larger than any that had existed before. The final major element in the development of modernity was commercial: marked by a special interest in the consumer and in ways of stimulating the consumption of goods and services. This process was complete, we should remember, before the first motion pictures appeared, before radio communication was possible, and long before television was invented and deployed—which is to say that it happened in a world of communications dominated by print, though later developments extended and modified it.

The mass media that first appeared in modernity were newspapers and magazines. The audiovisual mass media that are now so familiar all came later. But these matters need to be discussed with greater specificity in order to be clear. Let us focus on a particular stretch of time and a few places as marking a point at which modernity was clearly recognized as a social fact, and what we know as modernism was just as clearly emerging in response to that recognition. We do not wish to suggest, as Virginia Woolf once did in a semijocular way, that "human character changed" at a particular point in time, or even that modernity happened all at once. Modernity emerged in Europe and America during the latter half of the nineteenth century, though we will focus on the 1890s as the decade in which this new socioeconomic structure generated sufficient cultural power to provoke the emergence of modernism as a response. We must remember that Charles Baudelaire was writing about a "Painter of Modern Life" in the 1860s, in terms that are distinctly modernist, but Baudelaire was in Paris, and he was a leader in this new movement. In discussing the emergence of modernism in the English-speaking world, we are going to emphasize London and New York in the 1890s, though many other cities in other parts of the world, somewhat earlier or later, might have served as examples of this phenomenon.

The nineteenth century was marked by a major shift of population from the country to the urban centers, turning towns into cities and cities into metropolitan centers. In the census of 1801 greater London had a population of just over a million people, that number having doubled over the course of the preceding century. By 1891 the population had grown to 5,571,968 and by 1901 to 6,506,889. That is, in the last decade of the nineteenth century, the population of London grew almost twice as much as it had in the entire previous century. In the United States, New York City, which had only 76,000 citizens in 1800, grew to 2,445,000 by 1890 and 3,371,000 by 1900 (www.demographia.com), adding as many citizens in the last decade of the century as London did. What is important in both cases is the rate of growth, a process of urbanization that made each place a metropolis by 1890. Along with this shift in population came industrialization, driven by an astonishing array of new inventions—a story too familiar to need retelling here, though the parts of that story connected to the media are worth recalling.

Dozens of improvements in the process of printing alone were made during this century, but all these can be summed up in two specific developments: the rotary press and the linotype. The rotary press was developed in the nineteenth century and became the norm for newspapers and other large-scale printing projects by 1870. Rotary presses could feed sheets of paper through the printing process at speeds ten times faster than was possible with the older flat-bed machinery (Peterson, 5). But the printing process was still slowed by the pace of human typesetters, until the linotype machine was invented and manufactured in the 1880s (first used by the *New York Tribune* in 1886 and exported to Britain in the 1890s [Clair, 223]). The linotype allows the typesetter to use a keyboard something like that of a typewriter or word processor to select a brass matrix for each letter in a line, instead of having to select each letter by hand from boxes of type. When the matrix has been used to shape molten lead into the letter for printing, it can be used again and again, while the lead is melted down for recasting. Speed of typesetting had caught up with speed of printing—and speed is a major element of modernity. Developments in the printing of images also contributed to the rise of the mass media during this period. Photogravure, which has been described as "an intaglio process, a marriage between photography and mezzotint" (Clair, 262), made the printing of images easier and cheaper. This technique, too, was developed in the 1890s and began to be used extensively in the following decade in the print media.

Not only were people moving to the cities in multitudes during this period: they were also becoming better educated. In Britain, the Education Act of 1870, which made schooling compulsory to age twelve and provided the first truly "public" schools in England and Wales, produced a reading public—or at least a public that could read and write. Parish records show that in 1840 only half the brides and two-thirds of the grooms in England and Wales could sign their names; by 1900 almost all could (Mitch, 287). In America as well, literacy increased enormously over the course of the nineteenth century. But there wasn't much for this new mass reading public to read. While newspapers and magazines both contributed to the growth in literacy and benefited from it, in the United States in 1890 the public had to choose between a few expensive "quality" magazines and "the cheap weeklies, the sentimental story papers, the miscellanies. Between there were few magazines of popular price and general appeal" (Peterson, 3). This was a situation ripe for change.

Economic developments also played a role in the emergence of modernity. Department stores appeared in the great cities at the end of the nineteenth century as commerce began to emphasize retail selling, which focused on consumers. Focusing on consumers led to a vastly increased emphasis on ways of attracting them. As Ellen Gruber Garvey has described this process, "The *grand magasin* of the nineteenth century was that new and exciting development, the department store, where goods were arrayed in visually exciting, sensual displays within architecturally novel buildings and where new plate glass windows brought the displays onto the street, creating new habits of looking" (*Adman in the Parlor*, 3). The word *magazine* in both English and French meant "storehouse" before it ever referred to printed periodicals, and it is useful for us to recognize the connection between these two kinds of storehouse. For the new department stores were just one part of this commercial picture. Advertising was the other. Advertising was the textual side of the new commerce, and it took many forms, ranging from signs and bill-boards to sandwich men who walked the streets as living advertisements and also, of course, to displays in newspapers and magazines. There are sandwich men wandering around Dublin in 1904 in Joyce's *Ulysses,* and there is also a bill-sticker (Blazes Boylan). Even Leopold Bloom himself, the central figure in that text, is fascinated by advertising and makes a bit of money by selling ads. Joyce's novel, which was published in 1922, though set in 1904, was a quintessentially modernist text, not only in its experimental form but also in its fascination with modernity in all its social and economic aspects.

There had been ads in periodicals since their earliest days, even in the *Tatler* and *Spectator* of Addison and Steele. (The fact that modern readers are seldom allowed to see these ads in reprinted editions of these pioneering magazines will be a topic of discussion in Chapter 8.) But something new happened to magazine advertising in the 1890s—and this enabled something new to happen to the magazines themselves. As we have mentioned, there was a gap in the magazine world between expensive periodicals aimed at a very literate and affluent audience and cheaper periodicals aimed at the lowest levels of literacy—the level Pound was to call "verminous." But the spread of education had raised the lowest levels of literacy and produced a large potential audience for an intermediate kind of periodical. This rise in literacy was seen by some, of course, as a lowering of the overall level of literacy and a threat to culture. This feeling became more intense when certain entrepreneurs discovered a way to make the intermediate sort of periodical commercially viable. Here is how Theodore Peterson describes what happened:

> The big revolution in the magazine industry came almost at once, in October, 1893. The New York *Sun* proclaimed it in a big black advertisement which announced that *Munsey's Magazine* had cut its price from twenty-five to ten cents, its yearly subscription from three dollars to one dollar. . . .
>
> The revolutionist was Frank A. Munsey, who vividly demonstrated a basic principle of twentieth-century magazine publishing—a principle which McClure, Walker, Curtis, and others were discovering in the late nineteenth century.

It was simply this: One could achieve a large circulation by selling his magazine for much less than the cost of production and could take his profits from the high volume of advertising that a large circulation attracted. (7–8)

Thus appeared the new mass magazines, and the older "quality" magazines had to adapt or die, which indeed they did—both. Those that survived, like the new version of *Scribner's* magazine that was started in 1896, managed to follow the Munsey formula while publishing work of serious and talented writers and artists. Following this middle way, however, was not easy, because advertising revenues depended on circulation, and the need to keep circulation high led such magazines toward a star system of popular writers and artists whose names could be counted on to help keep sales high. By 1920 the number of ads in *Munsey* had fallen off drastically as circulation declined. In 1918, for example, *Scribner's* had far more ads per issue than *Munsey*. In any case, this dependence on advertising made it more difficult for new writers to get their work published in the major periodicals, creating a demand for alternative ways of getting into print. It is no accident that what we know as "little magazines" experienced an astonishing growth at the very moment when advertising changed periodical culture decisively.

In 1903 a bibliographer named Frederick Winthrop Faxon produced a list of what he called "Ephemeral Bibelots," introduced by the following paragraph:

The small, artistically printed periodicals variously called Chap-books, Ephemerals, Bibelots, Brownie Magazines, Fadazines, Magazettes, Freak Magazines, owe their origin probably to the success of the *Chap-Book,* a little semi-monthly magazine which was born in Cambridge on May 15, 1894, and which was at once in such great demand that all the early numbers were soon out of print, and were in demand by collectors at from 20 to 50 times the original issue price of five cents a copy. All sorts of "little magazines" were soon on the news-stands, competing for a part of the *Chap-Book*'s favor. They were, with few exceptions, easily distinguishable by their

appearance as well as by their names, which were apparently
carefully chosen to indicate the ephemeral character of the
publication. (3)

Faxon then mentioned *The Mahogany Tree* (1892), observing that it was
"considered by some collectors the beginning of this class." And, finally,
he proceeded to list well over two hundred "ephemeral bibelots" published in England and America between 1890 and 1903. For our purposes,
his quotation marks around the expression "little magazines" indicate
that the term was already in circulation by 1903, especially among bibliographers and collectors. And his full list reveals that these periodicals
were, for the most part, very small and very short-lived. Some were produced in the great cities of Britain and America, but others appeared in
small towns. In general, we wish to suggest, these tiny periodicals were
deliberately setting themselves against the mass magazines that appeared
in the same decade. These were often handprinted, proclaiming themselves to be the work of amateur craftsmen rather than laborers, and they
quickly attained the status of collectibles, instant antiques because of their
rarity. These early "ephemeral bibelots" were the now-forgotten precur-
sors of the "little magazines" that are more familiar to us, which kept
some of their artsy flavor, to be sure, but also aspired to greater visibil-
ity and durability than the first generation of this kind of periodical.
When we look into the matter, neither the little magazines of this period nor the large ones were purely and simply "little" or "large." And
though they were all modern, they were not all equally or consistently
modernist. Obviously, this will take some sorting out, starting with the
vexed and vexing word *modernist* itself.

    If we examine modernism as a response to modernity, it becomes
readily apparent that there was no single or simple response. We can bring
some perceptual clarity to this complex situation, however, by noting that
responses tended to take one of two main directions: writers and artists
either embraced modernity or fled from it. That is, they either tried to
capture and represent modern life, as Baudelaire suggested that the artist
Constantin Guys, his "Painter of Modern Life," had done, or they turned
away from both modernity and representation in the direction of an internal or spiritual world. These opposed modes of response to moder-

nity, loosely captured in the terms *naturalism* and *symbolism,* are obvious in the literature and art of the late nineteenth century. The young
James Joyce, for example, produced two kinds of short prose pieces he
called "epiphanies"—naturalist sketches of the vulgar people surrounding him and Symbolist musings about his own spiritual life. The art and
literature we know as "modernist" can be usefully seen as an attempt to
reconcile these two opposed modes in a new synthesis that would capture, in some fashion, the external realities of the modern world, but
would also seek ways to express psychic or spiritual conditions hidden
below the urban and technological surface of modernity. Such a synthesis was not easy, and the road to modernism is strewn with failed experiments, including those "deeply deep" epiphanies that Joyce mocked in
Ulysses.

The connection of modernism to symbolism has been noted often.
Edmund Wilson actually equated them in his groundbreaking book of
1931, *Axel's Castle,* linking Joyce, Eliot, and Stein to the French Symbolists. In this Wilson was following René Taupin, whose book of 1929, *L'Influence du symbolisme français sur la poésie américaine,* broke this particular ground—guided, as Taupin notes, by Ezra Pound, "dont les conseils
personnels et toute l'oeuvre ont eu sur moi la plus grande influence" (whose
personal advice and body of work have had the greatest influence on me
[4]). Noted less often, however, has been the turn of the English and
American modernists away from symbolism (after having passed through
it) and back toward naturalism—or rather toward some difficult if not
impossible fusion of symbolism and the naturalism against which it had
revolted. Joyce had to go through Pater, and Pound through Swinburne,
to arrive at their modernism. But Flaubert and Maupassant helped Joyce
accomplish this. With respect to Pound, A. David Moody gets it exactly
right in his recent biography. Speaking of Pound's interest in "Fiona
Macleod" and Ernest Dowson, he writes, "Pound's revolt amounted to
a complete turning around of the religion of beauty and its sacred books
of dreams and visions. He was directing it back to engage with the grey
world it was meant to be an escape from" (44). So was Joyce. No wonder they hit it off.

Joyce, of course, felt indebted to Édouard Dujardin, whom he credited with having invented the interior monologue in *Les Lauriers sont*

coupés. Dujardin, a disciple of Mallarmé and founding editor of the *Revue Wagnérienne,* was a poet and critic as well as a novelist. He was, in fact, one of the pivotal figures in the transition to modernism. In 1920 Richard Aldington reviewed in *Poetry* magazine a new work of Dujardin's entitled *De Stéphane Mallarmé au prophète Ezéchiel, et essai d'une théorie de réalisme symbolique* in which, according to Aldington, Dujardin developed a theory of symbolic realism that pointed directly to the work of the Imagists, so that H.D. became the ideal embodiment of Dujardin's theory (*Poetry* 16.3: 164–168). Aldington, who of course had an Imagist pedigree himself, ignores Dujardin's own prime example: the prophet Ezekiel. But the term *symbolic realism,* as Dujardin defined it, does indeed allow for Aldington's application of it to Imagism. In this book Dujardin discussed the move away from symbolism by the writers who called themselves "Unanimistes" and rejected symbolism in favor of a poetry that would be "direct . . . dénudé et sobre" (25, 26). This group coalesced around Jules Romain in 1908 and was active in France for the next decade. Dujardin accepted the Unanimistes's goal of directness in poetry, but he felt that achieving directness did not require poets to reject symbolism; indeed, he thought symbolism could enhance directness, a belief that led him to advocate what he called "réalisme symbolique."

Symbolic realism describes a work like *Ulysses* at least as well as the more frequently applied term *mythic realism,* and it will also serve to delineate a poet like Emily Dickinson, whom Harriet Monroe called "an unconscious and uncatalogued *Imagiste*" (*Poetry* 5.3: 138). The point is that an attempt to synthesize the symbolism and the realism of the nineteenth century characterized the rise of modernist literature in the twentieth, leading to the recognition of Joyce as a major figure in this movement and the elevation of Dickinson to the position of a major American poet. Very few artists and writers managed to come close to the perfect synthesis of realism and symbolism. What we need to understand is that modernism was not only the sum of those relatively successful solutions. It was the struggle between those two modes itself, in both artworks and criticism, combined with the struggle between reaching a broad audience and pleasing a small coterie, between seeking to create a "great audience" for "great poets," as *Poetry* magazine sought to do, and "making no compromise with the public taste," as *The Little Review* claimed it was doing.

It involved avant-gardists and cartoonists, neorealists and abstraction-
ists, and all the combinations of them that appeared. Modernism, we
want to insist, was not a "solution" but the struggle itself, and it took place
on many levels in the magazines.

We also need to be aware of another feature of modernism and the
manifestos associated with it. In the course of the nineteenth century,
there was a struggle over the marketing of visual art which became a
model for the verbal arts as well. In this struggle, new artists learned the
virtue of being grouped into schools or movements and positioning
themselves against those kinds of art that had gained public acceptance
in the past. Armed with this knowledge, literary and visual artists made
a virtue of rejection, of being refused by the dominant Salon in Paris or
rejected by established magazines. This led to claims like those we find
in the self-advertising of certain avant-garde periodicals, such as *The Egoist*'s "This journal is NOT a chatty literary review; its mission is NOT to
divert and amuse" (from an ad in *Poetry,* May 1918) and *The Little Review*'s rejection of "public taste." For a certain kind of extreme modernism, difficulty and unpopularity were badges of honor. But this is
not the whole story of modernism, though some have believed it to be
so. It was, in fact, as Robert Jensen has demonstrated in *Marketing Modernism in Fin-de-Siècle Europe,* a marketing strategy, a way of selling unpopularity and difficulty to resistant consumers as signs of artistic merit
and investment value.

In studying this field, we often take experimentalism to be a feature of modernist art, though experimentalism was mainly a byproduct
of the difficult synthesis of surface and depth in response to the conditions of modernity. As Pound put it succinctly in "Small Magazines,"
"One should dissociate the ideas of experiment and of significant achievement" (699). In British and American literature, we can see such works
as *The Waste Land* (1922), *Ulysses* (1922), *Jacob's Room* (1922), and *Mrs.
Dalloway* (1925) as major achievements of symbolic realism, and their
dates indicate that the period of experimentation was complete by the
early 1920s. Without going into any analytical depth, we can note that all
three of these writers (Eliot, Joyce, and Woolf) gave serious attention to
the surface of modern life in a great city but managed to express psychic
or spiritual conditions as well, whether through streams of consciousness

or surreal images—or both. But the three decades leading up to 1922 constitute a period of intense experimentation and debate about the proper mode of artistic response to modernity. The debate was conducted mainly in periodicals, where samples of modern art and literature regularly appeared, along with critical reviews and manifestos in which modernist values were articulated and debated. These debates and experiments, we should remember, were often accompanied by advertising—advertising of books, to be sure, but also advertising of things like "Plumtree's Potted Meat" (*Ulysses*) and "Socialist Cigarettes" (*NA* 5.21: 374). Which brings us to a major problem in the study of modernism through the magazines.

We should notice, to begin with, that some little magazines, like Lord Alfred Douglas's *Antidote*, were fiercely opposed to experimentalism in literature and the arts, as conservative in this way as the mass magazines, but without the advertising and the revenue of the bigger journals. The world of periodicals was complicated and fascinating, and for us the Arnoldian problem—of seeing this world both steadily and whole —is indeed a serious one. The first stage in any solution to this problem must involve actually seeing these journals as they were, not in bound copies with nearly half their pages stripped out as irrelevant or in reprints that include only the "text" and not the advertising. This is a crucial matter, as we shall discuss more fully.

Poetry, that ideal example of the little magazine, had some advertising, even in those early years when it was still, in Ezra Pound's view, "a forum" and not just "a meal-ticket." In *Poetry,* volume 2, number 4, of July 1913, for example, an advertisement for *The Art of Versification* appeared (figure 2.1). This advertisement is interesting not only because it tells us about one source of income for the magazine but because it connects *Poetry* to the world of popular periodicals. From 1907 to 1915 one author of this handbook, Mary Eleanor Roberts, published stories in *People's Magazine, The Cavalier, Harper's,* and *McCall's.* Her co-author in *The Art of Versification,* J. Berg Esenwein, is even more interesting. He wrote, with Dale Carnegie (then Carnagey), *The Art of Public Speaking.* Carnegie gained fame two decades later, of course, through his enormously popular book *How to Win Friends and Influence People,* published in 1936 and still in print. Esenwein also wrote *Writing the Photoplay* in

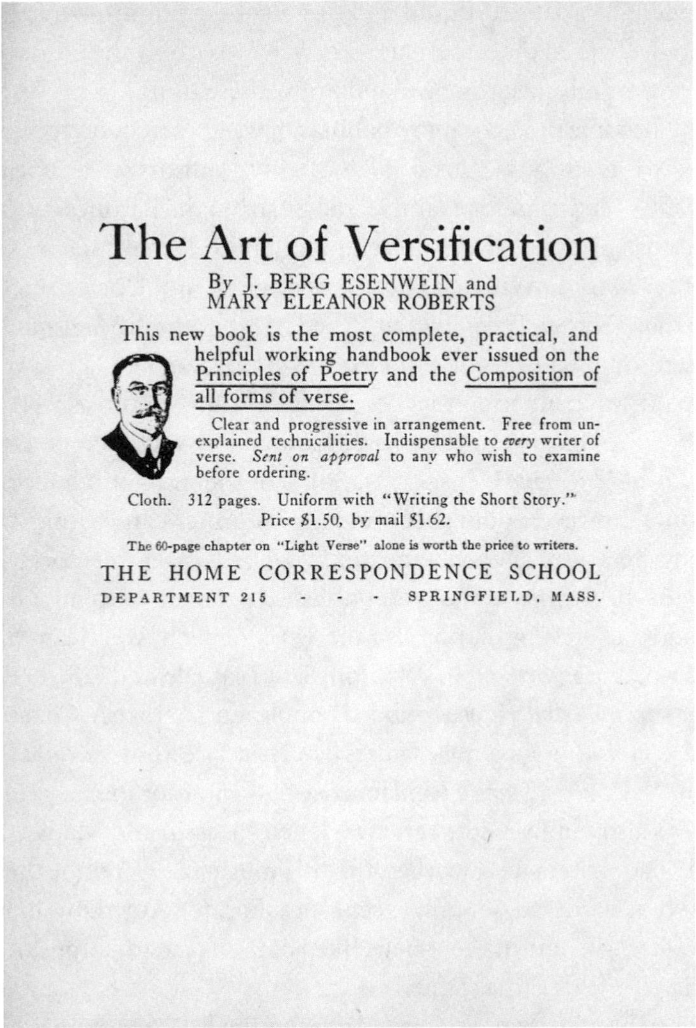

Fig. 2.1. Ad from *Poetry* magazine, July 1913

1913, one of the first books on writing for the movies. *Poetry,* itself, we should remember, was subtitled *A Magazine of Verse.* That is, this distinguished avant-garde little magazine did not, in its title, reject a connection with mere verse, though Harriet Monroe might not have wished to endorse this advertisement's stress on the book's "60-page chapter on 'Light Verse'" as being important to those submitting poems to her magazine. She accepted the ad and put a subscription form for *Poetry* itself on the back of the same page. People who see only the bound copies or reprints of this magazine will not know these things.

At the same time, the more popular magazines frequently published literary works and visual art of high quality. Authors who appeared in *Everybody's Magazine,* for example, ranged from the Baroness Orczy and Rafael Sabatini to Theodore Dreiser, Jack London, Frank Norris, Kipling, O. Henry, Mary E. Wilkins, Booth Tarkington, and Upton Sinclair. In 1914 Bernard Shaw's *Pygmalion* appeared in *Everybody's Magazine,* which had been founded in 1899 by the New York department store Wannamaker's. It was connected to a London publishing house as well, and it published a lot of material that had appeared previously in the London-based *Royal Magazine* (Mott 5: 72). Some of the mass and intermediate magazines, however, published much more American writing, though British writers were always in the mix. *Scribner's* magazine, for example, in the years between 1910 and 1922, published writing by Kipling, Galsworthy, and R. L. Stevenson, but also the work of such Americans as E. A. Robinson, Amy Lowell, Edith Wharton, Sara Teasdale, and F. Scott Fitzgerald. The mix in *Scribner's* also included popular authors like A. Conan Doyle and E. W. Hornung and public figures like Theodore Roosevelt and Fridtjof Nansen. N. C. Wyeth was a regular artist-illustrator for the magazine, but *Scribner's* also published images by Manet, Picasso, and Matisse in this period. The writers who worked for this magazine were not the modernist avant-garde, to be sure, except, perhaps, for Amy Lowell, but serious writers—some of them new, like Scott Fitzgerald—appeared regularly in this "elder" magazine.

The complexity of relations between the little magazines and the publishers of the big ones is perfectly embodied in an ad that appeared in John T. Frederick's regional little magazine, *The Midland.* Apparently Frederick had been soliciting advertising from Doubleday, Page and Company. It agreed to give him some and used the opportunity to advertise its own mass magazine, *Country Life in America* (figure 2.2). Several things about the appearance of this ad in *The Midland* are interesting for our purposes. For one, it shows that a little magazine might pursue advertising aggressively. For another, it shows the advertiser using the need of the little magazine for funds as an argument for buying its own bigger maga-

Will the Readers of The Midland Read Advertisements?

In an unusually persuasive letter from Mr. Frederick, the Managing Editor, we are told that they will. We believe he is right and this advertisement is a means to test his confidence. It is presented to call attention to what everyone agrees is the most beautiful publication in America:

COUNTRY LIFE IN AMERICA

It ought to interest every man or woman who takes THE MIDLAND. The smell of the soil is on every one of its pages —as well as the fine insight of writers who can see what the great world of nature holds and interpret it. The pictures have set a new standard in magazine illustration. We are so confident that the magazine will commend itself to you that we want to send you

A COPY WITH OUR COMPLIMENTS

If you like it, send us $1.00 and we will send you the four following issues—the five numbers would cost you on the news-stands $2.05. It is because we want to get you started as a reader of *Country Life* that we make this unusual offer to you at less than half price. We hope you will accept our invitation and draw up your chair to the *Country Life* fireside. This will be a source of pleasure to you and it will demonstrate to the publishers of THE MIDLAND that they have a magazine that pays advertisers.

Merely write your name and address in the margin, tear out this page and mail today to

DOUBLEDAY, PAGE & COMPANY, GARDEN CITY, N. Y.

OUR HOME IN THE COUNTRY

Fig. 2.2. Ad from *The Midland* magazine, February 1915

zine. Subscribe to our magazine, the ad says, and you will prove that we should continue to provide revenue to this little magazine that needs our support. And finally, it shows two modern magazines sharing an interest in country things. *Country Life in America* was edited by a Cornell University botanist, who said in its first number (November 1901) that the "growth of literature pertaining to plants and animals and the out-of-doors is one of the most emphatic and significant movements of the times" (quoted in Mott, 4: 338).

The first issue of *The Midland,* published in January 1915, had a healthy six pages of advertising and, among its contents, an indication of why John T. Frederick pursued advertising so zealously. The second item in this issue is a letter from Johnson Brigham, dated December 5, 1914, in which he tells us that "twenty-one years ago at this time I was toiling over the initial number of my *Midland Monthly* which was to bear the date, January 1894." Brigham's magazine ran for about five years, moving from Des Moines to St. Louis when he gave up the editorship, but never quite making it financially. In his letter to *The Midland* he explained this failure: "The weakness of the situation lay in my inability to obtain general advertising at paying prices" (vol. 1, no. 1, p. 4). Ezra Pound could never come to terms with the economic side of modern culture, which he felt suppressed individuality. Other modernists were less pure in their faith, and more willing to compromise with advertising, without allowing it to dominate them completely. But this is a story we can understand only if we see what was going on in the magazines themselves.

Modernism had everything to do with urbanization—which in turn generated a countermovement away from the cities, as surely as the rise of mass magazines involved a countermovement into little ones. That is, the emphasis on the city as the site of the modern, which we find in most theories of modernism, is just one side of a process that drove many modernist artists and writers into the country. For every Eliot there is a Frost, for every Joyce a Hemingway, and for every Picasso a Matisse. *The Midland* itself arose partly as a response to a lecture delivered by Josiah Royce at the State University of Iowa in 1902. In this lecture, later published as "Provincialism," Royce advised, "Let your province then be your first social idea. Cultivate its young men, and keep them near you. Foster provincial independence. Adorn your surroundings with the beauty of art. Serve faithfully your community and the nation will be served" (quoted in Hoffman, Allen, and Ulrich, 133). "There can be little doubt," say Hoffman and his colleagues, "that [John T.] Frederick was perfectly aware of Royce's Phi Beta Kappa address, delivered in the home town of *The Midland*" (133). And there is little doubt that a regional modernism existed alongside urban modernism, and a mass modernism alongside an elite modernism.

Our point is that we must study all these phenomena together if we are to have any hope of comprehending modernism. We must, in the phrase used to describe a memorable meeting at a conference of the Modernist Studies Association, go "beyond the little magazines" in order to understand them properly. And we must go to them as they were issued, and not rely on sanitized reprints or bound copies with the original ads stripped out and discarded. There is archival work to be done here, for only after we locate runs of the original issues of modern magazines can we hope for some digital editions of them that will allow us to encounter their pages as their first readers did, as products of a complex interaction between traditional and new, mass and elite, purity and impurity—an interaction of elements which was, in fact, modernism. This complexity is perfectly embodied in the early career of that archmodernist Ezra Pound. In 1905 Pound submitted one of his early poems, "Alba," to the elite little magazine edited by Thomas Mosher, *The Bibelot*. In August of that year, Mosher rejected the poem as insufficiently modern—"too old world," in fact (Moody, 42). But the following year one of Pound's first poems to be published—"Dawn Song"—appeared in the December 1906 issue of the large-circulation, advertising-oriented *Munsey's* (Gallup, 225).

And there is more. In 1908, when he was in Venice, Pound sent his father back in America some stories and travel writing with instructions to try to place them in the following magazines: "Try first on 'Outlook.' Then if not accepted Everybodies, McClure, Cosmopolitan, Book News in order" (Moody, 64). Later, in 1913, when he already had a connection with *Poetry*, he actually published some of the poems he had sent that magazine in *The Smart Set*, leaving Harriet Monroe to use the leftovers in her November 1913 issue (Williams, 48; *Poetry*, 3.2). Modernism happened in the magazines all right, but it didn't happen only in the little ones. And the little ones themselves were often quite different from one another and sometimes in direct competition, as was the case, for a time, with *Poetry* and *The Little Review*. The writers moved around, placing their work where they could. In the case of *The Smart Set*, Pound was impressed by the then editor, Willard Hunting Wright, and with the higher rates paid by his magazine. He also favored Wright, as he explained to Harriet Monroe, because "he has the good sense to divide all poets into two classes: Yeats and I are in one class and everybody else in the other" (Williams, 47). Wright, who would later produce books on Nietzsche and modern art, finally metamorphosed himself into S. S. Van Dine, the author of the very popular Philo Vance detective stories. But he edited *The Smart Set* from 1912 to 1914. And when H. L. Mencken took over in 1914, Pound corresponded with him, too. The point is that the roles of individual writers in the modern period were not fixed, and neither were the boundaries between different sorts of magazines.

Since we are engaged in studying the range of such periodicals ourselves, let us share with you a discovery we made about the current state of affairs in the archive of modernist periodicals. At the Modernist Journals Project (MJP), looking for periodicals important to the rise of modernism from 1890 to 1922, we learned of an appalling situation. Searching the Brown University Library for *Scribner's* magazine, we discovered that Brown's "complete" run of *Scribner's* consisted of copies that had been bound—with the advertising pages stripped out and discarded in the binding process. Further research demonstrated that this was the case with other periodicals in the Brown libraries and in other libraries as well. We will discuss this situation and its causes more fully in Chapter 8. But its importance to modernist studies can hardly be overestimated. For years, students have thought they were reading numbers of Addison and Steele's *Spectator* when what they were getting was the essays without the advertisements that accompanied them in every issue—offering us now a priceless window into the world of Queen Anne's England. In our courses and in our libraries we have been suppressing the cultural context in which our literary monuments first saw the light of day.

As we have seen, Ezra Pound knew how important advertising was, but he was getting his magazines at the newsstands in London. When we try to follow him now, and look at the magazines he was looking at, we are frustrated by our archival habits. And these habits have persisted so thoroughly and systematically that some of this crucial cultural information may be permanently lost to us. It is by no means certain that we can recover intact issues of many of the periodicals through which modern culture established itself. As Pound's own work has shown us, modernism was based on a struggle between popular and elite modes of cultural production, which means that our custodial habits of erasing the low side of the struggle—and advertising in particular—have left us with an impoverished notion of modernism itself. We know how important advertising was to the popular magazines, but we also know that behind every elite little magazine there is a story of a struggle for support, whether through direct patronage, or advertising, or both.

We know also that in 1935 the Conference of Eastern College Librarians addressed the issue of missing advertising. The conference brokered an agreement among thirty-four New England and New York City libraries to preserve at least one completely intact copy of the most widely held periodicals. But this means that for the period before 1935 there are not many intact copies out there. We shall return to the relationship of advertising and modernism in the magazines in Chapter 5 and to the hole in the archive in Chapter 8. For the moment it is enough to note that advertising was important to magazines of all types during the rise of modernism, and that our archives are poorly constructed to support research in this field. What is at stake here is the relationship between modernism and modernity—a relationship that is dynamic and complex, so that one can hardly be understood without the other. At present in our archives this relationship is obscure if not invisible, and we need to see it steadily and see it whole to understand modernism and our own present culture, which is, after all, an avatar of modernity. Modernism began in the magazines, and the magazines in which it began were—all of them —shaped by modernity. Pound, as we have seen, understood this perfectly. We later students of modernism must attend to this aspect of his thought as well as to others.

Rethinking Modernist Magazines

From Genres to Database

"—a magazine is a tricky individual!!"

—*Carolyn Ulrich, letter to F. H. Hoffman, 1944*

As we saw in Chapter 1, Ezra Pound gave some thought to magazine genres, comparing himself to "a simple-hearted anthropologist putting specimens into different large boxes—merely for present convenience tumbling things apparently similar into the same large box until a more scientific and accurate and mature arrangement is feasible." Pound's five "boxes" enabled him to sort the magazines by a combination of audience and ideology from his own critical perspective. Let us hasten to say that we are not going to propose a "more scientific and mature" version of such categories. Rather, we propose to review some attempts at categorization as a way of suggesting a different approach, made feasible by the digital resources becoming available to scholars working in this field. The subtitle of this chapter describes the change in approach—a move from ideological or cultural constructions to the collection of data that will enable scholars to group magazines in ways that will help answer the questions of interest to them and to search those magazines for appropriate information. But cultural genres are not the only boxes suitable for magazines. There are possible boxes based on simpler and more durable categories. Even that way of categorizing, however, has its problems. To understand them, we must begin by looking at the work of earlier students of periodicals.

There have been few attempts at a comprehensive theory of genres for printed periodicals. The best one we know of came from Frank Luther Mott, in the introduction to the first volume of what became his five-volume *History of American Magazines,* which began appearing in 1930. Mott knew more about American magazines than anybody, and he used that knowledge well in offering a brief discussion of "certain matters of definition" to be "cleared up at the outset" of his great project (1: 5). We will follow him as far as he can take us and then venture where he did not go. He began with the term *publication,* defined as "any issue of the press." From there he moved to a subcategory, *periodical,* defined as a publication possessing "periodicity," by virtue of being issued at regular or irregular intervals. Unlike the book, which is complete in itself, the periodical is not finished until its run has ended, which means, among other things, that a theory of reading based on the book will not work for the periodical. And there are other reasons, as we shall see, why this is so.

After defining periodicals as a subcategory of printed publications, Mott went on to isolate newspapers as a special case, arguing that usage had removed them from the category of periodicals even though etymology indicated that they belonged there. In making definitions, it is not a good idea to depart from etymology. Mott did so because he was on the way to making a case for *magazine* as the name for the objects of his inquiry, and he wanted newspapers out of that picture, along with annuals, formal reports, and foreign-language publications (1: 9). In any case, *magazine* is the name used by his followers in this field, whether studying American or British periodicals.

At this point we must pause and consider the usefulness of that word and the other terms regularly used to categorize periodicals—nouns like *magazine, review, paper,* and *journal,* along with adjectives like *little* and *mass.* A magazine was originally a periodical in which a miscellany of texts was collected and presented. Mott points out that the first use in English of the word *magazine* in this significance may be found in the British *Gentleman's Magazine* of 1731, where this new periodical was described as "a Monthly Collection, to treasure up, as in a Magazine, the most remarkable Pieces on the Subjects abovementioned, or at least impartial abridgements thereof" (quoted in Mott, 1: 6), and he glosses that use of the word with the subtitle of the American periodical *Massachusetts: Monthly Museum of Knowledge and Rational Entertainment, Containing Poetry, Musick, Biography, History, Physick, Geography, Morality, Criticism, Philosophy, Mathematicks, Agriculture, Architecture, Chemistry, Novels, Tales, Romances, Translations, News, Marriages and Deaths, Meteorological Observations, Etc., Etc.* This magazine also published "plays, essays, proceedings of Congress, and engravings," as well as an occasional page or two of music—clearly, *Massachusetts* meant to be inclusive. The words *magazine* and *museum* both denoted institutions where things were stored, though *magazine* connoted goods and *museum* connoted objects of knowledge. It is interesting, then, that the word with the more commercial connotations became the regular term for periodicals that collected and published a miscellany of textual objects, while the other, *museum,* became ever more tightly fixed to institutions with an educational purpose.

The word *review* has a slightly different history. As originally applied to periodicals in English, it referred to serious publications in which lengthy discussions based on books were the main form of content. The *Edinburgh Review* (1802–1929) can stand as a typical example of this genre. But the term gradually came to be used more loosely, as in *The English Review* (1908–1937), which featured poetry and fiction along with essays on current topics. As Mott put it, "For many years there was much rivalry between the miscellaneous, entertaining, and mercurial magazines on the one hand, and the dignified, learned, and lumbering reviews on the other" (1: 7). There is still, perhaps, a connotation of seriousness attached to the word *review* and of frivolity attached to *magazine.* No learned journal would call itself a magazine. The word *journal* itself is derived from *diurnal,* or daily, but it lost that specificity very early in both English and French and is now just a synonym for *periodical.*

Finally, as Mott pointed out, the word *paper* was used to denote periodicals that were not bound, stapled, or stitched, a significance retained in words like *newspaper* and *broadsheet.* But all these terms are inexact in their signification, to the point where they can scarcely be used for classification, though the addition of descriptive adjectives, as *little magazine*

Table 3.1: Information Provided in Studies of Magazines

Mott	Chielens	Sullivan
Title	Title and Changes	Title and Changes
Dates (first issue, last issue)	Volume and Issue Data	Volume and Issue Data
Periodicity	Frequency of Publication	Frequency of Publication
Publishers	Publishers	Publishers
Editors	Editors	Editors

or *mass magazine* or *weekly review,* helps a bit. If we are going to study periodicals, however, which will involve comparing and contrasting well-chosen samples of similar types, we will need something more reliable in the way of categorization. If we look into the data provided by Mott, Edward E. Chielens (*American Literary Magazines*), and Alvin Sullivan (*British Literary Magazines*), who all worked with the category *magazine,* we find a range of information regularly provided (see table 3.1).

All three provide exactly the same information, and omit the same information, from their basic categories. Mott set the standard here, and the others followed it. They all discuss the contents of their magazines as well, of course, but they do not offer other basic information of interest, such as price and circulation, or data on the role of advertising in the periodicals they list. Nor do they attempt to systematize the contents of their magazines in any way. Chielens and Sullivan deal only with "literary" magazines, of course. This adds a descriptive dimension to their work, but *literary* is a very loose descriptor. Circulation, on the other hand, is not always easy to determine, though Peterson, in *Magazines in the Twentieth Century,* offers tables of approximate circulation data for certain magazines, and he provides some data on advertising revenues as well. But there is no database in existence that offers all the information needed to put the study of modern periodicals on a firm footing. There is an old joke about a man who drops his wallet in a dark parking lot but searches for it only under a light because it is easier to search there.

We fear that bibliographical information often follows a similar pattern —offering information that is easy to find while ignoring more difficult things that it would be very good to know. In what follows here, we will explore all the sorts of information that would be useful for the study of periodicals connected to the rise of modernism.

The first and simplest consideration must be what Mott called periodicity—the interval between issues. This gives us a range of periodicals from daily through weekly, biweekly, monthly, quarterly, and annual to irregular, which may mean intervals of more than a year or less. We may indeed wish to give separate categorical names to some of these, like daily newspapers and annual volumes, but we must recognize that every publication issued periodically is a periodical. Though it is complicated enough, periodicity is actually the clearest and simplest of the categories we need to organize for studying the complex world of periodicals. Other basic considerations must be price, duration, dates, languages, size, audience, and content—and none of these is simple.

Price is relatively simple, though it often changes over the life of a periodical, and it is important. Price and periodicity could be used together as a rough-and-ready way of categorizing, as in Virginia Woolf's 1922 novel, *Jacob's Room*, in which Jacob (or the narrator) notices "on the table serious six-penny weeklies written by pale men in muddy boots —the weekly creak and screech of brains rinsed in cold water and wrung dry—melancholy papers" (35). To price and periodicity Woolf adds "serious" and "melancholy," along with her more imaginative and specific details. When she was writing, Woolf's category "sixpenny weekly" would probably have included *The Nation, The Spectator, The New Statesman,* and *The New Age.* Virginia's husband, Leonard, was at that time becoming an editor for *The Nation and The Athenaeum*—the result of a merger of two magazines in 1921—which adds a level of irony to her characterization of writers for these journals.

But the scene occurs when Jacob is at Cambridge, where he began his studies in 1906, so the date is probably 1907 or 1908, when *The New Age,* for example, was selling for one penny. Woolf may have been projecting backward, of course, using current prices erroneously to categorize magazines that sold for less in 1908. In this connection it would be helpful to know the prices of the other weeklies at that time. But *sixpenny* was a generic category, not necessarily to be taken literally. *The New States-man,* for example, had not been founded then, of course, but when it did appear in 1913 it was called a "sixpenny weekly" by its editor in a letter to *The New Age* (12.23: 17), which was then selling for threepence. Unfortunately, the bibliographical guides to periodicals, as we have seen, do not give us the information about price that would help us categorize them and thus learn to read Woolf's passage in a more informed manner. We can make an educated guess, however, that she had *The New Statesman* and its Fabian founders, Beatrice and Sidney Webb, squarely in her sights. Still, *sixpenny weekly* was a common term during this period. R. C. K. Ensor uses it in his monumental history, *England, 1870–1914:*

> A cheaper way for a rich man to become a maker of opinion was to publish a sixpenny weekly review. Publications of this class became now more numerous and various than ever before, and from first to last much of the period's best writing will be found in them. But only one (the unionist *Spectator*) paid solid dividends; the rest lived on their owners' money and their careers were apt to be brief or chequered. They took the place, to some degree, of the monthly and quarterly reviews, whose prosperity and influence after about 1904 went fast downhill. (536)

There is perhaps an intentional pun in "chequered"—hinting at the frequent support payments many magazines required. Woolf was not the only person to satirize sixpenny weeklies, nor the first. Lucy Lane Clifford (Mrs. W. K. Clifford) had done the job pretty well in the 1890s in one of her stories:

> *The Review* (there was no other worth mentioning in the opinion of those who conducted it, so the adjective was of no account) was a sixpenny weekly devoted to the patronage of politics, and the suppression of new books. It was sometimes brilliant, often amusing, and occasionally dull, for the simple reason that its staff could not be made to feel that anything contemporary with itself was of the slightest importance. It

thought most things vulgar and the rest foolish, went for the whole tribe of minor poets, the new school of everything it did not itself initiate, and all philosophical works that exceeded 300 pages. (12)

You have to like "the patronage of politics, and the suppression of new books." What we can learn from all this is that people who have discussed magazines have regularly attempted to classify them, and that this desire has led to the development of generic categories that are odd, and, as we shall see, often inadequate and misleading. In 1906 in Britain there were sixpenny monthlies as well as sixpenny weeklies. (Since a newer currency is in place now, we offer here a reminder: the pound was worth around five dollars during this period and consisted of twenty shillings, which in turn consisted of twelve pennies or pence each, so a sixpence was half a shilling and five shillings were called a crown.) Those monthlies offered mainly popular fiction to a large audience. And there were one-penny weeklies also catering to that audience. Knowing this we can see that the category "sixpenny weekly" names a weekly magazine selling at a monthly price, which, therefore, must be a weightier magazine containing deeper thought for a smaller audience. But we need the data to make these distinctions. The relationship between categories like sixpenny weekly and little magazine is not simple. *The New Age,* selling for whatever number of pennies, was a sixpenny weekly, but it published new writers like Katherine Mansfield and images by new artists like Jacob Epstein and Gaudier-Brzeska as well as work by established writers like Arnold Bennett and artists like Walter Sickert, both of whom thought of themselves as "modern" while others sought to deny them that status. *The New Age* was, in some way, both a sixpenny weekly and a little magazine, but it might just as well be called a weekly review, which is what it called itself—though it did occasionally publish fiction and poetry.

The distinction between a "review" and a "magazine" was meaningful when it was first used in the early nineteenth century, but it had lost its clarity by the time *The English Review* was founded in 1908. The monetary descriptors, however, which were regularly used in Britain but not in the United States, remain useful. *Blackwood's* magazine, founded in 1817, was a monthly selling for half a crown (two shillings sixpence) and persisted as such for more than a century, though it was challenged in the late nineteenth century by new "shilling monthlies" that aimed at a wider audience and reached it. *Blackwood's* was a true "magazine," glorying in its nickname, "Maga," and publishing a lot of fiction, including some famous serializations of novels. In 1917 Pound, of course, mocked its centennial issue as a stodgy relic of the Victorian past. In the 1890s the rising importance of advertising had changed the world of magazines again, allowing monthlies that could sell for as little as six or eight pence and survive, and they competed heavily for celebrity authors to help sustain circulation. Which meant that by 1917 *Blackwood's* was indeed on its last legs. (For an excellent collection of discussions of *Blackwood's*, see David Finkelstein's *Print Culture and the Blackwood Tradition*.)

Duration, which the bibliographical aids normally do consider, is both simple and crucial as a category. Did the periodical last for only a few months, a few years, a few decades, or many decades? This simple category can tell us much about a periodical, though it should not be taken as decisive with respect to the importance of any given journal. *Blast* ran for only two irregular issues in 1914 and 1915, but its importance and influence were great. Other periodicals ran for a century or more without making a major contribution to the culture in which they appeared. But we need to know about duration to know just what kind of periodical we are investigating. We may also be interested in the dates and places of publication. A journal of the 1890s will be significantly different from one of the twenties, even if all the other parameters are similar. And a journal published in Wausau, Wisconsin, or Iowa City, Iowa, will differ from one published in New York or Rome, even if all are in the English language, which is, of course, another basic categorical distinction. *The Little Review* (1914–1929) was published in Chicago, San Francisco, Chicago again, New York, and, finally, Paris—and it changed as it moved. It also changed from a monthly to a quarterly. The same journal may change drastically over the course of its life. There is a basic pattern of growth and decline, but imposed on this there are often radical shifts that are the result of changes in governance or editorial decisions.

Size, as a term, is not quite so simple. It can refer to the dimensions of covers and pages, or to the number of pages in a typical issue.

And both these sizes may change over the life of a particular periodical. Many of the ephemeral periodicals listed by Faxon in 1903 in his *"Ephemeral Bibelots": A Bibliography of Modern Chap-Books* changed their physical shape and size during their short runs, as Faxon carefully notes. And even a regular London weekly like *The New Age* changed its number of pages frequently over the fifteen years of Orage's editorship (1907–1922), starting at sixteen pages per issue, rising as high as thirty-two, and sinking as low as twelve. Still, the average number of pages per issue will prove to be a useful way of grouping certain periodicals for comparative study. A "little magazine" with a large number of pages is not exactly little, but some periodicals usually given this designation—such as *Blast*—were small in neither format nor pagination. The proportion of advertising to other matter in all kinds of magazines will also prove interesting as we begin to compare various periodicals within and across countries and periods or trace the lives of individual magazines—and so will the types and targets of such advertising.

In terms of audience, quantity is of great importance, especially in the period we are considering, where advertising revenues were tied to circulation. Circulation, where it can be determined accurately, is crucial, but other factors are interesting as well, though they may not always be easy to find. *Audience* can refer to the number of subscribers, the number of readers, or the education, class, race, or gender of the readership. It would be interesting to know, for example, how many people of one race, class, gender, or education level read periodicals ostensibly aimed at another. The proper study of periodicals is going to require some of the methods of the social sciences. Raw circulation figures are somewhat easier to find, though they are pretty vague for those magazines called "little." Categorization in terms of audience size will be a basic element in discussing periodical genres. Other refinements about the nature of such audiences must follow from this basic information. Still, as we shall see, looking closely at the advertising and other content of a given periodical can tell us a good deal about the intended audience.

All the bibliographers of periodicals provide the names of the editors and the publishers. This information is both obtainable and useful, though normally not of equal importance. With the larger magazines, information about the publisher may be of great importance (especially when it tells us where a given periodical was published), but with the smaller magazines it is the editor(s) and the staff of regular contributors who dominate. What the author is to a book, the editor(s) and staff are to a periodical—the major influence on the contents of the object. This is not to say that they are identical. A periodical, like a film, does not have a single "author," though the author function is so useful to criticism that critics have made the director of a film the *auteur* for their own critical purposes. We can't quite do that for periodicals, but editorship, especially for the smaller periodicals, is a crucial unifying element, which must be considered—and it has been so considered in books like Wallace Martin's *"The New Age" Under Orage*. *The New Age* ceased to be important when Orage left it in 1922; the first fifteen issues of *The English Review*, under the editorship of Ford Madox Hueffer (later Ford), are the stuff of legend. Periodicals change when an editor comes or goes, as can clearly be seen by tracing the presence of Ezra Pound on the mastheads of *Poetry*, *The Little Review*, and *The Egoist*. It will also be very useful, if it can be done, to categorize the types of contributors. Are they established, unknown, or transitional—and what is the mixture? Were they famous then and unknown now, or the reverse—or did they remain in one of these categories?

Content is, no doubt, the trickiest category of all. It can refer to the generic type of material published in a typical issue (reporting, reviewing, fiction, poetry, visual art, advertising, and so on) or to the topics regularly covered (public life or private lives, local or distant), or the quality of the work included—which is no doubt the most vexed category of all. The word *literary*, for instance, has been regularly used to designate a set of periodicals for study. But *literary* as a category may refer to both creative work and critical, or may be intended simply to connote the quality of writing in a given journal. And using *literary* as a category to describe whole magazines may result in works of literature that appeared in "nonliterary" journals being lost or ignored: some of James Joyce's first fiction appeared in an agricultural journal (*The Irish Homestead*). These difficulties never stopped editors of periodicals from making claims about quality, along with claims about audience size and type and other matters difficult to ascertain with any certainty. But scholars must proceed with a bit more caution and reliability. With respect to content, then, we think it important to note the textual genres appearing in a given journal, the presence and extent of advertising, and the presence and types of illustration. These things, too, often change over time. The life of a journal like *Munsey's* can be read in the rise and fall of pages devoted to advertisements in its issues. A single percentage for advertising versus text cannot be given for many magazines, though a high and low, with dates, may be possible, when research into these matters is taken far enough.

What we need, then, is a comprehensive set of data on magazines that can be searched in various ways and organized so as to allow grouping by common features, or sets of common features. We also need to know where to find original copies of these periodicals with their covers and advertising intact. Here is a version of the information we really need for the study of periodicals active during the rise of modernism:

- Periodicity: from daily to irregular
- Price per issue and per subscription, with changes (sample first, middle, and last issues)
- Duration: from a few issues to decades of regular publication
- Dates: year or years of publication
- Places: countries and cities of editing and publication, with dates
- Languages: the primary language and any others used in the journal
- Format: dimensions, type of paper, and the like (sample issues at regular intervals)
- Size: from a few pages per issue to many (sample issues at regular intervals)
- Readership: number, education, other significant factors (for sample issues at regular intervals, if these can be determined)
- Editor(s): names and dates, including staff, regulars
- Publisher(s): names, dates, and locations
- Contributors: type, whether established, unknown, transitional (names of most frequent and most important)

- Main types of content (sample issues at regular intervals for each of the following)
  - textual: social-political-public to artistic-critical-private
  - advertising: presence, quantity (percentage of pages), types
  - illustration: presence, quantity, types
- Availability: libraries with runs of original issues, with dates

The categories above require a good deal of information that we do not have at present. But they give us a template of what is required, so that we can begin trying to gather this information and develop the best ways to display and use it.

Meanwhile, we need to look more closely at the categories we have been using to group periodicals for study, which have been useful up to a point but are misleading and inadequate for further study. Hoffman, Allen, and Ulrich, for example, in their justly famous book, *The Little Magazine*, define "little" magazines by circulation (under one thousand, though they include *The Smart Set* at seventy-five thousand) and editorial selection (publication of new writing, especially experimental creative work that commercial periodicals will not accept, by writers not yet widely known). So far so good (except for ignoring their own limits), but then they go on to consider six subcategories of little magazine: poetry, exemplified by *Poetry;* leftist, exemplified by *The Masses;* regional, exemplified by *The Midland;* experimental, exemplified by *The Little Review;* critical, exemplified by *The Dial;* and eclectic, exemplified by *The Seven Arts* (8–9). From our inevitably postmodern perspective, these categories are a bit too much like Borges's definitions from "a certain Chinese Encyclopedia." That is, they do not connect; they do not even stay on the same level. We have one category based on a literary genre, "poetry," but nothing comparable for experiments in other literary genres. We have one political category, "leftist," but nothing for other brands of politics. And we have one geographical category, "regional," defined mainly as not from the East Coast of the United States. Then comes "experimental," which was supposed to be a characteristic of all little magazines but now defines a subcategory. This is followed by "critical," which is a potentially useful category, if there were others on the same level, and finally "eclectic," which is defined as less experimental than the others. And there is no category for ethnic, though there were small magazines like W. E. B. Du Bois's *Crisis* (which is not in Hoffman, Allen, and Ulrich), aimed at audiences of particular racial or religious background, that published interesting work.

We must make allowances for this groundbreaking and still useful book of 1946, but these subcategories are not helpful. There were, for example, rightist and antiexperimental little magazines, such as *The Antidote* (1912–1915), which appears in the book's bibliographical listing but apparently did not influence the definition section. Backed by Lord Alfred Douglas, *The Antidote* was resolutely antiexperimental—which threatens the definition of the whole category of little magazines as "experimental." Scholars of modernism have accepted a romanticized definition of little magazines as places where the aura of art was preserved by a modernist avant-garde of dedicated editors. But the situation was more complicated than that, and we shall need clear definitions and categories if we are to work our way through those complications.

Ezra Pound tried to shift that category to "Small Magazines" in his essay of that title, but he did not succeed. We should ask ourselves why he failed. The answer we wish to propose is that the *lit* in *little* suggests literariness in the context of magazines, and the notion of a "little magazine" connotes cuteness as well. In the world of periodicals, little magazines were perceived as handsome little Davids confronting ugly big Goliaths. (Think Donatello here, not Michelangelo or Bernini.) How could we not love and cherish them? *Small* captures neither the allusion to literature not the cuteness of *little*. But the notion of "little magazines" prevents us from seeing what was really going on in the world of modern periodicals. To undo this notion and correct our vision we need something like the "brains rinsed in cold water and wrung dry" that Woolf mocked in *Jacob's Room*. Such brains would start by unpacking *little* and following Pound's lead. We might start with a category of "small magazines" that allows for varieties in content: small literary magazines, small art magazines, small humor magazines, and so on. And perhaps we even need to unpack the word *small* and speak of "low-circulation literary magazines" and "short-lived literary magazines" and, in some cases, "short-lived, low-circulation literary magazines" or "short-lived, low-circulation art magazines." If our readers think we are getting too fanciful here, we can assure them that *The Apple (of Beauty and Discord)* was a short-lived, low-circulation, large-format art magazine published in 1920 and 1921 that published visual art by established artists as well as experimental newcomers and managed to get listed in the little magazine bibliography compiled by Carolyn Ulrich for the Hoffman book. Ezra Pound wrote critical essays for it, and a drawing of him by Wyndham Lewis appeared in it.

While we are looking at *The Little Magazine* we should note that Ulrich and Hoffman exchanged letters about what should be included in the bibliography. Their discussion is complicated, but the gist of it is that Ulrich, the librarian, wanted completeness and Hoffman, the critic, wanted selectivity, and Hoffman had the final decision about what went in. Ulrich wanted to start with 1890, but Hoffman wanted to start with 1912, so while Ulrich was allowed to include a few titles from before 1912, they were far from the two hundred or so she thought should be there. Hoffman also wrote the annotations that extended the bibliographic data with information about contents and judgments about quality, so many annotations, in fact, that his editor at the Princeton University Press had to ask him to tone down and reduce the number of value judgments he made (Hoffman archive at the University of Wisconsin–Milwaukee Library, correspondence). There remained, however, invisible value judgments about inclusion that were based, as Ulrich reminded Hoffman in the letter from which our epigraph is drawn, on his sample of only a few issues of many of the little magazines discussed in his notes to Ulrich's bibliography.

To put it simply, we need a bigger and better list, and we need to look harder at the notion of "little magazines" itself. Felix Pollak tried to look hard in his preface to Marion Sader's *Comprehensive Index to English-Language Little Magazines, 1890–1970*, where he discussed his criteria for selecting one hundred magazines out of the thousands that had appeared during this period:

> Above all, one had to pick not necessarily "the best," but the most characteristic. Nor could the factors determining inclu-

sion be the renown of contributors' names, the length of a
magazine's existence, or the place of its origin. In the end, the
decision always hinged on that undefinable quality known as
the "little magazine spirit" that emanated from the pages before me. . . .

One word should be said about a problem that faces
every bibliographer of little magazines: what to do with the
semi-big littles, the established journals within an anti-estab-
lishment genre, and how to treat the academic quarterlies?
When, in other words, does "little" cease and "big" begin,
when does "non-commercial" turn into "commercial"? It is
a problem that cannot be solved by "objective" criteria alone.
Make-up, illustrations, the number of pages, the kind of contributors, the price of subscription and single copies, are
merely factors that enter into the picture and need to be sub-
jectively appraised. . . . It is again the little-magazine spirit that
makes the big little difference. (ix–x)

We may note in passing that *objective* appears in quotation marks and
subjective does not, and that *little-magazine spirit* loses its quotes and becomes established by its repetition. Pollak, an experienced librarian,
points very clearly to the problem but really offers no solution. Furthermore, the selection, when it is investigated, does not help much with the
definition. Among the magazines excluded are *The English Review,* which
Ezra Pound listed among his "small magazines," and *The Mask,* which
was in Hoffman and colleagues' set of little magazines, while among those
included is *The London Mercury,* which resembled *The English Review*
in size, format, and circulation but not in "little-magazine spirit." *The
Smart Set* is excluded, though Hoffman and colleagues had included it
and Hoffman said that "from 1912 to December 1923" it was "an important magazine of modern letters" (374). Hoffman and colleagues had included *The Dial* from 1920 to 1929 among the little magazines, but not
its less well–financed earlier years in Chicago. Sader and Pollak exclude
it. Subjectivity is not the librarian's friend—or the scholar's.

Another, more recent attempt to define little magazines was made
by Suzanne Churchill and Adam McKible in the introduction to their

edited collection, *Little Magazines and Modernism: New Approaches.* Noting that "little magazines, like modernism itself, are vexingly difficult to define," they conclude that for their purposes, "aesthetic experimentation and political radicalism" will serve to define the modernist little magazine, noting that such periodicals are usually founded by individuals or small groups and are "non-commercial" in that they are not designed to make a profit (6). This is a noble attempt to solve the problem, but we find it ultimately inadequate. Harriet Monroe, for example, wanted to expand the definition of poetry in more than one direction, and she meant to educate an audience that could appreciate a whole range of poetry from Native American chants and Vachel Lindsay to Ezra Pound and Wallace Stevens. So if one looks at the whole first decade of *Poetry,* one finds not only works of aesthetic experimentation but also cowboy songs and other poems of the Southwest, and many poems by women (like Sara Teasdale and Edna St. Vincent Millay) that are not experimental but are nonetheless new voices in American poetry. Other magazines complicate the case even further. Gordon Craig's *Mask,* published in Florence from 1908 to 1929, was more aestheticist than modernist, and politically conservative (antisuffrage, for example), but quite properly has a place in *The Little Magazine.* Definitions in terms of attitude and values are as tricky as the magazines they seek to define. We propose, then, to go back to Pollak's warning and make an attempt to follow the less traveled road toward objective description by means of the mere "factors" that he mentions and some others that he doesn't.

The crucial categories required to unpack the concept of *little magazine,* then, would seem to be duration, circulation, and textual content, to which we might add the amount of advertising (relatively low) and the sort of contributors (usually, though not always, relatively new and unrecognized). Even here, however, we must be cautious. *New* can mean young, just coming on the scene, and doing something different, or it can mean previously unpublished but not necessarily doing something different or experimental. The fuzziness of "new" as a category helps explain, perhaps, the contradictory categories of "experimental" and "eclectic" in the discussion of little magazines by Hoffman, Allen, and Ulrich. We have not mentioned periodicity in connection with little magazines, but it is safe to say that those in Faxon's and Ulrich's bibliographies almost never published as frequently as weekly, and only a few as frequently as biweekly or semimonthly. They were mainly monthly, quarterly, or irregular, and often shifted among these modes of periodicity. *The Little Review,* for example, shifted from monthly to quarterly after its move to Paris. But we must learn to stop talking, writing, and thinking as if the category of "little magazines" represented something real in the textual world. It is a dream category, an attempt to unite periodicals of which the uniter approves and exclude those lacking such approval, as Pollak's discussion clearly reveals.

At the other end of the scale from what have been called little magazines lie what have been called mass magazines. As we indicated in Chapter 2, these two phenomena are simultaneous and linked, with the chapbooks, bibelots, and little magazines arising against the coming of the advertising-driven mass magazines. This means that advertising may be a key determinant in categorizing the differences between these two sorts of periodicals. A typical mass magazine of the late 1890s (our example is *McClure's* magazine for September 1898) might have about 90 pages of text (including illustrations) and another 90 of advertising. (In the June 1912 issue, we find 120 pages of text and about 80 of ads.) The small literary and art magazines rarely had as much as 10 percent advertising, while this large magazine had 50 percent, declining to 40 percent over a fourteen-year period. That is a major difference. The *McClure's* of September 1898 included several short works of fiction, but reporting and reminiscences dominated, with special emphasis on coverage of the war with Spain. Among less well–known authors, we find Hamlin Garland, giving an account of Custer's last battle from the perspective of an Indian chief, and Octave Thanet, with a short story, as well as Emily Todd Helm with reminiscences of her sister, who had been married to Abraham Lincoln. In the June 1912 issue the mix was similar, with fiction, poetry, and articles of various sorts, including one on "the new art of making Presidents by press bureau." A story by Willa Sibert Cather was announced for the next issue.

If we ask whether *McClure's* is a "literary" magazine, the answer is not simple, though it is clear that reporting dominates and that it included very little poetry (none in September 1898, and one poem by Kathryn Tynan in July 1912). But such authors as Kipling, Jack London,

A. C. Doyle, Stephen Crane, Willa Cather, and W. B. Yeats did write for *McClure's* in the two decades before America entered the First World War. A magazine not classified as "literary" might publish a number of authors considered to belong to "literature." Which means that generic categories (fiction, poetry, reporting) and quantitative measures (circulation, percent of pages devoted to advertising, and the like) may turn out to be more useful in trying to describe a periodical than a notion like *literary*, which combines a generic and a qualitative signification. Terms like *little* and *mass* magazines are in fact modernist notions, designed to make an invidious division into versions of "high" and "low" (as Robert Scholes has argued in *Paradoxy of Modernism*), and therefore very much in need of deconstruction, if we are to see modernism from outside its own perspectives.

In that connection, we can learn from the September 1898 number of *McClure's* that the magazine's circulation had increased over the previous year by more than 100,000 copies per issue, and that *McClure's* and Doubleday's *Ladies' Home Journal* had a combined total circulation of "more than 1,250,000 copies a month" (496) in 1898. This means that *McClure's* was selling around 400,000 copies a month, while *The Ladies' Home Journal* was nearing the million mark (a mark it finally passed in 1904 [Peterson, 56]). So *McClure's* had a large circulation, but not quite half as large as *The Ladies' Home Journal*. Were they both "mass" magazines? Clearly some periodicals were mass-ier than others. The category of *mass magazines* turns out to be no more precise than that of *little magazines*, and for the same reason: it combines a quantitative denotation with a qualitative connotation. We need ways to talk about periodicals and classify them, but we must seek terminology that is as descriptive as possible, which means that it must set aside considerations of quality and value for a later stage of analysis.

In this descriptive process, numbers are definitely going to be useful, even when we cannot obtain exact details, because they have the virtue of not implying quality—or the lack of it, as a word like *mass* so clearly does. We can begin, then, by using numbers to help define terms. Even here, however, we shall need to be very cautious and be alert for variations over the years. *McCall's*, for example, went from a circulation of around 200,000 in 1900 to more than a million in 1910 (Peterson, 60). *Poetry*, on the other hand, stayed between 1,000 and 2,000 for its entire first decade (Williams, 296), while *The New Age* ranged from a few thousand to a bit over 20,000 during the fifteen years of Orage's editorship (Martin, 10, 16, 122). Looking at these numbers, the *McCall's* circulation seems large in 1900 even though it grew enormously in the next decade. *The New Age's* was never large, though not exactly small. And *Poetry's* was always small, though not as small as that of some magazines that counted sales in the low hundreds. Most of what we have called "little" magazines had circulations from the low hundreds to a couple of thousand copies, and most of those we have called "mass" magazines had sales from near 100,000 copies per issue to up in the millions, with magazines that remained in that category between a few thousand and a hundred thousand or more as well. Let us call them, if we need names, small-, medium-, and large-circulation magazines: if it seems useful we can further divide those three categories, but let us start there and see what we get. Circulation numbers change over the course of a periodical's existence, but they usually change more slowly than other features—and perhaps less radically as well. Small does not become large overnight, though a change of editors may result in a relatively quick change in content. And large remains large, whether we are talking about hundreds of thousands or millions. Still, some combination of circulation, size, periodicity, duration, and content should enable us to get a start on categorizing most periodicals.

The fullest magazine data provided in any book about modern magazines is that in Mike Ashley's *Age of the Storytellers: British Popular Fiction Magazines, 1880–1950.* For every periodical discussed in the main section of this book, Ashley provides a rather detailed record:

Title(s)
Number of issues
Dates
Frequency
Publisher
Editor(s)
Format/Size
Price
References

Other editions
Holdings (in libraries, collections)
Collecting points

As the last field suggests, this book is aimed more directly at collectors than at scholars, but it comes closer to the ideal we have postulated above than do many scholarly works in this field. The rich notes for each journal also provide, in many cases, information on circulation, paper (pulp, slick, and so on), and the writers whose work appeared. Many writers we think of as belonging to "high literature" appeared in these journals, along with other writers who stayed resolutely within the popular field. It is a serious error for scholars to ignore such magazines in their studies of modernism, for the literary experiments that grace those magazines called "little" were in a symbiotic relationship with the more formulaic writing that readers sought in the magazines studied by Ashley. And new discoveries were made on both sides of this blurry line.

Another extremely useful step in providing data on periodicals was taken by David Reed in his book *The Popular Magazine in Britain and the United States, 1880–1960*. In his appendixes he offers information on the content of more than thirty magazines for certain years of their existence, at intervals of a decade. He samples *Scribner's*, for example, in 1890, 1900, and 1910, and *Cosmopolitan* in 1888, 1890, 1900, 1910, and 1920. For each of the years he studied, he offers percentages of pages for various types of content, based on an examination of at least six months' worth of issues. He lists percentages for twenty-nine different kinds of content, with subtotals for ten large categories. Table 3.2 shows Reed's large categories, with the figures in parentheses representing the (rounded off) percentage of each type in *Scribner's* magazine for 1910. Using data like this from Reed's book, we can see that the proportion of fiction in *Cosmopolitan*, for example, rose from 24 percent in 1890 to 81 percent in 1920, and in *Colliers* from 13 percent in 1900 to 50 percent in 1920, while rising at a more modest rate in *Scribner's* (33 percent in 1890 to 40 percent in 1910). These extremely useful figures are just enough to whet the appetite for more, however. One would like the data for *Scribner's* in 1920, for example, which Reed doesn't supply. But this is the kind of information we are going to need to study periodicals properly.

Table 3.2: Content as Assessed in Reed, *The Popular Magazine in Britain and the United States, 1880–1960*

Content Type	*Percentage Found in* Scribner's *1910*
fiction	(40%)
travel and adventure	(23%)
history and biography	(3%)
arts (including criticism)	(21%)
natural sciences	(0)
modern life	(10%)
religion	(0)
women's pages	(0)
humor and entertainment	(missing, with the ads, from the issues examined)
miscellaneous	(3%)

Or, to put it more precisely, we are going to need a refined version of such categories. For even these, when we look into them, have their problems—a major one being the separation of "fiction" from what Reed summarizes as "arts." The actual subcategories combined in "arts" are these:

> fine art
> decorative art
> literary comments
> verse
> theater
> music
> movies
> radio and TV
> dance

This categorization reflects the division we still find in old bookstores between "fiction" and "literature," and it puts poetry and criticism in a different group from fiction. Now, it is true that fiction was such an important element in popular magazines that it may deserve a category of its own, but when we turn to other magazines—especially those called "little"—we find fiction there as well. In the popular magazines, also, we will find fiction by Stephen Crane and Joseph Conrad alongside fiction by Kipling, Stevenson, H. G. Wells, H. Rider Haggard, and Rafael Sabatini. Just where would we draw the line here between "fiction" and "literature"? Reed, it is true, solves the problem by putting all fiction in a category of its own. But Reed devised his categories to deal with "popular magazines," while what we really need are categories that will enable us to trace similarities and differences among those magazines called popular and those we might call elite, as well as that large group of journals that straddle these two categories.

Reed himself begins his book by noting that his was "a mapping exercise," in which he would avoid "taking some general criteria as given without reflection" (9). He goes on to observe,

> To attempt a study of large-scale patterns is to confront the need to establish the parameters of the discussion and the terms in which it is couched. . . . The approach . . . should . . . promote coherence and accessibility so that commentaries use a vocabulary which will suggest similarities and highlight differences across barriers which frequently inhibit the understanding of generic qualities. . . .
>
> As this study covers eight decades, it is possible to subdivide the period in order to further the above objectives. By breaking it down into ten-year segments, the material is partitioned into elements which permit the consistent, recurrent analysis of magazines. Thus, by repeating particular procedures for each decade, a series of cross-sections can be built up which outline parts of the periodical press over time. (9)

Reed himself offers one example of how data such as that quoted above can be displayed in graphic form to indicate patterns in the content of periodicals. His graphs of *Cosmopolitan* for 1900, 1910, and 1920, for example, show the percentage of fiction increasing from around 30 percent to 80 percent of the magazine's pages, while all the other categories shrink. The graphs for *Scribner's Monthly/Century Illustrated*, on the other hand, show a more balanced set of categories, with fiction growing much more slowly. As he puts it in discussing his graphic display, "*Century Illustrated* was always a balanced publication, an approach reflected in the range of articles published in *Cosmopolitan* in 1900. But the extraordinary success of the *Saturday Evening Post* and its emphasis on fiction affected many editors and encouraged them to build on its example, as can be seen in *Cosmopolitan* by 1920" (caption to plate XI). We need data that will allow us to generate comparisons like this for various analytical purposes. And we need a set of content categories that will allow us to bring together a broader spectrum of journals than those studied by Reed.

Finally, what we need badly and do not find in Reed's categories is information about the percentage of advertising pages in all the magazines, popular and unpopular, large and small, during this period. And this needs to be combined with a refined version of Reed's categories to provide the data needed to study modernism in the magazines. Using such data we should be able to generate reliable categories that will enable us to group magazines for study, but we need fuller information before we can even begin to do this. Reed's form of decennial grid offers us a useful pattern to follow in gathering and displaying information. It is time to use digital technology to store such information and make it available in a variety of forms and groupings. Which means that it is time to move from notions of genres based, as they must be, on what Wittgenstein defined as family resemblance to the firmer and more orderly ground of digital databases that can support all sorts of ad hoc groupings based on the information they contain and interests of the investigator: the work of "brains rinsed in cold water and wrung dry" indeed.

We must begin this bracing work with reading. As we'll see in later chapters, reading an issue of a modern magazine is an enormously intertextual affair: one must be aware of the contemporary culture that surrounds the issue, and one must be able to see the issue as one installment in a sequence that unrolls over the lifetime of the magazine. It is reading, to be sure, but reading that requires perspectives that are difficult to achieve. There are many ways to read, of course, but we are arguing in this book that it is beneficial and rewarding to read magazines in a way that is informed by scholarship, if not precisely by criticism (indeed, in a way that is precisely *not* informed by criticism, because criticism is motivated by argument and perspective, and we are trying to develop a way of reading that suspends judgments). In other words, when we sit down to read a magazine, we pluck a single issue from an immense heap of twentieth-century culture. It might be useful to take on Ezra Pound's persona of "simple-hearted anthropologist" sitting in a warehouse with a hoard of magazines before us. We're going to have to make sense of this heap, and to do that we're almost certainly going to want to impose some order on it. Later we're going to look at the limitations of this approach and discover how to let multiple orders emerge from the material itself. But for now, let's start by making a list.

What is a list, exactly? Originally from an Old German word for a strip of paper, the word *list* in its early usage meant a catalog of people doing the same thing or associated with the same group, like soldiers in an army. A list, then, is the material trace of a winnowing, a ranking, or a classification of some kind, *for some purpose.* We need to bear that in mind as we go on: list making is motivated, even if the aim of the lister is to create something comprehensive. For now, our motive is rather simple, if audacious: we want to identify all the English-language magazines that were published at the dawn of modernism and that might be of interest to someone studying what we now call modern culture. It is obvious that our criteria are impossibly baggy: why English, to start with? Why not French, German, Italian, Spanish, or other European languages? Why confine ourselves to European and American culture, when modernism arose from an emerging global culture? And when is the dawn of modernism, exactly? Are there dates before and after which the magazines that were published are not of interest to us? Why?

And how can we possibly discard something on the grounds that it isn't of interest to someone studying modern culture? Even if we confine ourselves to magazines that publish "literature" or "art" (however we choose to define those), the very nature of magazines makes it likely that we'll find something of interest in almost every one, from the doggerel in a farm magazine to the dingbats in an accounting journal. So it is clear that no matter how catholic our intentions in creating a list of modern magazines, that list will be a trace of our biases, conceptions, and preconceptions. It is around such lists, or canons, that disciplines are formed, and we have learned to be suspicious of canons and disciplines. So we must regard this list-making business with skepticism. Yet for the moment there seems no other way to comprehend modernism in the magazines than to make a list of those magazines and study the modernism in them. So we will go on, retaining our skepticism while remaining pragmatic. (And eventually we'll return to some other possibilities besides lists.) Let us assume we have separated our wheat from the chaff and have some sort of list, whose confining parameters are as clearly articulated as we can make them. It is still a long, long list. How are we to get around it?

We have become used to computer-aided search and navigation by now, so some of the concerns with getting around a large list seem quaint. It was not always so, and it is perhaps useful to recall a time before computers, when compiling lists, indexes, and concordances was an important scholarly task, if dry as dust. Back then, these distillates of scholarly attention were durable: someone compiled them, typed or printed them, and published them; they sat on library shelves, usually in a reference room, where they were consulted (if they were consulted at all) with effort: one had to know where they were, get to that place, learn their conventions and use patterns, consult them, make handwritten notes from them, and then leave them. Indeed, knowing how to use indexes and concordances was one of the things that distinguished scholars from mere readers. In this way, reference books like these were vestiges of an almost-vanished culture of literacy, when books were rare commodities, and libraries were archives. Those conventions and use patterns derived from the constraints of print: lots of abbreviations (because transcribing and printing were time-consuming and expensive); many cross-references (because duplication was error-prone and similarly expensive); limited to one or two orderings (for the same reasons); seldom updated (ditto). This is why we now refer to it as hard copy: it is rigid and relatively immutable, though it can, of course, be mutilated—cut up and rearranged or, more important, annotated.

Choosing an ordering for a list was important, then, because you could have only a few of them. In a poetry index, for example, you might find a list of words, a list of titles, a list of authors, and a list of first lines;

but you would not find a list of poems containing words describing a rosy hue near words referring to dawn, because such a list would be too specialized: you would have to compile such a list yourself. And the list would be ordered to facilitate retrieval: an alphabetical ordering is the most sensible for languages that use alphabets, because alphabets have conventional rankings. This alphabetical arrangement is purely convenient; it represents no inherent ordering in the material itself: the fact that *The Bookman* comes right before *The Bookseller* in a list of nineteenth-century magazines says nothing about the publications themselves or the relationship between them (unlike, say, the name AAA Plumbing, which very likely was chosen precisely to put the business at the top of an alphabetical list).

So arranging our list of modern magazines poses any number of problems, because a simple alphabetical list doesn't tell us much. What we really want are lists ordered by those categories of information we itemized earlier: periodicity, duration, dates of publication, and so forth. We itemized more than a dozen categories, and those were just a start. That's a lot of lists, and in a precomputer era it was impractical to compile and maintain them. For this reason, among others, scholars have invented ways of lumping a bunch of important categories together, to make it easier to create, maintain, and study these texts: information scientists call these lumps *clusters;* literary scholars call them *genres.*

Classification is a problematic endeavor. Wordsworth wrote that "we murder to dissect," and in this he was responding to eighteenth-century rationalism: you can't see the forest for the trees might be another way of putting it. Analysis is under fire here: in attempting to understand by picking apart and/or classifying, you create false identities and distinctions. And so it is with attempts to classify modern magazines by means of categories like *little, mass, left,* and so on. These categories are prejudices, in the sense of prejudgment on the basis of preexisting, or *a priori,* concepts. To trace is to follow a path left behind; it is to reproduce. But tracing based on *a priori* distinctions yields a distorted picture: certain features are highlighted while others are repressed. So our problem with genres goes beyond the distinction between little magazines and mass magazines. As we've seen, the genres traditionally used to classify periodicals fail to distinguish where it matters, lumping too many distinct magazines under a single classification.

Modern computer technology can help us get around the problems posed by the imposition of genre on our magazines by allowing us to disaggregate the feature sets constituting genres and instead compile much more precise sets of features on the fly. This is the method linguists use when describing speech sounds: to describe the characteristics of speech, linguists identify a set of features (labial, dental, aspirated, voiced, and so on) that describe how a sound is produced. A feature set implies a matrix representing all the possible combinations of these features, denoted by their presence or absence. Each combination of feature-states in the matrix is the signature of a sound: a phoneme. So what we need are *magazine phonemes:* instead of assigning a single signifier to a magazine (*little* versus *mass,* for example), we need to identify a set of characteristics that contribute to our understanding of the magazines and then cluster them in different ways. In other words, we need to develop a *language of magazines.*

Language makes it possible for us to conceive and describe magazines with far greater subtlety and precision. We don't need to separate those magazines into generic lists or boxes, or put them into any particular order; instead, we need to identify the language for describing magazines and develop some tools for expressing that language. We have begun that first task by identifying the language of magazine description: that is, by proposing the information we need in order to study periodicals active during the rise of modernism. Let us now examine the choice of those categories more closely, and from two directions: from the data and from the questions we'd like to pose.

There is always more information to collect, but not all of it is of obvious use to researchers, and it can be expensive to get. On the one hand, then, we need to limit our collection to data that will help us answer our questions: "If I knew X, Y, and Z about modernist magazines, I would be able to answer the question Q." Question-driven discovery is, of course, the most common form of research, but its inverse, data-driven discovery, can be equally useful: some new category of information, or some new way of looking at that information, may spark questions one never thought to ask before. "Given that I know X, Y, and Z about modernist magazines, what can that information tell me that I don't already know?" Choosing what categories to use, then, involves a trade-off between cost and utility: how much it would cost to compile the information versus how useful having that information would be.

Let's begin with cheap information. Bibliographic information (title, editor, physical size, dates of publication, and the like) is cheap, relatively speaking: librarians have been cataloging it for years, as have researchers like Mott, Chielens, Sullivan, Ashley, and Reed; indeed, the work of these scholars may in this regard have been little more than compilation of existing data. And by transferring that data to an electronic database, we would be doing little more. That transfer, however, would reap dividends, because the speed of database queries would enable researchers to make new and better use of the information: they would be able to answer questions that would have been too expensive to ask before.

So it is worthwhile and relatively easy to put basic bibliographic information into our database. Now we come to more expensive information: expensive because it is difficult to obtain, or expensive because it is difficult to compile. In the first category are things like circulation figures and reader demographics; in the second are things like item-level cataloging of a magazine's contents: titles and authors of all "content" (articles, poetry, fiction, correspondence, and so on); some information about each advertisement that appears (the sponsor of the ad, and/or the product or service being advertised); and generic classification of each. Compiling this sort of information is labor intensive, and while some of it can be done using relatively cheap labor, some of it—especially the subject analysis and generic classification—requires trained catalogers or librarians, making the data very expensive to obtain.

This is where most efforts like the one we're imagining have stopped, because of the sheer magnitude and expense of compiling that detailed information, and because of the lack of adequate tools for making use of the information once compiled. Let's assume for the moment, though, that we had that information compiled into an electronic database: what sorts of questions would it enable us to ask? Perhaps the utility of the data justifies the cost of obtaining it.

Let's begin a list of questions, a list that we might begin to organize in order of complexity:

- For a given writer, in what magazines did his/her work appear, and with what frequency, over some span of time?
- What were the ratios of content types for a given magazine in a given year? How did those ratios change over time? How do they compare with other magazines?
- How many times did ads for Sanatogen appear beside works by Virginia Woolf?

Some of these questions can be answered using fielded data—data that can be explicitly (and precisely) named and represented as fields in a database, like the author of an article or the number of copies sold. Answers to other questions, though, like the Woolf question, cannot be derived simply from fielded data. Answering questions like these requires us to examine the text of the magazines. Still, the computer can help us. If we have marked the texts in some way—say, by indicating where articles begin and end and flagging advertisements where they occur in the text —we can with little effort construct a computer query that looks for the appearance of advertisements containing certain words and phrases (like the names of gun manufacturers) within articles by a certain author.

So there are some questions that a database is good at helping us answer, questions about circulation or about how often a writer appeared in different magazines, but there are other questions for which a database will not serve: for these we need a corpus of texts marked in ways that enable a computer to find patterns. We've now come full circle: we've returned to the pile of magazines on the floor. This time, though, the magazines can be read by computer programs as well as by people. As a result, we can move beyond the methodology of Pound's "simple-hearted anthropologist" (as have anthropologists everywhere) and dispense with boxes, large and small, altogether. To be sure, the fields we choose to compile in our databases and the markup we choose to apply to our transcriptions constitute a morcellation of their own. But, chopped finely enough (by brains rinsed and wrung dry enough), they are not the *disjecta membra* of a murderous dissection but constutute a pixelation of modernist magazines whose patterns can be read, like Woolf's atom-shower of impressions upon the mind, as a simulation of life.

Modernism in the Magazines

The Case of Visual Art

Humanity in art in the true sense needs humanity in criticism. To treat what
is being done to-day as something vital in the progress of art, which cannot fix
its eyes on yesterday and live; to see that the present is pregnant for the future,
rather than a revolt against the past; in creation to give expression to an art
that seeks out the strong things of life; in criticism to seek out the strong
things of that art—such is the aim of RHYTHM.
"Before art can be human it must learn to be brutal." Our intention is to
provide art, be it drawing, literature or criticism, which shall be vigorous,
determined, which shall have its roots below the surface, and be the
rhythmical echo of the life with which it is in touch. Both in its pity and its
brutality it shall be real. There are many aspects of life's victory, and the
aspects of the new art are manifold.
—*"Aims and Ideals," from the first issue of* Rhythm, *Summer 1911*

We have made the claim that modernism began in the magazines. We know, of course, that it began in other places
as well, including lecture halls, opera houses, art galleries,
and even books, but magazines were so central to mod-

ernism that it is hard to imagine this movement in literature and the arts without them. It is hard because modernism was a self-conscious movement, in which works of art and literature appeared together with manifestos and critical exegeses. Modernism can almost be defined as those visual and verbal texts that *need* manifestos and exegeses. And this is especially true of those modes of modernism often called "high"—which embraced visual abstraction and verbal complexity. The magazines provided a cultural space where these challenging new modes of literature and visual art could appear side by side with other, less extreme modernist modes of expression, and where artists, impresarios, critics, and philosophers could address one another directly, with a segment of the public listening in on those conversations about what kind of visual, verbal, and musical works were best suited for the modern world. The editor of *Rhythm,* J. M. Murry, was very well aware of the need for criticism to support modern art, as our epigraph from that magazine indicates. What is less visible, perhaps, is that he has quoted J. M. Synge, from the preface he wrote for his *Poems and Translations* (1911), but has transposed the word *verse* in Synge's text to *art* in *Rhythm* as the thing that needs to be "brutal." There were fierce debates about these matters, with cases being made for and against various modes and styles, along with reviews of shows in the galleries and performances in theaters and auditoriums. And this was modernism. These conversations and these works became what we think of as "modernist" art and literature. But it did not happen simply.

We are all aware of the importance of magazines to the emergence of literary modernism—especially those magazines usually called "little," which, as we have explained, means both low circulation and literary. James Joyce, for example, first published fiction in an agricultural magazine called *The Irish Homestead,* edited by the poet George Russell, known as AE, and first published poetry in the Irish little magazine *Dana,* edited by W. K. McGee under his pen name, John Eglinton. Later, both of these editors appeared as characters in *Ulysses.* Joyce's *Portrait of the Artist as a Young Man* was serialized in *The Egoist. Ulysses* ran in *The Little Review* until the censor stopped that, and even *Finnegans Wake* was serialized in *transition* under its working title of "Work in Progress." T. S. Eliot's most important early poems appeared first in *Poetry, The Egoist,* and *The Dial.* Katherine Mansfield's fiction began appearing in *The New Age* and continued in *Rhythm* and *The Blue Review*. And so it went for most of the writers we call modernists. But we are less aware, in general, of the importance of magazines to the rise of modernism in the visual arts—and that will be the main topic of this chapter.

We are more aware of the importance of magazines for literature than for visual art because of one crucial difference in these two modes of artistic expression—or, more precisely, because of our habits of thought with respect to these two modes. In the case of literature, we think of it as existing in the words, independent of any substantial form in which they may appear. That is, we think that a story in a magazine is the same story if it appears in a book—unless the words themselves have been changed—and we don't pay attention to what may have surrounded it on its first appearance, or what it looked like on the page. This, as George Bornstein demonstrated powerfully in *Material Modernism,* is an error. But we make a different and more subtle error in thinking about works of visual art. With these we think that only the "original" is real and that any reproduction of it is insignificant. Or, as Walter Benjamin pointed out long ago, we feel that original artworks have an "aura" that is lost in mechanical reproduction. This seems to us so obviously true that we can scarcely begin to question this way of thinking about art. But we want to begin by doing just that—which will take some explaining.

Imagine a person looking at Géricault's painting *Raft of the "Medusa"* in the Louvre. The painting is more than twelve feet high and twenty feet wide, and we would not wish to suggest that a black-and-white reproduction of it in a magazine is the same thing as the original—or even a color reproduction, or a slide projected on a screen in an art history classroom. But our imaginary person might have known *The Raft of the "Medusa"* for years before ever taking the trouble to visit that enormous and sparsely populated room in Paris where it hangs. That is, nothing in the actual painting would have surprised our visitor on seeing the real thing. Somehow, somewhere, in the course of a meandering life, this visitor had picked up a knowledge of that painting that was not vastly different from what any casual visitor to the Louvre might have acquired. We have used this painting as our example because it is an extreme case

—one of the largest canvases in anyone's mental repertory. We did this not in an attempt to prove that the real painting is not real but to suggest that, even in an extreme case, what we know of a work of visual art that we have not actually seen is not extremely different from what we know of it after having seen the real thing. Given a decent color reproduction and accurate information about the dimensions of the painting, we form an idea of what it actually looks like. And after we have seen the original, what do we have? Art historians, better trained in seeing such things, would probably disagree, but we wonder whether, aura aside, most of us have anything more than an idea of what the original looks like.

Géricault's painting is an extreme case of the difference between original and reproduction, but there are cases that are vastly less extreme. There are smaller paintings that are not so different in size from their reproductions. There are drawings that can be reproduced with a high level of fidelity. And there are prints of various types—engravings, etchings, woodcuts, lithographs—which exist in multiple copies by design. And, to consider the issue from the other side, face to face with original paintings in a museum, it is often not easy to really look at them. In several museums both of us have alarmed guards by getting our noses too close to paintings, trying to see details or look at brushwork. But we have actually gotten a better notion of Cézanne's brushwork from some digital reproductions than from the originals on museum walls, which could not be approached closely enough to do this. It is also the case that the "original" of an old masterpiece is never actually before our eyes. Simple age will darken the varnish on an oil painting and make frescos fade, and restorers not infrequently distort objects to conform to their own ideas of originality. What we are looking at in a museum is often the old age of something that was young long ago itself, and its youth is invisible to us.

George Bornstein has said that "if the *Mona Lisa* is in the Louvre, *King Lear* is on pages everywhere" (31). We are arguing that da Vinci's painting is more like Shakespeare's play than one might think. Actually, it has been stolen and returned to the museum, but that is not the point we are making. Rather, we are following John Berger's argument in *Ways of Seeing* to point out that framing, captioning, hanging position, and surrounding works all affect our perception of any particular work of art, and that time itself works crucial changes as well. We cannot call this a "bibliographic code," but it is definitely a semiotic one, and we do want to argue that time and situation change what we see when we look at a work of visual art. As Dawn Blizard has argued persuasively, when Virginia Woolf looked at the works of the first Post-Impressionist show in Roger Fry's home, with Fry at her side explaining things and a Watts portrait on the wall behind them before the paintings moved to the Grafton Gallery for exhibition, Woolf had a different experience of those paintings than that of the people who saw them in the gallery with a crowd of outraged viewers milling around, and complaining about this affront to public taste (chapter 2).

Once again, let us clarify the point we are trying to make, which is only a preliminary to our main argument. We are not saying that works of visual art are unreal for us, or that there is no difference between originals and copies. We are saying that what we know of a work of visual art is our mental copy of that work, and that the validity of that copy may have more to do with our individual minds and their training than with the source of that copy. We are also saying that in discussing a work of visual art, we deal mainly with ideas of the original, even if we are looking at the painting itself in a museum, but especially if we do not have the original before us, as is often the case when we actually are writing about it. And all this is just a fundamental point of visual semiotics—that what we see is simply our perception, a sign of a reality we can never quite reach. In a museum we may look at a painting from different distances and different angles, on different days, under different light. The result of all that looking is what we retain of the original, and it is, however scrupulously acquired and carefully retained, just a sign of the real thing. But let us move on to the main point, which has to do with modernist art and the magazines.

To begin with, we will need a working definition of modernism in the visual arts, and a sense of the history of this concept. Modernism has, by and large, defined itself in terms of its newness, its difference from some traditional practice. But this rejection of tradition can take more than one form. For example, in England in the nineteenth century, the main break with tradition took the form of Pre-Raphaelitism—that is, a rejection of the tradition established by Raphael in Renaissance Italy and continued by academic painters in England. Pre-Raphaelitism was, then, a newness that claimed to be going back to an older oldness for its inspiration. (The English do everything in their own way.) In France, on the other hand, the great break with tradition took the form of Impressionism, which developed amid a bitter conflict with the academy and its traditional salon. England might have developed its own impressionism, of course. Monet, in France, owed a debt to J. M. W. Turner, who is now regularly seen as a British precursor to the French Impressionists. But in England the artist who owed the most to Turner's work was Whistler, and Whistler's work was viciously attacked by Turner's great champion John Ruskin, who accused him of flinging a pot of paint in the face of the public. The subsequent lawsuit was a financial disaster for Whistler, though he was the nominal victor in it. But what the travails of the Pre-Raphaelites, the Impressionists, and Turner and Whistler demonstrated was that innovation in the visual arts had a serious need for verbal support.

When the next round of visual modernism came in both these countries—and in others as well—this lesson had been thoroughly assimilated. The new artists would come forward with verbal support, and that support would often take the form of periodical publications in which images were accompanied by words of explanation and justification. This happened in many places, but we shall mention two continental instances and then discuss at greater length some crucial British periodicals. Our instances will include *La Revue blanche,* in Belgium and Paris, which began in 1889; *Der Sturm,* in Berlin, which began in 1910; and two British periodicals: *The New Age,* in London, which began a new series in 1907, and *Rhythm,* which began in Paris but was based in London, and ran from 1911 to 1913.

Each of the first two of these journals was associated with a particular kind of visual art and came to be seen as a supporter of a certain set of artists. But *La Revue blanche* did not start out with that in mind. It was the offspring, initially, of four young men, two Belgian (Auguste Jeunhomme and Joë Hogge) and two French (Charles and Paul Leclercq), who met in a gaslit café in the town of Spa and shared their enthusiasm for new poetry and art. One of the Frenchmen had regularly attended the famous "Tuesdays" of Stéphane Mallarmé, and his brother declared himself to be "un symboliste enragé"—a fanatical Symbolist (Jackson, 12). We should pause here a moment to recognize that, for a certain period of time, "symbolism" was the name for modernism in general—crystallized in American critical discourse in 1931 by Edmund Wilson's use of it in his book *Axel's Castle* as a term under which he grouped the work of William Butler Yeats, Paul Valéry, T. S. Eliot, Marcel Proust, James Joyce, and Gertrude Stein—seeing them all as sharing a Symbolist aesthetic. But when Charles Leclercq declared himself a "fanatical Symbolist" in 1889 he was using a fashionable word of the moment—a name for works of verbal and visual art that moved away from naturalism in an attempt to get beyond the surface presented by the world, as in the poetry of Mallarmé, for example. As Georges Bernier pointed out in his catalogue of an exhibition devoted to the work of the artists connected with *La Revue blanche*, it exemplifies this very move:

> The first issue came out on December 1, 1889. It consisted of only a few pages under a long, narrow cover. The preamble, naturally, was a declaration of principles. It still bore the imprint of the naturalist movement although Symbolism already reigned in Belgium. Alfred Natanson was probably one of the drafters of this manifesto which set a guideline to be steadfastly adhered to: "That the *Revue* should remain open to every opinion and every school of thought." (Bernier, 8)

Natanson's position anticipated that of Orage in *The New Age,* though *La Revue blanche* came to be associated with one set of artists as *The New Age* never did. But *La Revue blanche* started in naturalism, aiming to publish authors who were "fidèles reproducteurs de la réalité" (from the opening page of the first issue, quoted in Jackson, 14), moved toward symbolism and ultimately toward that synthesis of the two that we call, simply, modernism.

The four young men who dreamed of a review in the dreamy town of Spa, though devoted to symbolism themselves, hoped to reach out to all the creative tendencies of their age. Noting that a *Revue bleu* and a *Revue rose* already existed, they decided to call theirs *La Revue blanche*

Fig. 4.1. *La Revue blanche* poster

Fig. 4.2. *L'Art moderne* poster

because white is the synthesis of all the colors—a Symbolist gesture par excellence, but not an exclusive one. Still, to turn their dream into reality they had to find financial backers, and there they really scored. They were able to enlist the aid of the three brothers Natanson, sons of a rich Polish banker who lived in Paris, and with the help of the Natanson family, this dream journal became a reality. An early poster for the magazine reveals traces of the art nouveau attitudes that lay behind it (figure 4.1). These traces derive, perhaps, from a preceding Belgian magazine called *L'Art moderne* (figure 4.2). At a certain moment l'art nouveau *was* modernism, and that style is still called "modernismo" in Spain.

As *La Revue blanche* started publishing it gradually found its proper form and content, and, on the way, became one of the first—and perhaps the greatest—of the modernist magazines. In 1913, *The New Age* published the following description:

> The "Revue Blanche" has won for itself a place in the history of French literature of yesterday. It contained the first efforts of many whose names have since become widely known and that not only in France. But the best thing about the "Revue Blanche" was its great editorial room. . . . It was an ever-

changing stream of people that met here, made appointments for the evening, exchanged the tittle-tattle of the day and discussed literary projects of every description. And when from all this busy trifling there emerged something of real worth the conversation ended in the room of the three chief editors with the ordering of an article. (*NA* 13.18: 507)

This description was translated from a German magazine called *Die neue Rundschau* (The new review); the scene it describes is not very different from descriptions of the editorial group of *The New Age* itself, and we would imagine that this translated piece appeared because it caught the fancy of *The New Age*'s editor by virtue of that very resemblance.

La Revue blanche kept getting larger as its circulation grew, and it moved its editorial offices from Belgium to Paris in 1890. And in 1893 Thadée Natanson began writing regular articles on art and reviews of the exhibitions of art in Paris. This banker's son turned out to be a gifted art critic, who observed, in 1895, that Cézanne "alone, or more than anyone else, has the glory of having shaped students and made a school, in the best and most profound sense of those words" (*La Revue blanche* no. 60; Jackson, 65). This was easy to observe fifteen years later, when Roger Fry organized the first Post-Impressionist show in London, but it was startling and prescient in 1895. Thadée Natanson did not only write about the painters. He brought their work into the magazine, which began publishing prints of artworks as the frontispiece to issues in May 1893, and these were collected in 1896 as *L'Album de "La Revue blanche."*

Figure 4.3 shows the back inside cover of the magazine for January 15, 1896. It advertises the artworks of artists associated with the magazine, including its own advertising posters. The artist-critic Maurice Denis also wrote for the magazine, producing a theoretical manifesto on behalf of the group of artists who called themselves "Prophets" or "Nabis." Among the other artists associated with this journal were Édouard Vuillard, Paul Signac, Maurice Denis, Félix Vallotton, and Kees van Dongen. Debussy, Gide, and Jarry also wrote frequently in the magazine, with Mallarmé and Proust contributing occasionally. And they published French translations of such writers as Tolstoy, Chekhov, Gorky, Ibsen, Kipling, Stevenson, Wilde, and Twain. The salon of Misia Natanson, wife of one of the three

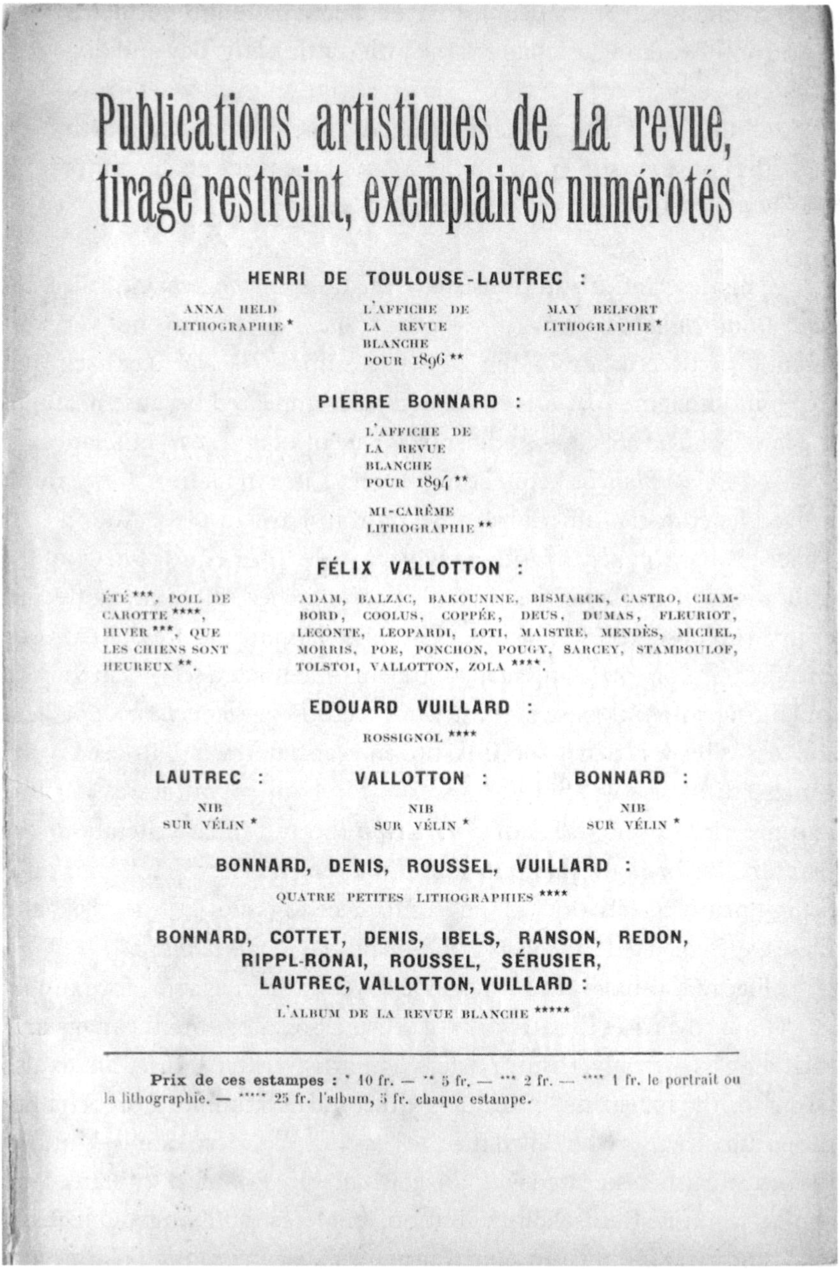

Publications artistiques de La revue, tirage restreint, exemplaires numérotés

HENRI DE TOULOUSE-LAUTREC :

ANNA HELD LITHOGRAPHIE *	L'AFFICHE DE LA REVUE BLANCHE POUR 1896 **	MAY BELFORT LITHOGRAPHIE *

PIERRE BONNARD :

L'AFFICHE DE LA REVUE BLANCHE POUR 1894 **

MI-CARÊME LITHOGRAPHIE **

FÉLIX VALLOTTON :

ÉTÉ ***, POIL DE CAROTTE ****, HIVER ***, QUE LES CHIENS SONT HEUREUX **.

ADAM, BALZAC, BAKOUNINE, BISMARCK, CASTRO, CHAMBORD, COOLUS, COPPÉE, DEUS, DUMAS, FLEURIOT, LECONTE, LEOPARDI, LOTI, MAISTRE, MENDÈS, MICHEL, MORRIS, POE, PONCHON, POUGY, SARCEY, STAMBOULOF, TOLSTOI, VALLOTTON, ZOLA ****.

EDOUARD VUILLARD :

ROSSIGNOL ****

LAUTREC :	VALLOTTON :	BONNARD :
NIB SUR VÉLIN *	NIB SUR VÉLIN *	NIB SUR VÉLIN *

BONNARD, DENIS, ROUSSEL, VUILLARD :

QUATRE PETITES LITHOGRAPHIES ****

BONNARD, COTTET, DENIS, IBELS, RANSON, REDON, RIPPL-RONAI, ROUSSEL, SÉRUSIER, LAUTREC, VALLOTTON, VUILLARD :

L'ALBUM DE LA REVUE BLANCHE *****

Prix de ces estampes : * 10 fr. — ** 5 fr. — *** 2 fr. — **** 1 fr. le portrait ou la lithographie. — ***** 25 fr. l'album, 5 fr. chaque estampe.

Fig. 4.3. *La Revue blanche*, back inside cover, January 15, 1896

Fig. 4.4. *Der Sturm* cover,
July 1910

brothers, brought the major contributors together regularly. Misia herself was a talented pianist, who had sat on Liszt's knee as a child and studied with Fauré, alongside Ravel. It is she whom we see on the famous
posters by Bonnard, Toulouse-Lautrec, and others advertising *La Revue
blanche. All* the painters painted her. But our point is that this magazine, which also played a prominent role in the Dreyfus affair—on the
correct side—showed the others how to do it and led directly to *La Nouvelle Revue française* in Paris and indirectly to *The English Review* in London and a host of other magazines in which the nature of modernity and
the art and literature appropriate for it were exemplified and debated.

In Germany the closest thing to *La Revue blanche* was started two
decades later, by a man named Georg Lewin, who was renamed Herwarth
Walden by his first wife, the poet Elsa Lasker-Schüler. Lasker-Schüler also
helped him start the magazine, for which she had provided the name—
Der Sturm—and which, like *La Revue blanche,* was more interested in literature than in visual art when it began. Walden, trained as a musician,
was widely acquainted with the world of theater and literature. One result
of this was that in July 1910 the magazine printed a play by a young Viennese writer who was also a visual artist: Oskar Kokoschka. The play was
called *Mörder, Hoffnung der Frauen* (Murder, hope of women), and the
issue containing it had a drawing by the author on the cover (figure 4.4).

The drawing, showing an ancient Greek husband attacking his wife with a knife, was in an aggressively modernist style. The publication of his work drew Kokoschka to *Der Sturm*.

Other artists followed. The process of attraction was aided greatly by Walden's second wife, Nell, who was a painter herself—she has been called the first abstract painter in Sweden—and a beautiful woman who caught the eyes of most of the young sculptors and painters in Berlin during those years. With her help Herwarth Walden added an art gallery to his enterprises, as well as a publishing house. There were readings and staged performances in the gallery. In 1919 Kurt Scwhitters wrote a poem accompanied by an image in her honor.

A 1919 poster by Schwitters gives an idea of the artists included in just one show at the Sturm gallery after the war (figure 4.5). The magazine paid more and more attention to visual art as it went along, changing its format in 1919 and including images in color. But before the war, from the summer of 1910 to that of 1914, *Der Sturm* brought modernism in the arts to the German public in a powerful and effective way. As with *La Revue blanche, Der Sturm* provided visual artists with the various forms of support required by a modernism that could not speak critically in its own behalf. The magazine helped to educate the public, and, in this case, it actually sold the pictures as well.

The third magazine we wish to discuss is *The New Age*. Started in 1894 as "A Weekly Record of Culture, Social Service and Literary Life," it had an undistinguished record under several editors for a dozen years, until a group of socialists backed by G. B. Shaw and others bought it and installed two young provincial intellectuals from Leeds as its editors. One of them, Holbrook Jackson, left after the first year. But under the editorship of A. R. Orage, for fifteen years *The New Age* spoke about modern life, politics, and the arts with a lively authority unmatched by any other journal in Britain. Though over the years it had important rivals and imitators like *The Freewoman/Egoist* and saw the rise of powerful literary monthlies like *The English Review* that captured some of its audience—and some of its writers—these rivals on the literary side never undertook what *The New Age* did on the side of the visual arts.

This had not been planned, but Orage and Jackson had been founders of the Leeds Art Club before moving to London, and that club

Fig. 4.5. *Der Sturm* collage poster

had a strong connection to modernism in the arts. The interest of *The New Age* in visual art came from a range of sources: commercial, social, and political before aesthetic. The first images to appear in the magazine were in advertisements for books and prints. These were followed by cartoons and drawings of people in the news, plus the very occasional photograph. Over the first several years of the journal's operation under Orage, more than twenty-five cartoons appeared before the first reproduction of a drawing was presented as a work of art in June 1911. But the magazine had begun to take an interest in the visual arts well before getting around to including images of artworks in its pages. *The New Age* did not have a regular art column until the first issue of volume 6, which appeared in November 1909, included one under the byline of Huntly

Carter. Carter was an interesting person, whose early life is still largely a mystery. From clues he dropped it seems as if he had been a medical student who lived for a time in a bohemia shared with art students. Like many of the editorial staff of the magazine, he was interested in spiritualism, and ultimately wrote a number of books on "The New Spirit" in drama, art, and even cinema. He had written a review or two in the magazine before he appeared as its art critic, but no one could have predicted his impact on the magazine's attention to visual art. In addition to writing regular columns attacking academic art and its institutions, he reviewed shows in the galleries, and finally in April 1910, he organized the first critical art supplement published by the magazine. There he encouraged artists and critics to join together and rise up against their oppressors: "Let us go out together, you and I, and rescue a brother artist or two from the circle of despair into which neglect has driven them. And then let us invite them into the arena which THE NEW AGE is offering to artists for their benefit, and there encourage them to jump on their iniquitous enemies. Then we shall see some real fun" (*NA* 6.23: sup. 2). In this supplement, which ran half a year before the now famous show organized by Roger Fry, "Manet and the Post-Impressionists," we find the first reasoned defense of Picasso as an artist in any English periodical, made by an art historian who was living in France, Victor Reynolds. In his regular columns on art, Carter quoted a number of letters he had received in support of the supplement—one of which, from the Scottish Impressionist painter James Guthrie, said, "Many things that needed to be said are finding their way into THE NEW AGE, thanks to your benign energy. I hope the obvious developments will follow; a mere supplement will not satisfy us for long, you know" (*NA* 6.26: 618). For the next year or so, Carter continued reviewing shows and salons, always searching for the new spirit in art, manifested in new subject matter and new ways of painting and drawing.

In the art supplement we also find Walter Sickert writing an essay on "Encouragement for Art," in which, among other things, he argues that what artists need is not some gift from taxes on working people but simply recognition that they themselves are working people, who must keep working to develop their talent. This essay itself is less important than the way that it brought Sickert into the editorial orbit of the magazine; a couple of issues later we find him publishing an article on what he called "Exhibititis" in the magazine, alongside Huntly Carter. Sickert's views about the form of art were more conservative than Carter's, but his views about the audience were not. In "Exhibititis," for example, he argued that painting large canvases for exhibitions was disastrous for artists, who should be in a more direct and healthy relationship with people who might like to own their works and hang them on their walls. In all his essays, Sickert argued for representing subjects from common life, painted and drawn in ways that suited modern subjects but were not aggressively modernist. Finally, six months after Fry's Post-Impressionist show closed, Sickert began to submit his own drawings to the magazine for publication, carrying on his own quarrel with Post-Impressionism by offering images in his own mode of modernism, which is a continuation of the sort of Impressionism practiced by Degas. This mode was called "Neo-Realism" by Sickert's friend and associate Charles Ginner, and that is as good a name for it as any, though Sickert himself rejected it.

The New Age ran four distinct sets of modern images in the period from 1911 to 1914. These have been discussed at some length by Robert Scholes in chapter 2 of *Paradoxy of Modernism* (available at www.modjourn) and described clearly by Dawn Blizard in "New Art in *The New Age:* What Was Modern?":

- 1911–1912, Sickert's work, submitted by himself;
- 1911–1912, Picasso, Herbin, and others, organized by Huntly Carter;
- 1914, "modern drawings," Sickert and others, organized by Sickert;
- 1914, "contemporary drawings," Epstein, Gaudier-Brzeska, and others, organized by T. E. Hulme.

As the dates indicate, the series came in two pairs, and, in each case, the second was a response to the first. Sickert's images led to those organized by Huntly Carter in 1911, and the set Sickert called "Modern" in 1914 led to T. E. Hulme's set of "Contemporary Drawings" in that year, though one of them, Epstein's *Rock Drill,* had appeared by itself in December of 1913. In each case, the neorealist version of modernism provoked something more aggressively modernist, tending toward abstraction, in response, though Epstein's image seems to have inspired Sickert's series, which led to Hulme's situating the Epstein as the first image in his "contemporary" series. This final set, with vigorous images like Gaudier-Brzeska's *Dancer,* supported by Hulme's powerful theoretical defense of abstraction, may be said to have won the day, but the story is more complicated than that, and we need to see modernism as defined more accurately by the struggle itself rather than by the "victory" of one side.

One of the things we need to know has been largely ignored by scholars of modernism, despite attempts by people like Faith Binckes (in Churchill and McKible, 21–35) to draw attention to it, and that is the role played by the magazine called *Rhythm* in the debates over visual art in the English-speaking world. *Rhythm* was founded by an Oxford undergraduate named John Middleton Murry in 1911. He had been visiting Paris on a winter vacation and there discovered the verbal Fantaisistes and the visual Fauves. He was twenty-two years old at the time, which makes his achievement with this magazine all the more astonishing. He edited others, later, but never reached this level again, which indicates that there was more to *Rhythm* than Murry himself. The story of this magazine is, in fact, an extremely complicated one, which has made it very difficult to tell. We will do our best, here, however, to follow the main threads of the narrative by looking at some of the individuals who were directly or indirectly involved and the roles that they played.

Huntly Carter and John Middleton Murry

Carter, as we have mentioned, was the art critic for *The New Age* when *Rhythm* began. He was searching for signs of a new spirit for the new age, and his search led him first to visual art, then to theater, and finally to film. It also led him from *The New Age* to *The New Freewoman/The Egoist* as a columnist. But in 1911 he was in Paris, attending to art, theater, and ideas, while writing, in particular, about Henri Bergson as one who "has an intense interest in symbolic poetry—a poetry of enormous suggestion; he has indeed been accepted by the symbolists as the philosopher of the new idea." In Carter's summary, Bergson's philosophy was the antithesis of academic logic:

It aims rather to remove the sluice-house of such logic from the life stream which flows through human beings; that hard mechanical check which continues human existence at the expense of the stream by damming its spontaneity and adulterating the purity of its elements, and to substitute an emotional aid to continuity through which the stream shall pass freely and unadulterated without being exhausted in the process. Bergson's system reduced to an aphorism says, mathematical reasoning is the last resort of the intuitionally destitute. (*NA* 9.2: 43–44)

Carter was attacked in the letters column of the magazine shortly thereafter, and then defended in a letter by J. Middleton Murry, who had never appeared in *The New Age* but must have been a regular reader to pick up so quickly on a short letter to the editor. Murry concluded his lengthy response by observing (of Bergson):

We have now at least a philosophy which can recognise the reality and truth of a creative evolution; which can allow for and comprehend a real progress, alike in every intellectual sphere. If every critic in England were sufficient of a philosopher to lay to heart the implications of the Bergsonian theories of time and change, creative art would receive a new lease of life. In France there can be no question that such a philosophy has had the most comprehensive and vital results, of which one alone, Post-Impressionism, has sufficed at once to enrage and confound its critics here. I can but feel that M. Hübener has but little of the faculty for feeling the pulse of the great cosmopolis [Paris], which Mr. Huntly Carter has so markedly shown. (*NA* 9.5: 116)

At the moment when Murry wrote this letter, he was just starting his own magazine—one devoted to Bergsonian ideas and the new forms of art and literature. The magazine was then a quarterly, and its first issue turned up on a riverboat in Germany, where Huntly Carter was on his way to an art show in Dresden. In a "Letter from Abroad" in *The New Age*

Carter praised Murry's take on Bergson (a nice quid pro quo, to be sure) and then imagined the artists of *Rhythm* attending the Dresden show with him: "The tour of the exhibition with the stalwarts of 'Rhythm,' J. D. Fergusson, S. J. Peploe, Othon Friesz, Picasso, Thomson, Estelle Rice, and Jessie Dismore [*sic*], was distinctly stimulating." He then imagines the Rhythmists as an art committee commenting on the Dresden show: "'They are doing good work, and must come to Paris. They ought not to be left too long in the vicinity of that vastly disappointing "Sistine Madonna," with which Dresden catches the traveller's eye: Dead masterpieces choke the waterspout of public artistic opinion.' With which remark, the artistic committee of 'Rhythm' exhausted its wisdom. The rest was silence" (*NA* 9.15: 346). In November 1911 Carter was back in London, attending art shows, but his thoughts were still with the Rhythmists. Here is the concluding paragraph of his discussion of a show at the Goupil Gallery:

> Now that the ideas of rhythmic expansion and vitality are in the air in this country, artists should read Mr. Lawrence Binyon's little book, "The Flight of the Dragon" (Murray, 1s.). The dragon has flown to England to expound the principles and ideas of rhythm expressed long ago by the Chinese. Its arrival synchronises with the birth of a movement of great importance in art and drama aiming consciously to bridge the gap left in European thought and action by the lack of an intelligent understanding of internal expansion. Some of the dragon's words of wisdom are as follow:—"The deepest intuitions of a race are deposited in its art"; "Rhythmic vitality is the Life-movement of the Spirit through the Rhythm of things"; "Whatever Rhythm is, it is something intimately connected with life, perhaps the secret of life and its most perfect expression"; "With the idea of Rhythm in our minds we are led to think, above all, of the relation between things." The book is for moderns who are interested in pictures rather than in prices. (*NA* 10.2: 36)

We should pause here for a moment to note that Laurence (the correct spelling) Binyon, as one might expect, wrote for *Rhythm,* and was praised at length (though faintly) by Ezra Pound in *Blast* 2. These three magazines are all closely linked. And, as Faith Binckes reminded us recently (Churchill and McKible, 21–34), there was a feud between *The New Age* and *Rhythm,* but Huntly Carter should not be blamed for this. In fact, when he started his own series of modernist images in the magazine, he quoted Murry (misspelling his name, to be sure) in support of a *Study* by Picasso that was one of his first modernist images to appear in the magazine:

> As a clue to what Picassoism really is and to what little extent it is related to geometry, I may quote from a letter which Mr. Middleton Murray sent me while in Paris. It seems that Oxford, no less than Paris and New York, is greatly impressed with the profoundly intellectual character of the French painter's work, and during a discussion on the subject Mr. Murray was led to put forward the following Plato-Picasso idea: "It will be remembered that Plato, in the sixth book of the Republic, turns all artists out of his ideal state on the ground that they merely copy objects in Nature, which are in their turn copies of the real reality—the Eternal Idea. Plato, who was a great artist and lover of art, did not turn artists out because he was a Philistine, but because he thought their form of art was superficial; 'photographic' we should call it now. There was no inward mastery of the profound meaning of the object expressed, so that the expression was merely 'a copy of a copy.' The fact is, Plato was looking for a different form of art, and that form was Picasso's art of essentials." Mr. Murray's contention is that Picassoism is the first intelligent advance upon Platoism, seeing that it is a practical application of Plato's theory. Thus the study submitted to the readers of this journal, and chosen for the purpose by M. Picasso from the Galerie Kahnweiler, demonstrates that painting has arrived at the point when, by extreme concentration, the artist attains an abstraction which to him is the soul of the subject, though this subject be composed only of ordinary objects— mandoline, wine-glass and table, as in the present instance.

It indicates, too, that painting is at the point of its greatest development. It is on the threshold of the will, and not at a halting place of men sick with inertia. (*NA* 10.4: 88)

The Picasso presented by Huntly Carter provoked cries of outrage and mockery in the letters pages of the magazine, along with a response from Murry that was elevated to article status, in which he praised Picasso highly and deprecated his own ability to comprehend him, beginning with this disarming sentence: "Mr. Huntly Carter has quoted some words of a letter of mine on the subject of Picasso's work; and as I read them again I am struck by a suspicion of intellectual arrogance and assumed finality from which I wish to clear myself."

The *Study* by Picasso was a distinctly Cubist effort, and it was the first image to appear in Carter's series, but we need to be aware that it was stimulated if not inspired by *Rhythm* and the Rhythmists, and that is was also a response to Sickert's neorealist series which had preceded it. When Carter listed the "stalwarts" of *Rhythm* in discussing the Dresden show, he mentioned J. D. Fergusson, S. J. Peploe, Othon Friesz, Pablo Picasso, Marguerite Thomson, Anne Estelle Rice, and Jessie Dismorr, which reveals that he was thinking of Picasso as a Rhythmist. All of them were, in fact, represented in the first number of that journal. Moreover, we find Murry and Carter, side by side, in the letters columns of *The New Age*, defending Picasso against various attacks. But it was one of the other works in Carter's series in *The New Age* that seemed to be the cause of the feud between the two magazines.

In January 1912, a reproduction of André Dunoyer de Segonzac's *Les Boxeurs* appeared in Carter's series (figure 4.6). This image provoked less outrage than Picasso's work had, but in *The New Age* for March 28, 1912 (10.22: 519), there was a ferocious attack on *Rhythm* ("no single page that is not stupid or crazed or vulgar—and most are all three"), almost certainly written by Beatrice Hastings, of whom we shall have more to say; the author claimed that *Rhythm* had published an early sketch of the *Boxeurs* image that had appeared in *The New Age*, thus proclaiming the magazine's derivative status. In the following number of *The New Age* "The Editor of 'Rhythm'" answered the charge, mentioning in passing that Huntly Carter had "consistently and unworthily belittled" the the-

LES BOXEURS.
By A. de SEGONZAC

Fig. 4.6. Segonzac, *Les Boxeurs*, from *The New Age*,
January 18, 1912, art supplement

atrical work of Gordon Craig. The "Editor" concluded with this entirely justified statement:

> Lastly, the same innuendo of "dutiful imitation" is maintained in your suggestion that you had already published the finished picture of the sketch by Dunoyer-Segonzac in "Rhythm." It is obvious that "art criticism is not your contributor's business." The treatment of the subject in the two drawings is absolutely different. It would be as reasonable and as puerile to suggest that, because "Rhythm" was the first paper in England to publish the work of Picasso and Herbin, THE NEW AGE had "dutifully imitated" "Rhythm." (*NA* 10.23: 551)

As we have already mentioned, it is clear that Huntly Carter had indeed taken the idea for his series from his encounter with *Rhythm* and

Fig. 4.7. Segonzac, *Les Boxeurs,* from *Rhythm,* Spring 1912, 22

its visual artists on that steamboat. But he was soon to be replaced as art critic for *The New Age* by Anthony Ludovici, who despised the modernists. We can see, however, that the *Boxeurs* in *Rhythm* was a sketch of a different sort from the image that had appeared in *The New Age* (figure 4.7).

The Two Couples: Hastings/Orage and Mansfield/Murry

Two couples were involved in the *New Age/Rhythm* dispute, and their interactions have been chronicled a number of times, once perceptively, in John Carswell's *Lives and Letters* (1978), and then more elaborately in Stephen Gray's *Beatrice Hastings: A Literary Life* (2004). They have also been touched on in various biographies of John Middleton Murry and Katherine Mansfield. We will not try to reproduce all this material here, but rather will make the connections that are relevant to modernist visual art and the dispute between the two journals. Beatrice Hastings and Katherine Mansfield have both been described as "wild Colonial girls" and the designation suited them in certain respects. They both led erotic lives more like those of their male contemporaries than women were supposed to do, and both paid a price for that. Mansfield was originally from New Zealand, and Hastings from South Africa, and both left failed marriages behind them, had changed their names, and were generally inventing themselves as writers at that time. Hastings lived with A. R. Orage, the editor of *The New Age*, during the first years from 1910 to 1914, and had significant co-editorial responsibilities, though the full extent of these has been debated. She may have been responsible for the acceptance of Ezra Pound's early contributions, as she later claimed, though she became his enemy and Pound hers, making some nasty comments about her in a letter to Margaret Anderson in 1918 (Scott and Friedman, 200). Hastings was also involved, in various ways, with Katherine Mansfield, whose early fiction was mainly published in *The New Age*, where she was coached as a writer by both Orage and Hastings. Mansfield became part of a ménage à trois with the *New Age* couple for a while.

These complex literary and erotic relations became more so when John Middleton Murry entered the picture. Murry had been reading Mansfield, probably in *The New Age*, and certainly when her first collection of *New Age* stories, *In a German Pension*, was published. He apparently solicited work from her (there are various versions of this), with the result that she left Orage and Hastings and moved in with Murry, eventually assuming visibly with *Rhythm* the role of co-editor that Hastings had held invisibly at *The New Age*. This defection, which was both erotic and literary, lay behind the magazine feud and added fuel to that fire. But the erotic entanglements did not end there. Murry and Mansfield were soon closely linked to the artist Henri Gaudier and his "sister" and mistress, Sophie Brzeska, whose name Gaudier added to his own. Gaudier was living in London then, in poor financial straits, and he asked Mansfield and Murry to take Sophie in and house her, producing a rather different sort of ménage à trois. At some point, for reasons that are still murky, a bitter quarrel broke out between the two couples, with the result that Gaudier became an enemy of Murry and Mansfield and then the close friend of Ezra Pound. Pound championed his work, which had been appearing in *Rhythm*, converting him from a Rhythmist into a Vorticist and writing a book about him after Gaudier's death at the front in 1914. We shall return to the relationships between *Rhythm* and the Vorticist

Blast a bit later, but now we must look deeper into what *Rhythm* was and how it came to be that way. The literary side, even with Mansfield leading the way, never matched the journal's contribution to visual modernism and the theories that surrounded it, becoming a vehicle, in its last issues, for the Georgian poetry despised by Pound and other modernists. On the art side, however, Murry, who was still an undergraduate at Oxford when he started *Rhythm*, got more than a little help from his friends.

Michael Sadleir and John Duncan Fergusson

While at Oxford, which he entered in 1908, Murry had met a number of other undergraduates, including Joyce Cary and Michael Sadleir. At that time Sadleir still used the family spelling—Sadler—which he later changed to avoid confusion with his father, also named Michael. The father was a prominent collector of modern art who moved to Leeds in 1911 to become vice chancellor of the university there. He also became a leader in the art club that had been founded by A. R. Orage and Holbrook Jackson in 1893, before they moved to London to take over *The New Age*. The young Sadleir was interested in all things modern, from Symbolist poetry to Post-Impressionist visual art, and he led the younger Murry in those directions, which culminated in Murry's visit to Paris on the Christmas vacation of 1910–1911. In Paris, as we have mentioned, Murry met the visual Fauves as well as the verbal Fantaisistes, and both got involved in his new magazine venture, making *Rhythm* in certain ways a successor to two distinguished nineteenth-century predecessors: *La Revue blanche*, which we have already discussed, and *The Yellow Book*, in which Aubrey Beardsley's visual art had regularly appeared. Where *La Revue blanche* had championed the Nabis visual artists and the Symbolists, *Rhythm* would champion the Fauves and the Fantaisistes. And from *The Yellow Book*, Murry's *Rhythm* learned to make a virtue of necessity and to feature strong artworks in black and white.

Paris, as Murry observed in writing to *The New Age*, was a cosmopolitan city, and among the Fauves were a number of native speakers of English, including the Scots John Duncan Fergusson, Samuel John Peploe, and Dorothy "Georges" Banks, the American Anne Estelle Rice, and the English Jessie (later Jessica) Dismorr. Fergusson was recognized as a Fauve

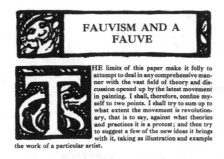

FAUVISM AND A
FAUVE

HE limits of this paper make it folly to
attempt to deal in any comprehensive manner with the vast field of theory and discussion opened up by the latest movement
in painting. I shall, therefore, confine myself to two points. I shall try to sum up to
what extent the movement is revolution-
ary, that is to say, against what theories
and practices it is a protest; and then try
to suggest a few of the new ideas it brings
with it, taking as illustration and example
the work of a particular artist.

Fig. 4.8. Fauvism, from *Rhythm,*
Summer 1911, 14

and was the leader of the group that joined *Rhythm,* becoming art editor of the magazine and bringing the others and a number of French
artists with him. His painting *Rhythm* became the motif of the journal,
with a version of it appearing as the regular cover. There is some dispute
over whether the painting preceded the cover or followed it, and whether
it gave its name to the magazine or took its title from it (see Binckes in
Churchill and McKible), but it clearly embodied the visual principles that
animated Murry's *Rhythm* (see plates 1 and 2).

The cover is more consciously Rhythmist than the painting. If Fergusson embodied the practical side of Rhythmist art, Michael Sadleir
(or Michael T. H. Sadler, as he signed himself in those days) embodied
the theoretical. The major statement about visual art in the first number
of *Rhythm* was "Fauvism and a Fauve," by Sadleir (as we shall continue
to call him). The entire essay needs to be read, but we can only summarize it here. In it Sadleir rejected the designation "Post-Impressionism"
and presented "Fauvism" as a useful "*nom d'école,*" or school designation for a group of artists, because it could be used as a tag, without "ul-
terior association." But we need to see how this article began to appreciate the flavor of the magazine (figure 4.8).

The article is embedded in art, and art is embedded in it. The Fauve
mentioned in the title is not, as we might expect, J. D. Fergusson, but
the American artist Anne Estelle Rice, whose brilliant work in the black-
and-white medium of the magazine makes her *the* Rhythmist Fauve
among a number of vigorous artists in that movement. In the article
Sadleir sums up Fauvism as "a reaction on the one hand against the life-

SCHÉHÉRAZADE. BY ANNE ESTELLE RICE

Fig. 4.9. Anne Estelle Rice, *Schéhérazade*, from *Rhythm*,
Summer 1911, 15

less mechanism of Pointillism, on the other against the moribund flick-
erings of the aesthetic movement" (*Rhythm* 1.1: 14), and he offers a sample of Rice's work as his prime example of Fauvist rhythm, "the one
fundamental desire with which all start—the desire for rhythm. Be it of
line or colour, be it simple or intricate, in every true product of Fauvism
it will be present." The image he presents is Rice's *Schéhérazade* (figure
4.9). The fictional character represented, of course, is the great storyteller

STUDY. BY OTHON FRIESZ

Fig. 4.10. Othon Friesz, *Study*, from *Rhythm*, Summer 1911, 4

of the *Thousand and One Nights,* who saved her life by dazzling power with the beauty of her art, and this image stands here not only for Fauvism and Rhythmism but for all women as artists, verbal and visual. *Rhythm* featured more of them than any contemporary journal, which is one of its achievements. Sadleir found in Rice's pictures a "rhythmic repose always on the edge of action and always ready for action—to borrow a phrase from Mr Holbrook Jackson" (18). There is strong work by other artists in this issue, including Picasso, Friesz, Peploe, Dismorr, Thomson, and Fergusson himself, but very few challenge Rice's power in this medium, though one *Study* by Friesz is very strong (figure 4.10). The works by Rice and Friesz are in totally different styles, to be sure, but they may be taken together to represent the range of *Rhythm,* which never went so far in the direction of abstraction as Hulme's sequence in *The New Age* or the Vorticist *Blast.*

Before we move on from Sadleir's contributions to the magazine, we must note a few more aspects of them. One was financial. His father was an original sponsor of the journal, without whom it would never have begun. And another also stems from the elder Sadler. His art collection lay behind Michael's interest in and knowledge of the contemporary art scene, which clearly extended beyond Fauvism. In the fourth quarterly issue of *Rhythm*, Michael Sadleir wrote an article called "After Gauguin," in which he emphasized the work of two followers going in different directions: André Derain and Wassily Kandinsky. Sadleir mentioned "a fine example of [Derain's] work," *Creation*, which had appeared in *Rhythm*, No. 3 (figure 4.11).

After Derain, Sadleir moved on to Kandinsky. He had seen some of Kandinsky's work with his father at Frank Rutter's Allied Artists Association exhibition in the Albert Hall in the summer of 1911, and had purchased a number of Kandinsky's woodcuts. This purchase led to further acquaintance with Kandinsky; an invitation to visit him in Murnau, which Sadleir and his father did in the summer of 1912; and ultimately to Sadleir's becoming the translator of Kandinsky's *Über das Geistige in der Kunst* (On the spiritual in art), which had appeared in German in 1912 (Steele, 179–181). Sadleir's English version, then called *The Art of Spiritual Harmony*, appeared in 1914. Selections from this work, translated by Edward Wadsworth, appeared in *Blast* 1, and a critical response to Kandinsky by Wyndham Lewis was published in *Blast* 2.

In the summer of 1912, however, London was introduced to Kandinsky's theories by Sadleir, who expounded them at some length in *Rhythm*, concluding with these paragraphs:

> While encouraging the new art to abandon the accepted aspect
> of nature, not to fear in fact the charge of bad drawing and im-
> possible colour, Kandinsky gives a wise and necessary warning.
> The process is attended by a double danger. Anti-naturalism
> may become pure pattern-making, and form and colour mere
> symbols. He should have added that the chief fault of such an

CREATION. BY ANDRÉ DERAIN.   By permission of M. Kahnweiler.

Fig. 4.11. André Derain, *Creation*, from *Rhythm*, Winter 1911, 28

art is that it leads nowhere. It is barren because it never touches reality, and reality is as essential as naturalism is deplorable. The other danger is the creation of an imaginary dream-world, which being also divorced from life is equally worthless to the future of art. The true way is the way of the inner *notwendigkeit*, and that can be found only by the true artist.

From a book full of suggestive thought, which touches

every aspect of the modern effort, I have extracted a few main ideas, with a view to making clear the aim towards which a large part of the art of today is striving; for though the book is one man's, he has voiced the inarticulate ideals of a multitude. (*Rhythm* 1.4: 29)

The other main point made by Sadleir in this article is that

Kandinsky argues that primitive art is a more direct expression of the soul of externals than is that of later periods, because it belongs to a time when life was simple, experience single-eyed, and when the fundamental *zusammenklang* was less obscured by the noise of the naturalistic appeal. For this reason the new art inclines at present to primitive technique, but such a tendency will be temporary only, because the feeling of the primitive artist for the inner reality, being more instinctive than educated, was soon overlaid, while the art of the future, once it has thrown off the chains of naturalism, can develop fresh methods of its own, unhampered by tradition. (25)

It should be clear, even from this brief summary, that Michael Sadleir brought into the discussions about modernist art in English features that were of great importance in the ongoing debates, including those taken up by T. E. Hulme in *The New Age* in 1914 and continued in *Blast* after that. And Sadleir was co-editor of the first issues of *Rhythm,* in which the visual arts were so important. We should add that he contributed poetry to *Rhythm* and became a well-known novelist later on, as well as a book collector and publisher.

Geocultural Interlude: London Bohemias

We shall return to the individual artists and critics involved in these visual matters, but first we must attend to something that underlay them. We know *Rhythm* started in bohemian Paris, but we need also to recognize the role played by bohemian London in artistic affairs, which is by no means simple. The best guide to all this is Peter Brooker's *Bohemia in Lon-*

don, which has a painting of the Vorticists on its cover. What we offer here will be simple and schematic, offering nothing like Brooker's fuller study. We can start by thinking of two different bohemias in London: one that we might call Bloomsbury and another that we might call Camden Town, using these geographical locators for things that were more complicated in various ways. Bloomsbury belonged to the cultural establishment, with roots in the Victorian world of Virginia Woolf's father, Leslie Stephen, and in the great universities, especially Cambridge. And we all know a lot about its membership and their achievements. What we are calling Camden Town includes artists with studios there, but we mean the term to include other bohemians who were outside the established system, like those who worked at *The New Age* and lived at various points around the city. There was a formal Camden Town Group of artists, and Wendy Baron has provided an excellent history of them, *Perfect Moderns.* Walter Sickert was the center of that group, which included many of those called neorealists by Charles Ginner, who was another member. But we want to use the term to include others who were less directly connected to the area. One might think of it as all the artistic and literary groups active in London in the period from 1910 to 1920 who were not part of Bloomsbury. But let us give some examples. T. S. Eliot, from Harvard, was clearly admitted to Bloomsbury, and called facetiously by Virginia Woolf "Great Tom," after a clock of that name. Ezra Pound, however, kept his distance from Bloomsbury—or was kept at a distance.

When Wyndham Lewis quarreled with Roger Fry about Fry's Omega Workshops, it was Camden Town against Bloomsbury. Orage and Hastings, Mansfield and Murry, Gaudier and Sophie Brzeska all belonged to what we are calling Camden Town. When Virginia Woolf and Katherine Mansfield met, they were respectful, but extremely wary of each other. It was Bloomsbury and Camden Town again. Nina Hamnett, the object of a nude torso sculpted by Henri Gaudier, was Camden Town. After she arranged to lose her burdensome virginity in a rented room, she discovered that the French poets Verlaine and Rimbaud had once shared a room in that very building. When she asked her friend Walter Sickert which event would get a plaque on the building, Sickert tactfully replied that there would be one in the front for her and one in the back for them (Hamnett, 44–45).

In both Bloomsbury and Camden Town a lot of the game we might call musical beds was played, and without much concern about the gender, number, or marital status of the partners. Virginia Woolf and Vita Sackville-West had a little erotic adventure, and so did Beatrice Hastings and Katherine Mansfield, but the boundaries that were not breached were those of affiliation and class. Bloomsbury tended to stay in Bloomsbury and Camden Town in Camden Town, though there were exceptions like Duncan Grant, who moved from the Camden Town Group to the Omega Workshops and the bed of Vanessa Bell. And there was a strong connection between Camden Town and Paris. Nina Hamnett introduced Beatrice Hastings to Amadeo Modigliani there, and Hastings lived with him in 1914 and 1915. Gaudier-Brzeska's sculpture was close to that of Modigliani in style, but one of the few people in England who owned any of it was Augustus John, a Slade School colleague of Wyndham Lewis, who was definitely a Camden Town type. He was also one of the artists whose work appeared in both *The New Age* and *Rhythm,* though few people would call him a modernist these days. Modigliani shifted his artistic emphasis from sculpture to visual art during the time when Hastings was with him. This happened too late for *Rhythm,* but it is not hard to see the Rhythmist tendencies in Modigliani's visual art. He painted Hastings a number of times, and Hastings was the archenemy of the Rhythmists, so this is not a connection she would have liked to acknowledge.

Ford Madox Ford, or Hueffer, as he was then called, and Violet Hunt were connected to the lower bohemia we are calling Camden Town, as was Rebecca West, who met Ezra Pound through Ford and Hunt and brought him into the pages of *The New Freewoman,* which became *The Egoist.* Pound, in turn, brought West into *Blast,* which he and Wyndham Lewis edited for its short run in 1914 and 1915. *Blast* was a production of Camden Town, though the artists who came to call themselves Vorticists for a time had by then split off from the original Camden Town Group and its larger successor, the London Group. Jacob Epstein, whose work was championed by Pound and T. E. Hulme, belonged to this bohemia, and Nina Hamnett recalled that in Paris she would go with the Epsteins and Brancusi to the Père Lachaise cemetery to pull the covers off of Epstein's monument to Oscar Wilde until the police made them stop (45).

It is worth noting at this point that when the American writer

Theodore Dreiser was introduced by the publisher Grant Richards to bohemian Paris, he met Fergusson and Anne Estelle Rice, whom he used as a model for the title character in the story "Ellen Adams Wrynn" in his *Gallery of Women* (1929). (A useful examination of this connection may be found in Carol A. Nathanson's article on the subject in the *Woman's Art Journal*, 13.2: 3–31.) There was an international bohemia that linked Americans like Dreiser and Rice to people like Pound and H. L. Mencken and James Huneker. Another figure in this bohemia was Frank Rutter, who organized the Allied Artists Association. Rutter, who was connected to the Parisian bohemia as well, had been editor of Jerome K. Jerome's magazine *To-Day* (later revived by Holbrook Jackson, who had been Orage's co-editor in the first year of *The New Age* and then wrote for *Rhythm*). Rutter was friendly with Michael Sadleir's father, and joined him in Leeds as director of the art gallery there (Steele, 181). The AAA was very much a Camden Town production, with Sickert aiding Rutter in the organization of art shows modeled on the Parisian Salon des Indépendants, which contributed to the introduction of modernism to England, along with Roger Fry's more famous Post-Impressionist shows. In this connection it is worth noting that Walter Sickert attacked Fry the impresario in the pages of *The New Age*, but had only praise for his painting.

We can conclude this brief account of London's bohemia by noting that Virginia Woolf, in her essay "Walter Sickert" in 1933, reported that Bloomsbury had concluded that the Camden Town artist was "probably the best painter now living in England" (*Captain's Death Bed*, 202). The two bohemias were aware of each other and even interacted occasionally. And both provided networks that generated modernism in the London of that period, with art shows, galleries, printing presses, and magazines. Bloomsbury had the Hogarth Press and the Omega Workshop. Camden Town had a whole range of formal and informal art groups, and magazines like *The New Age*, *Rhythm*, and *Blast*. But the major point of this excursion in bohemian culture is that this culture provided both the creators and the consumers of the literature and art produced there. Nina Hamnett, for example, was a reader of *The New Age*, which she considered "about the most interesting and well-written paper in London before the war" (69). And now we must return to its rival, *Rhythm*.

Fig. 4.12. Jessie Dismorr, *Izidora*, from *Rhythm*, Autumn 1911, 20

The Other Visual Rhythmists

As we have indicated, Rice and Fergusson (the art editor) were the dominant artists in *Rhythm,* but a number of others were also important. There was art throughout the pages of the magazine, full-page drawings and woodcuts like Rice's *Schéhérazade* and little fillers and decorations like those at the beginning of Sadleir's article on the Fauves. One of the artists who contributed most frequently was Jessie Dismorr, who later joined the Vorticists and contributed to both issues of *Blast* and to Wyndham Lewis's later publication, *The Tyro.* She is one of the two women represented in William Roberts's famous painting of the Vorticists at the bohemian Restaurant de la Tour Eiffel in London in the spring of 1915, which is on the cover of Brooker's *Bohemia in London.* She contributed fewer works to *Rhythm* than some of the other female artists, and her work for the magazine is not as interesting as that of Rice, but she caught

Fig. 4.13. Georges Banks, *Katherine Mansfield*,
from *Rhythm*, October 1912, 193

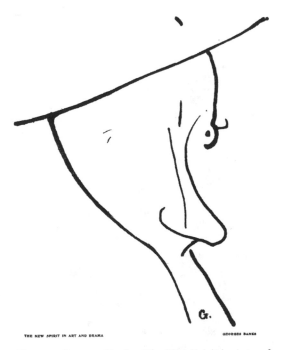

Fig.4.14. Georges Banks, *The New Spirit in Art and
Drama*, from *Rhythm*, January 1913, 339

Fig. 4.15. J. D. Fergusson, *Head of a Woman*,
from *Rhythm*, October 1912, 222

Fig. 4.16. J. D. Fergusson, *Seated Woman*,
from *Rhythm*, July 1912, 42

HENRI GAUDIER-BRZESKA

Fig. 4.17. Henri Gaudier-Brzeska, *Head of a Woman*, from *Rhythm*, September 1912, 143

HENRI GAUDIER-BRZESKA.

Fig. 4.18. Henri Gaudier-Brzeska, *Head of a Man*, from *Rhythm*, October 1912, 198

HENRI GAUDIER-BIZESKA.

Fig. 4.19. Henri Gaudier-
Brzeska, *Whitechapel Jew*, from
Rhythm, September 1912, 129

A DANCER. By GAUDIER-BRZESKA.

CONTEMPORARY DRAWINGS—NO. 1
EDITED BY T. E. HULME

Fig. 4.20. Henri Gaudier-Brzeska, *A Dancer*,
from *The New Age*, March 19, 1914, 625

something of the Rhythmist attitude in her image of Isadora Duncan (figure 4.12).

One of the other interesting female artists in *Rhythm* was Dorothy
"Georges" Banks, a caricaturist, who gave us a compelling sketch of
Katherine Mansfield and a delightful evocation of *The New Spirit in Art
and Drama* (figures 4.13, 4.14).

The artists in *Rhythm* all had a range from something like neoreal-
ism to something much more abstract, as we can see in two images by
J. D. Fergusson (figures 4.15, 4.16). Henri Gaudier-Brzeska had a similar
range, as in two heads from different issues of *Rhythm* (figures 4.17, 4.18).
His range is shown more clearly, perhaps, in one image (*Whitechapel Jew*)
from *Rhythm* and another (*A Dancer*) from Hulme's series in *The New
Age* (figures 4.19, 4.20).

Of all these artists, Gaudier-Brzeska is the one who links all three of these vital journals: *The New Age, Rhythm,* and *Blast.* To *The New Age* Gaudier-Brzeska contributed the art Hulme called "contemporary" in reaction to Sickert's claim of the title "modern" for the neorealists; he placed Rythmist art in Murry's journal; and, finally, a photograph of his Vorticist sculpture *Stags* appeared in *Blast.* His sculpture, too, ranged widely, as in his quite realistic torso of Nina Hamnett and his abstract bust of Ezra Pound. His loss in the war was a severe blow to the artistic side of modernism, as was that of T. E. Hulme to the theoretical side. For it was Hulme who started out as a Bergsonian and then followed Wilhelm Worringer's *Abstraction and Empathy* to a powerful argument for abstraction as the proper mode for modernist art. Pound and Lewis were strongly influenced by Hulme, and Pound included all Hulme's extant poems in a volume of his own (*Ripostes*), as he included as much of Gaudier-Brzeska's art as he could find in his book on that artist, thus giving similar posthumous tributes to both men.

Much more, of course, could be said about all this, but we must close this discussion after making two more observations. We have seen that the caricaturist Georges Banks was important in *Rhythm.* Similarly, the cartoonists Tom Titt and Will Dyson both weighed in on the aesthetic debates going on in *The New Age.* Titt responded to a drawing of London as beautiful with a satiric image of the commercial metropolis, as if to say, You think you high artists can represent the real London? Let me show you that only we cartoonists have what it takes for that (figures 4.21, 4.22). And Will Dyson, another *New Age* cartoonist, offered his own critique of art fashions (figure 4.23). The caption for Dyson's drawing, which occupied a full page in the original (as did Titt's cartoon and its inspiration), was "PROGRESS," and in it a "Post-Ellipsoidal Rhomboidist" is disparaging another artist for painting in "the old-fashioned manner of last Thursday." One of the terms being used to describe the new abstract art was "Geometrist," and Dyson runs with it: if you merge a Post-Impressionist with a Cubist and let them compete for new isms, Post-Ellipsoidal Rhomboidist is what you get. And the cartoon itself is rather rhomboidal in shape. So the cartoonists were really in on the debates in this magazine, and if we neglect them, we miss something important about modernist art.

ᴀLEICESTER SQUARE. Bʏ Cʜᴀʀʟᴇs Gɪɴɴᴇʀ.

ᴍᴏᴅᴇʀɴ ᴅʀᴀᴡɪɴɢꜱ—4
ᴇᴅɪᴛᴇᴅ ʙʏ ᴡᴀʟᴛᴇʀ ꜱɪᴄᴋᴇʀᴛ

Fig. 4.21. Charles Ginner, *Leicester Square*, from *The New Age*,
January 22, 1914, 369

The other aspect we should not miss is the connection of magazine modernism to advertising, which is especially visible in *Rhythm*. It
is visible in two ways. One is in the ads themselves, and the other is in
the aggressive defense of advertising presented by the editor in the third
quarterly number:

NEW OXFORD STREET AND HOLBORN.

Fig. 4.22. Tom Titt, *New Oxford Street,* from *The New Age,*
January 22, 1914, 384

The men who try to do something new for the most part
starve. They can only win to success by unity, by helping their
best friends and neglecting petty differences. If we all have the
same idea of revitalizing art, it matters not one straw against
the great question whether we deal with the same tailor, or
use our colours a little differently. And so it is always with

PROGRESS.

Post-Elliptical Rhomboidist: "Him a modern! Bah! He paints in the old-fashioned manner of
last Thursday !"

BY WILL DYSON.

Fig. 4.23. Will Dyson, *Progress*, from *The New Age*,
January 22, 1914, 376

unessentials. Advertisements are unessentials. There may be
some who will say that the admission of advertisements is a
degradation of an artistic magazine. These are the people who
are in love with the print and the paper. We have no use for
them. We believe we have something to say that no other magazine has ever said or had the courage to say. It is a thousand
times more important that we should live to say such things,
than that we should bow before the cries of artistic snobbery.

Fig. 4.24. Ad for Heal and Son, from *Rhythm*, June 1912, i

Those who are really for us, listeners or doers, know that the
life of art depends on free expression, not on the methods by
which that freedom is secured. (36)

Having been attacked for including advertising and not being a "pure"
little magazine, the editor of *Rhythm* replies by saying that the advertising was making the art and criticism presented in the magazine possible
and enabling it to survive. But *Rhythm* went beyond that. Its artists actually helped design the ads, so that they had their own Rhythmist quality (figures 4.24, 4.25). Even in drastically reduced images, we can see that
the ads in *Rhythm* were indeed a part of the magazine. Some were purely
practical, like that for the Heal and Son bed, but others, and they were
the majority, were for galleries like Hanfstaengle, which makes the con-

Fig. 4.25. Ad for Hanfstaengl, from *Rhythm*, June 1912, ii

nection between the magazines and the places where art was viewed and purchased as clear as it can be. Anne Estelle Rice's drawings of the Russian ballet in the magazine were not intended as advertising, but they functioned as such, and their technical links to the more overt ads are readily visible (figure 4.26). There was a culture in place, social and commercial, personal and aesthetic, in which the debates about modern art were ongoing. To understand that culture, we need to make the best use

Fig. 4.26. Anne Estelle Rice, *Russian Ballet*, from *Rhythm*,
March 1912, 481

possible of the magazines that can open it to us. And that means looking at the full range of the magazines and everything that was in them.
John Middleton Murry said that advertisements were "unessentials," even
as he was claiming that they were essential to the survival of his magazine. But as this paradoxical admission reveals, advertising was part of
the essence of modernism, and we shall look at it more carefully in the
next chapter.

Modernism's Other

The Art of Advertising

The Strand Magazine advertisements filled an average of a hundred pages
a month, representing more than two hundred and fifty advertisers.
They provided it with an envied revenue in its heyday. They indexed the
domestic and social life of its readers with something like encyclopedic
completeness. We become acquainted with the preferences, prejudices,
habits, and conventions of a wide section of society. A sociologist might
discover more about the period from those back and front pages of
The Strand than from the articles and stories between.
We follow the readers' evolving tastes in furnishings, fabrics, clothes,
wallpapers, carpets, perambulators, kitchen ware. We see the holiday
resorts bidding for their favours. We see the cars they coveted. We are
reminded of the cosmetics they used and the patent medicines they took.
Their secret dreams are laid bare to us.
—*Reginald Pound,* Mirror of the Century

Modernism has many "others." But one of the most powerful and persistent of these is advertising: that resolutely commercial and rhetorical mode of discourse against which modernism regularly defined itself. One way in which this distinction is situated in our critical discourse derives from Ezra Pound's positioning of little magazines like *Poetry* and *The Egoist* against those commercial magazines that depended on advertising revenue. Pound did this vigorously and persuasively in his essay "Small Magazines," which appeared in November 1930 in the *English Journal,* a publication of the National Council of Teachers of English—influencing, in this way, the critical approach to modernism in the magazines taken by subsequent generations of critics. Pound's own discussions of magazine advertising in *The New Age* have escaped the attention of most scholars because his "Studies in Contemporary Mentality" were not widely available before their appearance in the appendix of this book. The little magazines themselves, of course, often included advertising, and we have much to learn from looking at this aspect of those periodicals, but in this chapter we want to look in another direction, at the advertising in what Pound called an "elder" magazine—that is, an established monthly journal that had added advertising to meet the challenge of the newer mass magazines that arose at the turn of the nineteenth century and the beginning of the twentieth. Pound himself, as we have seen, looked at contemporary advertising, but with fierce hostility. From our later perspective, things look different.

We know that the ads in old magazines are fascinating. The most recent testimony to this phenomenon came in a *New York Times* editorial on November 6, 2005, welcoming the digital edition of *The New Yorker:*

> But the most visceral pleasure in these discs comes from the advertising. It is so interesting that you can be forgiven for confusing the real relation between advertising and editorial content, for supposing that ocean of warm, gray ink existed just to support those astonishing ads. Who remembered that Exxon made an "intelligent typewriter"? Why should an ad

for laser discs feel so cruelly ancient, more ancient than an
ad—"Ask the man who owns one"—for the Golden An-
niversary Packard? There is quicksand here, and some of us
are sinking fast.

To put this editorial comment in perspective we need to go back a century and look at what was being said in the magazines about advertising at that time. Here is a bit of dialect spoken by Finley Peter Dunne's
fictional Irish bartender, Mr. Dooley, in *The American Magazine* in
1909: "What I object to is whin I pay ten or fifteen cents f'r a magazine expectin' to spind me avenin' improvin' me mind with th' latest
thoughts in advertisin' to find more thin a quarter iv th' whole book
devoted to lithrachoor" ("Mr. Dooley on the Magazines," *American
Magazine,* September 1909, 539–542, quoted in Garvey, *Adman in the
Parlor,* 173). This view is a parodic echo of remarks made by Samuel
Hopkins Adams in *Colliers* a few months earlier, when he observed
that "advertising is, in its best development, literature of the most ex-
pert and technical, though not of the highest, type," adding that the
cost per word drove the composer of an ad "to say the most that can
be said, to say it with the highest degree of explicitness, to appeal, to
make it arrest, to make it convince, and all in the briefest compass. If
that isn't literary work, I don't know what is" (May 22, 1909, 14, quoted
ibid., 170).

Ironies abound here. One is that Hopkins's description of advertising is eerily close to the prescription for Imagist poetry developed by
Ezra Pound and others a few years after this. Pound would have abhorred
such a connection, but it is plainly there, as in these bits of advice from
an Imagist manifesto:

- Use the language of common speech, but employ the exact
  word, not the nearly-exact, nor the merely decorative word.
- Produce a poetry that is hard and clear, never blurred nor
  indefinite.
- Concentration is of the very essence of poetry. (Preface to
  Some Imagist Poets)

Compare these to Adams's description of advertising values:

- to say the most that can be said, to say it with the highest degree of explicitness;
- to appeal, to make it arrest, to make it convince;
- and all in the briefest compass.

Advertising, ironically enough, is inside modern poetry as well as all around it in the pages of the magazines. Yet another irony lies in the way Mr. Dooley's obvious preference for advertising over "lithrachoor" is based on the difference between them, while Adams insists on their similarity. It is Adams, not Dunne, who is being paradoxical here. But advertisers, in the period of the rise of modernism, had been arguing Mr. Dooley's case for a couple of decades before the Irish bartender expressed his opinions on the relationship between literary art and advertising. Here, for example, is a view from an advertising trade journal published in 1890, presented as an overheard remark:

> One of the gentlemen said he was convinced that there was a great number of people who always looked at this department first. "Did you ever notice," he said, "how a woman in the cars will read a magazine? She will take it up, look at it all over carefully to see she has the real thing, read the baking-powder advertisement on the back, start in from the end, look all through the advertising pages—stopping now and then to read some announcement of special allurement—until she strikes the text. She then gives a sigh, reaches toward her back hair for a superfluous pin, and begins to mutilate the pages in a languid quest for the month's poetry." (*Art in Advertising*, March 1890, 5, quoted in Garvey, *Adman in the Parlor*, 173)

These lines are attributed in the magazine to a Mr. Fulkerson, who is based on the character of that name in William Dean Howells's novel *A Hazard of New Fortunes,* which was first published that year. We can learn quite a bit from them. First of all, the pin. What this lady is doing is using a hairpin to open the text pages of a magazine, which were still uncut (technically "unopened") when the magazines were sold at that time. The advertising pages at the front and back of the magazine would have been cut open before distribution or never folded as the inner pages were for printing. They were also numbered separately from the text pages, which eased their integration at the time of printing but also, as it happened, made it easy for libraries (or the publishers themselves) to discard those pages when copies were bound for permanent collection. The usual practice was to number the text pages consecutively for an entire volume, anticipating their transformation to a bound book, while the advertising pages were consecutive for single issues only, anticipating their disappearance later. The *New York Times* of 2005 and the fictional woman in a railway car of 1890 seem to have the same view of the relationship between text and advertising in magazines. That is perhaps the supreme irony to be extracted from this comparison of views.

There are other ironies, however, in the world of modernist magazines that will help us understand just how intertwined modernist art and advertising actually were in the early twentieth century. Sometime around 1911 or 1912, when Harriet Monroe was trying to enlist support for a magazine devoted to modern poetry, she drafted a letter that included this crucial passage (located in her correspondence by John Timberman Newcomb):

> We feel that the magazine is the most important aesthetic advertisement Chicago ever had. We are doing the same kind of work for the city which is done by the Art Institute, the Orchestral Association, the Chicago Grand Opera co., the two endowed theaters, etc. Indeed, our work is of more far-reaching influence, as poetry travels more easily than any other art. (quoted in Churchill and McKible, 92)

With pitches of this sort, Monroe persuaded one hundred wealthy Chicagoans to pledge fifty dollars a year for five years to support her magazine. For our purposes, however, the important thing to notice is that *Poetry* itself, one of the greatest of the small magazines, was sold to Chicagoans as advertising for the city and its culture—and the literary genre that it promoted, the poems that were published in the magazine, were being sold in this document on the basis of their portability: "poetry travels more easily than any other art." Yes, indeed. Poetry *is* advertising, and it is also art, making it the aesthetic form best designed by the age of modernity, if it could generate properly modernist forms for properly modernist content—and if Harriet Monroe could accomplish what Walt Whitman said was necessary for poetry to succeed. In every issue, we can find these words of Whitman's, usually on the back cover: "To have great poets there must be great audiences too." Monroe's magazine took as its mission the creation of such an audience, and it succeeded. As Harriet Monroe observed herself in 1917,

> SOMEWHERE I have read a quaint old myth of a goblin who, blowing the fog out of his face, started a tempest which went careering around the world. Now and then I feel like that goblin. Is it possible that less than four years ago poetry was "the Cinderella of the arts"? Already a great wind is blowing her ashes away, and on the horizon are rolling dust-clouds which may conceal a coach and four or is it an automobile?
>
> For there must be some gift of the gods in the large and many-colored cloud of words which fills our eyes and ears. Never before was there so much talk about poetry in this western world, or so much precious print devoted to its schools and schisms. This is as it should be, no doubt. It may be evidence of that "poetic renaissance" which some of us profess already to be living in; or at least it may initiate that "great audience" which will be ready for the renaissance when it comes. A breach has been made, we may hope, in that stone wall of public apathy which tended to silence the singer ere he began. (*Poetry* 3.8: 140)

A final irony (as if more were needed) is that Harriet Monroe herself became a commodity as *Poetry* succeeded, and was marketed in advertising in the back pages of the magazine (figure 5.1). With Monroe as its ambassador, even "The New Movement in Poetry" could be marketed as a topic for lectures. And this cannot be separated from the professed goal of the

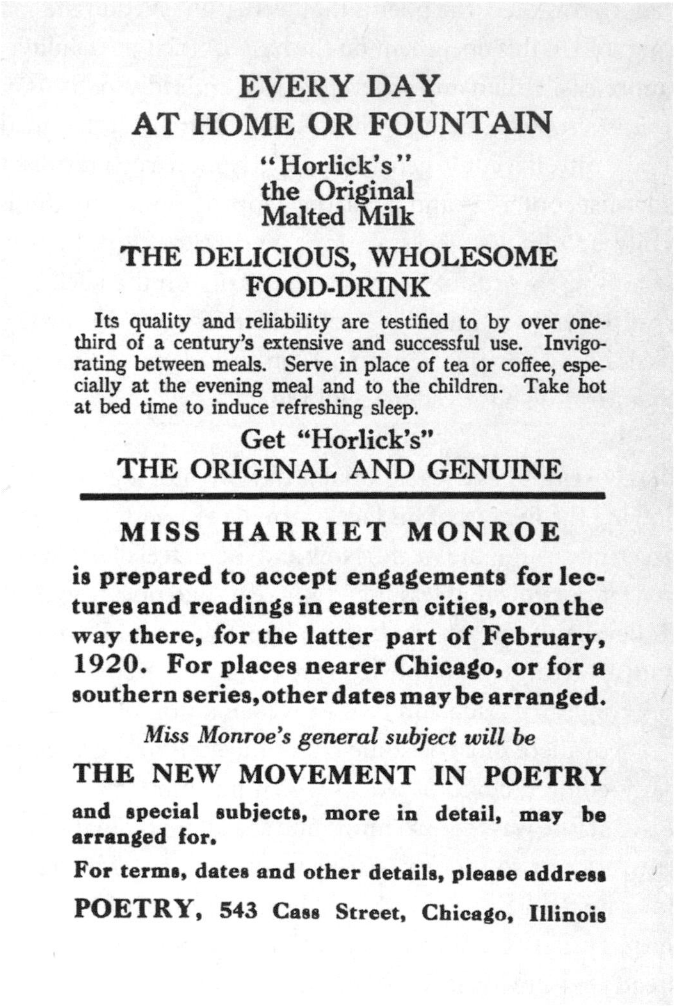

EVERY DAY
AT HOME OR FOUNTAIN

"Horlick's"
the Original
Malted Milk

THE DELICIOUS, WHOLESOME
FOOD-DRINK

Its quality and reliability are testified to by over one-third of a century's extensive and successful use. Invigorating between meals. Serve in place of tea or coffee, especially at the evening meal and to the children. Take hot at bed time to induce refreshing sleep.

Get "Horlick's"
THE ORIGINAL AND GENUINE

MISS HARRIET MONROE

is prepared to accept engagements for lectures and readings in eastern cities, or on the way there, for the latter part of February, 1920. For places nearer Chicago, or for a southern series, other dates may be arranged.

Miss Monroe's general subject will be

THE NEW MOVEMENT IN POETRY

and special subjects, more in detail, may be arranged for.

For terms, dates and other details, please address

POETRY, 543 Cass Street, Chicago, Illinois

Fig. 5.1. Ad for Harriet Monroe, from *Poetry,* January, 1920

magazine itself, expressed in Whitman's view that great poets required great audiences. We cannot be certain, of course, whether Whitman's second *great* referred to quality or size. But what Harriet Monroe was trying to do, in the pages of her magazine and in her lectures, was to produce both a larger and a more discriminating audience for modern poetry. She succeeded, but success required not a separation from the culture of commodities but an immersion in it, with art and commerce intricately entwined.

Monroe's main collaborator on *Poetry* was Alice Corbin Henderson, who produced poetry under her maiden name, Corbin, and criticism under her full name or, more often, over her full set of initials. In the June 1917 issue of the magazine she recounts an interesting experience that points, half-jokingly, toward a new way of reading poetry:

> I was passing a store window when I noticed an attractive cover on a magazine. Closer inspection revealed the fact that it was a reproduction of a painting by Edmund Dulac, fine enough to make one care to preserve it. So I gave the clerk a quarter for the March number of *Harper's Bazar* and began turning the pages to see if there were more illustrations by Dulac. As it happened, there was nothing with any direct reference to the Chinese lady on the cover, but there was an article on *The Hawk's Well*, the Noh play written by William Butler Yeats, with Dulac's designs for the costumes and for the masks worn by the two principal characters. This was interesting, and I congratulated myself on having bought the magazine, usually associated in one's mind with fashions, for which, being on the edge of the desert, I had no present use. The article and illustrations covered two full pages in the body of the magazine, and I fancied that that was all there was to it. Not until I reached home did I notice at the bottom of the second page of the article (which proved to be a preface by Mr. Yeats) a note in small type: *Continued on page 132;* and there, sure enough, between advertisements of Hair Restorers, Patent Leather Boots, Mrs. Vernon Castle, and Backlace Corsets, I found the text of *The Hawk's Well.* Perhaps there was something symbolic about it. Many may wait and fall asleep and know only by the wet stones that they have missed the perfect moment. I at least had luck—I found the play. But think of a Noh drama, born of the most ascetic theatre and convention, produced among such distractions! Is it not a reversal of all precedent? (*Poetry* 10.3: 163–164)

"Perhaps there was something symbolic," she suggests, about the location of Yeats's Noh play among the ads for "Hair Restorers, Patent

Leather Boots, Mrs. Vernon Castle, and Back-lace Corsets." She is just kidding, of course, but we may profit from taking her more literally than she intended. Ezra Pound himself, a few months later, would start connecting advertising to the other content of magazines in his "Studies in Contemporary Mentality." Reading in the magazines involves interpreting such symbolic juxtapositions, but we need to see the original pages (or a replica of them) in order to do this.

Advertising was all around the magazine world in the early twentieth century, but the most fascinating ads were certainly those in the larger magazines with the widest circulations, like the *Harper's Bazar* (this spelling persisted until 1929) that attracted Henderson's attention. In this chapter we propose to address this fascination in ways both practical and theoretical. That is, we want to look at a small sample of ads from an "elder" magazine of this period to see what kind of things we can learn from them, and we want to take at least the first steps toward a theory and method of investigating the rhetoric of these texts. In practice this will require something like the hermeneutic circle: that is, first a tentative theory, then some practical analysis, and then, perhaps, a more refined theory. On the theoretical side our starting point will be the changes wrought by time in the relationship between an advertisement and its readers. In the beginning, behind every ad there was a commodity, which the ad urged its readers to consume, whether this were an object to acquire or an opportunity to go somewhere or do something. Over time, however, the commodity and the original target of advertisements have faded away, leaving only a text that has a certain appeal that is partly aesthetic and partly historical, so that it is this process of change over time that makes such texts fascinating for us now, who live in another world, another time.

This changes the dynamic of response drastically. The fictional woman in the railroad car was drawn by the "special allurement" of new products and opportunities. Reading the same material a century later, we are drawn by nostalgia for a vanished past, for objects that have disappeared and opportunities that can no longer be seized. In looking at these old ads we are constantly reminded of the famous opening lines to E. P. Hartley's novel *The Go-Between*: "The past is a foreign country; they do things differently there." The lines resonate and linger in memory not because they see the past as strange but because they see it as alive, in the present tense. And this is just what we experience in looking at magazine advertising in the period of our investigations, 1890 to 1922. That *New York Times* editorial paragraph on the digital edition of the old *New Yorker* concludes its praise of the ads in the magazine with these words: "There is quicksand here, and some of us are sinking fast."

Clearly the *Times* writer was carried away, as the mixture of metaphors in the notion of a "visceral pleasure" in "sinking" into "quicksand" reveals, but was onto something very important nonetheless. As we have been suggesting, the old ads have gained aesthetically. That is, their power to please us has increased, as their power to persuade us has decreased. If we consider Adams's formulation—"to say the most that can be said, to say it with the highest degree of explicitness, to appeal, to make it arrest, to make it convince, and all in the briefest compass"—all the elements are still there except the power to convince, which has been removed by time, turning rhetoric into poetry. And, correspondingly, some of the old text has lost its power to please and become merely of historical interest, turning poetry into something more prosaic. During the rise of modernism, however, the power of advertising was seen mainly in a sinister light, as having an adverse effect on literature rather than competing with it aesthetically. Literary figures like Ezra Pound were only too aware of the power of advertising, not only in its own persuasiveness but in the ability of advertisers to influence the content of the magazines that advertising supported.

The sinister influence of advertising was noted in the magazine world as early as the 1890s, when publishers first found that advertising revenue could support journals that lost money on their actual sales— if they sold enough copies to suit the advertisers. This discovery led to the first of the real mass magazines, *Munsey's, McClure's,* and the like— and to their antithesis, the little magazines of small circulation, in which the literary and artistic forms we know as modernism arose. The rhetoric of modernism, drawn from such texts as Ezra Pound's "Small Magazines," was based on an absolute distinction between the high art of the little magazines and the low and boring stuff that was supposed to be in all the others, including what Pound called the "Elder Magazines," such as *The Atlantic Monthly* and *Scribner's.* But Pound himself knew that was not the whole story. We students and scholars of modernism have heard him selectively, ignoring his reminders that we need to consider the whole range of periodicals to understand modern culture and the texts it produced.

In particular (as Robert Scholes has argued in *Paradoxy of Modernism*), we need to understand the often excluded middle range of literature and the other arts, which, when we look into it, turns out to be a complex affair. It is not just middling texts produced by middling authors and artists for middlebrow audiences. In the magazines, it is also a rich mixture of the new and the traditional, of art and advertising, of the poetic and the rhetorical—a mixture that allowed new writers to reach a wider audience. The little magazines themselves took in advertising, and in some cases, this advertising helped promote the dissemination of modernist ideas to a wider audience. And they published manifestos in which the case for the new modes of art and writing was made as persuasively as possible. To understand this process we must recognize that a manifesto is itself a form of advertising. Moreover, as we have shown, Harriet Monroe's *Poetry* magazine carried advertising for a popular book on the art of versification. This book, in turn, added to its second edition a chapter on modernist free verse, with quotations from Ezra Pound and Amy Lowell in it. When we really look into the magazines of this period, we find authors now ignored being published next to Pound and other canonical modernists in the little magazines, and we find authors now enshrined in the modernist canon appearing in both the "elder" magazines and the "mass" magazines. The elders that survived in this period in fact took in substantial amounts of advertising and became almost indistinguishable from the larger magazines in that respect, though a study of the ads themselves may reveal interesting differences.

With that in mind, we propose to look at advertising in a single issue of a single elder magazine, to see what pleasures it may hold and what we may learn from taking advertising seriously. Our journal of choice will be *Scribner's* magazine for July 1918. This is practically a random choice, since it is based on the fact that we came upon it at an opportune moment, but it will be useful because it is from a time more than a year after the United States had entered World War I, but before the war had ended, which means that we can look at it with our own more re-

cent wars in mind. It is also from just a few months after Pound had
ended his survey of British popular magazines. This issue of *Scribner's*
contained 76 pages of advertising and 130 pages of text. That is, in fact, a
relatively low ratio of advertising to text, which in many earlier issues approached equality. The advertising section of the magazine, however, includes some text of its own—writing which is not part of any advertisement but is intended to situate and enhance the ads themselves. The
advertising in *Scribner's*, as in other magazines of this period, appears in
two sections, at the front and the back of each issue. One of the interesting segments of the front section is a nine-page sequence called "The Fifth
Avenue Section," containing ads from shops on the famous New York
avenue where the Scribner publishing house itself was located. This section includes a useful calendar of art shows and exhibitions in the local
galleries, but it is preceded by something even more interesting—a page
called "Midsummer on Fifth Avenue," which begins with the following
paragraphs:

> Long stretches of sun-baked asphalt, uninviting and weari-
> some; shop-window awnings scarcely stirring in the sporadic
> breeze, yet forming welcoming pools of shadow under which
> filmy summer finery lurked. Infrequently a sight-seeing bus
> creaked by on "a semaphore voyage up the Avenue," its barker
> droning out the landmarks, houses, and famous shops.
>
> Such was Fifth Avenue in former years when in mid-
> summer it resigned itself to dog-days, deserted and empty. To
> the influx of Western and Southern visitors it owed its chief
> animation, occasionally whirling by in taxis that seemed to
> have gathered up all the energy of the Avenue and concen-
> trated it in getting out of the heat.
>
> In contrast is Fifth Avenue in its second war sum-
> mer! . . .

The page includes three photographs of the avenue, with flags flying and
uniformed doughboys on the sidewalks, and the prose goes on to speak
of how war work is bringing women shoppers into the city. The war, it
seems, is good for business in New York. We can also get, if we attend to

Midsummer on Fifth Avenue

LONG stretches of sun-baked asphalt, uninviting and wearisome; shop-window awnings scarcely stirring in the sporadic breeze, yet forming welcome pools of shadow under which filmy summer finery lurked. Infrequently a sight-seeing bus creaked by on "a semaphore voyage up the Avenue," its barker droning out the landmarks, houses, and famous shops.

Photographs by J. B. Carrington

SUCH was Fifth Avenue in former years when in midsummer it resigned itself to dog-days, deserted and empty. To the influx of Western and Southern visitors it owed its chief animation, occasionally whirling by in taxis that seemed to have gathered up all the energy of the Avenue and concentrated it in getting out of the heat.

IN contrast is Fifth Avenue in its second war summer! For in war-time activities

there is a complete disregard of season. Fifth Avenue has been commandeered for service the calendar round! Many of its habitués are remaining in town for their first New York summer, while canteen service, committee meetings, and executive responsibilities for the Red Cross and other war activities are bringing women, accustomed only to infrequent shopping trips in town all summer, back daily all week. Back, too, they come with the officer members of their families under sailing orders, here to snatch a last precious gayety together with a round of the Fifth Avenue shops, roof-gardens, theatres, exhibitions, and restaurants.

DOG-days on Fifth Avenue? Ask the traffic officer! Still, we doubt if he will have time to mop his brow and chat. His traffic signals now in midsummer must be as frequent as in season!

Fig. 5.2. Midsummer on Fifth Avenue, from *Scribner's*, July 1918

this prose, a sense of the class of readers the magazine assumes it is reaching, as it speaks of these women coming to the city "with the officer members of their families under sailing orders, here to snatch a last precious gayety together with a round of the Fifth Avenue shops, roof-gardens, theatres, exhibitions, and restaurants" (figure 5.2). These shoppers come from the social class that produces commissioned officers rather than enlisted men—and Fifth Avenue is their street, as Scribner's is their publisher. The orientation of *Scribner's* to an upper (or at least moneyed) class is further exemplified by the ten advertising pages devoted to private schools, organized on a state-by-state basis, covering fifteen states and Washington, D.C. These ads betray an eastern orientation as well, with California's private schools being the only ones west of the Mississippi to appear in this section.

There are also eighteen pages that contain ads for banks or investment services. Clearly, *Scribner's* and its advertisers thought they were reaching the class of people who had money to invest as well as spend, who sent their children to private schools, bought expensive cars (with ads for Locomobile, Pierce-Arrow, Studebaker, and Apperson in this issue), and came to Fifth Avenue to shop. In fact, the attention to financial matters in the journal is almost shocking in its ubiquity and intensity. It is there in the fiction (Hansell Crenshaw's "Money Magic," richly illustrated by Arthur William Brown) and in the articles ("The Perils of Will-Making," by Robert Grant). We can even find war and finance united in a piece on "The Financial Situation: During the German Drive," by Alexander Dana Noyes, which runs into and through the advertising pages devoted to finance.

There were also ads for more homely products, to be sure, like Mazda lightbulbs and Swift's bacon, but even the bacon is "premium," and Mazda is presented as a research service that just happens to have developed a product sold by General Electric. There was a definite upward tilt to the advertising pages from beginning to end, as we might expect from a periodical that thought of itself as a leading member of "The Quality Group" of magazines (*Atlantic Monthly, Century, Harper's, Review of Reviews, Scribner's,* and *World's Work*). "The Quality Group" even had its own ad in this issue of *Scribner's,* addressed to potential advertisers (figure 5.3). This ad compares advertising in magazines of "The Quality

If You Were a Retail Merchant

YOU know that advertising is simply silent salesmanship—but do you put your knowledge into practice?

Do you apply to your advertising the same principles that you would apply to the management of a retail store?

Suppose that you as a merchant were offered a particularly good location on the most desirable street in town. Suppose you found that its rental was a great deal lower than one in another, more congested district. Which one would you take?

Suppose you also found out that you could keep open the well-located store every business day of the year, but that you would have to close up part of the time at the other location. Which one would you take?

Think of The Quality Group as the store in the best neighborhood. Think of being able to buy a page in every issue of every one of these six magazines *for a year* for a little over $17,000! Think of keeping your door open *every day in the year* to the three-quarters of a million families who are readers of the Atlantic Monthly, Century Magazine, Harper's Magazine, Review of Reviews, Scribner's Magazine, World's Work!

Strip advertising of its artificialities and be as hard-headed about buying advertising space as you would be about renting building space if you were a merchant. Tell your advertising manager that you are ready to hear his arguments for The Quality Group.

ATLANTIC MONTHLY
CENTURY MAGAZINE
HARPER'S MAGAZINE

REVIEW OF REVIEWS
SCRIBNER'S MAGAZINE
WORLD'S WORK

Fig. 5.3. Ad for Quality Magazines, from *Scribner's,* July 1918

Group" to doing business on "the most desirable street in town." The
ad offers a page in every issue of six magazines for one year—for "a little over $17,000."

The literary content of these magazines is not our topic on this occasion, but it is fair to say that in the issue of *Scribner's* we are considering, high economics does not equate with high modernist culture in fiction and poetry, though a short poem by Amy Lowell does appear on
page 79. Most of the fiction and poetry in this issue is quite forgettable
and, indeed, has been forgotten—though this is by no means the case
with all issues of *Scribner's* during this period. But the ads are still ready
and able to speak to us, if we attend to them. Let us look more closely at
a few.

The ad for Swift's bacon is typical of many in that it ties the product to the war, however it can (figure 5.4). And it is typical of *Scribner's*
in that there is a uniformed maid ("old Mary") bringing in the bacon to
the returned officer son of the household. But the visual quality of the
primary image is distinctly superior to that of many other illustrations in
the magazine. Look closely at the glasses on the table, the window, the
detail of the faces, and the handling of the light in general. This has all
the hyperrealism of a Norman Rockwell image, though Rockwell is probably not the artist involved. But the draftsmanship and the view of American home life presented are Rockwellian. He was in the early years of
his career at this time, doing advertising work, among other things, and
this is the aesthetic milieu from which his work emerged. Whoever the
artist, however, this is a higher order of art than that in the grotesque
frontispiece of this same issue, produced by the English academician John
da Costa (see plate 3). Here we see two warlike ladies, with their flags
and shields and emblems, "United after a century and a half," in *The New
Fourth of July, 1918*. This is the sort of academic blather that makes one
long for the modernist excesses of Futurists and Vorticists. And it is just
as much an example of the rhetoric of visual advertising as any of the
images in the advertising section, though it is propaganda rather than
consumer advertising.

The abstraction of the high modernist artists is just one response to
such academic banalities; the hyperrealism of the Swift ad is another. And
there is yet another in the fanciful images shared by certain magazine ads

How he enjoys
the home meal again

HOW delighted he is to be home —with his mother and old Mary making so much of him. They give him his favorite meal—the bacon he has loved from boyhood—and beam to see the relish with which he eats it.

It is Swift's Premium Bacon. His mother never served any other kind. She knows that this bacon has always the same even mixture of fat and lean, that cooks into almost-brittle curls of juiciness. She knows that only in Swift's Premium can she get that delicate, mellow flavor. For Swift's Premium Bacon is given a special cure that brings out all its deliciousness—until its very heart is mild, sweet and flavory.

Whenever you buy bacon, always look for the Swift's Premium brand which distinguishes this finer bacon.

Swift & Company, U. S. A.

Swift's Premium Bacon

Comes in three convenient forms; in the strip; sliced in the box; or sliced in glass jars

66

Fig. 5.4. Ad for Swift's, from *Scribner's,* July 1918

and the poster art of this period. Compare the patriotic colors of da Costa's painting, for example, to the imagery in an ad for Murad cigarettes (see plate 4). There are flags here, too, but just their corners are visible, and some are fanciful, it appears, though the Stars and Stripes and the Union Jack seem to be among them, and one resembles, though not exactly, the Confederate Stars and Bars. This is a "Turkish" cigarette, so the women in the foreground are wearing what were called "harem pants," an exotic version of bloomers introduced by the fashion designer Paul Poiret in 1909. In this case one is colored like a flag and the other in a softer version of military khaki. These garments connoted the eroticism of the harem and the freedom of the bloomer-wearing female cyclist. The only person actually smoking is a British-looking soldier, and there is also a French military man in the background, reminding us that there is, indeed, a war on. The whole thing is in poster style, and the colors are attractive, with deft handling of places where they are superimposed. Both Poiret's fashions and Murad's ads have, in fact, been compared to Leon Bakst's sets for the Russian ballet, which influenced both fashion and advertising artists during this period. What is perhaps most astonishing is that this commercial confection makes the da Costa painting look extremely heavy and even vulgar in comparison.

Turkey, of course, was an enemy of the Allies in this war, but it was just about to go under in the summer of 1918, having been despoiled of its Arabian possessions by T. E. Lawrence and his friends so that Britain and France could carve them up into the Syria, Lebanon, Palestine, and Iraq that we presently encounter. These "Turkish" cigarettes are attributed in the ad to a wealthy Greek, S. Anargyros, though they were actually manufactured by the New Jersey firm of Lorillard—a company owned by Pierre Lorillard, the man who in 1886 (the year the new *Scribner's* magazine was founded) had introduced a new kind of male evening dress to high society in Tuxedo Park, New York. Murad, and other "Turkish" cigarettes like Mogul, were made from blends of tobacco imported from the Near East and sold to the sort of people we have already identified as readers of *Scribner's*—or to people who wished to be like those readers—people who owned tuxedos, or those who rented them. Later in this issue there is another, smaller cigarette ad, with an art nouveau image of a smoking cigarette and the slogan "nobody ever changes from Rameses,

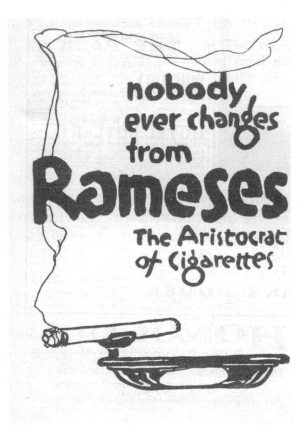

Fig. 5.5. Ad for Rameses cigarettes, from *Scribner's*,
July 1918

the Aristocrat of Cigarettes" (figure 5.5). It is clear, even from this relatively superficial investigation, that the magazine was resolutely upscale, and that every facet of this issue had to reflect that orientation.

There were other things going on in the advertising pages of the magazine, however, and one of the most interesting can be found in the Kodak ad shown in figure 5.6, which was spread over two pages. One hardly knows whether to laugh or cry over this astonishing blend of war propaganda and salesmanship. On the left-hand page is an image of what is said to be a pamphlet designed by the Association of German Amateur Photographers, with the text in German, and on the right a translation of that pamphlet. The problem the Germans were facing was that

Kodak had become a generic name for camera, and the German photographers' association wanted people to stop using both the name and
the cameras made by Eastman Kodak. Eastman promoters faced the same
problem from the other side and used the German propaganda to rein-
force their own brand's recognition factor, making it patriotic to buy their
product. It is hard to imagine a more effective way of getting attention
in 1918 America than starting with an image of the imperial eagle of the
enemy and a large text in his language.

The war was everywhere in the magazine, with articles on the U.S.
Naval Academy, on a Y.M.C.A. theater group at the front, on "The Great
Work of American Railroad Men in France," on "The Defensive Battle,"
and on "Defeat, Compromise, or Victory." But nowhere was it more visible than in the advertising pages. Consider the gem from the makers of
Havoline Motor Oil, shown in plate 5. The Stars and Stripes have metamorphosed here—the stars into aircraft and the stripes into the language
of Lincoln against a cloudy sky. And this new flag flies over a line of troops
moving up. But the text in this image is the most interesting part. Under
the large heading, "WARRIORS ALL!" we find writing that divides the population into the warriors—meaning those who fought, worked, or *bought*
for their country—and those who did not. In this text, those who "bought
Bonds" are equated with those who worked and those who actually went
to war, and those who did not do one of these things, we are told, "will
be marked well." The implied threat of retribution here is palpable. And
the Indian Refining Company and its product Havoline Oil want you to
know that they are on the side of the buyers, in that they bought this advertising space to threaten the nonbuyers with stigmatization. Investing
in war bonds and shopping on Fifth Avenue are both presented as patriotic activities in this *Scribner's*—giving us a look into the world from
which our own post-9/11 world emerged.

One ad that does not mention the war is the one for Remington
Steel Lined Wetproof shotgun shells, which is all about killing ducks in
wet weather. Remington, apparently, did not want to remind *Scribner's*
readers that guns also kill people. Even the *Christian Science Monitor*,
however, attuned its advertising to the conflict, arguing, in an ad headed
"To Win the War," that a "clear, calm, and exact" record of events supported the war effort. The world of 1918 was both like our own world

The illustration shows a pamphlet signed by the Association of German Amateur Photographers' Societies and dated Berlin, October, 1917. It is reproduced from a photographic copy lately received in this country. The translation in full is given on opposite page.

Fig. 5.6. Ad for Kodak cameras, from *Scribner's*, July 1918

—*If* <u>*it*</u> *isn't* <u>*an*</u> *Eastman* <u>*it*</u> *isn't* <u>*a*</u> *Kodak!*

A translation of the circular in full is as follows:

"It is the duty of every German to use only German products and to patronize thereby German industry. Therefore, use for photographic purposes only German cameras, German Dry Plates and German papers. Whoever purchases the products of enemy industries strengthens the economic power of our enemies.

"Germans! Remember for all times to come that with the aid of your patronage the American-English Kodak Co. subscribed before the war with the United States, the round sum of 50,000,000 marks of war loans of our enemies!

"There are no German 'Kodaks'. ('Kodak' as a collective noun for photographic products is misleading and indicates only the products of the Eastman Kodak Co.) Whoever speaks of a 'Kodak' and means thereby only a photographic camera, does not bear in mind that with the spreading of this word, he does harm to the German industry in favor of the American-English."

If it isn't an Eastman it isn't a Kodak!

EASTMAN KODAK COMPANY
Rochester, N. Y.   *The Kodak City*

and unlike it—and we have much to learn from both the resemblances
and the differences. The magazines of the period, we are suggesting, with
their mixture of materials, offer us one of the best possible windows into
that world.

Unfortunately, that window is far from wide open at present, because the copies in our libraries have regularly been bound without the
advertising. We will discuss this problem more thoroughly in Chapter
8. For now, we can only note that the result of this hole in the archive is
that we cannot just send students to the library and expect them to find
things like the ads we have been discussing. A remedy for this problem
will take some serious efforts by many people. We are going to have to
locate original issues of the magazines in libraries or elsewhere, and then
make digital versions of them widely available. When that work is done,
we will be able to compare the literature and advertising of one periodical with another, and to study these things as they change over time in
any given magazine. Interesting projects in cultural history will become
possible for scholars and for students working under the direction of such
scholars. Some of these projects, as we have already indicated, will be
cumulative if not quantitative, involving comparisons drawn over a range
of journals or a period of time. Others will be more analytical, and, for
these, we shall have to develop some new tools of analysis—or adapt
some old ones to new purposes.

Some of the work we must do tends toward the sociological. You
will have noticed our counting things like the number of pages devoted
to banking and investment, and the pages devoted to private schools. We
are going to have to count and compare ads from different periodicals
to get a sense of their audiences and their ideological positions. And we
must do the same things with individual magazines viewed over time,
to see how they changed. But we are also going to have to learn to *read*
advertising, to decode the images as well as the texts for both ideological
and aesthetic purposes. Long ago John Stuart Mill suggested that poetry
was "overheard"—not directly addressed to the reader—and later I. A.
Richards picked up that notion and incorporated it into his own poet-
ics. The transformation in magazine advertising that takes place as a magazine recedes from us in time moves it in this very direction. We—contemporary readers of old magazine advertising—are not being directly

addressed either. We have been put in the position of the audience for poetry, as Mill and Richards understood the matter. Which is to say that we have reached an aesthetic position with respect to these texts—and a historical position as well. To read these texts well we must acknowledge both of these positions and work from them. In our examples we have taken some first steps in this direction. Ezra Pound, of course, when he looked at the advertising in contemporary magazines, was in a very different position. He felt oppressed and offended by the way both the advertising and the other texts in the magazines he examined camouflaged the reality of his world. We, on the other hand, are interested in what they reveal about that world which is not ours.

When we have studied more ads, we will be able to do better at analyzing them, but we can already see, in the ads we have discussed, how the wartime ideology of 1918 can be extracted and compared to our own. We are perhaps better prepared to deal with ideology than with the aesthetic side of magazine advertising. For this we need to see these ads as antiques, in which craft has become art thanks to the passage of time. We need to situate their images in the artistic styles of the time, as we attempted to do by contrasting the ads in this issue of *Scribner's* with the da Costa painting in the same issue and connecting them to Rockwell and the Russian ballet artists.

The main thing we want to emphasize in concluding this chapter is the pedagogical value of such studies. We can offer students a path to learning something about the feel of a moment in our cultural history by their own direct analysis of magazine advertising. And we can offer them a way from the visual materials in such ads into the other modes of art that were alive in the past. There is a pleasure in contemplating things like the ad for Studebaker cars shown in plate 6—a pleasure that our students need simply to enjoy and also to analyze. Without trying to push this too far, we would suggest that our enjoyment in contemplating this ad comes from the Impressionist quality of the image itself (notice the haystacks and the tree), and from the sense it gives us of entering a scene. Actually, it is as if a realistic car had been driven into an Impressionist landscape, since the artist has blended these two modes deliberately in composing the image for the ad. These people are talking, enjoying themselves, because this lovely real machine has taken them to this charming dream landscape. We might be looking into a scene from *The Great Gatsby* here, though the novel itself did not appear until seven years later, as a world that is dead and gone comes alive in this commercial image.

The study of advertising in magazines like *Scribner's* will allow us to historicize more thoroughly, to understand the past more fully, by entering that past through the door provided by digital editions that include the original images and advertising in color. In these ads we can see how the rhetoric of commerce is mixed with that of politics and that of art. The roots of modern culture are here laid bare for studies that should ultimately help us understand ourselves and our present situation better—which is the main purpose of all historical investigation. This work —and these pleasures—are now waiting only for the digital editions of these magazines to be made available to scholars and students everywhere. And we can assure you that we are doing our best to make this happen.

How to Study a Modern Magazine

Blackwood's Magazine has ever had a corporate life of its own. It is not a mere
medley of heterogeneous articles. It is a single work, conducted by a single
mind, for a single purpose.

—*Charles Whibley, quoted in Finkelstein,* Print Culture and the
Blackwood Tradition, 1805–1930

Our epigraph is from the Centennial Issue of *Blackwood's* magazine, published in April 1917 and discussed by Ezra Pound in "Studies in Contemporary Mentality." Whibley is a fascinating figure, admired by Joseph Conrad and T. S. Eliot, though not, apparently, by Pound. He was as much of an elitist as Pound, however, though opposed to modernist experiments in art and literature and devoted to traditional values. He wrote a regular column for *Blackwood's,* for the first three decades of the twentieth century, which is as opinionated and lively as Pound's own writing, and he shared Pound's anti-Semitism and approval of Mussolini, though he died in 1930 and never saw where fascism led. Pound, in the second of his "Studies," attacked *Blackwood's* as the reactionary voice of the British Empire—which it was, and Whibley was the leading spokesman in that voice. We begin with this quotation, however, not for political reasons but because it makes an interesting point for the study of modernist periodicals, urging that we read one of them, at least, as a unified text. He overstates the case, in our judgment, but he points in a useful direction, and we should keep his view in mind as we embark on the study of modernist magazines. We should also note that the antimodernist *Blackwood's* is just as much a part of the study of modernism as the anarchist and experimental *Little Review*, and not just because *Blackwood's* published Conrad's *Heart of Darkness* and *Lord Jim*.

Because the study of magazines—as opposed to the literature or art that may be in them—is a relatively new academic discipline, we will seek in this chapter to provide a method or pattern for such study that can be adapted by individual scholars or teachers working with groups of students. This is not the only method or pattern, and it may not be the best one, but it is a place to start, a way to get into the domain of periodical studies by refining the pioneering steps of Ezra Pound, taken so long ago. Pound demonstrated two things: how to read a single magazine, looking at everything from advertising to fiction to editorials, and how to read a whole set of magazines as a way of understanding the "mentality" or culture represented in them. Pound, of course, had a critical or satirical intent, based on his own set of values. Our method must be more neutral, though it can certainly be adapted to more critical perspectives. We hope that other teachers and scholars will improve on it and share their improvements with the rest of us. In the next chapter we will look at methods for reading a set of contemporary magazines. In this one we will use as an example the very magazine for which Pound wrote "Studies in Contemporary Mentality": *The New Age*.

We know that we are not the audience that the magazines of modernism addressed. As our discussion of advertising in Chapter 5 suggested, we come back to them with a historical interest. We read them to recover the past, to study the culture, the ideology, and the values of the past. And this is especially important because journals, as the very word implies, are meant to be timely. They are very much of their moment, addressed to the audience of that moment. Newspapers are daily, presenting the news of the day, to an audience that is usually local. Even a "national" newspaper like the *New York Times* turns local—and partisan—on the sports page. Magazines have a different temporality—weekly, monthly, quarterly—and are usually intended to be less local, which makes the question of audience especially interesting. One of the first steps, then, in reading a magazine of a century ago, is to get a sense of the readership the magazine is trying to reach, so that we can imagine ourselves as members of that group without losing our own perspectives. An attempt to understand the audience of any journal will lead us to most of the other elements involved in reading a magazine from the past.

In seeking to understand the audience, as in every other phase of reading a magazine, we must remain aware of the nature of magazines in general. Magazines are more like soap operas than novels. They are intended to continue indefinitely, which in practice means as long as audiences are interested in them and advertisers (or patrons) support them. Every magazine must give the public what it wants, but different magazines have very different publics in mind. An elite literary or artistic magazine must try to please sophisticated readers, which often means addressing a small audience with support from a sympathetic patron or group of patrons. When a magazine calls itself *Coterie*, it is acknowledging that situation—even reveling in it. A shocking journal seeks an audience that wants to be shocked. A magazine like *Blast*, which lasted for two shocking issues, might have gone on for more with the right patronage, but for the shock of World War I, which put the editor in the trenches. But it is hard to produce a steady diet of shocks. And since this particular editor, Wyndham Lewis, edited two later journals that had lives of similar brevity, we may assume that he had limitations as an editor that prevented his journals from reaching an audience that actually existed. An interesting project, then, might be a reading of Lewis's three journals, *Blast, The Tyro,* and *The Enemy,* in an attempt to detect a pattern that accounts for their short lives. Is an audience implied that did not or could not exist? Is the journal too narrow in its appeal? Or does the editor himself seem to lose interest or run out of material after a couple of issues?

There is a larger possible project lurking behind a restricted investigation of Lewis's journals. What accounts for the duration of any magazine's existence? *Poetry*, which is usually called a "little" magazine, has lived from 1912 until now, while others founded at that time lasted only a few issues or a few years. Large-circulation magazines rise and fall too, with some lasting much longer than others. A Dutch scholar, A. J. van

Zuilen, wrote an interesting dissertation on *The Life Cycle of Magazines,*
published in the Netherlands in 1990 and subtitled *A Historical Study of
the Decline and Fall of the General Interest Mass Audience Magazine in
the United States During the Period 1946–1972.* (The competition of television for advertising revenue, coupled with the rise of niche magazines,
had a lot to do with the fall of the magazines van Zuilen studied: *Life,
Look, Colliers,* and *The Saturday Evening Post.*) In seeking out the implied
readership of any magazine, however, it will help to know the duration
of its existence and the frequency of publication, because a magazine's
readership may change over time if it lasts long enough.

Another "external" detail we can use is the actual circulation: how
many copies were printed and reached readers. Circulation numbers
themselves require interpretation. When *The New Age* reached a circulation of more than twenty thousand, which it did briefly near the
end of 1908 (*NA* 4.5: 81), that was a great success. For another magazine, falling to that level would mean that the end was near. In America *The Nation* and *The New Republic* were successful at circulations of
around thirty thousand in the 1950s. Such magazines are aimed at an
elite audience, but we need to look inside them to get a real sense of
this. It is time, then, to look inside a magazine with some care as the
first step in demonstrating how we think magazines should be read and
studied. In the following chapter, we will take this demonstration further, but we can start now with a single issue of a single weekly magazine. Knowing that we are not the audience the magazine intended to
reach, our first steps must lead us toward that audience. Who were they?
How did they differ from us? In what ways are their interests and concerns still ours? We offer here, then, a set of topics and questions designed to allow us to look into the world of our chosen magazine from
as many angles as possible, starting with those readers we must imagine from the clues in and around the magazine itself. We will proceed
by offering these as the basis for an assignment which we will then accept ourselves as a way of showing how the academic study of a modernist magazine might work.

    1. Implied reader
        • Study a single issue of the magazine—ads, articles,

stories, everything—and from that study arrive at a notion of the ideal reader implied by the magazine's contents: age, sex, economic class, intellectual class, race, political position, and anything else that seems important.

- Look at other issues of the same magazine to confirm or modify your first description. Does the magazine change over time? Does it fluctuate from issue to issue? Can you describe a consistent implied reader for a certain period of the magazine's existence?

2. Circulation
   - What can you find out about the circulation of the magazine? How would you characterize the circulation? How does this connect to the "implied reader"?

3. Regular contributors
   - Check the contents page of a substantial range of issues. Note authors who reappear regularly or frequently. Who are they? Reputations—then and now? What can you find out about them? What features do they have in common? Check for pseudonyms.

4. Contents
   - In a single issue, what kind of content gets the most pages (creative: fiction, poetry, drama, visual art, music; critical: cultural, aesthetic, social, political; informative: travel, biography, history, news)? What proportion of the total does this kind get? What proportions do other kinds get? Check other issues for range and trends.
   - In a single issue, what is the ratio of advertising to other forms of text? What kind of advertising gets the most space? What proportion of the total is this? What other kinds get significant amounts of space? Check other issues for ranges and trends.
   - If the magazine attends to social, political, or cultural issues, how would you describe its position? Again, check other issues for range and trends.

5. Editor
   - Does the magazine have the same editor for a range of time? If so, what can you find out about this person? What is his/her background, education, training? If the editor writes for this magazine, what kinds of things does he/she write? Check the editor's writing over a range of issues. What is the editor's reputation as editor, as writer? How important does the editor seem to be in shaping the magazine?
6. Format
   - Examine one issue for size and shape: physical dimensions and number of pages. Check for changes in earlier and later issues. Is there a pattern of change?
   - Consider the use of visual material in a single issue. How many images per page? Is color used? If so, how? Are images photographic or drawings? What methods are used to reproduce the images?
   - How are the images used? Do they illustrate articles or stories? Are they there for their own sake? How important are they?
   - Compare issues over time for changes and patterns.
7. History
   - When did the magazine begin? When did it end? How frequently was it published? If the frequency changed, can you determine why? What can you find out about the way it was regarded by the public and other magazines?
8. Putting it all together
   - Using the data you have gathered, produce a description of the magazine. Make it as brief as possible, but accurate and detailed enough to position the magazine among others, so that it can be connected to others like it but also distinguished from them.

We have numbered these points, but they need not—and probably cannot—be so neatly separated and taken up in this numerical order.

PLATE 1
Cover of *Rhythm* magazine, October 1912

PLATE 2

J. D. Fergusson, *Rhythm*, Fergusson Gallery, Perth and Kinross Council

Painted by John da Costa.

THE NEW FOURTH OF JULY, 1918.

United after nearly a century and a half.

PLATE 3

John Da Costa, *The New Fourth of July, 1918*, from *Scribner's*, July 1918

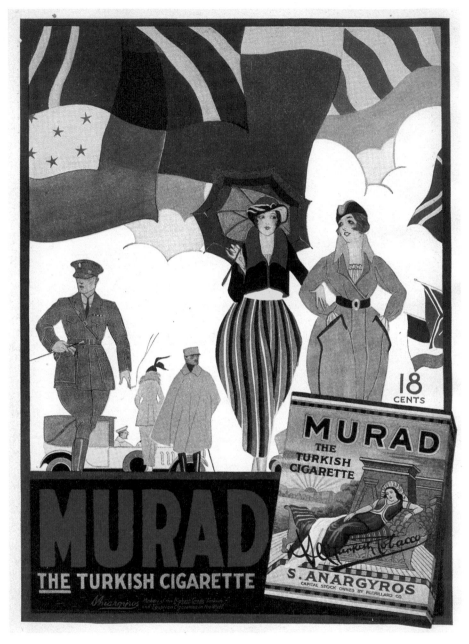

PLATE 4
Ad for Murad cigarettes, from *Scribner's,* July 1918

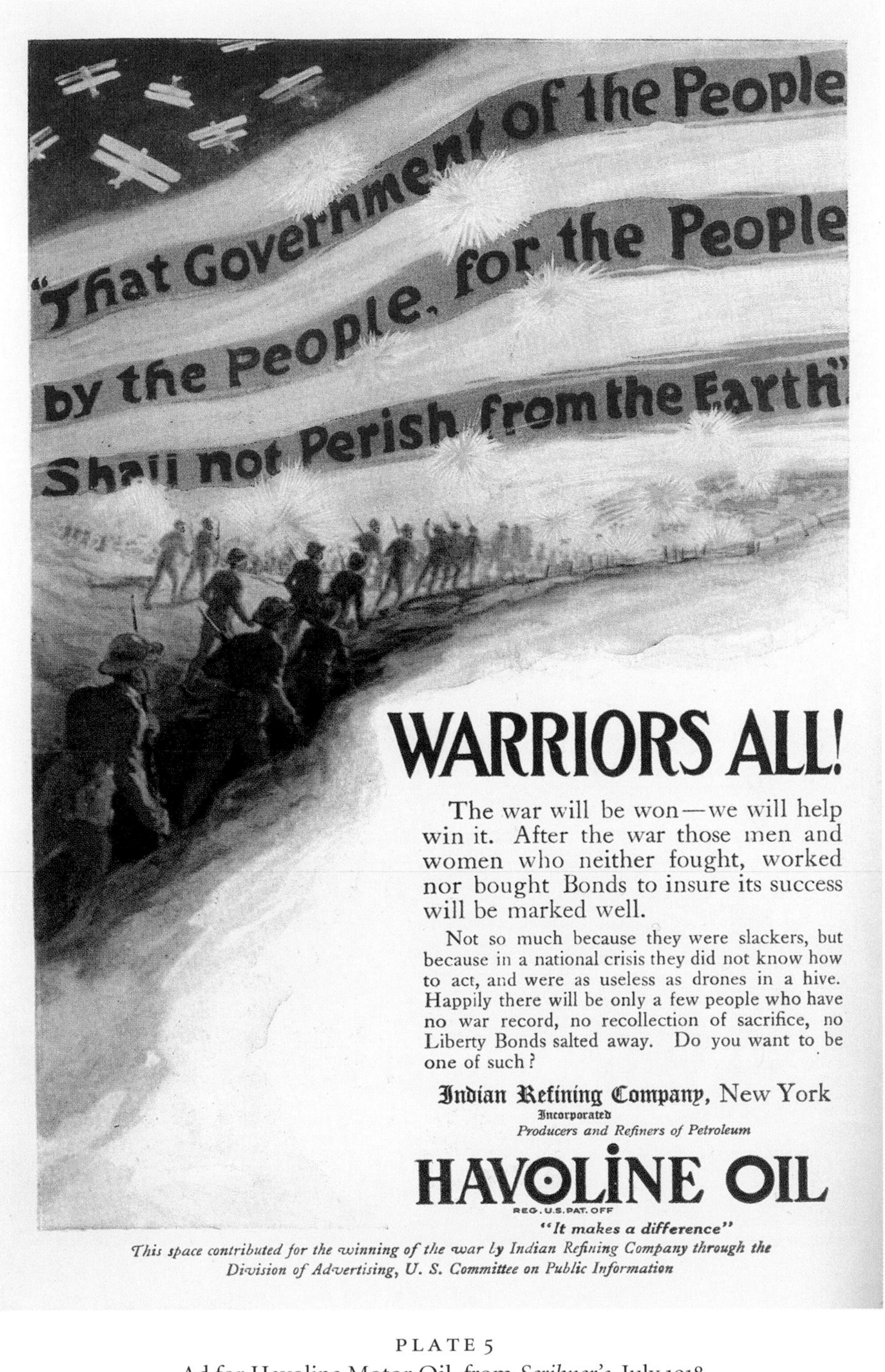

PLATE 5

Ad for Havoline Motor Oil, from *Scribner's*, July 1918

PLATE 6
Ad for Studebaker automobiles, from *Scribner's,* July 1918

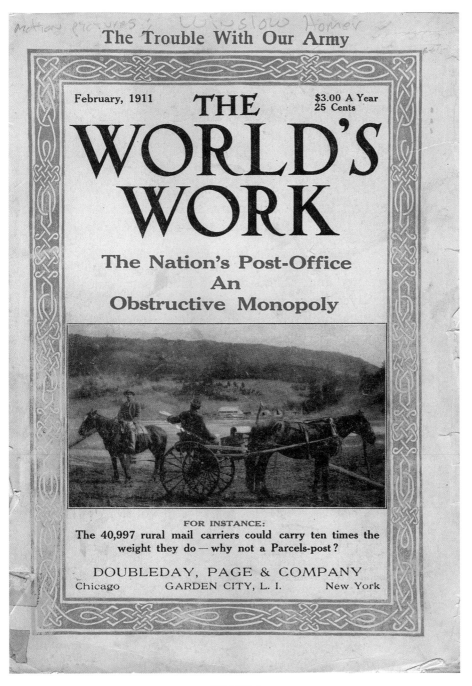

Written annotations at top: "Motion pictures:" "Winslow Homer"

The Trouble With Our Army

February, 1911

THE WORLD'S WORK

$3.00 A Year
25 Cents

The Nation's Post-Office
An
Obstructive Monopoly

FOR INSTANCE:
The 40,997 rural mail carriers could carry ten times the
weight they do — why not a Parcels-post?

DOUBLEDAY, PAGE & COMPANY
Chicago   GARDEN CITY, L. I.   New York

PLATE 7
Cover of *The World's Work*, February 1911

PLATE 8
Covers of some of the magazines discussed by Ezra Pound
in "Studies in Contemporary Mentality" (see appendix)

They are all points that should be covered in this kind of historical reading process, and they can be used as a checklist in the course of reading a magazine, but reading any magazine from the past must start by taking up a single issue of that magazine and reading it. This "taking up" ideally means holding the original in one's hands and turning the pages. The next best thing is to use a digital edition that enables one to see the entire magazine, with all its advertising, from cover to cover, and we will demonstrate the reading process outlined above by reading a single issue from the current digital edition of a weekly magazine published a century ago. We will be using one that we know very well, but we shall try not to lose sight of the problems confronting readers unfamiliar with their object of study. To that end, we will regularly indicate where one may go for information not contained in the issue we are reading.

For a weekly magazine, we may need to look at more than a single issue to get a plausible handle on its readership. (Obviously, the more issues of any magazine one attempts to read, the better that handle will be. As we have seen, David Reed developed a lot of useful data by examining six consecutive issues of monthlies at ten-year intervals.) We will now look at the weekly issue of *The New Age* for December 1, 1910, starting with an attempt to characterize the audience it was addressing. This will inevitably involve, as we shall see, an external investigation of the editor, writers, and visual artists (if any) involved, and an internal examination of their work in this particular issue—which may be different from their other work, as is apparent in the case of the writer Alfred Ollivant. In fact, a regular oscillation between internal and external perspectives is an absolute requirement for reading magazines of the past. We read them in order to learn about the past, but we read them better if we know enough about that past to grasp references and situate what is said in a cultural context. Secondary sources can help with this, but there is no getting out of the historian's circle: we must know some history in order to learn more about history. Magazines are part of a cultural web, which is one reason why they are so useful in studying the past. But historical and cultural background will help us read in a richer, fuller, and more accurate way.

The best way to begin reading a magazine like this is simply to read it—to read every page. Such a reading can begin with the table of con-

CONTENTS.

	PAGE			PAGE
NOTES OF THE WEEK...	97	AMERICAN NOTES. By Juvenal		108
MR. LLOYD GEORGE: THE PICT IN POLITICS ...	99	THE MAIDS' COMEDY.—V. ...		109
FOREIGN AFFAIRS. By S. Verdad...	101	BOOKS AND PERSONS. By Jacob Tonson...		110
BANKRUPT TURKEY.—III. By Allen Upward ...	102	EUGENICS AND EVIDENCE. By Alfred E. Randall		111
THE HOUSE UPON THE SAND. By Alfred Ollivant	102	MODERN DRAMATISTS: BRIEUX. By Ashley Dukes ...		114
SUFFRAGIST SEAT-BREAKING. By W. L. George...	105	ART AND CRAFT. By Huntly Carter		116
THE PARTING OF THE WAYS. By Judah P. Benjamin ...	106	LETTERS TO THE EDITOR FROM John Kirkby, E. Wake Cook,		
UNEDITED OPINIONS.—II. The Superman	107	Hugh Blaker, Eden Phillpotts, and J. Anderson ...		117

Fig. 6.1. Table of contents for *The New Age,* December 1, 1910

tents, but in the case of a magazine with a significant subtitle one should start with that, and in this issue of *The New Age* (but not in all issues) it is "A WEEKLY REVIEW OF POLITICS, LITERATURE, AND ART." The contents, as we can easily see, follow the categories in the subtitle, with topics that are obviously political, obviously literary, and obviously artistic (figure 6.1). Two questions follow from a mere look at the contents: (1) What kinds of writing do we actually find in the articles? and (2) Who are the authors of these pieces? The first question leads us deeper into the issue, while the second takes us outside. As we have already noted, this pattern of combining internal and external investigation is at the heart of periodical studies, and it is one of the things that make periodical studies different from normal literary critical or social-historical work. Because we are dealing with multiple authorship, we must read internal texts closely, and we must root around in other primary and secondary sources, too, putting these efforts together at every stage of studying a periodical.

The New Age, as it happens, has been edited, so a lot of the external work has been done for us and is readily available in the introductions that accompany every volume of the digital edition of the magazine, along with the list of pseudonyms assembled by the editorial staff. From these sources and others (including what we can find by Googling their names) we can learn something about nearly every writer mentioned in the contents for December 1, 1910. Even for us, however (and we know as much as anyone about this magazine), there are gaps that later scholars may fill. A preliminary investigation of the authors listed in the contents (along with some consultation of the editor's introduction for this volume and some Googling) will yield this information:

- Notes of the Week, unsigned. These were regularly written by the editor, A. R. Orage, and dealt mainly with British political and social matters.
- Lloyd George as Pict, by Anthropologist. Real name unknown, this person wrote four articles for this volume of the magazine.
- Foreign Affairs, by S. Verdad, a Spanish pun (es verdad) for "it's true." This name was used for a regular column on events outside of Britain, written by J. M. Kennedy, a mainstay of the magazine.
- Bankrupt Turkey, by Allen Upward. Upward was a poet, novelist, lawyer, and political commentator, contributing to the magazine a series on the Ottoman Empire after that government was taken over by the "Young Turks." The series continues in this issue with a discussion of financial trickery and corruption in this "military despotism."
- House upon the Sand, by Alfred Ollivant. Ollivant was a writer of fiction, best known for his 1898 novel about a heroic dog, *Bob, Son of Battle* (English title: *Owd Bob: Being the Story of Bob, Son of Battle, the Last of the Grey Dogs of Kenmuir*), but here has written an allegorical story critical of the House of Lords.
- Suffragist Seat-Breaking, by W. L. George. Best known for his fiction, George was sympathetic to the women's suffrage movement but here criticizes the suffragist tactics in challenging the parliamentary "seats" of their enemies.
- Parting of the Ways, by Judah P. Benjamin. There was a famous person of this name, a Jewish lawyer who was a U.S. senator from Louisiana and later held cabinet posts in the Confederate States of America. Moving to England after the Civil War, he practiced law there. But he died too early to be this unidentified writer, who used Benjamin's name to contribute frequently to the magazine from 1909 to 1911 on political subjects, in this case producing a spirited critique of English nobility and the House of Lords.

- Unedited Opinions, Superman, unsigned. The writer of this was almost certainly Orage, who here attacks the idea that a Nietzschean superman can be biologically produced.
- American Notes, by Juvenal. A Roman satirist's name was chosen by this writer for a series on being English in America that ran for two years in the magazine. In this issue he discusses the shift of literary power from Boston to New York and the West, mourns the death of William James, and praises the work of Mary Wilkins-Freeman and Finley Peter Dunn. It would be interesting to learn who is behind this name.
- The Maids' Comedy, unsigned. The editor of the volume tells us in his introduction that the author was Beatrice Hastings, a regular writer and an unofficial editor of the magazine—in this case offering the fifth chapter of a serialization of a picaresque romance, continued from the previous four issues.
- Books and Persons, by Jacob Tonson. The name of an eighteenth-century printer was used by the novelist Arnold Bennett for his regular column, of which this is a typical sample: a chatty, opinionated, good natured discussion of current books.
- Eugenics and Evidence, by Alfred E. Randall. Randall was a regular contributor, who later did drama reviews as John Francis Hope. Here he attacks the pretensions to science of the Eugenics Society.
- Modern Dramatists, by Ashley Dukes. Dukes was a playwright and critic who wrote regularly for the magazine on drama at this time, here offering the tenth in a series in the form of a severe critique of a French academician admired by G. B. Shaw.
- Art and Craft, by Huntly Carter. Carter was the regular art critic for the magazine at this time, here reviewing a book on hand weaving.
- Letters. It is unusual for letter writers' names to appear in on a magazine's contents page, which tells us that this mag-

azine took a special interest in the construction of an "active" readership.

- John Kirkby's letter is on Fabian tracts. All we know about him is that G. B. Shaw wrote him a letter in 1904.
- E. Wake Cook was a good traditional painter who hated Post-Impressionism.
- Hugh Blaker was an art critic and collector who supported Post-Impressionism.
- Eden Phillpotts, a popular novelist, here defends W. D. Howells against remarks in a previous issue by "Juvenal."
- J. Anderson writes to praise a novel by Allen Upward; the name may be a pseudonym for Upward himself.

What can we learn about the magazine and its readership from this preliminary investigation of the writers and their topics in this issue of *The New Age*? We can learn that the magazine's subtitle accurately reflects the proportions of the content, with political and social issues getting the most space, literature the next most, and art a smaller segment. (In other issues, we would find music replacing visual art.) Though reading a single issue won't show it, a reading of other issues as background for this one will reveal that a regular group of writers dominates the magazine and that dominance is visible in this issue. Orage, Kennedy, Hastings, Bennett, Randall, Dukes, and Carter were regulars, and Upward, "Juvenal," W. L. George, Alfred Ollivant, and "Anthropologist" all wrote for it more than once. We can also see that the letters section was important, and that people with reputations in their fields wrote letters, debating questions of the day, such as the art show "Manet and the Post-Impressionists, which had opened in November at the Grafton Gallery and been reviewed in the previous issue. Finally, we can see that the political inclination of the magazine is leftward and antiaristocratic. A closer reading of the articles will tell us more, but let us look at the advertising first.

The only ads in this issue appear on the back page, by themselves, which gives us a ratio of advertising pages to total pages in this issue of 1/24 and tells us that advertising could not have been a major source of income for the magazine. A wider survey will support this conclusion, yielding a maximum ratio of around 1/7 in early issues and a minimum of zero in many issues after 1913. In some earlier years ads were scattered over several pages toward the back of issues. There are no images in this issue; other issues contained cartoons, drawings, and/or photographs, though never very many. But figure 6.2 is a reproduction (reduced in size) of the advertising page in this issue. The page includes, in large print, ads for the previous volume of the magazine itself, for a new collection of essays on mysticism by Francis Grierson, and for Fry's Cocoa, the only large-print ad for a physically consumable item. There is also another book ad, and an ad for advertising in *The New Age*—a meta-ad, if you will—and one for lectures at the Central London Lodge of the Theosophical Society. The smaller print ads are perhaps even more interesting, resembling those in such early magazines as the *Tatler* and *Spectator*.

Here we find a company interested in buying old false teeth, especially those made with precious metals, and another offering "SOCIALIST CHRISTMAS AND NEW YEAR CARDS." Other ads offer instruction in printing, typing, and authoring—everything one might need to produce a magazine of one's own. There is also an ad for a private school-home, for "New" things in the writings of "Zion," for the "clever" writing offered by the London Literary Syndicate, and for Unitarianism. All together, this is a quirky if not zany set of ads, but they suggest, in their own way, the socialist and theosophical leanings of the editor, along with a search for new values, whether religious or political. Even the cocoa ad stresses health, and the Ashlet School-Home offers a "Reformed Diet" as well as preparation for examinations. There is more for the mind than for the body in these ads, but there also seems to be an assumption that the two are connected—and that they both need to be improved.

Armed with our reading of the ads, we can now return to the other contents of the magazine and read them more closely. NOTES OF THE WEEK sets the tone for the whole magazine. The prose is clear and supple but not simple, implying an intelligent reader eager to think about the major events of the week in Britain. As Lee Garver points out in his introduction to this volume of the digital edition of *The New Age*, the collapse, in the middle of November, of a conference designed to work out a com-

Fig. 6.2. Ads in *The New Age*, December 1, 1910

promise on limiting the power of the House of Lords in the British Parliament made that situation a live issue for the next few weeks. Orage therefore addressed it in the NOTES, and, as we have noted, it surfaces in Ollivant's fiction and Benjamin's essay as well. The Lords, and the aristocracy in general, do not fare well in these pages. But a Liberal cabinet minister, David Lloyd George, comes under serious attack as a primitive Pict (an ancient race of Britons) in the second article in the issue, and bomb-throwing anarchists and violent suffragists are also censured. Clearly, the audience addressed in these pages could not be unthinking members of any party, class, or group. The journal's attitude was critical, and the objects of the criticism came from all over the social, political, and artistic spectrum.

In terms of readership, a paragraph in S. Verdad's article is revealing:

> I am contemplating a slight change in the form of these notes on Foreign Affairs. When I began them about seven months ago, as I stated in a letter written subsequently in reply to criticism by Mr. Bax, it was my aim, to give the readers of THE NEW AGE the facts, and to let them deduce the conclusions therefrom. In the course of the summer and autumn, however, I have observed that this paper penetrates into certain quarters, notably crusty Conservative clubs and solemn Liberal clubs—not to speak of the Fabian Society—whose members, to say the least, cannot be trusted to apply their minds to an international problem and to arrive at a decision which stands far above the ordinary level of party politics. I hereby give notice, therefore, that in future I may save them this trouble if I think it necessary. In short, I propose to set forth principles as well as merely facts. (*NA* 8.5: 101)

Verdad/Kennedy claims a wide political spectrum of readers for the magazine—Conservative, Liberal, and Socialist—and insults them all as incapable of getting beyond party politics and in need of instruction on principles. *The New Age,* for a while at least, was like a restaurant where the waiters insult the customers—who love it and keep coming back for more. For this to work at all in a magazine, those waiter/writers had to be interesting, and the intellectual nourishment they provided had to be worthwhile. At the end of this article, Kennedy extends his critique to the periodicals of the moment, concluding with these words: "Apart from THE NEW AGE, I cannot call to mind a single English weekly or monthly in which Foreign Affairs are treated with impartiality, insight, or discrimination, much less all three. Mais nous changerons tout cela." That final sentence in French—"But we will change all that"—indicates just how ambitious (or arrogant) this periodical was, and shows that it assumed an audience able to comprehend a bit of French as well. Elite magazines in Britain at this time often had one article or newsletter entirely in French. It was a way of indicating the sort of readership they had in mind.

This readership was assumed to be interested in social and political issues of all sorts, as witnessed by Allen Upward's series on the problems of the Ottoman Empire under the rule of the Young Turks. Problems ranging from Albania to Baghdad and from Bulgaria to Crete are touched on in this article about Turkey's financial difficulties, reminding us that the heritage of the Ottoman Empire has contributed to the political and social problems of our own time. The positioning of this discussion of Turkey so that it ends on the page where Alfred Ollivant's allegory begins is far from accidental. We go directly from Turkish trickery to this:

> SOME Men built their House upon the Sand, and dwelt
> in it in Coronets.
> It was a lordly House with buttresses of gold, shining
> domes and pinnacles, and great pleasure gardens;
> and it shone in the sun so that everybody admired it,
> especially those who lived in it.

This "lordly House" is, of course, the House of Lords, and the story of its demise goes on for several pages and includes a character called "Little George," based on Lloyd George, who finally leads the Men in Coronets to their proper end, in which the readership of this magazine, it is assumed, will rejoice.

In the next article, W. L. George (no connection to Lloyd George), a self-professed Liberal and friend of the movement for women's suffrage, argues that the movement is in a state of chaos and not choosing well in contesting seats in Parliament: "Suffragists must choose their ground. Here is the crux of my argument," he writes. "Though I am a Liberal I am quite willing to agree that a Liberal Government must sometimes be forced to act, as must a Tory Government" (*NA* 8.5: 105). The

Liberals were in power at this time, but the Liberal writer of this article agrees they may have to be forced to act properly. He is sympathetic to the suffrage movement, but critical of its political tactics, arguing that the women of England and their supporters must "show, more clearly than they have done hitherto, that they have level heads as well as stout hearts." Level heads are advocated in the magazine, and its readership is credited with having them, though these readers are expected to enjoy an allegory of the end of the House of Lords as well.

A more direct critique of the Lords followed George's article on suffrage, written by the pseudonymous Judah P. Benjamin. The following passage from this article continues the theme of level-headedness:

> Most of our troubles arise from the fact that we find it almost impossible to understand another man's point of view. At no time in the history of England has the point of view been so exacting, so contradictory, so difficult, and so complex as it is at present. At no time in our history have sects and parties been so numerous. Even within the ranks of a single party the point of view can stand for so many fantastic whims, so many personal prejudices, that he who would conciliate the divers factions within his own following must needs possess something more than mere political prestige, something greater than ordinary statecraft. (*NA* 8.5: 106)

And beyond the need for level-headedness and leadership, we can find evidence of why the magazine was called *The New Age*:

> Nothing goes as of yore, nothing looks normal, social and political prestige is a thing that belonged to the mid-Victorian era, the varnish of make-believe has been rubbed off the religious picture, the veneer of gilt has gone from the framework of the most astute hypocrisy. Nothing remains but the crude figures amassed by Republicans, Democrats, Socialists, labour champions, and what not. While the nobility are engaged in horse racing, shooting pheasants or grouse, giving and re-

ceiving banquets, going and coming from the moors and pleasure resorts, the people's parties are awake and engaged in
ceaseless activity. The point of view of these latter is not now
a view seen through a mist. Rightly or wrongly they have made
up their minds. They have climbed the mount and discovered
Canaan in the distance. That is now *their* point of view. The
Canaan of our nobility lies behind them. (*NA* 8.5: 106)

Something new is happening, discernable to this writer as the awaken-
ing of "the people's parties" to their own interests and goals, with a corresponding lowering of the prestige of the aristocracy, who are now seen
as idlers with no real function in this society.

The motif of a new age is continued in the dialogue on Nietzsche's
Superman in the next article. The very fact that it is a dialogue, and written by the editor himself, tells us more about the magazine and its readership. Nietzsche's ideas were very much in the news at this time, a decade
after his death, and many of the *New Age* circle were involved in a mul-
tivolume translation of his works into English. In this dialogue, the voice
that says "I" in addressing the reader—presumably that of the editor—
is lectured by another person on the need to abandon the hope of breeding a Superman and turn to a notion of the Superman as "self-begotten
from within the mind of man" (*NA* 8.5: 107). One might say that a certain change in human nature is being advocated here, and we are invited
to see feminism as a sign of such a change:

I am prepared to maintain not only that feminism is a revolt
against feminism, but that the most intelligent feminists are
aware of it. Just when, in fact, the value of motherhood is seen
to be declining in the world-market, women who have no
other commodity begin to cry up its value. Of such women
there are, I admit, many in the feminist movement. But from
the same cause other women, with other commodities than
motherhood for sale, desire an amplified scope for themselves.
These are the real feminists and, as I say, they are averse from
procreation. (*NA* 8.5: 107)

G. B. Shaw's play *Man and Superman* had appeared in 1903, and the only role for an intelligent woman it seemed to offer was breeding with a superior man and giving birth to the Superman. *The New Age,* revived in 1907, partly with money provided by Shaw, regularly attacked him and his ideas, as Orage is doing here—and Orage apparently expects the audience for the magazine to be aware of Shaw's take on Nietzsche and to appreciate his own distinction between two kinds of feminists. (In this connection, we should remember, from Chapter 1, Pound's attempt, in his "Studies in Contemporary Mentality," to get below the level of magazine in which Shaw and Nietzsche were discussed.)

"Juvenal," the Englishman in America, gives us another clue about readership in this brief remark: "The death of Prof. William James was a rude loss to the thinking world here as elsewhere" (*NA* 8.5: 108). The notion of a "thinking world" is crucial to *The New Age.* This is the audience it will address—even if it has to create it first. The first paragraph of this article reveals something else:

> THIRTY years ago Boston set the literary pace for all America. The New England influence has been on the wane since the passing of the old idols—Emerson, Lowell, Holmes, to name only three. The Bostonian "tone" was Yankee in the true meaning of that much misunderstood word. It was more or less puritanical in spite of the Unitarians and the Freethinkers of Boston. The "Atlantic Monthly" was the recognised literary organ not only of New England but of the whole of America; and let it be said in passing that this magazine at its best was as near perfection as any publication of the kind has ever been. Its only failing was its disregard of the cosmopolitan spirit everywhere at work. (*NA* 8.5: 108)

There are two qualities to note here. One is that *The New Age* could praise a rival magazine generously, and the other is that it had a stake in what this writer called "the cosmopolitan spirit everywhere at work." The writer speaks as an individual, of course, but the interest shown in this issue of the magazine in America itself, in Canada, in Mexico, and in the Ottoman Empire offers evidence of what this phrase might mean. As does the report by Juvenal of a conversation with a New York politician who says, "We Americans are a new and primitive people, just like the Russians. . . . We are the two youngest of the great nations. Every year we become more Russian in our moods and our discontent. We are devoured by a spirit of unrest. . . . With all our common sense in America we are powerfully influenced by fanatical and passing fads." This is, to say the least, very interesting for 1910—and still interesting today. And it suggests a readership possessed by a cosmopolitan spirit as well.

The episode from *The Maids' Comedy* is something else altogether, as is its author, Beatrice Hastings, who used more pseudonyms than anyone else in *The New Age*, which is saying a lot. For *The New Age* she wrote fiction, poetry, articles on various topics, and letters. She helped with the editing. She argued with Ezra Pound. And in 1914 she wrote a series of letters from Paris that are her most enduring contribution to modernism, though they have never been collected for publication. She was raised in South Africa, as Emily Alice Haigh, came to England at an early age and was still quite young when she began to write for the magazine. *The Maids' Comedy* is a Cervantean story of a young woman and her maid in South Africa who set out on a series of picaresque adventures in search of a knight like their hero, Don Quixote. The chapters in *The New Age* are short, amusing episodes in this quest, full of exclamations in Afrikaans and quixotic adventures. The reader implied by these would be familiar enough with the Spanish original to appreciate the pastiche. And this reader would need to have the previous four installments of this serial in mind to comprehend the chapter 5 presented here—which implies a regular and faithful readership indeed. Monthly magazines that ran serial novels usually summarized what had gone before at the beginning of each new episode. But *The New Age* was a weekly, and it was different.

Arnold Bennett's column of literary chatter (he calls it "an occasional causerie") is light but clearly aimed at an educated audience. A. E. Randall's article "Eugenics and Evidence" is a weightier thing altogether. It is a devastating attack on the scientific pretensions of the Eugenics Education Society, who were arguing that poverty was caused by inborn qualities—a hereditary rather than a social condition—and that the bearers of such genetic defects should not be allowed to reproduce.

This is perhaps the most serious and certainly the longest piece in this issue of the magazine. And the conclusions Randall draws are devastating: The Eugenics Education Society "has collected evidence of pauperism, but not of hereditary defect; it has not shown that pauperism results from defect, and its cool proposal that pauper stocks should be eliminated by segregation and sterilisation is seen to be the fatuous impertinence of self-satisfied people" (*NA* 8.5: 114). Eugenic thinking contributed to the Nazism that would arise in later years, but the opposition to it here is already thoughtful and vigorous—as is the audience implied by the text. Taken together with Orage's critique of any attempt to breed a superman, these articles give us an indication of why Hitler's brand of racism gained few adherents in England—and those mainly from the upper classes.

Ashley Dukes shows us another facet of this magazine in his critical comments on the French playwright Eugène Brieux. Dukes explores the connection between the social views of the playwright and the quality of his plays, coming to this conclusion: "Blanchette" pointed the way for M. Brieux, and at the same time defined his limitations. "Conventional domestic comedy was always his trade, and his social and political views are only window-dressing. There need be no doubt of the sincerity of M. Brieux's opinions, but they are for the most part so trivially expressed that they carry no conviction. In becoming a reformer, he ceased to be an artist" (*NA* 8.5: 114). And that is a crucial point for understanding this magazine. Political or social correctness will not satisfy this reviewer, and since he is a regular, we must assume he speaks, to some extent, for the journal itself. He wants art. That is, he wants a play to be aesthetically satisfying and not merely deliver the right message. In the present case, several of the author's plays had been banned in England for political or social reasons, which brought G. B. Shaw to Brieux's defense. But Ashley Dukes and *The New Age* held up Ibsen and Chekhov as a standard which Brieux failed to meet, in particular with respect to the creation of character. "Rebecca West and Dr. Stockmann [Ibsen's characters] we know," he says, but we do not know the characters of Brieux, who are "ill-digested scraps of blue-books, manifestoes, Charity Organization leaflets," given names (*NA* 8.5: 115).

In the final article in this issue, Huntly Carter reviews a book on hand weaving, written in the tradition of William Morris—a book that argues for a return of the medieval craft to present-day England. Carter is sympathetic but says that this "book needs supplementing on the sociological side by chapters discussing how its methods may be adapted to modern domestic requirements; how they may be made sufficiently attractive to be brought into modern homes" (*NA* 8.5: 117). In this case, art is not enough. But Carter is not contradicting Ashley Dukes. Taken together, they are saying that art and social values must be united to bring a new age into existence. And that is what the magazine seems to be saying to an audience it gave credit for considerable intelligence and a genuine concern for the future not just of Britain but of the world. The question of art comes up again in the letters section, allowing us to investigate it further.

Two of the letters in this section are responses to a review in the previous issue by George Calderon of the show "Manet and the Post-Impressionists" at the Grafton Gallery in London. To understand these letters properly, we must go back to that issue and read Calderon's review. Calderon was not a regular writer for the magazine, though he might have written more for it had he not died at Gallipoli in 1914. To understand where he was coming from in this review, however, we need to know that he had recently returned from Tahiti and was working on a book (with drawings) about his time in those islands, which was published posthumously. His interest in Tahiti may have been a motive behind his undertaking this review, since he spends a good deal of time criticizing Gauguin's paintings of that world and its people. But here are two short passages from Calderon's review which, taken together, should give us another angle on the readership of the magazine. One comes from near the beginning and the other from near the end of his review, but we will put them together here:

> At the Gallery itself it is all titter and cackle; well-dressed women go about saying "How awful! A perfect nightmare, my dear!" "Did you ever? Too killing! How they can!" They are like dogs to music; it makes them howl, but they can't keep away. Men in tall hats are funny over the exhibits, saying: "This is a horse; this is a man." All through the galleries I am pursued by the ceaseless hee-haw of a stage duke in an eye glass.

> If there is still time, fly to the Grafton. To judge by clothes, there were no readers of THE NEW AGE in the gallery when I was there. (*NA* 8.4: 89, 90)

The first passage tells us that the show is full of well-dressed women and men in top hats, including one who is excessively aristocratic ("a stage duke"), all of whom despise what they are seeing. The second tells us that a look at the clothing indicates that the readership of the magazine was not in attendance, with an implication that their opinions of the show would be as different from those of the viewers Calderon encountered as their clothing would be. They would not be "well-dressed" in the way that the tittering, cackling women are, nor would they wear top hats or sport monocles. After telling these readers to go and look at Laprade, Cézanne, and Sérusier, he concludes with this advice:

> See Marquet's admirable "Sands at Havre," with all the racket and bunting of a real holiday at the seaside, and his grim grey "Notre Dame," a tragic rendering of the rocky loneliness of a great cathedral in a city, the two mouse-coloured towers with their crumbling outline, and the big empty square made alive by the two yellow tramcars that stand, little patches down there in the distance, waiting for passengers. Then go forth and pass along the streets about and note how flat, stale and unprofitable have become all those engravings, pictures and statues in the art dealers' windows, that represent the bare photographic semblance of reality, with dramatic meanings laid on it, not drawn out from it. (*NA* 8.4: 90)

In this review, though he is critical of many works in the show, Calderon says that he, "a plain man from the country," found more than a hundred pictures of real interest. We know he is not exactly a plain man from the country. (He went to the Rugby School, after all, and had traveled to Tahiti, and he alludes to *Hamlet* in passing with those "flat, stale and unprofitable" engravings.) But that is the role he has chosen on this occasion, trying, rather, to suggest that one doesn't have to be a specialist to find value in these pictures. His praise of Marquet and others is praise for a new way of seeing and painting suitable for a new age, and he expects this magazine's readership to appreciate them as he does. The two writers of letters in response to this review, which appeared in the next issue, both disagree with him. E. Wake Cook thinks he shouldn't have given these "Newists" any support, and Hugh Blaker, while praising the magazine for being "one of the few papers to treat the exhibition intelligently," disagrees with Calderon about Gauguin. Both writers were themselves artists, though Cook was much better known and Blaker is remembered mainly as a curator and collector. What these letters tell us is that the readership of the magazine had varying opinions and saw *The New Age* letters section as a place where they could express them. It was an active, rather than a passive, readership, and the other letters deliver a similar message, most of them arguing with things that were said in the journal or offering different perspectives on those things.

It is time, now, to return to the checklist offered at the beginning of this chapter, to see what we have learned by reading this issue.

1. Implied reader: left-leaning, antiaristocratic, intellectual.
2. Circulation: maximum just over 20,000, minimum 3,000–4,000.
3. Regular contributors: a tight inner circle and a looser outer circle, and the magazine depended on both; they have been described as provincial intellectuals—not from the great universities or residing in Bloomsbury, but intellectual nonetheless.
4. Contents: political-social articles dominate, followed by literature and art criticism, some fiction; low ratio of advertising to text; books and lectures dominate; political position is leftish but critical of all parties and movements.
5. Editor: one editor for fifteen years—a provincial intellectual with interests in Nietzsche, theosophy, and socialism; he wrote on political, philosophical, and literary matters; when he left, the magazine ceased to be of interest. He is usually credited with being one of the best editors of his time.
6. Format: very simple, with large two-column pages, rang-

ing from twelve to thirty-two pages per issue; no images
in this issue, one cartoon is the norm for others, but one
or two drawings sometimes appear, and, very occasionally,
a photograph. They are not used to illustrate texts but are
sometimes the object of discussion. No color, ever. Ratio
of advertising pages to others in this issue is 1/24.

7. History: an existing magazine in 1907, it was bought and a
new series begun then under Orage's editorship; after he
left at the end of 1922, it lasted until 1938.

8. Putting it all together: . . .

We have done this above, in the course of reading a single issue, but
let us summarize it here. A reading of the December 1, 1910, issue of *The
New Age* demonstrates powerfully the serial nature of periodical texts.
There is much in this issue that continues from or refers to previous issues of this magazine. Our reading also reveals that, in place of the single
author of most books, what we have here is a powerful editor, whose interests shape the magazine, surrounded by an inner circle of regular contributors, who become a kind of collective author, and an outer circle of
less regular but known contributors. Only occasionally does an entirely
new author contribute an article or other piece. These regularities provide
coherence for what would otherwise be a very heterogeneous text.

In terms of content we find a mixture of genres and modes: reports,
reviews, fiction, allegory, social and literary criticism, plus letters in which
readers become writers, engaging the regulars in dialogue. There is a di-
alogic spirit operating here, evident in the editor's dialogue on Nietzsche
and in other texts as well. Even Hastings's *Maids' Comedy* is in dialogue
with Cervantes. There is also, in general, an attempt to live up to the name
of the journal. This issue is all about what is new in the world and what
should be new. It is about what is right and what is wrong with the new
conditions of life in Britain and the rest of the world, and about what is
good and bad in attempts to capture this world in literature and art.
Nothing is finished here because everything is part of a dialogue that will
be continued in other issues of this magazine and in other places as well,
such as the "crusty Conservative clubs and solemn Liberal clubs" mentioned by Verdad/Kennedy in his article, or in the Grafton Gallery—if

the *New Age* readers go to see "Manet and the Post-Impressionists" and challenge the social snobbery of the viewers described by Calderon with their own intellectual snobbery, as indeed he urges them to do.

To read an issue of this magazine—to really read it—is to enter a world and begin to learn its language. It is to follow the connections that link certain political views and certain views of art and literature. Judah Benjamin says that "the people's parties are awake." *The New Age* presents itself as their alarm clock and guide through the perplexing world that they must master. The nature—and the reliability—of that guidance may change over the life of the magazine, but in December 1910 the magazine offers a coherent, nuanced view of the world from a leftish perspective. The British Labour Party, so visible now, was established in 1906, just a year before Orage and his group took over *The New Age*. The magazine does not speak for that party, though it may speak as Orage and his group hoped the Labour Party would speak, if only it were smart enough and had the visionary range the magazine attempted to provide. What reading a single issue allows us to see, however, is that a single issue is not enough. There is a narrative here—of rise and fall, perhaps—that can be seen only by following the magazine through the twists and turns that constitute its life as a force in British culture, through its rise to cultural prominence and its decline to eccentricity and mediocrity at the end of Orage's tenure as editor. Above all, such a reading will allow us to perceive the issues of the day as live issues. Magazines from an earlier period have a unique ability to bring social, political, and aesthetic history to life for those who read them with energy and care.

QED? Probably not, though we hope we have gone some distance toward a method for modernist periodical studies. In any case this ends our demonstration for the time being. In the next chapter we will extend this method to other magazines with more advertising and visual material, and we shall return to this issue of *The New Age* as part of our discussion of the December 1910 project and its possible uses in teaching and research.

"On or About December 1910"

"On or about December 1910 human character changed."

—*Virginia Woolf,* Mr. Bennett and Mrs. Brown

Virginia Woolf's jocoserious remark about human character having changed at the end of 1910 was made in her essay *Mr. Bennett and Mrs. Brown,* published as a pamphlet by the Hogarth Press in 1924—so it was not an immediate observation but a retrospective judgment. Woolf's own fiction had made a significant change to a modernist emphasis on internal thoughts and feelings during those years, but this change was fully visible for the first time in her 1922 novel *Jacob's Room.* The essay in which her observation about this change appeared was an attack on the old realism or naturalism of external detail, embodied in the work of Arnold Bennett and other writers whom she labeled Edwardians—that is, authors who came to prominence during the reign of Edward VII, which ended with his death in 1910. Edward's successor, George V, was officially crowned in 1911. Between these two events, for Woolf, human character had changed, becoming internalized, less embodied in material things, thus requiring the new literary methods practiced by Woolf and the other writers she called Georgians.

All this is well known, and many literary scholars and critics have been content to follow Woolf and date the start of modernism in Britain around 1910. We are not going to argue with Woolf here. How, in any case, do you argue with someone being jocoserious, without putting on a clown's motley to do so? If pressed, we would propose a longer and less drastic process—a timid and academically "safe" position. But what we wish to do in this chapter is discuss a digital experiment we have begun that is designed to allow scholars and their students to examine the period around December 1910 for themselves, to see what they can learn about the state of human character—or, perhaps more accurately, the state of human culture—in Britain and America at that time. This project grew out of our work with the Modernist Journals Project and, in particular, our experience of the hole in the archive: the advertising missing from the bound copies of early-twentieth-century periodicals in the stacks of most of our libraries, which we will discuss in the next chapter.

Because of the care with which we work in our major projects, and the small number of journals we can actually hope to locate and digitize, we began to consider providing single samples of a wider range of early-twentieth-century magazines. Not wanting to do this in a merely random manner, we discussed particular dates that might function as the locus for a wide range of sample issues. Here, Virginia Woolf came to our rescue and provided a date worthy of examination. So we decided to collect single issues of British and American periodicals published within a year or so of December 1910, in order to provide digital versions of them, with all the advertising and other material visible for scholars and students to investigate. We did not stick strictly to December 1910, because it is impossible to find enough journals from that month that run from cover to cover, but we did find samples of more than twenty magazines published within a year or so of that date. (Woolf's "about" had already indicated that she did not really mean to be that precise.) These sample magazines are now available on the MJP Web site, and more will be added as copies are discovered. What we wish to do in this chapter, however, is to give some indications about the possible uses of this material, without preempting too much of the research that scholars and students may perform for themselves. To that end, we will look at one of these sample issues with some care, glance at others, and use this examination to propose some general suggestions for projects and lines of research that should prove interesting and instructive to those who pursue them.

In the previous chapter we used, as an example of reading a modernist magazine, an issue of a British weekly review, *The New Age,* from that fateful month December 1910. There, we showed how reading a single issue leads to a concern for the entire span of a magazine's existence and the implied narrative of the magazine's life. Keeping that basic lesson in mind, here we shift to a method of reading that compares samples of many magazines that are closely related in time. The structuralists would call the first method diachronic and the second one synchronic. The focus of this kind of synchronic reading should be not the story of any single magazine but the composite picture of a historical slice of culture provided by a group of nearly simultaneous magazines. Ezra Pound did something like that in his "Studies in Contemporary Mentality," though he never quite put the whole picture together at the end. In what follows here, we will try to develop a method for the production of such a picture—pieces of the puzzle constituted by the cultures of Britain and America within a year or so of December 1910. We can begin by rethinking that weekly issue of *The New Age* from a synchronic perspective.

Among the topics of interest in that issue there are some that will clearly repay further investigation. Among them are these:

- eugenics;
- Post-Impressionism and modernism in visual art;
- women's suffrage and other suffrage questions;
- trade unions and other labor problems;
- the situation of the House of Lords in the British Parliament;
- the political situation in Turkey.

Searches of the set of 1910 issues made available by the MJP will turn up other perspectives on these topics and encourage further study, as will online research of other sorts. People mentioned prominently and the authors of articles will also provide topics to pursue further, by means of similar searches. Among those mentioned in the issues of *The New Age* whom we considered are these:

- Lloyd George;
- Balfour;
- Asquith;
- Cézanne;
- Gauguin;
- Matisse;
- Nietzsche;
- the Young Turks;
- Beatrice Hastings (anonymous author of *The Maids' Comedy*);
- Allen Upward;
- A. R. Orage;
- Alfred E. Randall;
- Huntly Carter.

The New Age is not rich in advertising, but there is at least one topic mentioned that will repay further study:

- Mysticism and Theosophy.

Culture is a web, which is one reason why it lends itself to digital representation and study. A magazine like *The New Age* offers threads from the cultural web, such that scholars and students who follow one of them will be led deeper into modern culture and come to a richer understanding of it. But *The New Age* was a British weekly magazine, with a relatively small audience and very little advertising. Another way into the cultural web is offered by monthly magazines from the other side of the Atlantic.

We can begin the approach from the American side by looking at a monthly magazine, *The World's Work*, for February 1911 (plate 7). The magazine had a circulation of around 100,000 in 1911 before rising during the First World War and then sinking afterward (http://www.time.com/time/magazine/article/0,9171,744048,00.html). Like most monthly magazines of the period, this one is ten inches by seven inches in size, is about a half-inch thick, and uses color sparingly. It contains about 120 pages of content: printed text and images—mainly photographs. And it has, in the front and back, a total of about 110 pages of advertising. The magazine was published by Doubleday, Page, and Company, based in Garden City, Long Island, New York, and it was edited by Walter Hines Page himself at this time. One does not have to go deeply into the table of contents to discover that this monthly is the voice of an aggressive American capitalism. Even the cover emphasizes an attack on the U.S. Post Office, "The Nation's Post-Office: An Obstructive Monopoly," and the contents include other articles on "The Pension Carnival" and "Wasting the Government's Money." These are perhaps not the most useful articles in the magazine for studying human character as it was in February 1911, though they certainly tell us something about the culture of capitalism. *The World's Work* was not, it should be obvious, a mainly "literary" magazine: it did not feature fiction or poetry. But as a window into the culture of this period it is superb. Nor did it entirely neglect the arts. There is an article on "Winslow Homer: A Painter of the Sea" in this issue, with eight halftone illustrations that show as much of Homer as one could hope for in the absence of full-color reproductions. (Homer's death in September 1910 probably inspired this attention from the magazine.) And there is a profusely illustrated piece called "The Moving Picture Show."

"The Moving Picture Show" offers a history of cinema from the "nickel-in-the-slot device" exhibited by Thomas A. Edison at the Chicago World's Fair in 1893 to more recent times when "store shows" proliferated rapidly.

> The year 1908 was one of phenomenal growth in the amusement. With the beginning of 1909 there were 10,000 shows and a daily attendance of 3,000,000 people. The estimated expenditure by spectators was $57,500,000 a year. . . .
>
> Yesterday, 4,000,000 Americans visited 13,000 pictureshows. They do so every day. One man, woman, or child in twenty-three, every afternoon or evening, visits a cinematograph. They pay an average of seven cents each, or more than $102,000,000 a year. (*World's Work* [hereafter *WW*] 21.4: 14020)

The World's Work, true to its character, is more interested in the financial aspect of this new amusement than anything else, but it gives us an indicator of how this technological development is beginning to change human behavior, if not human character itself. And this, let us remember, was long before films had sound or color. They were silent and colorless, but still were proving irresistible to old and young people in the years around 1910.

Even more interesting for our purposes is an article by the future editor, Arthur W. Page (son of Walter H. Page), entitled "What Is 'Scientific Management'?" In this piece Arthur Page discusses what the subtitle calls "THE RESULT OF MR. FREDERICK W. TAYLOR'S TWENTY-SIX YEARS OF SUCCESSFUL WORK IN THE STEEL BUSINESS—A SYSTEM TO IMPROVE THE CONDITION OF LABOR AND TO DECREASE THE COST OF PRODUCTION." Page recounts Taylor's study of "the science of shoveling." At the Midvale Steel Works in Philadelphia, Taylor studied the methods used in basic acts of laboring, such as shoveling coal, ashes, and sand. He was then asked to bring these methods to Bethlehem Steel.

> Mr. Taylor's analysis showed that a first-class man working at normal speed could handle more material on a shovel that held a 21-pound load than on any other. A lighter load necessitated too high a speed, and a heavier load meant too much strain on the man. He determined how much more quickly and easily a man could load his shovel with material from an iron or wooden floor than from the ground. There were several other things Mr. Taylor learned about the science of shoveling, but these will do by way of example. There is nothing occult about it, and it is hard to say whether it is more remarkable that Mr. Taylor should have thought to do such a thing or that no one else had thought to do it before. (*WW* 21.4: 14045)

Page continues his discussion of Taylor's work and its importance, noting that wage increases must accompany any shift to this form of labor, to accompany the increases in productivity, and concluding with these words:

Among the 50,000 men now working in some twenty different kinds of industrial plants under "scientific management,"
there has not been a single strike. The men are making more
money than they could make elsewhere, and the companies
are getting their work done more cheaply. The Midvale Steel
Works, where the system was evolved, has not had a strike
for thirty years. On the other hand, in several places where the
introduction of "scientific management" was undertaken all
at once—where the system was forced upon men before they
understood it—strikes occurred immediately and prevented
its adoption. Mr. Taylor's principles can not be applied like
cocaine to give instant relief. They form a constructive system
and take time to introduce; but their introduction would be
a long, long step forward in our industrial and labor worlds.
(*WW* 21.4: 14050)

Page's casual mention of cocaine as a painkiller tells us something
about the world of 1911, to be sure, reminding us that Freud had been an
advocate of the drug a couple of decades earlier, but the main thing we
need to notice here is that "Taylorism" (or "scientific management") was
a growing force in the world at this time and an aspect of the changes in
human character and culture that were taking place in that world. There
is, in fact, a photo-portrait of Taylor among the "great men" whose images appear at the beginning of this issue. The regimentation of labor
involved in Taylor's mode of manufacture was exported to England,
where Yevgeny Zamyatin experienced it in the Tyne shipyards before
writing his dystopian novel *We* (1921)—a book that later influenced
George Orwell's *1984*. The main point, however, is that this single article
in a single magazine of 1911 opens the way for students to become interested in and pursue an understanding of a major process in the cultural
history of America and England. Human character among the working
class was having a certain change imposed upon it in the interest of efficiency. In the name of "science," men were being made more machine-
like. Charlie Chaplin's movie *Modern Times* would take this process up
with a vengeance in 1936. But in 1911 the movies were still in their infancy.

They were not too young, however, for *The World's Work* to register their importance.

The article on "The Moving-Picture Show" that we have already mentioned offers not only a history of this nascent medium but a detailed and profusely illustrated discussion of how films were currently being made:

> The manufacture of films has created a new profession whose proportions are undreamed of by the public—the business of enacting plays before the camera. For this business, studios and stages as elaborate as those in a pretentious city theatre have been established. A visit to one of these disclosed what the industry has grown to be.
>
> The plant has a stage sixty feet wide and forty feet deep —approximately that of a large theatre. It is entirely enclosed in glass. Daylight is supplemented by forty-two hanging and standing electric lamps, affording 82,000 candle-power. Under the stage is a tank filled with water for aquatic scenes. As the cameras record no color-values, all of the scenery is painted in black, white, and gray to obtain sharply defined outlines.

One of the many illustrations for the article is entitled "A DOMESTIC DRAMA IN THE CORNER, WITH A SMALL BUT IMPORTANT AUDIENCE OF CAMERA-MEN AND ELECTRICIANS" (figure 7.1). It shows, from a point behind the camera, a scene being shot in a building that is constructed like a greenhouse. The main camera is fixed on a tripod, though there seems to be another on a makeshift dolly. As the magazine's title proclaims, it is about the world's *work,* and it is film as *manufacture* and *industry* that is being discussed here, rather than film as art. For art we have Winslow Homer. Still, this magazine has much to teach us about aspects of human character in the United States just two months after December 1910.

One of the things *The World's Work* can teach us about is racial prejudice. The subject comes up in the issue of February 1911 in the section

A DOMESTIC DRAMA IN THE CORNER, WITH A SMALL BUT IMPORTANT AUDIENCE OF
CAMERA - MEN AND ELECTRICIANS

Fig. 7.1. Photo from *The World's Work,* February 1911

of Booker T. Washington's *My Larger Education, Being Chapters from My Experience* (a book published by Doubleday and Page) that appeared in this issue. After discussing a dinner he had with Theodore Roosevelt, Washington reports and reflects upon an incident in Florida, when a farmer saw him on a train and spoke with him about President Roosevelt. Washington said that he considered Roosevelt a great man and got this reply:

> "Huh! Roosevelt?" he replied with considerable emphasis in his voice. "I used to think that Roosevelt was a great man until he ate dinner with you. That settled him for me."
>
> This remark of a Florida farmer is but one of the many experiences which have taught me something of the curious nature of this thing that we call prejudice—social prejudice, race prejudice, and all the rest. I have come to the conclusion

that these prejudices are something that it does not pay to disturb. It is best to "let sleeping dogs lie." All sections of the
United States, like all other parts of the world, have their own
peculiar customs and prejudices. For that reason it is the part
of common-sense to respect them. When one goes to European countries or into the Far West, or into India or China,
he meets certain customs and certain prejudices which he is
bound to respect and, to a certain extent, comply with. The
same holds good regarding conditions in the North and in the
South. In the South it is not the custom for colored and white
people to be entertained at the same hotel; it is not the custom for black and white children to attend the same school.
In most parts of the North a different custom prevails. I have
never stopped to question or quarrel with the customs of the
people in the part of the country in which I found myself.
(*WW* 21.4: 14038–14039)

Washington was fifty-five years old when he wrote this, and he lived only
four more years, but it is clear that his views on prejudice belong to his
time and not to ours. It is easy to be impatient with his calm acceptance
of prejudice as simply the custom of the country, but we need to see it as
a form of pragmatism, a philosophy that developed during his lifetime
and is still with us. It was also the view of a man who had earned the
right to his opinion by his own experience. Nevertheless, we must see
Washington's view as anchored in the world of 1911, a world in which,
apparently, human character had not changed much, and did not look
likely to change, when it came to matters of racial prejudice. It took another half-century for that part of human character to begin changing,
and that change is far from complete at the present time, though progress
is clearly being made. But this excerpt from Washington's memoirs opens
the way to a study of racial attitudes around December 1910, which can
be continued in both the advertising and content pages of this and other
magazines.

Another ethnic group receives attention in this issue of *The World's
Work*: the Irish. They appear in a short piece called "How to Choose a
Public-School Teacher," by William McAndrew, the principal of Wash-

ington Irving High School in New York City. McAndrew's notion is simple: "If you seek a female teacher, choose an Irish girl."

> An Irish teacher won't be imposed upon. Forty boys some-
> times get the devil into each one of them, all at once. The rules
> nowadays prevent you from driving him out by muscle. The
> Irish girl laughs at him. If any boy takes a mean advantage of
> her, she can launch an outburst of sarcasm, invective, and cor-
> rection in perfect taste—and in a few moments you will hear
> the whole company, teacher and children, laughing together.
> Your typical New England woman, with her ingrowing con-
> science, would be resentful all the rest of the day. The Irish
> teacher counts more on affection than on system. (*WW* 21.4:
> 13965)

McAndrew's little essay needs to be read in full. He thinks teachers should
be good looking and that they should "radiate interest and inspiration,"
and he concludes with some remarks that resonate today:

> Lastly, find out where she is teaching. Go and test her children
> to see whether they have learned anything. Don't rely on any
> official record about a teacher. Not one report in a thousand
> is made after any testing of the work that she has done. You
> choose every other worker on the basis of the results of per-
> formance. But no one keeps "the batting average" of a teacher;
> no one records what her pupils can do. The most that the of-
> ficial record will show regarding a teacher is that she ought
> to be able to teach. Whether her children are taught or not—
> only a test of the children can show that. (*WW* 21.4: 13966)

Some things in this magazine seem to come from another world altogether,
like Booker T. Washington's remarks on prejudice. Others seem much
closer to us in some respects. McAndrew's insistence on giving the Irish a
racial character that apparently applies to all of them is clearly dated. But
his suspicion of official records and his insistence on measuring teaching
by student performance seem quite current, though one might wish to add

a warning about the kind of testing that might be used, since Taylorized testing will generate Taylorized teaching. Taken together, his emphasis on testing and his distrust of "system" betray an unresolved conflict in the mind of William McAndrew, if not in the whole culture.

Teaching at the college level is also taken up in this issue, in connection with a report by M. L. Cooke of the Carnegie Foundation for the Advancement of Teaching, comparing the efficiency of college teaching with that of industrial works. This report is discussed by the editor, W. H. Page, in the opening section of the magazine. Some of his observations resonate today:

> But, even after the teacher is left free to teach, it will be necessary to have a standard for teaching, which is now almost entirely lacking; and, because it is lacking, few men achieve success purely upon teaching. Teaching-power is often unrecognized. Research, on the other hand, is recognized because it can be measured. Mr. Cooke points out, "One reason for the demand for research-workers is just a demand for established efficiency. I think if methods can be developed by which the success which a professor may be achieving—in teaching—may be measured and recorded, that he will be in demand as research workers are in demand." (WW 21.4: 13959)

We still lack any reliable measure of the quality of teaching, and we still favor research over teaching in our colleges and universities—and we still lament this fact. In this respect human character seems not to have budged since 1911. But the common thread of measurement and the need to measure everything from teaching to shoveling runs through the entire issue of this magazine. Something, indeed, appears to be changing, if we can judge by this American magazine. What we are seeing here is the pressure of modernity on human character and culture—a pressure in the direction of greater measurement, greater quantification of human activities: measuring the success of the film industry by numbers of viewers and dollars, measuring the success of teachers by testing their pupils, measuring waste in the post office and other government activities against the standards of profitable industries.

We can also find in this issue an interesting discussion of the problem of representing the lives of great figures. Dorothy Lamon Teillard, in "Lincoln in Myth and Fact," takes up the problem of such representation by discussing the persecution of her father for writing what she calls "the most faithful history of Mr. Lincoln's life from his birth to his first inauguration." In this article the author quotes extensively from the attacks on her father's biography and also from letters praising it, written by people with some knowledge of the man and his life. She also discusses the impact of the criticism on her father, who finally suppressed the second volume he had intended to produce. She also calmly discusses the reasons why the book was found so offensive:

> Many things combined against the acceptance of the truth then. First and perhaps the most important was the fact that so short a time had elapsed since the death of Mr. Lincoln. The memory of the hideous tragedy was still fresh. The reading public regarded it as an offense to trace his wonderful growth from so humble an origin. Then there was the religious world, which was shocked that he was described as unorthodox. What may be called the sectional public took exception to the unprejudiced attitude toward the South. (*WW* 21.4: 14042)

Articles about public figures like Lincoln and Napoleon were popular in the periodicals of this time. A culture of celebrity was forming, and this article registers the resistance of the public and the media to facts that disturbed their views. This, too, is a part of the developing culture of modernity, just as much as "scientific management" and "progress." By formulating this as an opposition of "fact" and "myth," Teillard directed attention to one of the great problems of modernism.

Virginia Woolf's modernism was all about the inability of facts to capture the truth, but she was not one of those who embraced myth as the proper alternative. The modernist media, with their powerful advertisements and potential for propaganda, constituted part of the modernity that Woolf's own work opposed. She wrote in reaction against what industry and science were doing to human life, offering a form of resistance to a modernity which had molded the "modern" works of the

Edwardian writers and was now being opposed and resisted in her own work and that of her Georgian friends. Much of modern art and literature can be usefully seen as positioned against modernity, seeking some truth obscured by the polarity of fact and myth. But *The World's Work* has more to tell us about modernism and modernity. Let us look at some of the advertising. The advertising pages in this magazine are unnumbered and confined to the front and back of the issue. At the front, full-page ads for Victor Records and Tiffany and Company are followed by ten pages of advertising by publishers, a few miscellaneous pages, a four-page set of ads for schools, more miscellaneous pages, four pages on the eleventh edition of *The Encyclopaedia Britannica*, then a full eighteen pages labeled "INVESTMENTS," devoted mainly to stocks and bonds, followed by "CITIES AND LANDS OF OPPORTUNITY"—four pages on places like Houston, Texas, and Des Moines, Iowa ("Des Moines is the Young Man's City"), along with an ad in which the magazine announces its own "plan of city advertising that will interest every city in America." After this come a few pages of insurance ads, and the section concludes with full-page ads for White automobiles, Swift hams, Steinway pianos, Royal baking powder, and Gold Medal flour.

Taken as a group, these ads tell us something about the readership aimed at by *The World's Work*. The dominance of investment advertising over everything else is perhaps the most revealing feature of this section, but this harmonizes with the upscale products offered by Tiffany, Steinway, Victor, and the other companies, and the general emphasis on opportunity and prosperity. All this is perhaps more revealing of *American* character in 1911 than of human character in general. Which opens the way to one possible line of research involving a comparison in the "character" revealed by American as opposed to British periodicals at this time, using the advertising in British and American periodicals as primary sources. But we must hold off on proposing general lines of research for the moment and continue looking into the advertising of this one American magazine. There are some fascinating things in the section of ads at the back of *The World's Work*. We can begin by looking at a complete list of what is on these advertising pages (table 7.1).

Just a glance at this list should help us realize what we miss when we look at bound copies of a periodical like this in our libraries or at the san-

Table 7.1: List of Advertisements on the Final Pages of *The World's Work*, February 1911 (Each Item Represents a Full Page Unless Otherwise Noted)

Postum (an alternative to coffee)	Pearline washing powder/Buffalo Lithia Springs Water	Pianola pianos
Pacific Mail SS Company	Hotel Chamberlin, Virginia	California Limited
Royal Mail Winter Cruises/ Burpee Seeds/Doubleday	Welch's Grape Juice	White Rock Water/ Prophylactic Tooth Brush/Codliver Oil
Pebeco Tooth Paste	Horlick's Malted Milk/Cedarcroft Sanitarium	Everett Piano/Dreer's Garden Book/Smith Granite Monuments
Lea & Perrins Sauce/ Atwood Grapefruit	G & S Neverbreak Trunks/Shur-On Eyeglass Mountings	Doubleday
Jos. A Richards (two-page spread)	Doubleday	Howard Watch Works
(Information about automobiles)	Rambler Motor Cars	Goodyear Tires
Winton Motor Cars	Kelly-Springfield Tires	(start clothing section)
Griffon Razor Stropper/ Doubleday	Rogers Peet clothing Best & Co. clothing	American Woolen Company
(start business helps section)	Smith & Bros. Typewriters	International Time Recording Company
Belknap Rapid Addressing Machine/Hampshire Paper Company	The Dictaphone	Mabie, Todd Fountpen/Safe-Cabinet/ PaperFastners/Rebuilding Typewriters/Prentiss Clocks
Strathmore Business Stationery	Moore's Fountain Pen/Neostyle Self-Inking Stencils	Oliver Typewriters
Shaw-Walker Filing Cabinets/Miscellaneous small ads	Globe-Wernicke Co. Office Equipment	Marsh-Capron Concrete Mixers

(*continued*)

Table 7.1 (*continued*)

Sargent Hardware	Natco Hollow Tile Fireproofing	Grand Rapids Furniture Company
Wood Mantel Manufacturers Assoc./ Wroe Stationery	Yale Locks	Fay & Bowen Electric Lighting/Monroe Refrigeration/Suck Concrete
AT&T Telephone Etiquette	Cabot's Shingles/ Rogers Bros. Silver Plate/Doubleday	The Architectural Record/Carter White Lead painters
Reeco electric hot air pumps/American Bankers Assoc. Traveller's Cheques	Berkey & Gay Furniture	Macbeth Lighting Glass
Murphy Varnish Co.	Dahlstrom Builders (two-page spread)	Barrett Roofing
National Lead Co. Paints	Standard Bathroom Fixtures	Kodak Film Tank
Bauer Chemical Co. Sanatogen	Fairy Soap	Pierce Arrow cars (color—back cover)

itized versions provided online by companies like ProQuest. From it we can readily see what has changed and what has not in the past century. Bottled water is still with us, and so are automobiles and their tires, though the tire companies seem to have lasted better than the car manufacturers themselves. But this new form of travel was one technological development that would leave a lasting imprint on human culture. Yale locks are still with us today, as is the American Telephone and Telegraph Company (AT&T), though it has changed a lot since 1911. The new office technology was based on fountain pens, typewriters, stencil machines, and the Dictaphone—all of which have been replaced by technological advances, though their functions have remained, for the most part. The Worcestershire sauce of Lee and Perrin has endured, however, proving tougher than lead paint, and much less dangerous to your health. Speaking of health, one of the

most interesting items in this list is the Bauer Chemical Company's
"Sanatogen" (figure 7.2). The student who follows the trail of this diet supplement will discover many interesting things, including a more recent
product that has adopted the same name. The ad itself must be seen to be
appreciated. The "case" diagnosed by those twelve thousand doctors, and
represented by the testimonials scattered around the edges of the main text,
is based on the way that "our present mode of living creates nervous dis-
orders" for which Sanatogen is the best remedy. The "case" is that of
modernity itself, which makes Sanatogen a form of modernism—a chemical response to what Matthew Arnold had diagnosed a half-century earlier as "this strange disease of modern life, / With its sick hurry, its divided aims, / Its heads o'ertax'd, its palsied hearts" ("The Scholar Gypsy,"
lines 203–205), which had clearly become more acute by 1911. The disease,
then, was not something that changed in 1910, but this cure was new.
Introduced in 1908 by a German chemical company, it flourished in the
English-speaking world until World War I made German products unpopular. Like the cocaine mentioned casually by Arthur Page in his discussion of "scientific management," Sanatogen was a chemical remedy
for a psychic problem, for a form of distress caused by modernity itself. The
young Virginia Stephen (before she married Leonard Woolf) wrote to Violet Dickinson in a letter, "Do you take Sanatogen? I find it very warming
to the brain" (Woolf, *Letters,* 438).

The ads in the back of *The World's Work* offer another remedy for
the stresses of modern life: advertising itself. Yes, the most interesting ad
of all is the two-page spread promoting the services of "Jos. A. Richards &
Staff, Advertising Agent, Tribune Building, New York." This ad is addressed
to the managerial class assumed to be the readers of this magazine:

> If you don't advertise, I don't see how you have time for any-
> thing except work, work, work.
>
> You are the world's workers, of course, or you would not
> be reading these pages. Most likely you are men who work
> on your own initiative, men who plan campaigns, and put
> them in work, appoint your captains of industry, commit to
> them the administration of details, stand back and look on
> with a kindly critical eye to see the enterprise rise from the

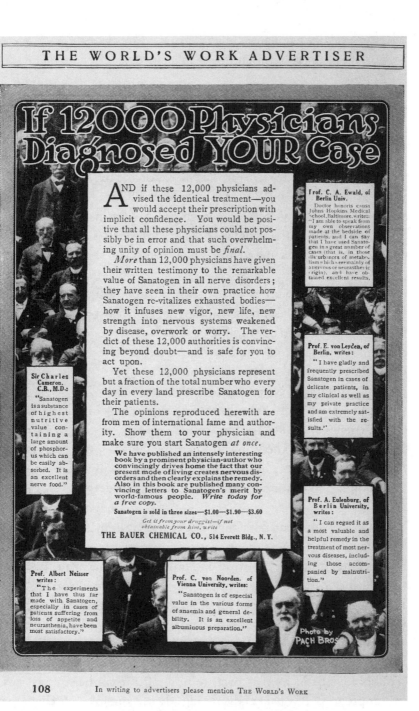
Fig. 7.2. Sanatogen ad from *The World's Work*, February 1911

ground like a biplane and go soaring off to success.

That's you, isn't it? (*WW* 21.4: adv67)

This is not the audience Marx and Engels addressed as "Workers of the world," is it? *The World's Work* has taken that phrase from *The Communist Manifesto* and has stood it on its head, and nowhere is that more apparent than in this bit of advertising, which goes on to praise the magazine itself, advising the reader to "fertilize, rest and refresh your mind for a half hour with the big business ideas you will find recorded on every page of the World's Work." After much praise of the magazine's contents, and some advice on the right way to play golf, which is also the right way to succeed in business, the ad itself finally gets down to its own business:

> If you don't advertise, you hard-worked brainworking World's Worker, I don't see how you can play or rest—provided you propose to keep up with the progress of the age.
>
> I'm sure I have to advertise in order to rest well nights and Sundays and play well Saturdays.
>
> And now comes my advertisement.
>
> If you don't know how to advertise, why I have the experience and will advertise you.
>
> If you do know how to advertise, there is something else which you know how to do better, and it will still be economical to let me advertise you. (*WW* 21.4: adv68)

This is a fascinating and revealing piece of writing. Maybe Jos. A. Richards really knew what he was doing. For our purposes, however, this ad ties together everything we have been looking at in this magazine. It explains the title: the World's Workers are the "hard-worked brainworking" CEOs of companies and their top-level management who aspire to such positions—along with those, perhaps, who want to know what people at the top are thinking. This ad also sounds the theme of "the progress of the age," which is a crucial aspect of American ideology at this moment. And it offers advertising itself as a way to find relief from the stresses caused by this progress. If you take advertising advice from Jos. A. Richards, you won't need Sanatogen.

But the ads in this magazine offer us many threads into the cultural web of modernism. A search of other magazines for Sanatogen will provide a number of full-page ads for this elixir, and a comparison of advertising in different kinds of periodicals from both Britain and America will provide a way into modern culture at this moment when change was in the air. Other topics that emerge from this issue of *The World's Work* and offer opportunities for further study include the following:

- moving pictures (not yet called "movies" or "film");
- scientific management (or Taylorism) and "efficiency" in general;
- race and racial prejudice;
- the election of U.S. Senators (compare House of Lords);
- teaching and education;
- military training and preparedness.

Among the editors, contributors, and people discussed in these pages are the following:

- Winslow Homer;
- Booker T. Washington;
- Abraham Lincoln;
- Dorothy Lamon Teillard;
- Walter W. Page and Arthur W. Page;
- Don C. Seitz;
- William McAndrew;
- Hubert Bruce Fuller;
- William Bayard Hale;
- Arthur Hoeber.

The less well-known names on this list are contributors to this issue, and, though they are not currently famous, they were people whose careers can teach us something about modernity and modernism.

One of the things *The World's Work* does not have that many other magazines of this time—including *The New Age*—had was fiction. A survey of these magazines to see which writers of fiction were being published or discussed, followed up by some research on who they were and how their reputations have changed since that time, can tell us a good deal about that moment in modern culture. And the same sort of thing can be done with poetry or verse, and with drama and the theater. Some of the periodicals in this sample published a lot of fiction. If we look at one such magazine—*Cosmopolitan* for June 1911—we can learn something about the writing of fiction at this time.

The fiction in this issue of *Cosmopolitan* begins with an installment of a romantic novel by Robert W. Chambers that was being serialized in the magazine, with many illustrations by Charles W. Gibson—the creator of "the Gibson Girl," an image of feminine beauty that dominated America for two decades. The Gibson Girl was described this way by Susan E. Meyer, in her book *America's Great Illustrators:* "She was taller than the other women currently seen in the pages of magazines . . . infinitely more spirited and independent, yet altogether feminine. She appeared in a stiff shirtwaist, her soft hair piled into a chignon, topped by a big plumed hat. Her flowing skirt was hiked up in back with just a hint of a bustle. She was poised and patrician. Though always well bred, there often lurked a flash of mischief in her eyes" (217). The Gibson Girl was a part of "human character" in America in 1911—a part that changed not in December of 1910 but after World War I, when John Held's images of flappers replaced her in the public eye. After the serial novel in this issue comes a section that includes short fiction by the following:

- Jack London;
- Bruno Lessing;
- Charles Belmont Davis;
- George Randolph Chester;
- Arthur B. Reeve;
- Paul West;
- Maurice Leblanc.

Jack London is the best known of this group, and Maurice Leblanc's detective fiction about Arsène Lupin is still remembered, but some of the other writers are interesting enough to repay some research. "Bruno Lessing" was the writing name of Rudolph Edgar Block. The story included here is a sympathetic—even sentimental—look at a New York City ghetto. Block wrote frequently on Jewish-American themes, for the movies as well as the magazines. Charles Belmont Davis and his brother Richard Harding Davis were sons of the American realist Rebecca Harding Davis, who wrote *Life in the Iron Mills*. Charles Davis's story in this magazine is part of "The Octopus," subtitled "Conclusion of the two-part story which shows the lure of money in New York City and pushes aside the screen for some glimpses behind the glitter of wealth." George Randolph Chester's story is about a con man named Wallingford, who was the protagonist of four novels by Chester published between 1908 and 1913. The first of them was presented in a stage version by George M. Cohan in 1910. Arthur B. Reeve, a lawyer who graduated from Princeton, wrote eighteen books of detective fiction about Craig Kennedy, of which this story is a sample. Most of them can be downloaded from Project Gutenberg. Paul West is apparently another pseudonym, attached to stories in several magazines in the period 1909 to 1915, but there is still some mystery about just who he was. The amount of fiction in this issue of *Cosmopolitan* was well over 50 percent of the content pages, up from just over 30 percent in 1900. By 1920, as David Reed has demonstrated, it would exceed 80 percent (245).

One of the changes going on at this moment in modernism was an increasing interest in fiction in magazines addressed to a wide audience. Since such magazines were driven by advertising, and advertising revenue depended on circulation, we can conclude that the great mass of readers wanted more fiction—and they wanted it illustrated, too, if they could get it. *Cosmopolitan* clearly tried to give them what they wanted. But the very popularity of fiction put pressure on certain writers to demonstrate that they were artists and not hacks, pushing them away from the norms that we find in magazines like this. On the other hand, the income from these magazines drew those same writers who hoped to live by their work back in. We thus find some writers trying to live in two aesthetic worlds, with varying degrees of success—and others going to extremes in one direction or the other. All of which sets up some interesting possibilities for scholarly investigation, involving the following questions:

- Whose work appeared in these magazines?
- Whose work was discussed in these magazines?
- What norms or formulas seem to govern this fiction?
- How good—or bad—is it?
- Can we distinguish clearly between artists and hacks?
- Do different magazines have clearly different standards?
- Is there a middle ground?
- What is the role of illustration in this fiction?

To address such matters, one first will have to list the works and authors in the magazines, learn more about the authors, actually read the works, and then try to make the required judgments about them. This sort of study will lend itself to team investigation, with individuals following the work of particular writers and reporting on them. Similar projects can be established for other genres of writing and images in these periodicals, with a goal of putting it all together ultimately to make a picture of the culture at this crucial moment in modernism.

Obviously, one can scarcely scratch the surface of these cultural riches in a single chapter of a book like this one. We would like to close, however, by showing what may be discovered by following just one of the topics mentioned above in discussing *The World's Work*. We also hope to demonstrate how one may go about following such a topic, using "race and racial prejudice" as our sample. This topic surfaced in Booker T. Washington's memoir in *The World's Work* with respect to the Negro race, and in a more benign form in the article about hiring an Irish teacher. One can start looking into the subject, then, by searching these magazines for the word *Negro*. Such a search will turn up Washington's article and two other mentions of Negroes in the same issue of *The World's Work*: one in the article on Winslow Homer, noting that after the Civil War, Homer "painted the Negro life of the South" for a while, and one in a caption to a photograph of well-trained Negro troops in the article on the sorry current state of the U.S. Army. A search for *Negro* will also locate a number of items of interest in the *Atlantic Monthly* for December 1910:

- In an article on Robert E. Lee, the Confederate general is quoted thus: "'I have always observed,' he writes, 'that wherever you find the Negro, you see everything going down around him, and wherever you find the white man, you see everything around him improving.'"

- An article about a mining disaster describes a powerful Negro who escaped only because the blast that sent him through the air caused him to land on his head—apparently his most durable feature.
- A favorable review of a novel by Octave Thanet makes a case for the separation of the races by telling of the bad effect a Harvard education had on a black man.
- An installment of a "Diary of the Reconstruction" chronicles events of the years after the Civil War. The diary, by Gideon Welles, secretary of the navy under Lincoln and Andrew Johnson, was published by his son, Edgar T. Welles. It is clear from this that the Civil War, the problems of Reconstruction, and the situation of Negroes after the war were still live issues in 1910.
- Finally, the index for the volume *The Atlantic Monthly* points to an article by Ray Stannard Baker on "Negro Suffrage in a Democracy." A copy of this article may be found at the University of Virginia's library Web site. In it, Baker, who gained fame as a muckraking journalist at *McClure's,* makes the case for the rightness of Negro suffrage, after going into the history of limits on suffrage in the United States, including current bans on Asian suffrage and women's suffrage.

These are the kinds of things we will find if we pursue that one word —*Negro*—through these magazines. To find everything relevant, however, we need to consider additional search terms, such as *black race,* for example, or words distasteful now but in common use then. If we search for those words, we will find an article in *Fry's Magazine* for December 1910 by the sports promoter Hugh D. McIntosh called "My Reminiscences, and the Search for a White Champion." He recounts some fights of the black heavyweight champion Jack Johnson and speaks respectfully of Johnson as a man and a fighter, but also notes the political implications of Johnson's victories. He recounts the reception of films of Johnson's victories among black audiences in various countries, concluding that a white champion should be found and would be found to replace Johnson. For McIntosh, the political mastery of the whites over other races must be maintained. Following the word *nigger* leads us to references to a contemporary play called *The Nigger* by Edward Sheldon, and to other instances of the word in both British and American magazines, where it is used often, but without the intense quality of disparagement attached to it in current usage. For students of race and racism, there are many fruitful trails in these old magazines.

We should note in this connection that W. E. B. Du Bois founded a magazine in November 1910 that is still running today, as the official journal of the NAACP. It was called *The Crisis: A Record of the Darker Races,* and in his opening editorial Du Bois defined his intentions this way: "The object of this publication is to set forth those facts and arguments which show the danger of race prejudice, particularly as manifested today toward colored people. It takes its name from the fact that the editors believe that this is a critical time in the history of the advancement of men." This is a very different position from that of Booker T. Washington, and it needs to be seen as part of what was happening to modern culture in 1910. Original issues of this journal are extremely rare, but the Modernist Journals Project hopes to offer a digital edition in the near future.

Another possible direction based on questions of race is the geographical one. A search for the word *Africa* in these issues will produce hits in nineteen journals, and following these leads will result in the location of whole articles and stories devoted to Africa, and illustrations as well. All of these are revealing about the attitudes of British and American writers toward Africa and Africans. If we do not remember that we are within a decade of the publication of Joseph Conrad's *Heart of Darkness* here, the articles in these magazines will remind us of that fact. A search for other geographical locations will also turn up interesting patterns of thought, feeling, and representation. The issue of *The Wide World* in this group of magazines manages to include photographs of bare-breasted, dark-skinned women from both Africa and Papua, along with images of a grizzly bear attacking a man and the collapse of a tunnel that trapped workers in Switzerland. One can, in fact, start with almost any one of these magazines, as we started with *The World's Work,* and follow the topics encountered there to construct part of the "character" of the world of 1910 and 1911.

Another fruitful topic that can be developed using these periodical resources has to do with the issues around votes for women and suffrage in general. A search through these issues for the word *suffrage* will turn up more than a hundred hits in eleven issues:

- an article on "Negro Suffrage" in *The Atlantic;*
- a cartoon about women's suffrage in *Cosmopolitan;*
- an article on "Woman: The Line of Progress" that offers a balanced view of women's suffrage in *The Forum;*
- a hostile view of women's suffrage in "Civic Pride in Amityville" in *Good Housekeeping;*
- an ad in *Harper's* for an article by Max Eastman, "Is Woman Suffrage Important?" forthcoming in the *North American Review;*
- a long and unfavorable report on what women voters actually achieved in four U.S. states where they had the vote, in *The Lady's Realm;*
- support for the Anti-Suffrage League in Britain, in the pages of *The Mask,* a little magazine of the theater;
- an ad in *Mother Earth* for Emma Goldman's book *Woman Suffrage;*
- a long and serious article on women's suffrage in Finland, "Where Women Vote," in *The National Geographic;*
- rich and nuanced discussion of the issue from many perspectives throughout W. T. Stead's columns in *The Review of Reviews,* which mentions other sources;
- an antisuffrage short story, "Votes for Women," in *The Smart Set.*

For students who want to find out what people really thought about the issue of Women's Suffrage and the tactics being used to attain it in the period around December 1910, these magazines, plus what can be found in *The New Age, The English Review,* and the full run of *Scribner's* for these years, offer a rich array of perspectives, and the fact that we know how this came out in Britain and America some years later makes these struggles all the more interesting. The rise of women from a position of dependence if not servitude is one of the major changes in human character that we can find happening around December 1910.

At the beginning of this chapter we raised the issue of synchronic reading as a way of studying the culture of modernism. This has always been a theoretical possibility. That is, one could always pursue a topic across many sources within a relatively short time span. But this has been easier with indexed books than with magazines, which often lack comprehensive indexes. For periodicals we have had certain resources like Marion Sader's eight-volume *Comprehensive Index to English-Language Little Magazines, 1890–1970,* which claims to have provided "complete bibliographic control to the contents of one hundred little magazine titles" (1: xiii). In this case "complete control" consists of the names of people who were the "contributor" or "subject" of an article in one of the hundred magazines selected for inclusion. If the object of your interest is a topic and not a person, you will not find it in this index. Nor will you find any information about advertising in these magazines. Thus was completeness defined in 1976. Many things have changed since then, but none more so than our notion of searching for information in texts; digitization has enabled our searches to go "out of control."

The ability to search across a range of texts for words and phrases is something that we have gained only recently, as part of the digital revolution in scholarship. And this ability is enabling new ways of reading —or, at the very least, allowing many more people to perform old ways of reading at a higher level, making connections that might have been missed and drawing conclusions that might have been impossible before the digital age. To read a topic synchronically, then, across a range of magazines, is an experience that is being brought within the reach of students and scholars who could not have done this even a few decades ago. What this means for reading modern magazines is that the whole web of modern culture as it existed a century ago is becoming visible, providing students with an opportunity to become engaged in our history in ways that will enable them to understand better who we are and how we became what we are today. The tools for this are being constructed now, but the work is far from done and must be continued at the highest levels possible if the promise of this opportunity is to be realized.

The Hole in the Archive and the Study of Modernist Magazines

We have mentioned the hole in the archive before, but now it is time to consider more thoroughly how it got there and what we can do about it as students and scholars of modernism. Most of our libraries simply do not have copies of the fragile but important magazines that published the work of writers like Ezra Pound and other young modernists in the first decades of the twentieth century. Because so many had small circulations and short runs, today these magazines are rare, preserved in a scattering of archives around the world but inevitably crumbling as century-old acidic paper consumes itself. Although reprints of some of these magazines are more widely available, they are not always complete, so for many who wish to study them, the magazines are simply not available. And even when a library owns a full run of a magazine, it may be irredeemably mutilated. In order to preserve magazine issues and ensure that their runs remain complete, libraries often bind periodicals into volumes that combine several months of publication into one large tome. But something happened when our libraries bound periodicals, and we need to understand how that happened and why it happened before we can consider possible remedies.

Most publishers of magazines, large circulation or small, thought of them as containing two distinct sorts of material: what was permanent and what was ephemeral. This conceptual distinction was (and still is) supported by material conditions. "Content" (the articles, features, and illustrations the publishers paid for) was acquired and managed by an editor, who might know months in advance what would appear in an issue; advertisements, on the other hand (for which the publisher received fees), were rather unpredictable and could be assembled only near the time of printing. So publishers numbered content and advertising pages separately. They gave the "permanent" material continuous pagination from issue to issue for some regular period of time (usually six months, but sometimes more or less), anticipating that the issues would be united into a single volume. To the ephemeral advertising pages they gave no numbering at all, or they gave them a different sequence of numbers or letters that started over with every new issue. When the time came to bind a volume of a magazine, libraries, which are perpetually strapped for shelf space, were able to strip away the advertising pages (who would ever want to look at them again?) and put between hard covers a slimmer, more respectable, sequentially numbered series of pages from which it seemed nothing had been lost. As we have seen, however, a lot was lost, since those ephemeral pages have become more interesting with every passing decade. There is no point in blaming the librarians for this; they simply followed what the publishers expected and planned for them to do. Publishers and librarians shared a centuries-old assumption about what should go into bound volumes. Printed editions of *The Spectator* after its original publication in 1711–1714 never included the advertisements that had appeared in every original issue. The growth of advertising in the magazines from the 1890s on also meant that binding unabridged issues could as much as double the size of the volumes and the space required to store them. And very few people in the first decades of the twentieth century had any idea that advertising might be worth noticing. Ezra Pound, as we have shown, was one of the few. He hated advertising, but he knew how important it was, and he turned his critical gaze on it in the "Studies in Contemporary Mentality," appended to this volume. In the ninety and more years since his study, these early ads have become even more important, because of what they tell us about the magazines themselves and the world in which they appeared.

The hole in the archive forces us to consider how today's researchers can come close to seeing what Pound saw when he picked up an issue of *The Strand,* or what the readers of *Poetry* saw when they read Pound's poem "In a Station of the Metro" in April 1913, with the original spacing of Pound's words and the five pages of advertising that conclude the issue. Unbound copies of *Poetry* are extremely scarce; bound copies may lack the ads. Reprints and microfilms based on the bound copies will perpetuate the lack, as will digital editions based on those bound copies. That is why librarians, scholars, and information architects have begun to work together seeking digital solutions to the problem caused by the hole in the archive. In this chapter we intend to discuss, with a necessary minimum of technical jargon, the production of digital replicas or editions of those scarce original editions of modernist magazines.

We are talking about copying, which is an ancient process now finding a new form in the digital world. For centuries people have been making copies of their writings in order to preserve and disseminate them, first through the use of scribes and more recently through photography. These two methods—making scribal copies and taking pictures of existing pages—produce very different sorts of reproductions, and the difference is crucial for scholarship. The scribal copy aims at fidelity to the words on the page—what was once simply called the text. Over the centuries, fidelity to the text has been measured to different degrees of exactness. Under some circumstances, a paraphrase of the original text could function as a copy of the text; under others, a transcription with great variation in abbreviation, punctuation, spelling, and even word choice still counted as a faithful copy; in some cases, only a strict character-by-character, line-by-line match between the texts would do. All of these kinds of copying may be grouped together under the rubric of transcription.

In more recent times, our concept of text has broadened to include not only the words indicated by marks on a surface but the marks and surfaces themselves. Being faithful to this notion of text is a much different affair, which we will call simulation. A simulation must replicate the appearance of the page as it was written or printed: the shapes of the letters and other marks that make up the words and their placement on the page, along with all the other things that accompany them, including accents, punctuation, decoration, and illustrations. Fidelity of this kind awaited the advent of photography to become practical, but since then photographic reproduction has become the standard way to make copies.

The distinction between transcription and simulation is preserved in the digital domain, though we are not always aware of this as we work. When you use a word processor to copy your handwritten notes, you are making a transcription from pencil marks on a scrap of paper to character codes (which are in turn represented as discrete points of difference in a computer's memory). What these character codes look like is of secondary importance: they may be rendered as pixelated characters on a screen, or ink on a page, or quavers over a fax line. What is of primary importance is that these character codes must be consistent and distinguishable by the computer programs that duplicate, transmit, and search for patterns in immense strings of them. It is for this reason that text encoded as character codes is often called computer-readable text.

A simulated text, on the other hand, is a digital image: a very large table, or bitmap, of color values corresponding to specific locations on a page or a screen. While programs have been written to distinguish patterns in pixelated maps (optical character recognition [OCR] programs provide one example), they are far from perfectly accurate, and the ability of computers to "read" pictures of words on pages falls far short of their ability to process character codes. The difference here is that between a scanned image of a page, for example, and the text of the same page copied and pasted by a word processor. A word processor can read —or search—only the copied text. The scanned image is just a picture. We human beings can make words from that picture, which is to say that we can "read" it, but a word processor cannot. To transform a scanned image of a page into the text of that page, we must put that image through an OCR program that will turn the marks on that picture into computer-readable letters and words. Once that is done we will have a text to work with that is both readable and searchable. And, for many purposes, that may be all we want or need. For reading the magazines of modernism, as it happens, the text is not enough. We need to see the pages as well as read the words that are on those pages, since these pages contain images as well as words, and we need to read the whole amalgam of words in various fonts and sizes along with illustrations, decorations, and advertisements, noticing their placement on the pages and their connections to one another. All these things must be brought together in a new kind of semiotic reading for those of us who study modernism in the magazines.

This means that an edition of a modern periodical must allow for and even encourage this kind of reading. When literary criticism and analysis are foremost, an edition's value is measured by its selection of source texts, the fidelity with which it transcribes those texts, the ease with which they may be read, and the quality of the glosses and commentary that support them. When reading broadens to become a more general activity of semiotic interpretation, an edition must be further measured by its fidelity to the whole sign—to the artifact itself—as well as by its ease of use and the quality of its scholarly apparatus. In the former case, transcription is most important; in the latter, simulation is key. And because the reading of signs in general necessarily encompasses the careful reading of linguistic signs, a generally useful edition must comprise both transcription and simulation. In the realm of print, most late-twentieth-century readers were familiar with both sorts of edition. Annotated transcriptions were the typical product of publishing houses, and the prevalence of photocopiers made it easy to create a simulated version of many kinds of texts (assuming, of course, that you could get your hands on an original copy). Occasionally publishers would produce volumes that combined both: side-by-side editions that paired a high-quality photograph of a page with an annotated diplomatic transcription. Books like these are expensive to produce, however, so they are usually reserved for editions of manuscripts or early printed materials.

Both transcription and simulation may be found in the digital realm. Transcriptions—simple character encodings—have been available since the earliest days of computers. But as storage capacity has expanded and inexpensive digital photography has become a reality, the mass creation of image books has blossomed. And the development of optical character recognition—the ability of software to scan a photograph of a page and translate the pictures of characters into letters and words—has accelerated the production not only of simple transcriptions but of hybrid texts that combine a photographic simulation of the original page with a word-by-word transcription of its contents linked to the location of the words on the page, as in many texts encoded in portable document format (PDF).

The importance of this latter sort of edition for the study of modern magazines can hardly be overstated. First of all, this kind of edition allows us to see what the original pages actually looked like. The storage capacity of today's personal computers, combined with improvements in image-compression software, make it possible for users to download and store many digital pages on their own computers and so examine many texts at once, an invaluable activity not always possible in rare-book rooms. For all but the most exacting bibliographic readings, high-quality digital images of pages are equivalent and in some cases superior to originals: they can easily be magnified and filtered to make faded text more legible. From a photographic page reproduction, readers are able to see a text in its original context: the typography used to print it, where it was placed on the page, the kind and content of the articles and advertisements that surrounded it.

Furthermore, when a digital image of a page is combined with a word-by-word transcription of its contents, readers can enact a powerful fiction: that they and the computer are reading the same page. When a reader types a word into the search box in a hybrid edition, the computer instantly scrolls the pages to the first occurrence of the word and highlights it, just as a word processor or a Web browser does. What happens behind the scenes is quite different. The search program is not examining a picture of the page but a character encoding of the page, a character encoding in which the position of each word in the image is recorded as a set of coordinates. When it finds the word in the character-encoded transcript, the program uses the accompanying coordinates to position the found word behind the image of that word on the visible page. The success of this simulation depends on the quality of the transcription: if the transcription is truly letter-perfect, and the coordinates are exactly correct, then there will be no discrepancy between the two versions, preserving the illusion that both the user and the computer are "reading" the same text. If the transcription is flawed the simulation falters. If the coordinates are inaccurate, the highlight may be a bit off the visible word in the image—or even some distance from it. If the transcription has errors in spelling or other textual features, the word may not be found in searching, even though it is visible in the image. And, since OCR programs are dictionary based, proper names that are not in the dictionary, along with other unusual words, are the words most likely to be missed, even though they are often just what the searcher wants to find. Searches are a vital feature of digital editions, but we need to use them with caution. Just because a search didn't find a word or a name, that doesn't mean that it isn't there. If the OCR process is hand corrected, such errors are much rarer, but this is an expensive task, avoided by most large-scale digital editions.

Even with faulty transcriptions, however, hybrid editions are powerful resources. If they are composed as actual issues (as in a PDF), they become simulacra of the original magazines: they can be read like magazines, with the reader moving from page to page or issue to issue. But the power of digital editions is compounded when they are collected, cataloged, and encoded, like their paper progenitors. Making a catalog of a magazine's contents—compiling the authors and titles of all the articles, poems, and artwork, and classifying all of the advertisements—takes considerable work to do well. But it makes it possible to perform fielded searches—searches within a particular part of the database for specific kinds of information, like authors or titles—an important complement to full-text search and retrieval. When hybrid editions are brought together into indexed, cataloged collections, they become a searchable, readable database.

It is clear now what a digital edition of a magazine must be designed to do:

- It should reproduce the appearance of the original with sufficient fidelity that the original seldom needs to be consulted: this allows digitization to function at least in part as a preservation method.
- It should reproduce the entire issue, including covers and advertisements. Modern scholarship and modern reading practices require that texts be seen in the context in which they originally appeared.
- It should reproduce the entire run, whenever possible. Not only should all issues be presented in their entirety, adver-

tisements and all; the entire run of a magazine should be available to researchers so that they can comprehend the periodical as a sequential whole, if this is possible.

- It should be broadly searchable. Sometimes a researcher will want to look up an article, a letter, or an image by its creator's name or its title; other times the reader will want to zero in on a discussion by searching the entire text for key words.

- It should be readable. This almost goes without saying, but many digital delivery systems treat everything as though it were an image. Digital simulacra of historical magazines should preserve the "look and feel" of their originals: pages should be legible and turnable; readers should be able to navigate quickly among articles and issues; they should be able to magnify pages to zoom in on small visual details.

With these goals in mind, we can see that producing a really useful digital edition is far from easy, and that it requires the cooperative efforts of people with a variety of skills and backgrounds. Constraints and difficulties must be acknowledged, ranging from issues of copyright to matters of time and money. Given both the ideal and the realities, how should this process be managed? We will make some recommendations about these matters before we end this book, but first we want to share with you some of our experiences with the Modernist Journals Project (MJP, http://www.modjourn.org), since our recommendations are largely based on those experiences.

The MJP began in 1999 with another name: the New Age Project, which had as its goal the production of a digital edition of the weekly review edited by A. R. Orage from 1907 through 1922. Having little experience with digital production, we thought this would not be difficult. At first we hoped to scan from microfilm versions at the British Museum and the Library of Congress. This proved difficult at first and then impossible. The British Museum would not give us permission to do this, and then we found that we could not produce copies from microfilm that would allow for reliable OCR to be performed on them. We might have been able to produce simulations, but not transcriptions, and we wanted both, since we had decided to use the combination of visible image and searchable text offered by PDF for this edition. With microfilm ruled out, we had to find original issues of the magazine, and we were lucky to find a nearly complete set of bound copies in London. The copies we lacked we borrowed from libraries, since we could find none of them for sale.

As the New Age Project progressed, we learned things we had not known when we started. We learned, for example, that OCR accuracy depends on scanning resolution (it needs to be 300 dots per inch or better), and we learned that page images need substantial cleaning up after scanning. We learned that all OCR software is not equal. It gradually became clear that the simple flat-bed scanner and off-the-shelf OCR software we owned had not been designed for the kind of use we were giving it: the processes of image capture and correction, of OCR and its correction, and of binding the results into a format that could be used and delivered via the World Wide Web was both time-consuming and expensive. We used up a substantial starter gift in this process and were fortunate enough to get a grant from the National Endowment for the Humanities to complete the work. Fifty-two issues a year, averaging around twenty pages per issue, for fifteen years—that's a lot of pages to be scanned, OCR'd, and turned into PDFs. We also provided introductions to every six-month volume, and other sorts of supporting scholarship. For example, since artists and artworks were mentioned from time to time, we began generating biographical sketches of artists, along with copies of works mentioned or other typical work by those artists, and linking their names to these biographies. Before we were finished we had more than a thousand such biographical sketches and thousands of digital images of artworks. A digital edition of an important magazine is a complex endeavor, requiring time, energy, ingenuity, and money. Such projects should not be undertaken lightly. While we realized, at some stage in this process, that we should have started with something smaller, we also discovered an enthusiastic base of users for our work, and we knew that we should continue with other projects that would make modernist periodical studies a real possibility for scholars and students everywhere. And so we have. At the close of 2009 the MJP had put online almost a thousand issues of thirty-seven magazines, with more to come.

In the course of this work, we have learned a lot. When we started, for example, we thought that a combined text-and-image PDF would suffice for search and delivery. We soon learned, however, that our work would be much more useful with the sort of metadata that would allow for more complex searches, and with the possibility of other sorts of display, such as thumbnail images of pages and single-page viewing along with the PDFs. Having learned this, we went back and produced the metadata for our earliest editions and changed our methods, so that now the metadata is produced along with the PDFs.

We will discuss metadata more fully later on, but for the moment we must outline the effort that producing it requires. We produce two main types of metadata: descriptive metadata, which records such information as the titles, authors, and genres of each item in an issue, and structural metadata, which describes the arrangement of each issue (on what pages items appear, for example). In addition, we produce a minimally encoded transcription of each issue, one that notes generic information and page breaks. Performing these tasks requires at least a working knowledge of descriptive cataloging and extensible markup language (XML) technology. What all this means is that the whole process—from scanning and the production of images suitable for OCR, the OCR correction, and the generation of metadata—is neither easy nor cheap.

After the massive effort required to produce a digital version of *The New Age,* we found that elite magazines with short runs were much easier to produce, which made them attractive, but our studies of modernism helped us to understand that scholars and students also need access to the large-circulation magazines full of advertising that dominated the modernist period. And that is when we first became aware of the hole in the archive. Brown University has a full run of *Scribner's,* we thought, so let's begin there and do a substantial run of that magazine. When we looked at what was there, however, we discovered that these were bound copies, with all the advertising removed. We then turned to Princeton, where the Scribner Archive is located, only to discover the same thing. Princeton, however, had a substantial number of individual copies and undertook to search for those they lacked in an attempt to assemble a complete run from 1910 through 1922 for digitization by the MJP. That edition is now in progress, though as of this writing there are still some issues we have been unable to locate in unstripped condition. The hole in the archive seems likely to prove extremely difficult to fill. And the catalogs do not always give accurate information about what is there, since they do not distinguish between bound copies and unbound originals. With this in mind, the Brown University Library has started the Cover-to-Cover Initiative, in association with the MJP—a Web page where libraries may share information about holdings of modernist periodicals that are indeed complete, starting with a list of twenty magazines provided by the MJP.

In the course of working on *Scribner's*, we have learned that within the larger holes in the archive there are little ones. Many of the issues that we have lack a few pages at one point or another, the victims of unscrupulous razor blade–wielding collectors or patrons. Frontispieces by artists like Wyeth and Remington go missing from these magazines, and even pages of advertising occasionally are lacking. Where these pages are numbered, as they are in *Scribner's*, we can usually tell when something is gone—but not always, because sometimes the advertising pages are numbered subsequentially (for example, 16a, 16b, 16c), making it difficult to know whether a sequence of pages is complete without comparing several issues. This means that the effort involved in making digital editions of large, advertising-laden magazines will be considerable.

Even when the advertising pages are intact, they can be difficult to digitize. The typography of advertising copy is much more fluid than that of body text, and their wildly varying typefaces, point sizes, and orientations make ads the bane of OCR programs. With advertising making up more than half of a typical issue of magazines like *Scribner's*, it is simply too expensive to hand-correct advertising copy to the same level of accuracy as body copy. At the MJP we have compromised: we make sure that in each ad, every product name is captured correctly at least once. That means a search for "Hupmobile" will not find every instance of that character string, but it will find all the advertisements for that now-forgotten automobile.

We are a long way from the ideal of cover-to-cover digital editions of all the significant modernist magazines, but we must do what we can when we can. For example, if a full run of a magazine is not possible, something less than a full run may still be useful. At the MJP, we digitized *The New Age* not for its entire run but for the fifteen years of Orage's editorship, and, so far, we have digitized *The English Review* only for the fifteen months of Ford's editorship, though we would like to add the continuation of that journal under Austin Harrison from 1910 through 1922. In some cases, it will make sense to do a year, or a decade, or some other coherent period, if a longer run is not available. With the short-lived elite journals, a complete run is essential, and we have done that with all of those we have digitized. With the longer-running magazines a representative, coherent segment will be much better than nothing, so long as the job is done properly, and that is what we have tried to do.

The lessons learned from a decade of digitization, then, inform the recommendations we are going to make here. This is the part of our book that is most tentative, and if past technical recommendations are any indication, the least likely to hold good over the long term. What follows, then, are guidelines and not prescriptions. Ideally, the standards should be high enough to withstand the most exacting use while still being achievable by most digitization projects, but it is important that some standards be followed. Creating the archive we envision must be a collective endeavor: no individual researcher or institution can hope to do it all. But for that archive to be coherent—for it to be searchable and browsable through a single interface, for example—it must be made up of digital editions that share common formats.

Selection

The choice of what magazines to digitize, and when, will best be made by a consortium of interested parties: scholars, librarians, and digitizers. Individual scholars will have their own research agendas that will dictate the kind and degree of their participation; individual libraries will likewise have collections with different strengths. The most important criterion is that the digital editions be complete, at least within the bounds of copyright: the entire run of the magazine, cover to cover. It will be the job of librarians to assess the condition of their collections, which means that a comprehensive clearinghouse of such information that supplements the information already in library catalogs will be essential. Such a clearinghouse will aid scholars in finding intact originals when digital editions are not available, and it will guide digitizers as they assemble complete runs. Often, it will be necessary to combine holdings from a number of libraries in order to put together a full run of original issues of a magazine.

But if full runs are the ideal, constraints often make that ideal unattainable. If, because of copyright, or availability, or sheer size, the entirety of a magazine cannot be digitized, or cannot be digitized at once, then a selection based on significance and coherence should be made. The duration of a powerful editor's reign is usually both significant and coherent: Wallace Martin's book "*The New Age*" *Under Orage* was our inspiration in selecting that fifteen-year run to edit; Ford Madox Ford's (Hueffer's) legendary editorship of the first fifteen issues of *The English Review* constitutes a significant and coherent part of that magazine's life. Austin Harrison's subsequent editorship of *The English Review* is another coherent and significant unit, but it runs past the 1923 copyright line, and so would have to be cleared or curtailed. The point at which a magazine changes its name, or merges with another magazine, is another useful milestone. Thematic coherence can also be taken into account: for *McClure's,* the years 1900–1910 are significant and coherent because those are the great muckraking years.

At this point it is important to realize that there are two sorts of digital projects being undertaken at the present time. There are vast projects for digitizing virtually everything on the shelves of major libraries and making the results available commercially. There are also smaller, more selective projects that offer their results without charge to the scholarly world. At first glance, this may look like a replication of the "mass" versus "little" classification of magazines, but that is really not the case. The large, commercial digitization projects are going to provide only what is on the shelves—not what is carefully preserved in rarebook rooms and similar archives. These projects will omit most of the advertising that was in any magazines they may reproduce. It is the smaller projects that will locate original issues in the archives and reproduce them with all their covers and advertising visible. Both sorts of projects will have their uses, but the users need to be aware of just what they are getting—and not getting—when they are given access to digital editions of modernist magazines. Our discussion, of course, is especially concerned with the smaller, more selective projects, but our hope is that these projects may add up to something that is of major importance to modernist studies.

While individual aims may be specific, the overall goals of the community of modernist scholars, teachers, and their students must be general: to build a comprehensive digital corpus of modernist magazines. Comprehension simplifies things: one need not choose, only prioritize. A number of fine catalogs have been compiled—they are noted in the bibliography—and these can serve as guides, supplemented by continuing research and discovery. Issues of cost, availability, and effort aside, however, there remains the issue of copyright. Digitization is transforming the copyright landscape all over the world, and there are no clear solutions yet to the conflict between protecting the rights of creators and enabling scholarly, noncommercial uses of art and ideas. At present, copyright law in the United States protects everything published after the year 1922, which confines most digital editions of magazines to the years before 1923. As it happens, however, 1922 was a crucial year for modernism, and whole books (like Michael North's *Reading 1922*) have been written about that year and that other landmark year, 1910 (Peter Stansky's *On or About December 1910*). A magazine published after 1922 that owns its own copyright, like *The New Yorker,* can offer for sale a digital edition of its entire run, from 1925 to the present. But scholars who must work in the public domain have to stay in the years before 1923, until the copyright coverage opens up the later years, which will take some time to happen. For the time being, then, we must make a virtue of necessity and recognize 1922 as an important landmark in modernism, which also happens to be the last year for which all published texts are out of copyright in the United States. That year did not mark the end of modernism, of course, but it may be said to mark the end of the beginning—the year by which modernist works in all the genres and media of the time achieved what Gilbert Seldes called "a complete expression of the spirit which will be 'modern' for the next generation" (quoted in North, 3).

Accepting this boundary for digital activities, then, what should be the criteria for ordering and selecting magazines to digitize?

SCHOLARLY VALUE. In few fields might it seem more true that one person's trash is another's treasure. The scholar of

W. B. Yeats's poetry seemingly has little need for Back-lace Corsets, while the student researching advertise-ments for Sanatogen seems to have little call to consult the writings of Virginia Woolf, but, as we have already shown, these things are indeed connected. We have been arguing in this book that all of these parts constitute a whole, because magazines are just what the term says they are—collections or storehouses that include many kinds of visual and verbal texts. It is precisely this vari-ety that makes them such a valuable window into the world of modernism. As Pound warned us so long ago, "You can't know an era merely by knowing its best." We would go further and add that you can't even be sure where the best will be found or what company it keeps. The notion of "scholarly value," then, is not an absolute. It depends, among other things, on pedagogical value. What do we want to learn and what do we want to teach —and which magazines will aid the most in these en-deavors? Those principles must guide us in selecting what to do, and we must be flexible and opportunistic when it comes to making choices. Such choices will quite properly be influenced by local needs and opportunities as they add to the collective effort.

NEED. This is not a simple category. One might think that we need most what we do not have, but there are different levels of having. For example, many libraries have reprint editions of important elite magazines. Does this reduce our need for digital editions of those magazines? In a sense, it does, but if the reprints lack ads that were there in the original (and some reprints, though not all, do indeed lack these) we still need a version of the full original in order to read it properly. But we may not need it as badly as we need a magazine for which there are no reprints available. It may also be extremely useful to add a journal to our searchable database even though printed copies are not especially rare, since searching is a driving force in this whole process. Once again, a local interest may give a particular need more force in choosing what digital projects to undertake. What do you and your students want to study and learn about the world of modernism, and which magazines will contribute the most to that?

BALANCE. As it is being constructed, the whole corpus should contain a healthy mixture of magazines of all sorts, to enable the widest possible use and to discourage accretion of the sort of false generic distinctions we discussed in Chapter 3. Big, little; mass and coterie: the archive should grow in ways that encourage both depth and breadth of scholarship and promote a continuing reassessment of the period. Cooperation among schools and libraries and regular communication about projects and possibilities should be a feature of the entire process.

RANGE. We have indicated why 1922 is a reasonable end date for digital editions of magazines of the modern period, allowing for extension when copyright permits. But what is a reasonable starting date? When did modernism begin? There is no good, decisive answer to this question, though Virginia Woolf's December 1910 offers one firm response. Certainly, magazines from 1910 through 1922 offer a rich field of study. One might wish to start with that period and expand backward and forward. But we would suggest that it makes more sense to start around 1890, since the major transition to magazines supported by advertising revenue begins in the nineties, along with the first flurry of "ephemeral bibelots." Modernism began amid the naturalism and symbolism of the nineties. For all these reasons, we propose 1890 through 1922 as the working dates for digital editions of modernist magazines.

Imaging

If the history of technology is any guide, digital photography will continue to improve, but resolution and overall image quality is already quite high. In 2001–2002, the Digital Library Federation published a specification for what it called faithful digital reproductions: a description of the minimal technical standards that should be applied to digital master copies of monographs and serials. The specification detailed minimum color ranges for page-image masters: black-and-white for text pages, line drawings, and descreened halftones; grayscale for covers and black-and-white illustrations; and full color for covers and "meaningful text or illustrations printed in color." This so-called benchmark is already dated; today most libraries routinely digitize everything in color. The general guideline must be to aim at producing archival-quality images, but libraries should not make the mistake of throwing the originals away once they have been photographed, as the bar of what constitutes archival quality will continue to be raised as technology improves, and it is not unlikely someone will eventually want to photograph these pages again.

Cataloging

Along with the data itself—the page images and the OCR'd text of those pages—it will be extremely important to have good metadata: data about the data, like the title of an article, who wrote it, and when it appeared. As we have shown in earlier chapters, researchers of this material must not only be able to read the pages; they must be able to find them in the first place, and they must be able to perform sophisticated queries about authors, titles, accompanying texts, genres, and other extratextual information. Compiling this quantity of information about a single issue of a magazine is an activity not usually undertaken by libraries: it requires far too much costly work by trained catalogers. The current standards for cataloging periodicals, then, are not adequate for the kinds of search and retrieval enabled by digital editions. Nevertheless, this sort of bibliographic detail is absolutely necessary for the corpus we wish to create.

Among the first things libraries must do is to revise the catalogs they already have to include more detailed information about the condition of their collections: whether the issues have been bound and whether the covers and advertisements have been left intact. And libraries must work closely with digitizers to guide the production of complete and consistent item-level metadata. Consistent adherence to existing metadata standards will facilitate information sharing and searching across repositories. An example is the consistent use of names: if all projects use a common database of names to refer to authors and subjects, it will be possible to conduct searches across the entire corpus. The Library of Congress has just such a database, used by librarians around the world. Using a common, "authorized" form of a name also makes it possible to link supporting materials like glosses and biographical sketches to diverse occurrences of the name. And designing browsing tools to use authority records like the Library of Congress's to broaden name searches to all the known forms of a name will make those tools much more useful. Anyone who has ever searched for Chekhov and missed references to Tchekhov or Checkov will know what we mean.

Metadata Representation

Over the past few years, the library and digital humanities communities have begun to settle on standards for encoding bibliographic information. The emergence of XML as a lingua franca for data representation and text encoding has made this consolidation possible.

Extensible markup language (XML) is simply a set of conventions for annotating text or data so that it may be interpreted. For example, this sequence of digits is hard to make sense of:

241136

But if it is marked up properly its meaning can be much clearer:

```
<lockCombination>
<left>24</left>
<right>11</right>
<left>36</left>
</lockCombination>
```

XML is not, in fact, a complete language in the traditional sense of that word. It is really a grammar, a set of rules that specify, for example, that one must signal the beginnings and ends of things with tags, which are written as sequences of letters between angle brackets, but it doesn't specify what those sequences of letters must be. We are referring to "sequences" instead of "words" because not all the sequences used in XML are words in English. A particular set of sequences, however, and rules about how they may be combined constitutes a language in XML. Figure 8.1 provides an example from a language librarians use to describe bibliographic entries.

There are, of course, other, less verbose ways to represent the bibliographic information about this poem, but this format has the advantage of being readable by both programs and human beings: if you know this language (a language called MODS, for Metadata Object Description Schema), then you will be able to interpret this statement about Pound's poem. More important, perhaps, is the fact that a search engine can read this language and take a reader to the issue of *Blast* in which Pound's poem appeared. MODS is one of several XML description languages that have emerged as standards in the digital library community. Any project in the digital humanities will do well to adopt these standards as closely as possible, so that painstaking research and work can be shared with others, which is, after all, the chief aim of scholarship.

Annotation

It is important to remember that producing digital editions of modern magazines should not simply be a preservation exercise, the digital equivalent of a microfilming campaign. Useful though such an exercise would be in providing broader access to rare materials to a larger audience of scholars, it would do little to make those magazines accessible to students with scant knowledge of the past century. That is why the production of such editions must be a cooperative effort among digital preservationists and scholars, and why the technical infrastructure on which this corpus is built must enable the development of a critical apparatus of notes and glosses. With proper guidance, students at all levels can be involved in

```xml
<?xml version="1.0" encoding="UTF-8"?>
<mods xmlns="http://www.loc.gov/mods/v3">
  <titleInfo>
    <title>Salutation the Third</title>
  </titleInfo>
  <name type="personal">
    <namePart type="given">Ezra</namePart>
    <namePart type="family">Pound</namePart>
    <role>
      <roleTerm>creator</roleTerm>
    </role>
  </name>
  <relatedItem type="host">
    <titleInfo>
      <title>Blast</title>
      <subTitle>Review of the Great English Vortex</subTitle>
      <partNumber>Number 1</partNumber>
    </titleInfo>
    <name type="personal">
      <namePart type="family">Lewis</namePart>
      <namePart type="given">Wyndham</namePart>
      <role>
        <roleTerm>editor</roleTerm>
      </role>
    </name>
    <originInfo>
      <place>
        <placeTerm>London</placeTerm>
      </place>
      <publisher>John Lane, the Bodley Head</publisher>
      <dateIssued>1914-06-20</dateIssued>
    </originInfo>
    <part>
      <extent unit="pages">
        <start>45</start>
        <end>45</end>
      </extent>
    </part>
  </relatedItem>
</mods>
```

Fig. 8.1. A sample record, slightly simplified, showing bibliographic information (often called metadata by librarians) about an item in a magazine encoded in an XML schema called MODS.

the research necessary to bring the modernist past to life. We all have things to learn about that foreign country that is the past.

Collective scholarship like this makes some librarians and scholars uneasy. Librarians, in general, like to keep their authority files to themselves so they can manage and protect them, and most professional academics prefer to publish their work in refereed journals or with serious academic presses, so that they can be rewarded with professional credit. Futurists have been predicting the demise of academic presses and the rise of digital publishing for some time, but an online academic publishing establishment seems unlikely to appear any time soon. Instead, there is the World Wide Web, with its exhilarating and bewildering hodgepodge of uncorrected information sources, and expensive commercial databases, access to which is often restricted to students and affiliates of research universities willing to pay for them.

What is needed, then, is a widely accessible scholarly editorial apparatus that is closely linked to the digitized magazines, a comprehensive database of information about the world of modernism whose content is as easy to retrieve as Wikipedia's while retaining the virtues of accuracy and consistency. This apparatus can be built by students and scholars working with programmers, so that the information generated is indeed accurate and also linked to the digital editions of modernist magazines and accessible from those editions.

Storage

There is no doubt that a comprehensive collection of digitized magazines will require large amounts of digital storage. Because the costs and capacities of storage devices continue to change so rapidly, however, there is little reason to discuss hardware here. More important is the strategy for storage and retrieval of digital assets. Initiatives like LOCKSS (Lots of Copies Keep Stuff Safe), based at Stanford University (http://www .lockss.org/), promote a decentralized model for storage, in which copies of files are housed and preserved by a number of participating institutions, so that the loss or corruption of one archive does not destroy their materials. As long as there is an agreed-upon reference scheme, the corpus of digital editions can be distributed across many sites and the work of producing them can proceed like any other work of scholarship: the piece-by-piece assembly of a whole.

Reproduction

Mass digitization projects, like Google Books and others, have demonstrated that it is feasible to produce page images that are backed by uncorrected OCR transcriptions in very large quantities at reasonable cost. Are such objects adequate? They certainly are better than nothing. With nothing else added, they fulfill a number of our criteria for digitized magazines: objects like these are discoverable, searchable, and readable. They get the issues into the hands of readers, which is of first importance. But as we have seen, the modernist scholarly community could benefit from a corpus of magazines that is focused on modernity and modernism. What is needed, to begin with, is a body of digital texts, providing both images of the original pages and a searchable text based on corrected OCR and cataloged using a common set of encoding standards. These, in turn, can be the basis of scholarly and editorial work extending into the future.

For we are talking about phased work here. Network-based distribution has changed the nature of publishing: no longer must publication of important scholarly resources await the completion of exhaustive and painstaking editorial work so that it may all appear at once, between the same covers. The same editorial care must be applied to materials that are published digitally, but the continuing work of editors can be released incrementally, while the initial fruits of their labors are made available to readers as soon as they are ripe.

This means that a complete corpus of full-fledged hybrid editions of magazines, with full descriptive metadata and text encoding, should be the goal of the modernist magazine community. But we must be willing to achieve that goal, not just one magazine at a time but one level of detail at a time. A complete, cover-to-cover digital reproduction of a magazine, with page images produced to a consistent standard and with corrected OCR, is preferable to a partial run with more elaborate metadata. We should aim for breadth of coverage over depth of metadata in the first place, followed as quickly as possible by detailed description and encoding.

Retrieval

So far we have been concerned with the production of a modern magazine corpus. Of lesser importance is the way this corpus is made available to its users, and it is to this concern that we turn next.

But why is it of lesser importance? The reason is not that preservation trumps use: there would be little reason to create these artifacts if no one were going to read them in one fashion or another. No, the reason we are less concerned with delivery systems and interfaces is that the technology behind them continues to change very rapidly, while the data and the metadata, once captured and created, remain relatively constant. We have already cautioned against throwing any magazines away after they have been photographed, because digital image capture will certainly continue to improve. Similarly, optical character recognition still has a long way to go. And while libraries have a long history of cataloging and describing periodical literature, we have seen that they have seldom allocated resources to producing the kinds of descriptions we require, so the metadata about modern magazines will certainly need to be revised. Still, the technologies for representing and storing information are far more settled than those for retrieving, delivering, and presenting it. User interface technologies—existing display devices like screens and emerging technologies like digital paper; existing input devices like keyboards and mice and improving technologies like voice recognition—are likely to be unrecognizable in a few years: optimistic futurists have been saying this for decades, but this time, so far, they've been right. They've been right, too, about the continuing increase in bandwidth, or the speed with which information can be transmitted. And the software of user interfaces—the methods for searching texts and images, the techniques for visualizing quantitative information, and the tools for viewing and navigating digital images and hybrid texts—is still in a very primitive state. It is therefore premature to give any specific recommendations or guidelines about how to deliver the digital corpus to scholars, students, and readers. Still, we can provide some general criteria.

- Readers should be able to see reflections of the original pages in the highest fidelity possible, so the interface must be able to present high-resolution copies of the magazines in readable ways: the pages must be navigable (basic page turning, plus other ways of skipping around in an issue and among issues), and they must be magnifiable (so that a reader may zoom in on small visual details).

- Because users will have different bandwidth connections to the information (different kinds of displays, different kinds of network connections), content-delivery software will need to provide the magazines in different formats.

- Besides reading the texts, researchers must be able to treat the body of magazines as a corpus and as a database. They must be able to make sophisticated queries against the full text of the corpus as a matter of course, but they should also be able to treat it as a mine of information, and a good user interface should provide tools for extracting that information and making sense of it, through visualizations of various sorts.

No single system will provide all the tools researchers require. The diversity of uses to which scholars, researchers, and readers will put this information makes it imperative that it be maintained in open systems whose contents and metadata can be queried and harvested by other systems. The idea of federated systems with many portals, rather than monolithic systems with a single point of entry, has become more widespread in recent years with the advent of new techniques for pushing and pulling information around the Web. This means the information architects designing and fashioning this corpus/database should carefully consider data- and information-exchange protocols, so that they can provide a variety of ways for people and programs to query and retrieve information.

Rights Management

We have mentioned the complex issue of global copyright, and we have suggested that in the short term digitizers confine their efforts to the period before 1923 in order to remain safely within the law. In the long term, however, such a conservative approach to intellectual property rights will inevitably hamper research and scholarly inquiry. Those individuals and institutions digitizing the modern magazine corpus should closely monitor developments in the legal realm, and they should also be mindful of developments in digital rights management software and techniques. Proper encoding and metadata creation make it possible to restrict access to portions of a magazine protected by copyright while making the rest available.

We've reiterated throughout this chapter the collective, cooperative nature of this endeavor. It won't be accomplished by a single scholar, clearly, or even by a single institution. And it won't be achieved overnight. This, like so many acts of scholarship, is a long-term task, a structure that will be built by many hands. It doesn't have to be a tightly coordinated effort, but it will benefit enormously from a common set of standards and practices, so that each digitized magazine fits well into a growing whole. We have spent some time in this chapter describing, in outline, what those standards and common practices should be.

What can individual students and scholars of modernism do? In most cases, they should not run the scanners themselves; the equipment for doing the job right is very expensive, and scholars should resist the temptation to engage in amateur digitization projects. They may put a lot of work into producing something that will not be very useful to the scholarly community as a whole. But there are many other tasks besides producing actual digital reproductions that can contribute to the enterprise.

One of the most important tasks, early on, is locating or establishing full and complete runs of magazines. In the simplest case, a full run is held, intact, in a single archive, where it may be studied—and digitized —as a whole. But in many cases libraries and archives will have scattered holdings, and full runs will have to be constructed by piecing together the holdings of a number of archives and libraries. Individual scholars can make a useful contribution simply by canvassing the holdings in their institutions and reporting the findings to a central location where this information can be shared.

Another important task that can be distributed across the scholarly and library communities is generating metadata for the magazines:

the issue-by-issue compilation of authors and titles that facilitates searching and browsing the archive. The work of cataloging does not need to
coordinate closely with that of digitization, if the digital images of magazines are made available to scholars as they are completed. Libraries are
surprisingly ill-equipped to generate the needed metadata: they cannot
afford it, and there is, in fact, little precedent for performing detailed cataloging on periodicals. But the standards for metadata capture (like
MODS) are sufficiently well established that the work could be performed
by students with proper guidance. In the best case, their work would be
aided by software tools and library supervision for quality control, and
the results of that work would be submitted to the modernist journals
archive.

In other words, like much scholarship, these digital editions can
grow organically. The combination of ubiquitous networks and standard
forms of representation will make distributed yet coordinated work possible, if the following principles are adopted:

- *An architecture for distributed editions.* The community will
  need to work with information technologists to devise or
  adopt a suite of protocols that allow data and metadata to
  flow freely among cooperating scholars and institutions.
  There need not be a single, monolithic repository for all of
  these materials, but there must be ways to browse, search,
  and access the archive as though it were a unified whole.
- *An architecture for preservation.* The project of digitizing
  modern magazines needs to be coordinated with other
  preservation efforts, in order to avoid duplicated effort and
  to ensure the long-term availability of the digital editions.
- *Authority control.* In order to coordinate the scholarly apparatus that supports these materials (so they may be in-
  terlinked and cross-referenced easily and reliably, for example), there must be agreement on terms of reference.
  Agencies like the Library of Congress can serve as the authority for established names, but because this work delves
  into obscure regions of twentieth-century culture, general
  authority databases will be insufficient. The community of

modernist periodical scholars must establish its own authority and agree to abide by it, just as it does with so many other aspects of scholarly publication.

Clearly, there is still much work to be done in dealing with the hole in the archive, and we have tried to suggest just how this work should proceed. But we also want to insist that enough has been done already to make the study of modernist magazines a real possibility. And we wish to conclude by urging scholars and teachers to make the most of the digital resources that are now becoming available in this area. The period in which modernism arose in the English-speaking world was the last moment when print was the dominant medium of communication. It was the moment in which the new audiovisual media began their rise to dominance; the moment in which the automobile and the airplane changed transportation drastically; the moment in which advertising achieved a new prominence in human affairs; and, finally, it was a moment in which literature and the other traditional arts were more important than they will ever be again, allowing Ezra Pound and his friends to flourish. The magazines of this moment offer us an unsurpassed way of introducing students to this world, from which our own emerged. And now, thanks to digital editions of these magazines, we can open that world to our students, so that they can discover it for themselves and connect it to their own lives. Let us not miss this opportunity.

Appendix

Studies in Contemporary Mentality

EZRA POUND

Note:

These twenty articles, which constitute a series that appeared in *The New Age* from August 1917 to January 1918, are reprinted with text reproduced accurately except for spacing changes due to the shift from narrow columns to these pages. (This is a transcription, not a facsimile. For a facsimile of the original, see the digital edition at www.modjourn.org.) Pound's series was pioneering work in that branch of cultural criticism now recognized as "periodical studies." In it, Pound looked at the magazines of the day in England, ranging from small religious papers to grand quarterlies and popular monthlies. It is more like a contemporary blog than a formal essay in criticism, with Pound taking up one or more magazines every week and recounting his adventures in both seeking them out and actually reading them. But he also aspired to use the whole group as a way of exposing for critical attention what he called "contemporary mentality," which we might describe as the dominant ideology of Britain in 1917–1918. He referred to these articles as "a series of satires" and a "*sottisier*" or collection of stupidities. They are those things, but they are also more, as the attentive reader will discover.

Because this study is resolutely "contemporary" and also nearly a century old, there are many names and other references that may be unfamiliar to current readers. The past is, indeed, another country. Experts in modernism will need no assistance with this material, but students may feel lost occasionally in the contemporary mentality of 1917. Our suggestion is that these articles be used as a point of entry into that other world, with students dividing up the articles for annotation, and Googling or searching in more traditional ways for references like "Anthony Comstock." The story of Comstock and the censorship associated with his name is too long for a footnote and worthy of a full report in the classroom, as an interesting piece of "contemporary mentality" in the America of 1917. And this information is not hard to find. Unlike many of the references in Pound's long poem *The Cantos,* these are not personal and obscure allusions but are public references and widely available.

Some of these references, of course, lead outside the English-speaking world. For example, Unanimism, which Pound mentions more than once, was the doctrine of a group of French poets led by Jules Romain, who believed that poetry should express a collective consciousness. Pound was interested in it but opposed. He was an individualist, as these articles certainly demonstrate. But Britain in the time of the First World War is the main focus of Pound's articles. His bitter critique opens one window onto that world. It is not the only viewpoint, to be sure, but it has the value of being internal to this time and place as well as emotionally engaged with it. He was there, and he was not happy with the way the media were representing that world at that time. These articles are his report on what he found in the popular periodicals of the day, as he read them in "the Metropolis," London. (A sampling of covers from these magazines may be seen in plate 8.)

1. "The Hibbert"
AUGUST 16, 1917
[SEE PLATE 8 FOR AN IMAGE OF THE COVER.]

UNANIMISM would counsel me to regard "The Hibbert" as a personality or "un dieu"; introspection permits me only the feeling that it is a vague tract, a nebulous aggregate stretching in no well-defined dimension "somewhere" between Mr. Balfour's lighter moments and the high seriousness of the Countess of Warwick. The name has been familiar to me for some years. Since my arrival in the Metropolis I have been ac-

customed, among what Mr. H——— calls "those few over-cultured people," to hear the phrase "an article in 'The Hibbert.'" I had never read
"The Hibbert"; I had never opened "The Hibbert" until about a year ago
when I was asked to review a single number of it in a bundle of review-
books for the "International Journal of Ethics." Vaguely I imagined "The
Hibbert" going its way in Mayfair, lying upon tables in political country
houses, proceeding from "libraries" to the humbler houses of the Ken-
singtons West and South-West and thence into the provinces. Never, to
my recollection, was the "article in 'The Hibbert'" baptized. It was "an
article in 'The Hibbert'"; it had no name and no author.

"The Hibbert" is "a Quarterly Review of Religion, Theology, and
Philosophy." My earliest distinct and, I venture to say, durable, if not permanent, impression of it is of the Countess of Warwick discoursing on
the joys of maternity: abundant breasts, of rather the Viennese pattern,
the pressing of small reddish hands, a facile and boundless fruitfulness.
The memory of her enthusiasm has led me again to "The Hibbert" as a
starting-point for this research. "Of that Pierian spring I would again . . . ."
I rise disappointed. The pasture in the Hibbertian Helicon is less rich than
I had supposed.

One gentleman recommends that the local post-office should bear the
national coat of arms duly and properly blazoned, in order that the divorce
between art and life be somewhat healed, and the wounds to sensibility,
caused by our being familiar with the coat of arms only in vilely engraved
advertisements, be filled with improving balsam. (Current number.)

The Dean of St. Paul's, a master of technique, opens his broadminded—I am not sure that for ecclesiastics the word should not be
spelled without the hyphen, thus, broadminded article: "The recrudes-
cence of superstition in England was plain to all observers many years
before the war." The reader is at once intrigued to know how the Dean
of St. Paul's is going to justify his own job and existence. It is, however,
only an aniseed-bag, a rhetorical device, a wagging of the legs to draw an-
telope. We go on to "the absorption of society in gain and pleasure" and
an attack on clairvoyants and mediums, whose existence "proves that the
Christian hope of immortality burns very dimly among us." (I have not
deciphered the function of the sectarian adjective in this sentence, but
the reader can seek at the source.)

Secondly, he, the Dean, says: "the clerical demagogue showed more interest in the unemployed than in the unconverted." Whether this "interest" was platonic or watchful he does not state. He proceeds until he reaches contact with the recent democratisation of Heaven. I am there on a firmer footing; I have perused (I think "peruse" is the verb one applies in such cases), perused a recent theological work which deplores the excessive use of "monarchical metaphor" in descriptions of deity. Let me return to Dean Inge. He does not believe that Eternity is an Eternal Now. He considers that "A Christian must feel that the absence of any clear revelation about a *future* (italics his, not mine) state is an indication that we are not meant to make it a principal subject of our thoughts."

The bulk of this number is concerned with "Survival" and "Immortality," whereanent Laurent Tailhade years since on Stanislas de Guaita (not in "The Hibbert"): "Les gens tiennent à conserver leur *moi,* en raison directe de son insignifiance. Un fait bien digne de remarque, c'est l'acharnement à maintainir sans fin leur vie intellectuelle de ceux qui n'ont jamais vécu par le cerveau." I am convinced that many good Hibbertians have read "Raymond."

The Rev. Canon Rawnsley says: "The increase of juvenile delinquents demands the serious attention of all the churches." He endorses some people who "agree with the Leeds commission in deploring the passion for the kinema show among juveniles."

And yet, "and yet," despite their peculiar dialect, the perusal of several numbers of the magazine leaves one with the impression that for both the lay and reverend members of its contributariat the prevailing opinion is that "the Church" is definitely worn out, ready only for the scrap heap, BUT that *the* question is: Here are a lot of fat jobs or at least "comfortable livings." Leisure is excellent, we must maintain as many people of leisure as possible. A gentleman (of sorts) in every village. The kindly and tired black back of the elderly cleric must not totally disappear from the islands in the street crossings. We are all very tired. New blood is wanted, and sought, me hercule! sought, in far distant Montana, whence an "English Professor," or Professor of English, assures them that he is "convinced that the average college man is giving far more thought to the question of religion than the average non-college man of the same age." "Of college girls" he "can not say so much." The undergraduate seems inclined to regard the Scriptures as fairy tales, but "let no one think religion is a dead issue in American colleges." (Now we know where it has gone to. It has not, like the "English Review," sought asylum in the genteel parlours of Edinburgh; it has nestled into the American colleges.) So much for the Quarterly Review of Religion. The Hibbertian Theology I am but ill fitted to cope with.

I find a thoughtful article by A. D. McLaren on German Hate. Mr. Edward M. Chapman, of New London, Conn., U.S.A., indulges the national passion—I mean the lust for quotation. He heaps up his Pelions on his Ossas. "War," says he, in his opening,—

" "War," says Emerson, "quoting Heraclitus"" . . .

No, I am not quite through with "The Hibbert's" religion and vocabulary. The Rt. Rev. J. W. Diggle, D.D., says: "In its widest connotation the term sacrament is immeasurably vast; for it includes all cognizable signs of the presence and attributes of the Invisible God." In his two opening paragraphs (about two-thirds of a page) I find the following symptoms: "scrolls of the ages"; "stability of righteousness"; "providential dealings"; "unseen Hand"; "all these—the starry heavens, the rainbow . . . the feeding of sparrows, the moral constitution of the world"; "the certificates of His presence with them"; "His faithful soldiers."

But let us proceed to "education" and the prominent Mr. Begbie. "The task of the schoolmaster is therefore to quicken the intelligence of children while at the same time he develops the fundamental qualities of their English character." (Drake? Hawkins? or Mr. Begbie?)

"Now there are three things which the State demands directly or indirectly in its citizens. It demands that they shall be moral, intelligent and healthy." "No parent ought to be allowed to interfere with a system which is a State system of education."

He sets forth the "ineradicable individualism"; although great intelligence "is not the shining quality" of the English, yet the "germ of it" is to survive the non-by-parent-interfered-with cram-gewissenschaft of the State, whereto the "apathy of the public" is at present the gravest danger or obstacle. It is, in his ideal England, "for the Board of Education to prevent" millions of people from living as if there were "no Wordsworth . . . no Shelley . . . no Dickens," millions who now (in the unregenerate now) eat shrimps "out of paper bags at Blackpool, Yarmouth, and Skegness," despite the "very gracious, tolerant and attractive aristocracy of intelligence" which ornaments this collection of islands, as we know them.

Despite Mr. Begbie's effort to compensate me for the absence of new anti-Malthusian dithyrambics from the Countess, it is only Mr. Crozier (page 572) who presents me with the quintessence of Hibbertism, and rewards my morning of patience.

"With Mr. Wells' new book on Religion—'God the Invisible King'—flaming like a comet in the sky," begins Mr. John Beattie Crozier, who next sets forth some "thoughts that have taken definite form" in his mind on Practical Religion. He asks what "a given human individual" (male, evidently) is to "do in the matter of religion," and decides that it should not be a straight line but a "rising and falling curve rather like the sun in the heavens." "As an infant he will start as a mere blank point or zero emerging from Eternity," as a boy, "an animal mainly thinking of his food." (Shakespeare's mighty line hovers behind Mr. C.) In early life as Matthew Arnold's "barbarian" he "plays the game."

"Later still, let us say as a public school boy (who has always been my ideal for this time of life), let him still 'play the game,' but under stricter control, with religion still a dribblet, but combined with the beginning of real education and culture," "inflexible personal honour." "As a young man" (and so he plays his part) "he is now to put on all his 'feathers' and seek to gain the favourable glances of the fair sex, which he can not do with all his mere knowledge and rough physical prowess" (Kama Sutra, Mr. C. ?) "unless he adds to them gentleness and grace of manners and of form and even of personal adornment" as a "stepping stone to the ideal." (Kama Sutra or Mrs. Hodgson Burnett? We must remember the specification about the rising and falling curve, like the sun in, etc. . . .)

Then Mr. C. prescribes a transition stage in which "the society of a g. and v. woman must be his tutor." His religion the "decent," the "right thing." "It must be that of the 'gentleman' and 'man of honour' in Captain Hawtrey's sense of the term." "But if at this stage he could add to this the attitude of mind of a really Christian 'converted man,'" etc., "that indeed, in my judgment, would be well-nigh perfection itself!"

The exclamation point is Mr. Crozier's. He then goes on to Phaeton, the Kaiser, renunciation, but despite his Phaetons, and their possible, profound, arcane connection with the flaming comets and sun-symbols of his outset, "The Hibbert" is not so entertaining as the Countess had led me in hope to suppose.

2. "Blackwood's"
AUGUST 23, 1917
[SEE PLATE 8.]

"UNANIMISM," as I said of "The Hibbert," would counsel me to regard "Blackwood's" as a personality or un dieu, introspection presents me with a brown cover, printed closely, very closely, in fact, and double columns. The object rests on the magazine rack, always on the magazine rack of a club or a library, any club, any library. I can conscientiously state that I have never seen a copy of Blackwood's in any private house whatsoever. Many people would cavil at its inclusion under my general heading. Never till now, never until this time when a passion to carry realism further than Zola has led me to record the details of human utterance as carefully as he recorded the newspaper details relative to "La Débàcle," have I read a copy of "Blackwood's," never has my eye performed the Gargantuan feat of penetrating its double-columns.

Eight years ago, M., who is not always truthful, alleged that he had met a mythical Blackwood, "Old Blackwood," a man such as we are; and that this man was pleasing, and a cynic, and that he printed N. not because he believed in N.'s work or liked it, but solely because "people like that sort of thing."

But I repeat, M. is not always truthful, and I have even forgotten whether it was really N. who had been so lavishly paid for appearing in "Blackwood's." Neither M. nor any other man I have met has ever claimed to have preceded me in the reading of this review. I am, for all I know to the contrary, a lonely De Gama doubling an uncharted cape.

(Parenthesis: Since writing the above I have pushed inquiry further. One of the most learned officials of the Museum Britannicum assured me that "No one ever read 'Blackwood's.'" Not content with this, I sought an officer of the old Army, who to my question replied firmly: "Yes, I have read 'Blackwood's,' and damn dull it was, too. I hear, since the war, they have gained a good deal of kudos by a sort of Chauvinism which nothing in Germany matches."

He has been wounded in earlier wars than the present, but I consider his statement exaggerated. I think he underestimates the Hun power.)

"Blackwood's" bears on its cover the following statement: "'Blackwood's' represents and appeals to all that is best in the undying genius of the race."—The "Times," Feb. 1, 1913.

I should hardly have expected to catch the "Times" in such an orgy of misanthropy. However, let us examine literature, the deathless voice of all the world, as presented in "Blackwood's."

"Isn't to-day sweet enough for you, mon ami? Just you and I and a punt and a perfect summer's day. Do be reasonable, and let's enjoy the present while we may."—P. 2, "Blackwood's" short story.

Opening of p. 4.—"How could anyone of ordinary flesh and blood be reasonable in a punt with Nan?, How altogether desirable she looked, half sitting, half lying, etc. . . . one graceful bare arm, etc. Nan's fingers would make anything infinitely precious."

P. 10.—"The fair, sparse moustache. . . ."

P. 11.—"What a boy he looked!"

P. 16.—"Only five times this week."

P. 17.—"Asked you to marry me."

P. 12 of it, second column.—"Thank the Lord he was dead before the Askaris reached him. He struck a match to light his pipe."

P. 14 column 2.—"He had tried again and again to forget."

Last page.—"Then as she stood up arranging her hair."

NEXT STORY.

"Typical seamen of the British Mercantile Marine, bronzed and breezy."

"It was plain he regarded the packet as of great importance."

"No worthy woman would willingly part for an hour, etc. . . ."

"His tears are very near; his throat chokes: what memories."

"Gentle Jesus, meek and mild,
Look upon this little child."

"Even so, Lord Jesus."—Still "Blackwood's."

POESY.

"I wish that I could be a Hun, to dive about the sea,
I wouldn't go for merchant men—a man-of-war for me.

. . . . . .

And help our eyes at the periscope as the High Seas Fleet goes by."

Anonymous, page 173, "Blackwood's," possibly not by Kipling.

TRAVEL BROADENS THE MIND.

"A summer's dawn in Kashmir is a lovely thing . . . My own destination is the Chasuma Shahi . . . I drive along the barred highway. . . ."

THOUGHT.

"We are in the midst of the greatest war of history."—June, 1917.

"The proposal to hold all elections upon one day is another sop to
the Radicals and a resolute attempt to make the plural vote of no effect . . . etc. . . . mere trick to win the approval of the Labour Party . . . etc.
If we are electing members to the unpaid service of their country, we
should not have a word to say against it. But as we provide the successful candidate with sinecure appointments of £400 a year, we think that
they should risk their own money in competing for the prize. . . ."

ETC.

"Bagpipe Ballads," "Roving Lads," "Adventures of an Ensign" (sic).

"The veteran acted as his own cook . . . parti carre dined under an
apple-tree, beneath the stars, off three young ducks and two young chick-
ens, with delicious fresh peas and new potatoes."

THE ADVENTURES OF AN ENSIGN.

"The battalion arrived at B———."

MORE THOUGHT.

"Such a man as M. Cailloux, whose activities do not seem to be at
an end, could flourish only in the close atmosphere of a democracy."

This year is of especial interest to the readers of "Blackwood's"—
it celebrates its century; thus, in the April number:—

"It is given to few enterprises to look back with pride and compla-
cency upon a history of 100 years, to contemplate a long work well
achieved, to one end and with one unbroken policy. . . .

"Hand to hand in ceaseless succession the lamp has been passed, alight
and duly trimmed; and we who are the lantern-bearers of to-day run our

course the more gladly because a 'Blackwood' still leads us, and because
the rugged face of George Buchanan still frowns upon our standard. . . ."

(Note: This possibly explains the curious cover.)

The writer of the above then goes on to the magazine's tradition;
recalls the "almost mythical heroes," Lockhart, Coleridge, de Quincey;
leaps upon Trollope, mentions Reade, and, again, in his inspiriting ore
rotundo, addresses us:—

"No better example, then, of the force of tradition could be found
in the annals of letters than the House of Blackwood. Its continuity is unbroken."

Its continuity is indeed unbroken. Mr. Whibley has a hard case to
make out for his suzerains. In the whole pageant of English literature
since the days of Coleridge and de Quincey, the one notable name he
can seize upon is that of Anthony Trollope, the one name his compla-
cent finger can point to, the one lamppost to which he can cling in his
"contemplation." Since Trollope; no one! not only among the men under
forty, but among our elders and among the generation of their fathers!
Dickens, God knows he was popular enough not to have been ruled out
on mere grounds of rapacity; Thackeray, Browning, Meredith, Fitzgerald, Rosetti, Swinburne, Henry James, Thomas Hardy?

Tradition at its best, tradition of which no better example is to be
found, has excluded them all from the pages of "Blackwood's." Let us,
therefore, join the Conservative party, let us leave off being moderns,
let us no longer be the young knocking at the door; we have this perfect
paragon of a publishing house looking after the national literature. We
may go our ways in deep silence. Since de Quincey there has been only
Trollope and Charles Reade. Synge was a Celt and a foreigner. Hawthorne
worked in a Customs house. France is on the other side of the Channel,
but the house of Blackwood remains.

Its magazine "represents and appeals to all that is best in the undying genius of the race." The responsible ministers of the "Times" have
gone bail for it.

"Blackwood's" represents all the best. We are wearied with mediocrity, let us drink of this pure Castalian, let us have only Falernian, let us
cease to ask for periodicals other than those whose perenniality is assured
by the continuity of town libraries and club libraries as subscribers. Let us

be orthodox, let us seek "sound opinion," let us annihilate ourselves before this triumphal centennial car, let us prostrate before Mr. Whibley.

3. On Quarterly Publications
AUGUST 30, 1917
[SEE PLATE 8.]

"THE Quarterly" must be done in extenso, or not at all. One cannot approach it on the basis of scattered paragraphs. It is a very solid review. One must take a centennial survey. It does not indulge, at least, it does not appear to indulge, in the facile imbecilities and crankism of "The Hibbert," or in the braggadocio of the Centennial "Blackwood." Its staff do not write about themselves as "light-bearers," etc. I must give my notes upon it time to mature.

The "Edinburgh" differs from it, superficially, in that it prints Gosse. The "Quarterly" does not, or at least has not, for some time printed Gosse. More anon.

The "London Quarterly" (current) divides itself between Gosse, Swinburne; God and Mr. Wells.

The "Church Quarterly" (Art. II, headed in the manner of Quarterlies, "Art., etc."), treats "De Partu Virginis," not in the manner of Sannazaro, but under the title, "The Virgin Birth from a Biological Standpoint." Sir Francis Champneys, M.D., F.R.C.P., says that

"Having been asked a short time ago to speak on the subject of the Virgin Birth, and having been urged to put into writing what I then said, I have decided to attempt to do so. The audience which I addressed was a Christian audience; and, indeed, nothing would have induced me to speak on this subject as I have done to any other sort of assembly. Nor do I now address my remarks except to those who are able to repeat the Creeds *ex animo* or who desire to be able to do so."

He was asked because of "having spent a long professional life among the mysteries of generation and birth." He continues:—

"It cannot therefore be because the mystery of generation is known that the difficulty arises with the birth of Christ. The difficulty arises in the way of *Experience*. In the human species two parents are (as a matter of experience) necessary."

This is not however "universal law," *vide* the Parthenogenesis of Aphides or Green Blight during the summer months.

"Also in the human body many tissues (bones, teeth, hair, etc.), are commonly produced in certain ovarian tumours."

Sir Francis, however, does not wish to be taken as declaring that the Saviour of Mankind was produced after this fashion. He merely illustrates that "exuberance of growth is a sign of life in all tissues." He points out that Luke, "himself a physician," bears testimony to the original events. But he weakens his argument (at least, in my own opinion, it is weakened) by going back to William Harvey A.D. 1653) for further corroboration. He considers the parthenogenesis an "outpost" of incarnation, and believes it should not be given up unless one is prepared to abandon or endanger "incarnation."

(Parenthesis: For those who are sincerely anxious to be able to repeat the Creeds *ex animo* we suggest the use of an ephemeris. It will be noted that many people are born each year "under Virgo." Astrology is much older than modern microscopical science. A slight misunderstanding of case-forms is enough to account for miraculous statements, especially as the story comes to us not in the language of Jerusalem, but in a suburban, hyper-colonial Greek. It places no strain on anyone's credulity to suppose that astrological statements about a nativity might have become a little distorted in the transcription, or even oral tradition, into a foreign tongue. The shifting of the date to coincide with that of the Saturnalia occurred, we presume, somewhat later.)

What Sir Francis' abuse of the Hun and his allusions to the "spiritual home" at the end of his essay "De Partu" have to do with that subject on either a biological or theological basis, I am unable to descry.

He is followed by the Baron Fr. von Hügel, who asks, "What Do We Mean by Hell?" One is inclined to refer him to Billy Sunday, who alone, among moderns, appears to hold definite views. However, the "Church Quarterly" has punctuated this query rather curiously; it reads, verbatim:—

"What Do We Mean by Heaven? And What Do We Mean by Hell? A synthetic attempt by Baron F. von Hugel."

That answer may do as well as another. Ten years ago the "Church

Quarterly" reduced its price from 6s. to 3s. the copy; now, owing to the increased cost (150 per cent. on paper) it has been forced to rise again to 4s.

I deeply regret that our town library does not file the back numbers of this highly interesting publication.

The "Edinburgh" is aware both of literature and theology. Sir A. Quiller-Couch begins upon Gosse (Edmund, C.B.) (a man of whom no young man will speak evil) as follows:—

"It is always a pleasure to read a book by a man who knows how books should be written, and Mr. Gosse's eagerly awaited 'Life of Swinburne' tells the tale vividly, tactfully, adequately . . . etc."

Sir Arthur, almost alone among strident voices, shows the true sense of solidarity which has up to now distinguished his generation.

W. R. Inge is concerned with more civic matters, thus:—

"In every modern civilised country population is restricted by deliberate postponement of marriage. In many cases this does no harm whatever; but in many others it gravely diminishes the happiness of young people, and may even cause minor disturbances of health. Moreover, it would not be so widely adopted but for the tolerance on one part of society of the 'great social evil,' the opprobrium of our civilisation. In spite of the failure hitherto of priests, moralists and legislators to root it out, and in spite of the acceptance of it as inevitable by the majority of Continental opinion, I believe that this abomination will not long be tolerated by the conscience of free and progressive nations. It is notorious that the whole body of women deeply resents the wrong and contumely done by it to their sex."

The Dean further states that medical methods against "a certain disease" are not enough. Early marriage is to become the rule in all cases. The results to be tempered by an "Imperial Board of Emigration."

He, however, deplores the "Comstock" legislation in America. And declares, quite sanely, that it has done "unmixed harm."

In this gargantuan attempt to learn what England and America are thinking one must not fly to conclusions, one must not confuse different shades of opinion. One must also remember that the number of people who implicitly agree both with Dean Inge and with the late Anthony Comstock is infinitely greater than the number of people who read the present periodical, or any or all other periodicals devoted to the affairs of the intellect.

It is extremely difficult for the "ordinarily cultured person" to realise the number of Christians per million of the population.

In October, 1916, the "Edinburgh" took note of Remy de Gourmont; in April, 1916, of Ch. van Lerberghe. They also published a long article by Havelock Ellis. The editor of the "Edinburgh" contributes regularly to "The Sunday Times." Among his contributors are found the editor of "Truth," and the editor, or late editor, of "The Dublin Review."

Against this must be recorded the fact that they devoted 17 pages to Maurice Barrès and, in contrast, 8 to De Gourmont. Mr. Thorold ends his article on Barrès as follows:—

"Among the influences that will go to form the new and emancipated France none will be more important than that of Maurice Barrès."

For all Mr. Gosse's name having become more or less of a jest and by-word, we must at this point commend and support Mr. Gosse against Mr. Thorold.

One cannot kit-kat about in the present pages of the "Edinburgh" and light upon transparent imbecilities. Quiller-Couch is in the main sane in what he has to say about Swinburne. The "Edinburgh" can print the word "bastardy" without endangering a strike of their printers. (Which is something, in England.) There is a reasonable divergence of opinion among its contributors. They took note of Carducci in April, 1914, of Stendhal in January of that year.

They are not always wholly tactful and prescient, to wit (January, 1914):—

"Few men have achieved a literary success equal to that of Houston Stewart Chamberlain, and Englishmen may well be proud of a fellow-countryman who is recognised in Germany as one of the most brilliant writers and profound thinkers of the day."

But they had heard of Péguy *before he was killed.* On the other hand they show a tendency to take up with Claudel and that kind of messiness, and its English equivalent (the later Tagore, Katharine Tynan, etc.).

It is to be noted that they have been "stirred" by the war. As early as October, 1914, they were talking about "War and Literature." It was perhaps a little early to be drawing conclusions. *But* they have been better since the war than immediately before it. In fact I find the earlier numbers rather unreadable. About the middle of 1912 they enlarged their type, the editor boldly put his name on the cover, and articles began to be "signed."

They wrote of the "sovereignty of the air" in 1912; of Oliver Wendell Holmes and E. A. Poe in 1910. In 1906 Wells, May Sinclair, Mabel Dearmer and Hitchens ("Garden of Allah") have their novels grouped in an article on "Novels with a Philosophy." Even at that date they seem to have been aware of the French XVIIIth Century, and of a book called Mayne's "Ancient Law." My impression—I do not wish to record it as more than an impression—is that their "tone" at that period is to be found in frequent phrases like "*no less a figure than*" or "a no less interesting figure of Madame de Maine's court at its later period was Madame du Deffand." I feel Madame de Stael forming a "family group" with Mrs. and Mr. Nekker, décor à la daguerreotype. But I do not feel it fair to judge the present "Edinburgh," i.e., the magazine since 1914, by its issues of the preceding decade.

Purely personal reflection, after having surveyed the last ten volumes of the "Edinburgh Review": I have not been a "good boy" or a "suitable curate" as these modes of existence are understood in the British literary episcopacy.

Impersonal or general reflection: Many people who are obviously and undeniably stupid are, it appears, able to write long articles without making "gaffes"; without in any egregious way displaying any of their particular mental limitations or their stupidities. This is because there are in England, perhaps more than in any other country, a great number of people who, without thinking, without any constructive or divinitive mental process of their own, manage to find out what ought to be thought upon any given subject or subjects. And they acquire a suitable and convenient proficiency in the expression of these suitable "thoughts."

4. The "Spectator"
SEPTEMBER 6, 1917

THE "Spectator" is something peculiar. I must put this thing *dans son cadre*. Approaching the centre of English Kultur, one enters gradually a state of awareness to certain forces or properties of that centre, and among them the "Spectator." This publication greeted me courteously. I cannot quite remember how I learned that the "Spectator" was a sort of parochial joke, a "paper printed in London for circulation in the provinces." All I know is that the "Spectator" is an unfailing butt. You can raise a smile, a pale and disdainful smile anywhere, veritably anywhere, as far as my experience goes, by the mere mention of the "Spectator." At the present moment (for I am writing this prologue before making my usual inspection of the "mentality" to be analysed) I do not know why the "Spectator" is so greatly and unfailingly a fountain of merriment.

In a way, even vaguer, I know that it emanates from some people called "Stracheys,"* called generically and comprehensively "Stracheys." I know by hearsay that they differ among themselves; that they exist in generational strata; that they are "militarist" and "conscientious," etc.; that they speak with peculiar voices; that they are "beings apart," despite the fact that one of them, perhaps more than one, looks like a banker. The only one I ever saw did not look like a banker. I cannot conceive him on the Exchange.

The "Spectator" is by hearsay "conservative." It has "dictated the conservative policy," whatever that phrase may mean. Save that it has given me one, or perhaps it is two, favourable reviews, I know absolutely nothing about it. For prejudging this paper or these people I have no more reason than the Athenian citizen who said, "I am tired of hearing him called Aristides the Just"; save perhaps this, that I did hear of a rural vicar of eighty who refused to write *any more* for the "Spectator" "Because it really was too *arrière*."

Thus we shall at least learn what the vicar of eighty or sixty or fifty or whatever his age was, thought "*too arrière*." Commençons!

"Spectator," No. 4,650, first page:

*A returning traveller recounts the following dialogue:—
Scene: A distant part of the English seaboard.
Precocious little girl, aged nine: "Mother, what is a Strachey?"
Mother: "Oh, it will take too long! It's too boring to explain it all to you."
Child (having been "told," and possibly labouring under a misapprehension): "But, mummy, I'll have to know some day."
I offer this with no comment. I am assured of its actuality.

"We do not know on what authority the 'Daily Mail' bases its figures, but they seem to us inherently improbable . . ."

"This is a situation which demands the whole determination and all the skill and resource of the Navy . . ."

"When American vessels are built in large numbers they will be needed to transport the great American Army, etc. . ."

"We want Labour to be solid in support of the Government policy in the future as it has been in the past; if therefore the Government, who have, etc. . . come t.t.c. that etc. Br. delegates g.t. Stockholm, we should not protest t.w.s.h.s. misgivings. . . ."

"Another reason . . . Government must accept the responsibility . . ."

"No demand is really 'popular' unless all the constituent parts of the people are behind it. We all belong to the people . . . We are all the people. The Government represents us all . . ."

"The Government must act with a proper sense, etc. . . ."

Page 2.—The P.M. made a v.g. speech o.t.w. at Queen's Hall last Sat., the 3d aniv. of G.B. entry i.t.c.:

"Sir W.R.'s *rugged* optimism *shines* out . . ." (italics mine.)

"The Germans have not turned O. and Z. into such m. fortresses without g.r."

"Those who talk lightly of the military advantages of autocracy . ."

"But as we all know only too well, incomes are not equal in this or in any other country, and the case, etc."

(Watch this carefully.)

"Indeed, by imposing adequate taxation the State assists the operations of war, because the taxes themselves, etc. . ."

"Frankly, we believe it would be difficult to the point of impossibility to say whether a man had or had not used his money dishonestly to procure his own social distinction . . ."

"The 'Gillie Dhu,' for instance, who inhabits Ross-shire is a merry little fellow . . ."

"The Control of Uric Acid . . . Hints to the Middle-Aged." (Advt.)

"Y.M.C.A. Headquarters."

"Spectator," No. 4,649:

"Our aeroplanes played a.g.p. i.t.v."

"Throughout the week the French have had m.h.f. on the C.d.D."

"The Allied Governments were strongly represented at a Conference on Balkan affairs held in Paris last week."

No. 4,648:

"A military disaster has befallen o.R.a."

"The Government doubtless have been further shaken in their position and authority by their handling of the Mesopotamian affair."

"Bismarck's tradition holds . . ."

"The Fellows of the Royal Societies have had a Dining club since 1743."

No. 4,646.

"The 'Times' military correspondent suggests, we do not know with what authority . . ."

"There is generally some drawback to the pleasure to be got out of a garden. . . ."

"We have spoken of the large numbers of letters written; their name is legion. The daily outgoing mail of the British Armies in France needs a considerable force to cope with it. It may, at first sight, seem strange that the unlettered portion of the community should put on record such an enormous amount of literature."

(This is what might be termed in Arizona, "a fair chunk of it.")

It continues:—

"Their ideas are few, their vocabulary limited, but their letters as the sands of the sea-shore for number, it is not as if there were anything of more than usual interest to say."

(Apparently not). And there, my dear Watson, we have it. I knew that if I searched long enough I should come upon some clue to this mystery. The magnetism of this stupendous vacuity! The sweet reasonableness, the measured tone, the really utter undeniability of so much that one might read in this paper! Prestigious, astounding! There are no disconcerting jets and out-rushes of thought. The reader is not unpleasantly and suddenly hustled with novelties. No idea is hurled at him with unmannerly impetus. Observe in the last quoted passage the gradual development of the idea of multitude. How tenderly the writer circles about it, from "large" to "legion," with its scriptural and familiar allusiveness; from "considerable" to "enormous," and then this stately climax, this old but never outworn or outcast comparison with the number of the sands of the sea-shore—measuredly refraining from exaggeration, from the exaggeration of including such sand as might be supposed to rest at the bottom or middle of the Neptunian couch, rather than being dumped and disposed round its border.

That is really all there is to it. One might learn to do it oneself: There is "nothing of more than usual interest." The problem is to present this at length, and without startling the reader. Others have done it. The "New Statesman" is what might be called a shining (if not rugged) example, in action, incipient, under weigh. Aimed at the generation which read Bennett, Wells, Shaw, Galsworthy, rather than Lord Macaulay, this weekly has done, is doing, the "same stunt," if we by so gutter-snipish and saltimbanquic a phrase may describe anything so deliberate as the on-glide of the successful and lasting "Spectator." The "New Statesman" is a prime exemplar of the species, leading the sheltered life behind a phalanx of immobile ideas; leading the sheltered thought behind a phalanx of immobile phrases. This sort of thing cannot fail. Such a mass of printed statements in every issue to which no "normal, right-minded" man can possibly take exception! Familiar, but all the dearer for that. Ce sont les vieilles chansons. The "New Statesman" gives the same sense of security, of static unchanging existence, of a mental realm without any volcanoes, of a population in almost strenuous agreement with a norm. It is, perhaps, not the Spectatorial norm. Of this I have no means of judging. It is indubitably a norm of similar or identical species. The gap between Macaulay and Galsworthy is merely a temporal gap.

"It is not" let me return once again to the key-note, "It is not as if there were anything of more than usual interest to say."

5. "The Strand," or How the Thing May Be Done

SEPTEMBER 13, 1917

[SEE PLATE 8.]

FOR those who have not followed the sign "Seek Safety First! Read the 'Spectator'!" there remains the great heart of the people. Not receiving comfort in the groves of academicians, I have gone "out into the open"; to the popular font. In the wideness and wildness of adventure I feel like

Captain Kettle and Don Kishótee. Heaven knows what I shall come upon next!

"The Strand" is a successful, and obviously successful, magazine. It carries 58 pages of ads. in double column, 50 before and the remainder at the back of its "reading matter," to say nothing of the cover with ads. on three sides and a modest statement, or command, concerning "FRY'S COCOA" neatly fitted into its belettered façade. It does not contain pictures of actresses or of Mlle. Règine Montparnasse in the act of saying that she wears beach stockings because sand is disagreeable to the feet. It is thicker and uses a slightly better paper than the other 8d. and 6d. (olim 6d. and 4½d.) magazines on the stand where I found it.

Putting aside my personal preferences for "literature," thought, etc., and other specialised forms of activity, we (and again obviously so) will find here a display of technique, of efficiency. This, No. 321, vol. 54, is manifestly what a vast number of people want; what a vast number of people spend the requisite 8d. to obtain. This is the "solid and wholesome." The ads. proclaim it. The absence of actresses' legs is a sign of power. "The Strand" can sell without their assistance . . not only to those who despise or disapprove of the legs, torses, etc., of our actresses, but also to the dissolute who know that these delicacies can be more effectively "conveyed" in the pages of the large illustrated weeklies than in small-paged monthly magazines. I suspect that "The Strand" is "soundly" imperialist; believes in the invincibility of Britain (odds ten to one under *all* circumstances); does not present Americans in an unfavourable light —for is not the language more or less common to both countries, are there not American readers to be thought of? In normal times I think the comic characters might have about them a "foreign touch." However, let us come to the facts. Let us see "what carries the ads."

1. "Sherlock Holmes Outwits a German Spy." Red band on the cover. "His Last Bow, The War-Service of Sherlock Holmes." This is what business managers of periodicals call "the real thing." Sir A. Conan Doyle has never stooped to literature. Wells, Benett, and the rest of them have wobbled about in penumbras, but here is the man who has "done it," who has contributed a word to the language, a "character" to the fiction of the Caucasian world, for there is no European language in which the

"Great Detective" can be hid under any disguise. Herlock Sholmes, spell it as you like, is KNOWN. Caines and Corellis lie by the wayside. Sherlock has held us all spellbound. Let us see what is requisite. Let us see what we are asked to believe.

In the first place, there is a residue in the minds of everyone who sees this name on the magazine cover. We all know something about Mr. Holmes. We have no difficulty in calling to mind this figure. He is perfectly fearless, possessed of inordinate strength, is absolutely impervious to the action of all known drugs and narcotics, and possessed, if not of eternal youth, at least of an eternal prime, of an invulnerable energy. He is also an eunuch (though I have no doubt that Sir Arthur would fit him out with a past full of romance if ever the public desire it).

In the present story we are asked to believe that two years before the war (i.e., 1912), Mr. Asquith and Sir Edward Grey visited Sherlock, who had then retired to the South Downs to study bee-culture. "The Foreign Minister alone I could have withstood, but when the Premier also, etc.," says Sherlock, with his usual modesty. These dignitaries asked him to round up the Chief German spy. (For the Empire was then alert to these matters.) Sherlock at once went to America and grew a real Amurikun beard.

When the action takes place, he has not seen his dear Watson for some time. In fact, they stop in a breathless passage to see how time has mutually treated them, and find themselves unmarked by his ravages. Nevertheless, when Holmes telegraphs Watson to appear at Harwich "with the car," Watson appears. What djinn could be more obedient to his Aladdin? In the midst of a most vital affair, you naturally do trust someone you haven't seen for several years to arrive on the instant with "the car" in response to a telegram which is bound to find him at home. (After all, the car is only a "Ford." The German Embassy had a Benz motor.)

Let us examine the modus. Let us see what is left to the imagination or credulity of the reader, and just what the author is most careful NOT to trust to the intelligence of the reader.

1. The exposition of the position of things by the German head spy and the Chief Secretary of the Legation (? I forget whether this is von

Kühlmann), at any rate, they are very explicit, and the documents in the safe are clearly labelled, "Harbour-Defences," "Naval Signals," etc.

2. When Sherlock (who is, of course, the chief spy's most trusted assistant) arrives, they begin to talk rather freely, before the reader is assured that Watson, the chauffeur, is well out of hearing. However, it might be assured that he is. Sherlock, in delivering all the naval signals, is careful to say, "a copy, mind you, not the originals." But this is not trusted to the reader in so simple a form. Two paragraphs are taken to explain (*between the assistant Sherlock and the boss spy*) that the originals would have been missed.

That is the sort of thing that the reader is *not* trusted to see for himself.

3. Sherlock chloroforms the chief spy. This is about all the action there is in the story. He suddenly produces a sponge soaked in chloroform. This chloroform is so strong that he and Watson have to ventilate the room a few moments later, yet no whiff of this chloroform has aroused the suspicions of Von Bork. Of course, he had it in a specially constructed thermos flask, or something of that sort, but this detail is left to the reader's "imagination" or inattention. Time required for extraction and use on Von Bork's mouth and nose equals three-fifths of a second.

I am reminded of a little story in the Italian comic paper, "Quattro cento venti." Alpine traveller having missed his shot at a bear, and being at the end of his ammunition, remembers that he has seen bears dance to a tambourine. He at once begins to play a tambourine, and the bear dances. He is saved.

Friend: "But where did you get the tambourine?"

Traveller (unabashed): "Made it out of the bear's hide."

4. Further details: Sherlock has taken to Claridge's. The Imperial Tokay they drink at the spy's expense is from Franz Joseph's special cellar. Sherlock still has (p. 234) "his long, nervous fingers." Sherlock recalls his triumphs over Prof. Moriarty and Col. Moran (p. 234). Further on we find the true steam calliope: "It was I who brought about, etc., and late King of Bohemia, when, etc., Imperial Envoy . . . etc. nihilist Klopman, Count Von und Zu Grafen . . . etc." So like that pretty little song:

"I'm the guy wot put de salt in de ocean."

"There is only one man," said Von Bork.

We must really agree with Von Bork. Sherlock is unique, but mankind remains amazingly unaltered and unalterable. He likes a relief from reality, he likes fairy stories, he likes stories of giants, he likes genii from bottles. Sherlock with his superhuman strength, his marvellous acumen, his deductive reasoning (which is certainly not shared with the reader), has all the charms of the giant. He is also a moral Titan: right is never too right. The logical end of these likes is, or was, God. The first clever Semite who went out for monotheism made a corner in giantness. He got a giant "really" bigger than all other possible giants. Whenever art gets beyond itself, and laps up too great a public, it at once degenerates into religion. Sherlock is on the way to religion, a modern worship of efficiency, acumen, inhumanity. Only a man on familiar terms with his public as Sir Arthur, as habituated to writing for that public, would dare "lay it on so thick." His Sherlock's peroration (supposedly, August 2, 1914) is a mixture of moving—prognostication of the "cold and bitter" wind which will blow over England and wither many in its blast, and a hurry to cash a £500 cheque before the arrested spy (then actually in their Ford motor-car, and about to be taken to Scotland Yard) has time to stop payment. Watson is urged to "start her up."

Sir Arthur is as illogical as any other sort of fanatic. He is loud in praise of Sherlock's faculty for reason, but his own flesh or mind, or whatever it is, falls a little short of divinity.

So much for the red-label story. It undoubtedly sells the magazine. BUT it is not all the art of making a magazine, and, besides, one can NOT count on such a draw as Sherlock for every issue. There is a lot more in the technique of successful magazine making than in getting an occasional story from Sir A. Conan Doyle.

The next item is "Confessions of a Censor-Fighter," by William G. Shepherd. This is clean, hard copy, six to seven pages of the first-hand experience of a newspaper correspondent during the present war, and much the best thing in the number.

Next item. Luxurious room, light such as "Rembrandt," etc., burglar, quelled by tremendous willpower and "concentrated lightning" from the "flint-blue eyes" of a blind man. Blind man very noble, burglar very base, and has deeply injured the blind man and the lady of his de- votion. Bell rung in the last paragraph when the blindness is discovered.

Next Item: Comic story, bell in last paragraph but one.

Next Item: Mark Hambourg tells how to play the piano.

Next Item, in smaller print, end of continued story (résumé of the first half given in black print). Killer Ames, the wicked pearl-fishing cap- tain, terribly wicked, hero terribly noble, tremendous passions, tremen- dous situations. Very readable. Very probably quite impressive if read without too close attention. Point: Nobility is exalted. One must always remember this point in any study of melodrama. And, moreover, one must not scoff at it. In this story the fundamental life values are right. By this rightness the author is able to "move" the reader, despite his sur- face exaggerations, *à la* Hyper-Conrad. Of course, one skips large para- graphs to "get on."

The most wildly romantic and melodramatic writer always has this one advantage over the professed "realist," that whenever anything "hap- pens" in real life it is often different from, and often in excess of "fiction," of the patterns of life already portrayed.

The dull writer, seeking only verisimilitude, possibly writing without experience or imagination, does not take this into account, and his work lacks a real profundity. I am not saying melodrama is profound. But the "unlikely" element in romance has a profound value, a value that no aes- thetic, no theory of literature, can afford to omit from its scheme of things.

Next Item: "The Tanks," described at the request of the authori- ties by Col. E. D. Swinton, who is obviously put to it, to make an "ac- count" without saying very much. The editors say he has written "mas- terly" stories. He is probably busy with other matters, and it is unfair to look at his article too closely. The beginning is verbose, a predicate does the split over six lines, etc. He says "*Schutzengrabenvernichtungsautomo- bil*" is not likely to be used as a topical refrain in vaudeville song. Toward the end he conveys some interesting information.

Next Item: Story, young man called "The Wastrel," worst recorded act that of distinguishing himself at football, gives his life for a cad who, we are assured, is very brilliant, although he behaves like an ass and dis- plays no intellectual gifts.

Next Item: "Lion-Kings," in the smaller print. Brief biographies of Pezon family, possibly left over from before the war stock of copy.

Next Item: Story translated from the French. With the aid of its illustrations, we are to believe that "little milliners" in Paris are equipped with rather nice evening gowns, and that the way to strangle cruel Russian ex-Governors is with long gloves which leave no mark on the throat.

Next Item (small italics): Paragraph on "Improvement on Double Dummy."

Next Item: "For Greater Italy!" (in the smaller print). Descriptive writing of the Italian front, all the usual words, presumably conveys nothing which might not have been left to camera and cinematograph. We are expected to read through such important bits of conversation as "*Buon' giorno, signor capitano.*" Life is too short to read this article. With the exception of the paragraph on "Double Dummy," it is, however, the only unreadable thing in the magazine. (Note: Author writes of D'Annunzio as if he were greater than Leopardi. This, however, may be merely a slip of the pen; by "modern poet" he may mean "living poet." It is, however, quite possible that Leopardi's name is unknown to him.)

Next Item: Acrostics (half page).

Next Item: "Funny Pictures" for children (4 pages).

Next Item: "Perplexities," one page of puzzles. Very good puzzles, too.

Next Item: "The Acting Duchess," usual farce about charming people *with* titles and egregious bounder without. Probably not based on a very close study of "the aristocracy," and would "do on the stage."

Next Item: Curiosities. One page.

Then comes Notice (as on front cover) that "The Strand Magazine" can be sent post free to the troops. (This postal regulation applies equally to all other periodicals.)

Finis: Johnny Walker, Secrets of Beauty, Jaeger, Protective Knickers, Eno's, etc.

6. "The Sphere," and Reflections on Letter-Press
SEPTEMBER 20, 1917

THIS study like any other branch of natural science demands great endurance. The individual specimens must, or at least should, be examined with microscopic attention; otherwise one's generalities will descend into mere jeux-d'esprit, and the patient student of contemporary misfortune will derive from them nothing more than a transient amusement.

Not as a theologian interpreting the Divine Will in infallible dogma, but as a simple-hearted anthropologist putting specimens into different large boxes—merely for present convenience tumbling things apparently similar into the same large box until a more scientific and accurate and mature arrangement is feasible, let me attempt a very general classification of such periodicals as have yet obtruded themselves in my research: There are, or seem to be:

First: "B. & S." periodicals, i.e., those designed to keep thought in safe channels; to prevent acrimonious discussion in old gentlemen's clubs. e.g., respectable quarterlies, "The Spectator," e.h.g.o.

Second: Periodicals designed to inculcate useful and mercantile virtues in the middle and lower middle classes or strata, e.g., "The Strand," and "Cocoa" in general.

Third: Trade journals, such as "The Bookman," "The Tailor and Cutter," "Colour," etc.

Fourth: Crank papers. Possibly one should include here as a subheading "religious periodicals," but I do not wish to press this classification; I do not feel the need of two categories, and my general term will cover a number of crank papers which are not definitely religious, though often based on "superstition," i.e., left-overs of religions and taboos.

Fifth: Papers and parts of papers designed to stop thought altogether.

This last group is obviously quite distinct from the four groups that precede it. I do not mean to say that one can tell at a glance which papers belong to it, but its aim is radically different. The first group desires only to "stop down" thought, to prevent its leading any man into any unusual or "untoward" action. The second group aims to make its reader a self-helping and undisturbing member of the commercial community, law-abiding, with enough virtue to be self-content. The third group is a specialisation of the second. It aims to do in particular trades and groups what the second does for the salaried and wage-earning order in general, i.e., to tell it or show it what sort of work is demanded; where one can get the best price, etc., e.g., "Colour" presents monthly sample illustrations (free of cost to its editors) by people who more or less obviously desire to be transferred from the "main text" to the advertising section of the paper. It also tells you about Mrs. Gumps' "Place in Art" or Mr. R. Roe's "Place in Art," patiently explaining each month just which follower of Mr. Brangwyn is the true successor to Botticelli, Monticelli, Mantegna, Boucher, Watteau, Conder, Manet, Albrecht Dürer, Velasquez, or whoever it may be who most needs an inheritor at the moment. (By the kindness of such and such "Galleries.")

This is essentially the scheme of "The Bookman," although Messrs. Hodder and Stoughton and Dr. Robertson Nicoll both need careful scrutiny on their own account. "The Lives of Publishers, a careful and comparative study by one not in their employ," is a book we have long been in need of.

The fourth group expresses those of the community who desire all people to "do something." Regardless of the individual temperaments with which nature has endowed us, these people desire us to behave in a particular way. For example, some of them earnestly desire us all to procreate in abundance, others desire that we cease wholly from procreation; others demand that people uninstructed in Confucianism go at great expense into far parts of the earth to prevent Orientals from remaining Confucians. Still others demand that we desist from alcohol in all forms, substituting food, coffee, tobacco; others demand that we substitute one form of alcohol for another. Others demand that laws be arranged in a book with an intelligible system, still others demand that laws *must* essentially be without any system whatever. Some demand the "suppression of all brothels in Rangoon and other stations in Burmah" ("The Shield," July, 1916, a very interesting periodical). Others desire that we believe in "God." Others desire that we should not "believe in God."

These periodicals must be distinguished from other propaganda for shifting the taxes, for a shifting of the taxes must almost of necessity bring, at least temporary, advantage to certain interested groups of individuals; but in many cases the "crank" periodical is more or less without "interest," for it can make no possible difference to Mrs. Crabbee of Hocking whether Lo Hi Li of Canton believes or disbelieves in Confucius, or whether the young men in Burmah cleave to, or eschew, the customs of their fathers.

Now in the face of these papers and on the grave of the Victorian era, it is by no means surprising that many people should have desired to stop thought altogether, or that there should have sprung up many papers like "The Sketch," whose obvious aim is to console the inane for inanity.

It is perfectly natural that people overwearied with being asked to decide at what age the female shop assistant of Hammersmith shall be judged fit to mislead the butcher-boy; overwearied with being asked to support missionaries to keep the Fijians sufficiently friendly to trade with the vendors of spirits, and to decide which sect shall morally uplift which islanders; overwearied with being asked to decide the necessary ratio between bathtubs, work hours, salvations of various brands; overwearied, etc. . . . it is perfectly natural that these people should desire "surcease" from thinking at all; just as after a period of frumpery and too many petticoats worn at once, it is perfectly natural that people should take delight in "Eve" with no petticoats whatsoever, and in similar mental ricochets.

It seems unlikely that anyone else has ever read the letter-press of illustrated weeklies, i.e., more than enough to learn who it is who is "chatting" . . . for someone always is "chatting." It is being done in the current numbers of three of them. I take "The Sphere" because it appears to be about "middlesize." [See plate 8.] It eschews the simple aphrodisiacs of the "brighter" papers; it has fewer cross-sections of dissected ships showing little compartments marked: coal, whale-oil, ballast, engines, crew, etc., than are published in the "Ill. London News." This last, "The Sketch," and "The Sphere" are familiar to me because I used to dine occasionally in a restaurant where veal "Milanese" was 1/3, the same being now 1/9. I judge these papers are aimed at people who paid 1/3 for veal cutlet before the War, and who are still able to afford the same dish, slightly smaller at an advance of 40 per cent. That is, I should say, about the average economic range of the 6d. (now 7d.) weekly. And "The Sphere" is about the average weekly, having fewer salients than the others. Current number 11 3/4 by 16 3/8 inches. Cover: Soldiers in waterproof blankets, looking at camera, but labelled "Fighting"; Fry, Shoolbred's, "Army Club." Full page illustration. Books received: "Harry Lauder's Logic," 1s., etc. "Plays Worth Seeing," are described as follows:—

1. Most attractive musical comedy, with some pleasant songs and picturesque scenes.

2. Irresponsible company provide an excellent night's entertainment. Play continues very popular, and the Song . . . is spreading far and wide over the Kingdom.

5. ———— looks very chic as the heroine.

First text page, Editorial.

"It is curious that certain people should allow themselves to formulate such an ignorant and careless question as 'What are we Fighting For?'"

"Mr. Wells has perhaps forgotten . . . famous pledge . . . Asquith . . . never sheathe the sword . . . ultimatum, . . . Serbia . . . Belloc. . . ."

Usual picture of "chatting." Fourteen pages of war pictures and maps. These things are of interest, are to be found in various weeklies. One wishes the editors would stick to photographs and not employ "artists."

Usual "science" page or half-page: "164,000,000 miles," etc. Mr. Lucas: "But apart from money, which has nothing to do with the pleasures of craftsmanship, it must be great fun to write aphorisms." Sketch of "Tommy in Italy, like Tommy in France, is on the best of terms with his Allies."

A LITERARY LETTER.

"Personally, I care nothing. . . I do not mind whether Shakespeare wrote the plays assigned. . . . I do not care a single jot about the authorship of Elizabethan drama. . . . A playwright never hesitated to borrow. . . ."

"Anyone who can write a book on the Elizabethan drama, one feels to be a friend with whom one would like to discuss various problems. . . . I would fain have gone through, in this or another Letter, the eight volumes of Middleton (every line of which I have read)."

Mehercule!!!

"And have endeavoured to demonstrate the essential greatness. . . ."

"I paid for my edition of the works of Webster in four volumes, published by Pickering in 1830, edited by Alexander Dyce, not less than £4 10s., and a friend paid £7 or £8 for a copy rendered additionally valuable by a wider margin. I paid a guinea for the plays of Tourneur edited by Churton Collins."

"Dyce's one volume edition—an uncomfortable book to read. . . ."

"The Elizabethan dramatists are not really available to-day to any but those who, like myself, spend more money than prudence justifies upon books."

"One of my favourites among the Elizabethans. . ."

"Further, it may interest those who remember the discussion about the German word, *Kadaver*. . ."

"Now, I have great admiration for Sir Arthur Quiller-Couch as a novelist, and I count him one of the most attractive men I know."

"If I were giving advice to a young student of literature (and my correspondence indicates that this Letter fulfils some such purpose in countless cases)."

SISTE VIATOR.

Gentle friend, let us pause, let us drop a modest and not too prominent tear for the adolescent and countless correspondent.

There is more of this, there is even a part page headed "Literature." Blind worship of Shakespeare is deplored, but "The Tempest" is said to be better than Dekker's "Shoemaker's Holiday." Then follows a full page of the Pope, as damning a piece of evidence as even the most rabid atheist could desire.

In "Literature" we learn that, "Here Dion Cosway found his cousin Myola." "In the Petrol World," *sono profano,* I am unfit to discuss things, but the foot-pump seems an admirable, pain-saving invention.

WOMAN'S SPHERE IN WAR-TIME.

Here we note the repetition of the paper's own title, "Sphere," and:—

"Three years of the tangled web of war have passed away, with all our preconceived notions knocked to bits . . . timely Zepp . . . flattened purses and forced simplicity . . . infuse dashes of decorativeness into our attire . . . inexpensive devices . . . clever fingers . . . ordinary frock . . . absurdly simple . . decorative withal." (Surely this last must be the editor ipse.)

"Jersey of powder-blue tricot, . . . autumn toilette, dainty decoration . . . out of the commonplace . . ."

There is more of this both here and in other weeklies; but I am more concerned about the "countless" correspondent than with the problem of introducing literary archaism into the female dress paragraph.

7. Far from the Expensive Veal Cutlet
SEPTEMBER 27, 1917

WEARIED with the familiar scene, I mounted a 'bus at Picadilly Circus and proceeded via Vauxhall to Clapham, and thence by another 'bus via "The Borough" and Hackney to a bridge spanning, I believe, the Lea River. Here beneath the rain stretched northward a desolate, flat and more or less Dutch landscape. Below the west side of the bridge was a yard and dock for regenerating canal boats. It was not unlike a Venetian *squero*. On the other side of the bridge, and stuffed almost under it, was the copy of a poorish German bier-garten; in the forty-foot stream were a few disconsolate row-boats of the familiar Serpentine pattern. The bridge was largely surmounted by a policeman. He decided my wife was innocent, and warned me in a glooming and ominous silence, with a sort of projected taciturnity of the eye, that I was to commit no foul play in that neighbourhood.

I offered no explanation of my presence. If I had said "I came because I saw LEA BRIDGE on a 'bus-sign," he would have considered the explanation inadequate. Certain social gulfs are unbridgeable. I am convinced the policeman did not and does not yet understand my presence overlooking his disconsolate river. I am equally certain, after having traversed those 'bus routes, that the millions are unplumbed by our "literature." What! Beyond the scope of Conan Doyle, or Hall Caine, millions indifferent to Mr. Wells' views upon God; millions unexpressed in the pages of Bennett, and even in the pages of Jacobs; sunk in vice? No, surely, only a few of them sunk in vice, and the rest of them sunk deep in virtue, as deep as their specific weight will permit; but at any rate terra incognita, unknown to the most popular writer, inarticulate, unreceptive.

I am perfectly certain these people do not read "The Sketch," or "Blackwood," or even "Truth," though I am assured that this latter paper circulates widely among the nonconformists of North London. And what, in God's name, do they read? What data can they provide save to takers of census, to compilers and statisticians? And what sort of an image of the "social order" has anyone been able to form; even the most social of novelists? In a flight and fury of Galsworthian phantasy we might suggest a flabby but decorative poppy: the slightly pathetic "aristocracy," some

of whose "photos" appear in the illustrated Press; and below this a sort
of pustulent dough, the plutocracy, the hog-class, depicted by Belloc and
other writers, hated from above and below, but tolerated in its upper layer
by the "aristocracy" whom it appears to support, though in reality our
metaphorical Galsworthian flower is held up by a slender stiff stem: people whose males dress for dinner, habitually and without thought for
the changing of raiment; below them people to whom the boiled shirt is
a symbol of gaiety, gaiety more or less rare, to whom the evening black
is a compensation for emptiness of the pocket, to whom the low-cut
waistcoat is friendly, familiar; below them, in the "stem," people who
regard their evening costume with something like reverence, with just a
touch of the continental superstition for the "frac" and for "smok'ing."

There are also the followers and companions of Mr. Shaw, who advocate personal cleanliness but eschew the boiled shirt on principle, and
below them the followers of reformers who begin their economy on the
laundry-bill; who regard the body as the tawdry, rather despicable servant
of the civic instrument fixed in the head. There is also organised labour.

But with all these one has come nowhere near "The Great Heart of
the People." There must be, in all this waste of low dung-coloured brick,
"the people" undependable, irrational, a quicksand upon which nothing can build, and which engulfs everything that settles into it; docile, ap-
athetic, de-energised, or, rather, unacquainted with energy, simply The
Quicksand. About them we are ignorant, we are as ignorant, or more
ignorant than we were about Dublin before James Joyce wrote "A Portrait of the Artist"; we have had a few books "about them"; the books
from them are unwritten, or unprintable. Even the manuscripts I have
in mind are not of them, they are of Whitechapel, with a tinge of foreign, Yiddish, Polish, expressiveness. They divulge only something alien
in the mass, they are not the mass expressing itself.

With the exception of "The Strand," I have as yet, unthinkingly,
been concerned only with "Reading Matter for the West End." Last
evening I began to ask the questions: What do the people read? Answer:
Had I ever heard of the "Quiver"? No, I had not heard of the "Quiver";
I had heard of the "Shield," the "Clarion," and a curious American and
religious paper called the "Ram's Horn." (This latter has, or had, a cover
portraying a priest or levite of Israel blowing the instrument.)

Knowledge or opinions regarding the "Quiver":

My first informant: It had knitting patterns. It was widely known. Informant believed that no *man* had ever read the "Quiver." [See plate 8.]

Second informant (a woman of thirty): "Oh yes, when I was about ten, the cook used to have it."

Third informant (newsvendor), would get it for me, did not believe me likely to find a copy in Kensington; looked it up on a list, price 7d. I felt it could not be as popular as I had hoped.

Fourth informant (newsvendor): Oh yes, used to have it. What was it like? "Oh it had . . . it was more intellectual . . . er . . er . . perhaps you might say more scriptural. It had good reading in it. Servants read it. A friend of theirs used to get it: read it first." (I did not make out its ultimate destination.) It is not "more scriptural."

THE QUIVER (price 8d. . . . published La Belle Sauvage).

(A large pile of them discovered at "Smiths") "Mlle. Gaby Deslys (heavy black type for the name), famous Parisian artiste, writes (anent Saltrates):—I find that a handful dissolved in the bath makes the water Oh! so fragrant, refreshing and invigorating. A teaspoonful in the foot-bath quickly fills the water with oxygen, etc., foot troubles disappear."

(autograph reproduced.)

Animadversion: Gaby has been mugging up chemistry.

"Mr. Harry Pilcer (black for name as above), the well-known dancer, writes:—In one week I was able to walk without discomfort, etc."

FIRST STORY. Young female journalist ascends from flat or "diggings" through sky-light, descends through another after losing herself upon roofs; finds young man seated before a revolver.

Result, the Altar!! No, gentle reader, I was about to fly to that conclusion myself, but we both show our ignorance of popular writing. We forget that the unexpected is often the key-note of interest. "Result, the altar" is crude, it is too simple for the popular mind. Result young man sulky (despite the luxury of the illustrations), young man with literary ambitions resents interruption in suicide, tells of his failure, conversation on suicide and on the beauty of his literature lasts until morning, he shaves, she is about to leave in order to prevent her "char-lady" "having a fit on the spot." Postman knocks: two letters, for these things do not occur one at a time, the first requests author to call on theatre manager, the second announces legacy of £20,000 from uncle in Australia. Result: the altar, plus "brilliant" literary collaboration, and they become "owners of one of the most charming little houses in town, with several successful plays, and as many 'best sellers' and no failures to their credit," "and are something of celebrities in their way."

What *do* Wells, Bennett, and Doyle know of the great popular heart? The events of this narrative occupy five pages, leaving one-fourth of a page for magazine heading and title. The illustrations are of the school used by "The Century." The sub-headings are: On the Leads; Stella Intrudes; An All-night Sitting; The Postman's Knock.

SECOND ITEM: My Girls and the New Times, a frank talk, by a middle-aged mother.

She wished the home to be "a refuge and an inspiration," but the girls desired the great city. Declaration of present War made them realise "for the first time what it meant to have a home." "They realised in the flesh the comfort and the beauty of a common life." "Hard work has proved their salvation." "Love and the quiet and the pleasant surroundings of their home proved grateful comforts" after hospital and farm labour. Her "daughters have become domesticated. They have not had time to study cookery or housecraft in detail, but they have acquired the real domestic spirit." One of the maids left and they had to turn to. "If they do not marry they will still want homes of their own" even if only a cheap flat or rooms. "To know something of the practical side of homemaking, to grasp the art of shopping and to know the value of foodstuffs, etc., will be of immense value to girls living alone." "The war has shown my girls, and the girls of hundreds of other mothers, not only to appreciate their homes, but to be able to make homes."

The logic of this—it is part of a passage headed "Close to Pain, but far from Pessimism" is not quite clear to me. The point has been overlooked by Von Bernhardi and other Teutonic praisers of War, but I have no doubt that they will be grateful for the hint, and will use it in future appendices to their works. They will also delight in revelation of Britannia.

The mother wishes her girls to marry, but why their sundry accomplishments could not have been acquired under the reign of Saturn is nowhere explained to us. The healing hand of Mars has wrought this metamorphosis and solved her domestic perplexities. "Because of the War," she says, "I have lost—and found my girls. It is a paradox, but immeasurably true."

There are further exhortations to "let our girls bring their men friends to tea or dinner, and let us welcome them with perfect naturalness." We are told that "Most men are too ready to take it for granted that their girls will marry." Parents are exhorted to help towards this consummation . . . "The colonies need women. Our daughters need husbands." The mother is going to write to friends in New Zealand to ask them to offer hospitality to her youngest. She is not going to wait for official action even though the price of fares has gone up. 4 pages.

THIRD ITEM: Chapter XXVI (copyright in U.S.A. by Mrs. Baillie Reynolds), "The night of the Orenfels ball . . . . He was a gentleman—an English gentleman; then what was he doing masquerading as a peasant at Orenfels." Decore: marble seat, tennis lawn, faultless behaviour.

"Conscious—as what girl is not conscious—of being admirably gowned, and looking remarkably nice . . . mine arms . . . bearing you down river bank . . . I wish you would not! In England we do not talk like that . . . limpid eyes . . . Was not Otho a foreigner . ."

Illustration, à la Prisoner of Zenda, "There is much the music shall plead for me."
"actually preferred her, little Betty." 12 pages.

FOURTH ITEM: The Woman's Harvest . . with photos. Photos for the most part show female harvesters wearing broad expressions of pleasure. "On the banks of the Nile, with its periodic overflowings to make the desert blossom as the rose, gangs of slaves, etc." Continental females also have tilled, etc. 7 pages, counting the illustrations.

FIFTH ITEM: "The Duchess of Grandone must have been an interesting lady—Auntie often speaks of her to me." "Call me Louis, he murmured." £50,000 worth of jewels, villain plans theft, or abduction of heiress. Villain's manners much more polished than those of handsome young knight of the shires. 6 pages.

SIXTH ITEM: Village comedy, sub-Jacobs, verbs in present tense, "thank-ee . . . better like . . . do complain a bit . . . that there . . ." 3 pages.

SEVENTH ITEM: Tale of the French revolution, Tricolour, old Versailles days, Marquis de . . .

(Loose leaf folder on "Wiping away tears," inserted at this juncture.)

"I am Jeannot Fouron—butcher by trade, and, faith, I'm not ashamed of it! I've butchered to some purpose to-day." "He glanced with an evil laugh." Danger from mob, revolution: bloody monster. Lovers united.

EIGHTH ITEM. Informs us that "Before the War, fox-hunting was certainly one of the most familiar of British rural sports. Zoographical data re foxes translated into idiom of "Sometimes papa will make his appearance, but he never joins in the gambols of his family," 2^1/$_2$ pages, plus 4 photos, three of which display foxes; in the other I can discern no fox, but one may be imagined lurking in the underbrush.

NINTH ITEM: But no! These four letters from a Holiday Worker to her friend, beginning "Dear Mate," and continuing "When the call to national service rang throughout the length and breadth of the land"; these and the beating heart of the magazine demand more than a brief and hurried notice.

There is another story about a boy scout. There are three full pale page reproductions of the Piazzetta, the Bridge of Sighs, the Dome of St. Mark's, labelled "Venice the Queen of Cities." And there is something about the possibilities of potatoes, but the beating heart of the magazine is in its competitions and personal correspondence, and in "The League of Young British Citizens," Patron in Chief H. R. H. Princess Patricia of Connaught. These things cannot be scamped, they cannot be lightly passed over. No wind will cleave this Red Sea before us. I have been all, alas all, too brief in my consideration of the middle-aged mother. I trust the reader will turn to her for himself. She cannot be compressed in an extract. The wine of Mt. Bazillac will not travel. You should smell this aroma from the petal and not from the distillation.

8. The Beating Heart of the Magazine
OCTOBER 11, 1917

I RETURN with interest undiminished to the "frank" and middle-aged mother—my periscope for surveying the no-man's land of the unexplored popular heart.

"Those days of peace which now seem so remote were not altogether happy for parents." I take this sentence from near her beginning. For the word "peace" substitute almost any other temporal designation, for "parents" substitute any other noun indicating any other group of humanity, the sense of the statement will remain, I think, unimpaired. "Cliché," as generally used, has meant a set phrase; we have here something slightly different; it may be called the "gapped linotype."

From style we proceed to matter: mother states that there was restlessness and vague discontent finding expression in the crudest form of violence. Home was the last place where her girls cared to spend their time. The home of the "gapped linotype" had ceased to allure them. They preferred to study "pharmacy," "music seriously," and "secretarial work"; the one desire common to all the three daughters was that of escaping the home of gapped linotype and reaching London. Mother felt that she had "ceased to play a part that mattered in the lives" of her daughters. Can we deduce from this that there is still a large section of the community which has not accepted the idea that the human offspring must at some period of its development cease sucking at the mental dugs of its parents; or at least a vast area in which this idea comes as a shock—a shock to the middle-aged maternal, and perhaps paternal, parent?

I say, advisedly, "large section of the community," for the moot points in "The Quiver" must be the moot points of its extensive audience; just as the moot points of an art journal are the moot points of a certain number of artists. I mean that obviously the people who read this drivel must be people to whom these questions are of interest, people who get a certain thrill of satisfaction, a certain stimulus to their self-confidence or relief from their self-diffidence, in reading that Mary ought to have her own latch-key, or may stay out until ten, or that (as further in this "Frank Talk") Mary should be not only allowed but encouraged to bring James home to dinner, or to invite him "to the house."

Mother in the present case of offspring-desiring London was distressed, her helplessness was "disheartening," she could but wait, "ready always with patience and sympathy and understanding." We should, perhaps, add "with an almost overwhelming assurance of modesty." We deduce from this last quotation that there are numerous readers who are not surprised that an author, speaking as one of a great number, as one who knows, "of course, that most mothers have felt these fears"; that such a representative of maternity should believe herself fully endowed with these three superhuman endowments. Mother, in this case, is fully convinced that she possessed "patience, sympathy and understanding"; her equipment has never been subject to self-suspicion.

In the next sentence, she hopes "that in the bitter struggle of life, and with the coming bitter experiences, they might be glad to return as wanderers to their home." It is perhaps over-severe to translate this formulation of the unconscious into: "Hoping life would be so dam'd hard that daughters would be driven back to the locus of the gapped linotype."

Note that we have attained an almost peasant or folk pessimism in the forecast of "the struggle of life," and "coming bitter experiences." This is deeper than the scriptural turn at the end: "Wanderers to their etc."

When the war came, the family was preparing for separate holidays; war, however, united 'em; they realised what it meant to have a home (herd instinct in presence of danger?). Mother does not mean home in the material sense. (Nor did Lord Haldane, but we must stick to the point.) Family "realised in the flesh the comfort and beauty of a common life." (Immaterial flesh?) "They saw that, when all is said and done, blood is stronger than water."

Does the popular "common sense" consist in the huddling together of proverbial phrases (often indisputable facts, or, at least, relatively indisputable metaphor), with incoherent deductions, contradictions, etc., leading to yet other proverbial phrases; giving the whole fabric a glamour of soundness? The popular reader gets a proverbial phrase which he accepts; he then passes through something which is but a blurr to his mind; he is worried for a moment, then he comes on the next proverbial phrase, is soothed, thinks the "whole thing is all right."

"Just as the coming of war linked up our far-flung" (not battle-line, but) "dominions, so it gathered together the members of my family, glad to have the common centre of a beloved home." The action of the adjective "beloved" is a little hard to determine. However, we must accept the metamorphosis from centrifugal to centripedal. The family mobilised. Pharmacy was, "of course," useful in hospital. Brothers become "adored brothers," home-surroundings become "pleasant surroundings." I am

not, however, concerned with an extraordinary condition. I am searching for the popular intellection. Mother also is looking towards the end
of the war, despite the fact that it has so embellished her home life. After
declaring on p. 891 that all her three female offsprings were anxious to
escape from the home, via the diverse channels of pharmacy, etc., she
states on p. 892, that "It is the restless, wavering temperament that seeks
escape from home." She forebodes that this family characteristic will
burst out again after the war, or no, she forebodes that it may be necessary, despite their war-acquired domesticity, for them to go. The pre-
bellum characteristic of the junior members of the family was indubitably, according to the trend of her statement, "restless and wavering";
the middle-aged maternal characteristic was "patient, sympathetic, understanding."

Another popular assumption soon follows, or, rather, several, in
the lines "helpless woman, living alone in diggings," "dishonest land-
lady." Before the war the girls made beds, darned stockings, occasionally went to market, but "were too busy with intellectual experiments to
come down to home-making." "They would discuss Shaw and Nietzsche,
but they would not discuss a leak in a gas-pipe, or the making of a simple soup." The verb "discuss" is most interesting. "They still find time
to read the best in to-day's literature. But they are not concerned with intellectual freaks or bizarre ways of thought."

Ah, mes amis, we must go further. We must find some family where
they did not read Shaw and Nietzsche. However, let us keep on with this
stratum, the stratum where the middle-aged "discuss" the leak in the gas-
pipe, and the daughters abstain from "bizarre" ways of thought. This designation is very helpful. It clarifies very considerably our concept of the
"Quiver" readers. To the gas-leak-discussing mother "The Question of
Marriage" brings the following words: "I want my girls to marry. The
wise Creator did not intend man or woman to live alone. I am old-fashioned enough, etc."

Note possessive "my" before girls; "wise" before Creator. Tribal possessive. Primitive, folk or peasant pessimism as to bitterness of life, overlaid with unhellenic belief in wisdom of Creator. Stand made for the "old-
fashioned" wifehood and motherhood. Note the association of "virtue"
with old custom. This association dates at least from the Roman era.

Mother however approves of wage-earning by wives. "If a woman has special talents let her exercise them after marriage and earn money for herself." The tincture of modern theoryism has not left mother unscathed. This overlay is of extreme interest to us. She opines (I believe that word is correct) that no "woman is the happier for deliberately refusing wifehood and motherhood because of the possibilities of a great career." Greatest women have not so refused. "Their work is better, not worse, because they have known the joy of motherhood." We note here the introduction of dogmatism: the more or less quiet introduction of dogmatism. The dogmatic element is, we note, wholly unconnected with the "fruits of experience" and other matter of the "talk" that has preceded.

However, mother proceeds to say that a woman writer told her "my best work has been done since baby came." Mother, because of her belief in "these things," substantiated by woman writer's improvement on advent of "baby," proposes to match-make as hard as she can, and to lose no time in setting about it. "The nation must have mothers." Note here the tendency to State concept. The need of the State tending to coerce the act of the individual. The greatest "peace work" for middle-aged mothers is, according to our authoress, "to help their daughters to find husbands with whom they can lead happy, nationally useful lives." We note here that internationalism has not reached the gas-leak stratum.

The next paragraph is most interesting:

"I know, as a middle-aged woman, that it is not always easy to be polite and genial to the friends of our children who come in at all sorts of unexpected times."

Deductions: 1. Politeness is not habitual, or at least it is not second nature, in the gas-leak stratum. It presents difficulties to the middle-aged mother.

2. Politeness is in some way confused with, or associated with, "geniality."

3. The simple method of letting said friends of offspring alone has not occurred to gas-leaking mother.

3a. Housing accommodation probably not sufficiently ample to permit or facilitate such non-intervention.

4. "Friends of our children" enter at "all sorts of unexpected times."

Note this last as indication of habits of the stratum. Mother was discussing marriageable and suitable males. These appear to be free and idle at "all sorts of unexpected times." Do they call on the way to employment? Are they employed? Are they "travellers" whose hours of employment are unfixed? Does the remark refer to schoolboys and students, or to female friends? In the latter case, how does it connect with potential husbands? It is easiest to suppose the Shaw-reading daughters are to marry into the student stratum. But will they?

Mother continues: "We would much rather read the evening paper and settle down to a quiet evening than make ourselves charming." The implication is that such settling down would irrevocably damage daughter's chances of matrimony. However, mother advocates "most informal hospitality," "men friends to tea or dinner," make them feel at home, any time, never a nuisance, not to be welcomed with scowls. But must not let every man who comes to house think you regard him as possible husband. This is the narrow bridge, the hair stretched over the chasm.

But preventing "his" feeling this, is not enough; there is "more in matchmaking" than just this one bit of camouflage. The male population is less numerous than the female. Deterrent causes of matrimony; as per mother: 1. Men afraid girl's standard of comfort too high (this to be remedied by the war); 2. Men have not, "in hundreds of cases, the chance of meeting women of their own position"—this "obstacle will remain unless the mothers of the country overcome it." Mother once heard a young business man say the only women he met were barmaids and girls in tobacconists' shops. "Father could be useful here. Both parents should help more." Foreign ideal of match-making utterly repugnant to English mind, not suggested that father should deliberately seek potential husbands among his friends. Simple hospitality to lonely young employees and colleagues. Riches not to be expected of the young male, provided he "has ambition." Father should not frown on every y. m. not making £500 per annum.

Mother has another plan; does not think girls should marry Australians and Canadians until they have crossed waters and inspected colonial life. Suggests exchange hospitalities between parents of Dominions (sic) for one son rec'd in Eng. one daughter to be entertained in colony. (cf., Roman hospitium) Mother says that "before the war such exchanges of hospitality were frequently arranged between French and English parents." (This interesting point has been overlooked by many hurried sociologists.)

Mother thinks Empire League and Agents-General should do something about it—she does not say what. She does not, as I indicated in a former chapter, intend to wait for the Agents-General. Cost would not be greater than sending girl to cheap German school, or French family. Better do with fewer servants, etc., than deny chance of marriage and motherhood. £100 total cost of long visit to Australia or New Zealand, and "money spent on travel is never money wasted."

This is the first indication we have of economic status of mother's family, and those for whom she writes. Families with £100 epargnes chance it on Australian bridegroom. Canadian chances cheaper. Cost of emigration to domestic servant, until recently, £3 to Australia. Better grade female now wanted. Reduced passage rates to ladies investigating colonies, with probable motherhood, highly recommended. War has brought colonies nearer, with "flaming patriotism"; cheaper travel will bring them still nearer.

(Note: Nothing could possibly be sounder than this last contention.)

Girls brought back to home-circle by war, mothers should seek to provide them with (peroration à la the Countess of Warwick) "another home in which to dwell, there to hear the laughter of little children about their firesides as we heard it in the long ago." Observe that this scheme is slightly different from the procreation tempered with emigration scheme which we noted in an earlier study.

So much for what mother has put down on the printed pages (four pages double column). Note the ground tone. The ground tone not only of this little "frank talk," but of all this sort of writing. Whether the talk is "frank" makes little difference; if it is not the talk of a mother, or of someone expressing her own personal and typical mentality, but merely the tour de force of someone writing for a given audience, it is at least a successful tour de force. It represents the mentality of the not innumerous readers who accept it. This sort of didacticism proceeds by general statement, it is specifically ignorant of individual differences, it takes no count of the divergence of personalities and of temperaments. Before its swish and sweep the individual has no existence. There are but two conclusions: 1. That these people do not perceive individuality as existing; 2. That individual differences in this stratum are so faint as to be imperceptible.

Compare this abstract sort of writing with an earlier form of abstraction, to wit, the Morality Plays. In the morality of "Everyman" the abstract or generalised Everyman is confronted with Death, Pleasure, Riches, etc. Both he and they become strangely and powerfully "humanised." They become so humanised in fact, that a later generation insists on having "Iago" instead of "Cunning," and "Hamlet" instead of "Hesitation" or "Dubiousness." The equations of the Morality Play are basic equations of life.

It is perfectly possible to contend that there is a basic equation under mother's "talk": the difference lies in the treatment. Traduisons!

In our allegory or morality play, youth (female) desires to be exposed to the attack of the male; to exercise its predatory capacity for being seized. Middle-age (female) equally desires youth (female) to be mated, but desires herself (Middle-age) to be surrounded by youth (female), desires stimulus of young female's magnetic whirr, desires male, if possible, to make its spring in vicinity of Middle-age; this, however, can be dispensed with, so long as youth (female) is somewhere or somehow mated, plus more or less assurance of lifelong sustenance. All this is however weakened, covered with sickly pall of circumstance, state-theory, matriarchal sentimentality, minute attritions, mental inexactitudes. Similes of weaning and severance of umbilical cord, arise in the critic's mind. Maze of incoherence and proverbial statements. Fundamental element reduced to a minimum by the stylistic treatment. Sex-heave of the individual entirely circumlocuted, passion of the individual with its infinite ricochets untouched.

Question again arises: Is this critical estimate correct, or are the people, for whom this stuff is poured out, so devitalised that question of individual passion, individual drive, is not a factor in their existence? At any rate, the tension of "Everyman," or of the hero of the Morality Play, is obviously absent from anything presented by this modern general and aphoristic treatment of situation.

Many questions flow round one: Is this stratum maintained, re produced, by multitudes verging on impotence? One cannot ask the ratio between impotence and genteelness, for even genteelness is absent; we are in the presence of almost every vulgarity. We might ask the ratio between lack of mental grip and vulgarity; but that question does not reach anything. Lack of mental grip is equally consonant with good manners. Yet good breeding and the gutter both make for some sort of mental directness. The "gas leak" stratum is obviously in a gap between gutter and breeding. I don't know that we can determine much else.

I have not yet come to the end of the "Heart Throbs." Besides, we *must* get lower than the strata that reads Shaw and Nietzsche.

Note in the first method of abstraction mentioned above, the emphasis is on the fact of certain similarities or universals in the lives of all men, however superficially diverse; in the latter method there is the assumption of a lack of divergence. No mediaeval writer ever thought or wrote of any man as "a unit" in the modern sociological or statistical fashion. Apart from the tax-roll ancient empires had no statistics. The individual might be murdered for a whim, but modern democracy has invented the present method of melting him into a compost. Or is it merely a recognition of compost—compost actually existing in nature? An unconscious, or semi-conscious recognition?

9. Further Heart Throbs
OCTOBER 18, 1917

INTIMATE and touching as "mother's" talk may have seemed, we have not yet exhausted the possibilities of the magazine. "Hitch your waggon to a star" is enjoined only by one advertisement; other objects please hitch to the competitions. "Daphne" is pleased, "very pleased with the result of the 'Heading Competition.'" "Chrissie Potts very much wants to find a girl about her own age to correspond with. She is 15, fond of painting, photography, and reading." Various correspondents recommend books by Gene Stratton Porter, William J. Locke, and other authors. All this under the aegis of "Daphne." The "League of Young British Citizens" (Patron-in-Chief, Princess Patricia of Connaught) draws the pageant to its close. The editor takes this in hand as "Alison" has departed. "Daphne" ends by assuring her readers that she will always be pleased to hear from

them, and then the editor takes up the tale: "My Dear companions,—I
have a surprise for you, and an unpleasant one! Our good friend 'Alison,'" etc., is torn from them. She shrinks from farewells; the companions should feel and say "a great big thank you to Alison for all she has
done for us." She had taken an individual interest. The editor, now that
Alison has gone, has been "pondering deeply over the future of the
League."

"Years ago, in times of national crisis, 'The Quiver,' was ever at the
front with good works." Miss Woolf rendered invaluable service about
the Deep Sea Fisherman, married, and went to Ceylon. She is now stepping into the breach left by Alison, but competitions will be left entirely
to Daphne. The companions are, however, to write to Mrs. L., née Woolf,
and wish her well. Then follow letters from an ex-postal censor, a "gal-
lant sailor boy," Lieutenant———, and from William———, who is
very glad that Lena, Violet, David, and Philip are doing well, living a beautiful life, etc. Another "companion" is congratulated on Higher Grade
School examination.

These things appear slight enough, but they must not pass by us unheeded. The well-connected family with the large scrapbook on its draw-
ing-room table is no more symptomatic. We know that the family photograph album bound in red leather (and, a grade higher, in black leather)
no longer, at least we presume that it no longer, abounds in Mayfair; but
the scrap-book, the scrap-book with illustrations from the "Sketch" and
the "Tatler," showing the distinguished family in all its splendours, seats,
and positions, is extant, if it have not replaced its precursor.

The yearn of "mother's" daughters to escape the gapped linotype
repeats itself in the yearn of the suburb for companionship; hence Leagues
of Companions; hence simple-hearted epistles; hence church congrega-
tions; the difference being that Mayfair is nearer the top, and passably
conscious of itself, its possibilities, the number of meetable persons, and
the derivative advantage per person.

The theoretic sociologist is prone to pass over these things; the
politician, or practising sociologist, is aware of them, perhaps without
much formulation; the anthropologist will attempt to envisage them
calmly, as he would envisage the customs of exogamy among more primitive tribes; to him it is little matter whether the female young are taken

to the centre of Africa, to reserved places where they dance for hours on end until their muscles are abnormally strengthened; whether they patrol the passeo at Arles; whether they be taken to dances indoors, more or less tribally organised; whether they are "waited for" after church; or whether they are left, where the tribal organisation is deficient, to family or individual efforts, more or less unsystematic, more or less veiled. It is his business to classify, to make, if he can, "head or tail of it." As the anthropologist starts without a sense of "ought" he has one more chance, or several more chances, of making head or tail of it, than has the theorist who wants to fit mankind or "future society" to a model.

All we can postulate is that in certain strata the desire for encounter is sufficient to make these numerous correspondence columns, "leagues," etc., lucrative to their managers. I have not sufficient data at hand to determine much else concerning the correspondents. I do not know whether they, as a mass, read, like "mother's" offspring, Shaw and Nietzsche. But I have spent enough time on these suburbs for the present.

In the hope of getting below the Shaw-Nietzsche zone I purchased the "Family Herald." [See plate 8.] This paper I had often heard mentioned. Whenever a stylist wishes to damn a contemporary, especially a contemporary novelist, he suggests that said novelist is specifically fit to "write for the 'Family Herald.'" The phrase is as familiar as are the terms "Strachey" and "Spectator." The "Family Herald," No. 3881, Vol. CXIX, price One Penny, is not at first sight distinct from various other penny weeklies on the bookstalls. Why its name is more familiar, why it is the accepted symbol of debasement among hyper-sensitised literati, I have no present means of discerning. Twenty pages, treble col., paper as used in daily newspapers, ads. 4 pp. and 1 col. It sub-heads itself "The Household Magazine of Useful Information and Entertainment."

First item. Poem. Far from the worst I have seen, and mildly suggestive of Longfellow with his fancy lightly turned amorous.

Second item. Story beginning with statement that "The two roses . . . were having one of their tiffs." This is a little confusing, but I take it to be a sort of horticultu-allegorical prelude to the love-interest and the lovely day that follows. (5 cols.)

Third item. Chap. IV of continued effort. Lady Agatha, Madame de

Grespignan (Gareth's mother), Joan Lady So-and-So, relatives of the late Earl, etc. (12 cols.)

Fourth item. Chap. IV. Chas. Wynn, of good family, who has had to go to Australia on account of "gambling propensities," the Earl, Molly, Mary (known as Minnie), etc. (8 cols.)

Fifth item. Answers to Correspondence re "Zabern," "Liverpudlian," "Dorking," and a judicial separation. One page. Other answers deferred.

Sixth item. Editorial. "The Influence of Government on National Character." This is a perfectly sane and clear editorial, quite as good as any other editorial in any British periodical. There is no nonsense about it, no humbug, no quackery. It is informative. It explains to its readers the state of the franchise in Germany; administrative organisation of German towns, etc.; lack of local control, etc. It points out that local control is more highly developed in England. It does not broach the "dangerous" question of universal suffrage, or of manhood suffrage, but it is perfectly fair in its comparison of present actualities. It contains the kind of knowledge about a foreign country that is good to disseminate. It is the kind of popular education that a more sensitive, more intelligent capital would have been disseminating for years past concerning Germany and other foreign States. The disease of the Press is that it never will disseminate such information "beforehand." A more intelligent race would have been aware of these symptoms, stati, facts concerning neighbouring peoples. It would not wait for an Armageddon to awaken it into curiosity, into inspecting the nature of its neighbours. Six years ago only a crank would have tried to publish in a popular paper an essay on German local government. Only a recognition of the unity of this planet will lead future people to pay any attention to the nature and symptoms of their neighbours.

Next page: Moral Reflections, quarter col. Statistics, about a quarter col. "Scientific and Useful," remainder of col. Varieties, 2 cols.

Next page: Jokes, much the same sort of jokes as you find at the back of "The Century" or "Harper's" or in "Punch." In fact, this sort of small jab would seem to be the one feature common to the periodicals aimed at all zones of society. Let us note this polybious element. The "joke," the "humorous anecdote," is a usually minute dénouement, it is a dash of the unexpected or "the incongruous," it is a letting of the cat, usually an almost infinitesimal cat, out of the bag. Note this in comparison with the periodicals for the "stopping down" of thought. The joke is a letting out of the unimportant or trifling cat. Nobody minds what little Mary said to the Curate. Realist literature is a letting out the big cat. It is giving away the gigantic or established show, when the show is an hypocrisy; it is giving away with an ultimate precision. Shakespeare's "Histories" give away the show of absolute monarchy. They are the greatest indictment ever written. The realist novelists let out the cats of modernity, many forms of many oppressions, personal tyrannies, and group tyrannies. The slime will not tolerate the great gestes; they insist on the dribble of "humour," as it is called; they like people who are "funny." Note, for example, that "Punch" has never been on the side of a minority. It is, for all its pleasantry and nice behaviour, the most cowardly organ in England.

Note also that the "Family Herald," with its perfectly sane editorial, is a cut above "Punch." The "Herald" has no section devoted to the degradation of letters. It does not use its circulation for the deliberate debasement of any part of literature, as does "Punch" its review column for the consistent besmirching of every serious attempt of English novelists to paint the thing as it is.

Sir Owen Seaman is presumably neither a yahoo nor a mattoid; there is some moral tinge in his status. The law being what it is, perhaps we had better allow the man Seaman to find and apply to himself the suitable word for one who having a certain position, carrying with it a more or less fortuitous power to further or hinder good writing, definitely uses that position for the degradation of letters. This insult is deliberate and impersonal. I have never written a novel. I am therefore a fit person to deliver it. "Punch," originally a broken-nosed, broken-backed cuckold, is strangely overblown; has strangely puffed himself up into a symbol of national magnitude. We see him heraldic in Tabard, leading in a new dynasty upon horseback. I pass over the poor devils who have to be "funny" once a week for a living; they keep to the original rôle of jesters and society entertainers; but this pomposity of "Punch," as an "organ," "Punch" the "serious" is in no need of sympathy. It is time he was taken back to his bauble (Knighthood and a' that).

Return to the "Family Herald." Next item:—Children's Hour. Sunshine Guild (charity). Motto for the week, eight lines of rhyme, repeating the two lines—

"Back of the gloom—
The bloom!"

(Optimism spreading from Ella and Marie to ???)

Next item (skipping ads.): Woman's Sphere (*cf.* Mr. Shorter's paper). The "Family Herald" is not quite so gushing as "The Sphere" in this dept., or as Vogue, Frilly, etc. There is in the "Herald's" dress col. no archaic English, such as is found in "The Sphere."

Next item. "At Home," recipes, etc., chess, draughts, and lastly the key or distinctive feature, "Helps to Health." I had at first mistaken this for an ad. column, but no, the "Herald's" family physician replies to correspondents. This is the first such column I have found. A. B. S. is addressed as follows: "Do not be silly and make such an exhibition of yourself." Auntie Bee receives these instructions: "I fear you will have a difficult task. Medicines are no avail, only moral suasion on your part and the exercise of a free and a firm will on her part can do any good. A strong argument for her would be the 'comparative' one—viz., to put before her the condition of society generally if all were similarly affected, for you must never allow it to be named 'affliction.' Change of air, scene, and society will play a useful part . . . iron jelloids, etc." Archie has perhaps "an excess of natural waxy secretion in the ears"; white curd soap is recommended. Exercise, air, washing of various parts are suggested to other correspondents. The family physician seems possessed of good sense. The column is doubtless useful, and other weeklies might profit by similar methods.

As an indication of stratum note that the "Family Herald" is the first paper in which I have found ads. relative to "nits and vermin in the hair," and the ad. beginning "IF YOUR CHILD has nits or head pests." It is arguable, by these portents, that the "Family Herald" reaches, or at least approaches, the verminous level, but still it is a cut above "Punch." The "family physician" is useful, and "Punch's" book reviews are of no use whatever, though they be camouflaged by Punch's "pleasantry."

10. The Backbone of the Empire
OCTOBER 25, 1917

IN the periodicals we have examined hitherto we have found every evidence for the loss of Antwerp and the Gallipoli muddle; and no sign of a reason why England should have won the battle of the Marne or held the Ypres salient. The virtues recommended or implied by "The Strand Magazine" might have helped with the commissariat; the "Edinburgh" is but one voice, and a slow one; the editorial in the "Family Herald" is retrospective, and counterbalanced by the concurrent fiction in its pages. But I am morally certain that the Kaiser had never opened a copy of "Chambers' Journal," for no monarch who had ever perused this phenomenon could have hoped to starve England with U-boats or permanently to have wrested to himself the scarred soil of Belgium. The Hohenzollern may for three generations have subscribed to many English periodicals; from the bulk of them the decadence of the Anglo-Saxon race was a not unlikely conclusion; people fed on these things would "plump dead for neutrality." The poor simple German!! Thorough in so many things, he had neglected, to his cost, "Chambers' Journal."

The tone of this paper is indicated in such sentences as:

"On these the boy set to work with a quiet, dogged resolution that, after a while, met with its due reward."

or:

"Buckle was a conscientious student, and worked ten hours daily for seventeen years before publishing."

Madame, one copy of this paper is sufficient to form your boy's character—and irrevocably. It is the Nelson Column, the Bull-dog breed, the backbone of the Empire, the Trafalgar Square among papers. I do not make mock of it. For three hours after first opening its pages I sat spellbound, tense, muttering to myself the lines:—

"and man in tail-less terror
Fled shrieking to the hills."

At last we have escaped Shaw and Nietzsche. It is mentioned, in a curious article on President Wilson, that his parents read him Scott and Dickens in his boyhood. Since the date of these authors, the readers of "Chambers' Journal" must have read, I think, "Chambers' Journal" exclusively.

There is in this paper no intellectual vacillation, no Russian irresolution. I am glad to say that even God is almost eliminated. He is, I admit, referred to vaguely and occasionally, but, on the whole, He is metaphysical, and He has been, in practicality, replaced by the king, who says a few choice words over the body.

"'I regret to inform you, sir,' the captain said, addressing the king as his admiral. . . ."

"'Mc . . . was a brave man,' the King said, returning the captain's salute."

The officers and men stand rigidly to attention regretting that they had not shown more foresight in appreciating their paymaster's assistant.

A rear-admiral has congratulated "Chambers" on a former serial, in the words: "The 'Navy' as shown in the story is absolutely photographic." Of course the Navy *is* just the least shade, jest-the-wee-little-least shade "photographic." The rear-admiral is, unsuspectingly, a master of English. I should have searched for that word a long time.

However, let us turn backward to "Chambers' Journal." It is a dam fine thing that a man should have grit enough to die for his duty as he conceives it; or even that he should stick at something or other until he makes a good job of it. That is the beginning of "Chambers."

The "Strand" might have inculcated a few commercial virtues, but the "Strand" is a puny weakling compared with the strenuous "Chambers," Sam Smiles is a laggard and sluggard; he would have approved and despaired.

Style, of course, is not for them; they are wholly impervious; to rally them on their rhetoric would be as useless as trying to persuade a bronze lion with argument. No true Chambersite would regard a problem of style as anything but immoral, a sort of absinthe, an aestheticism in the worst sense of the term. We must meet them on their own ground, on the high moral tone of their subject matter.

Madame, one copy of this periodical . . . boy's character . . . and irrevocably!! Consider this outline of a story.

Will, sickly and the dullard of the class, had a stutter, and limped, but once having come upon a noble French motto, he was enabled to translate the same later and save his form from detention. This lit within his breast the spark of ambition. He diligently ascended the school to the tune of "On these the boy, etc." Issuing from school he was denied the advantages of a University education, but set to learn modern languages; he also took a course in non-stammer, and courses in physical exercise—"Ossa upon Pelion—Muller upon Sandow," is the phrase. The family noticed his improvement. The reader looks to the ad. col. There is, however, no ad. for the curing of stammer, only "Wincarnis," "Electricity Victorious (infinite joy of health)," "Could you lift a ton?" Mind and Memory, Don't wear a truss, and Eno's as usual.

However, "Will" is not content with these mentioned advances; his lame leg still handicaps him; he consults a doctor; he does not want his family to be worried; his father gives him a vacation; he conceals his whereabouts, and has the limp rectified. Possibly the long leg is sawed off a bit to bring it level with the short one. Anyhow, war is declared. One expects it (from the tone of the sentences) to be the Crimean, but we come on a mention of khaki. It must be the Boer war! But no! it is our own Armageddon. "Will" turns up in uniform to the unmingled delight and wonder of his admiring family. "Stutter, limp, rotten chest, no muscle," what of it? Invictis! Dogged as does it! Let no man despair.

We are next told that "The Discoveries of Genius Alone Remain." Buckle's steadfastness is cited, also the marvellous padded passage of Buckle containing this sentence. Breechloaders and percussion-caps seem to be the "discoveries" most in the mind's eye of the writer. The dilatoriness of the War Office in recognising inventions is sternly censured.

Hold this in mind, I shall refer to it later. Or no, let us turn at once to the article "Agriculture as a fine art." I had thought arts beneath them, but the art of the hedger and ditcher is proclaimed for its craftiness. "Canopied by azure glimpsed between a shower of snowy petals decked with virginal green," the virtuous agriculturist perseveres in skill far surpassing that of the theoretical layman. Excellent, excellent. The plowman replete with primaeval virtues, etc.

This is really dam fine. These people whom I thought so stern in their cult of efficiency have wrought round Hodge this mantle of poesy. They have rebuked the War Office for inefficiency. Their strenuous hold on tradition has led them to ignore the existence of steam ploughs, of steam tractors, or of any of the modern farm implements. They are truly a wonderful people.

One had best take their paper in due order.

Item 1. Story in the manner, more or less, of Walter Scott. "The air seemed truly to merit the epithet of filthy bestowed on it by one of Shakespeare's witches."

Item 2. Agriculture, as mentioned.

Item 3. Chap. XXXVII., of continued story, begins with farce Dickens, introduces a rough diamond, little cripple girl,

"'Oh, my God!' and huddling to the fence, Spike broke into a fierce and anguished sobbing" (The term "righteous ire" occurs not in this tale but in item 1). Continued effort contains also love interest "between those quivering, parted lips came a murmur of passionate prayer and pleading." Heroine legally married, presumably to high class gent. boxer, long resists consummating her marriage on the ground that her brother's intention or attempt to murder her spouse has declassed her for such honours of wedlock. Finest possible feelings displayed by all the "good" participants in the story.

Item 4. "Civilizing influence of Buffalo Bill." *Finale verbatim sic:* "Guess Bill's a greater civilizer than Julius Caesar himself or any noble Roman of them all. Perhaps he was." Bill had succeeded in roping a few bronchos inside the precincts of the Coliseum, despite police prohibition.

Item 5. The self-helpful tale of the lame boy who began with a stammer and ended in uniform.

Item 6. Discoveries of genius, as mentioned.

Item 7. A Chaplain describes the front.

Item 8. The continued effort intrudes itself again.

Item 9. Typical British traveller from the wilds describes the relative merits of black races as servants, "get through a deal of hard work on very little food, etc." "Variety of rickshaw boys and found them willing enough. Bearing the white man's burden, why shouldn't the beggars . . . ?"

Item 10. Continuation of Item 1.

Item 11. Shark stories.

Item 12. Effusion, by Mr. Bart Kennedy, beginning "Wine of the grape is good, but wine of the earth is better." "The most delicious I have ever tasted. . . . Finer was it than the finest wine of the grape that I have ever tasted. . . . We used to go to the Alhambra to drink it when day was nearing its close. It was an Italian count who first put me on to it. . . . A time will come to pass when the wine of the earth will have gone. . . . Man and his works and his heroes and his gods will be as nothing that has gone nowhere. And the earth will roll, a thing of desolation. When gone is the earth wine."

FOOTNOTE.—Mon Cher Bart, the scriptural prophecy refers only to more briny varieties of the liquid; the good book declares that the "sea" shall be no longer extant. You cannot possibly have been imbibing sea-water in the Alhambra gardens. The total absence of fresh water is specified only in hell; around the throne of the Redeemer the ever-flowing water of life will doubtless be found an apératif, palatable substitute.
—E. P.

This prose is followed by a poem beginning with "sweet violets," running on through "sward," "dawning of each happy day," "glories manifold," "yonder" and "rill." However, the pseudo Wordsworth has no more inversions in his rhyme than Mr. Bart Kennedy has in his prose dithyrambics on the potation of the aqueous fluid.

Item 14. Story of the man who hadn't the naval style and on whose corpse the King placed a verbal wreath.

Item 15. Effect of war on the nation's gold.

Further sections of items already mentioned.

Item 18. German doings in South America. The ethics of the Chançon de Roland. "The pagans are wrong the French are right," applied rather heavily to the Bosche.

Item 19. "A million a year down London drains."

Item 20. Poem.

Item 21 is devoted to President Wilson as follows: "In time so distant that even the history of this ghastly and fateful world-convulsion will be condensed by the historians into a page or two, the peroration of Woodrow Wilson's address to Congress will be given in full." "No man is more devoted to home life." P.S.—Considerations of space tore me from the contemplation of "Chambers."

The Empire owes its status to its moral priority. I mean that Herbert of Cherbury, or someone from whom he cribbed it, perceived before continental nations the advantage of some sort of probity. That Hesperian bloom, Benj. Franklin, condensed it into his aphorism on "Best policy," but long before his day England had seen the superiority of a moral claim to naïve Machiavellianism, such as lately practised by the Bosche. So long as you have a strong moral case you are, perforce, either a conqueror or a martyr, and the bones of the martyrs are excellent fuel for rebellions. The children's children of the oppressors, however efficient, may at any moment be called on to pay. "Chambers," which is more full of self-helpful maxims than any German possibly could be, has taken a firm stand on this pedestal. Its moral foregoneness is most bracing. Heroes are bred on such reading matter, and possibly blockheads.

The only other problem that faces us is that of rhetoric. Is it necessary to drug the young with such doses of it, in order to bring them up to the scratch? I dare say it is. "Chambers" has lasted a long time. The mind, set like a rock, and immobile as to two thirds of its possible excursions and activities, may be driven concentrated into the remaining territory, OR it may acquire the habit of immobility.

If anyone wants to know how people wrote and thought in 1832, "Chambers" is available; and if anyone is so naïve an utopian that he imagines that people no longer think in exactly that manner, there is the continued circulation of "Chambers" to confute him.

The ethic of "Chambers" is enough to terrorise any foreign nation to the point of a declaration of war; its tone, its lack of mental flexibility is enough to terrify them from it. It is so obvious that people, thinking as they do, can conceive nothing short of owning *all* the earth. It seems so likely that, having acquired it, they would permit no artist to live; would permit no mental experiments, no questioning of their excellent Lacedaemonian dogma; only in their one great gleam of stupidity (their ignorance of farm machinery in the year 1917) can one take comfort. They are dangerous if unwatched, but such stupidity, though a peril to neighbouring States, will probably be unable to close *all* the loopholes wherethrough an intelligent man might escape. As a wall of brass around Britain, i.e., on the purely defensive, I can conceive nothing superior, save foresight and intelligence, qualities much too rare to be counted on.

11. The Bright and Snappy
NOVEMBER 1, 1917

INADEQUATELY, most inadequately, have I dealt with the moral fibre of the weekly called "Chambers' Journal." No moderate modern man could give any idea of this fibre. Still, I have done my poor best. I have compared it to Nelson's column. Its gerants doubtless admired Carlyle.

A little more light may be cast upon it by comparing it with a younger weekly named "Answers"—the reader remembering in the meanwhile that we are searching for the psychology of the nation, and not seeking to advertise any paper to the detriment of the rest.

"Chambers" started a little before the accession of her late Majesty Queen Victoria; "Answers" anteceded her son by a few brief tremulous years. We are unfair to the great Victorian era unless we know a little of the mental atmosphere that preceded it. I open Mavor's collection of "English Classical Poetry" (pub. A.D. 1828); it is full of purposeless ululation. By its light one descries a reason for popular optimism, the optimism of Browning, the optimism of Ella. It takes at least a century for these reactions to drift through the public. I am not sure there is any "swing of the pendulum"; the idea, or the mood, seems to rise from one man or from a small group and flows out like mud or lava over the people, overcovering and making its strata upon similar effluvia antecedent.

Junius in his letters talks of the "melancholy madness of poesy." "The Family Herald" does the "Back-of-the-gloom-the-bloom" trick.

When the editor of a "bright-snappy" weekly applied to me for a bright snappy obituary notice of Emile Verhaeren, I rashly mentioned the nature of Verhaeren's muse, and said the correct amount of bright-snappiness might be hard to attain. Answer: "What, eh gloomy cuss, wuz he? Oh, we'd better not touch it at all."

The fashion of this world passeth away. The contemporaries of Mrs. Barbauld would have "taken theirs" melancholy. As with mood, so with the fervour of morals; "Chambers" shows none of the listlessness of "The Nineties." The bright-snappy papers show none of the Lacedaemonian firmness of "Chambers' Journal."

The first page of "Answers" leads me to classify it, at least for the present, under the general heading "Bright and Snappy." By taking the

Bright-and-Snappy at a penny I may be able to cover the ground in one article, whereas if I began at the bright and snappy more expensive (a shilling or thereabouts) I should have, later, to seek the bright and snappy for the masses. [See plate 8.]

The cover addresses me in these terms: "It will be a red-letter day for you when you receive the corsets, because it will be the beginning of new life. From the moment when you put them on a ceaseless stream of magnetism permeates the whole body from head to heel. The joy of New Life, of New Health . . . You feel a different woman. Your outlook on life is different—brighter, happier, and more hopeful." Even before this we are told "it gives splendid health, tireless energy, and an attractive personality."

I cannot argue this upon facts; my reader must wait for the discussion in a future chapter on almanacks and religion. Power to win by refraining from blushing and trembling is advertised inside the cover. The snappy-and-bright proper begins on the first page of the text: The last blows of summer, the short skirt, the man who wasn't good enough for the girl, the boy who wanted to get dirtier before being washed, the author whose play aroused the house, all obtrude their unvarying faces, brisk as ever. Note the humour, not of disclosure, but of the "sharp" irrelevant reply; then comes the humour of the jest based on special or local knowledge. "Have we any Gerards? asks a contemporary. Try the telephone girl for an answer."

This is a periodical for "Home and Train." We are not really on the trail of a force; we are not digging up a basis of action, mass action; we are not getting at the understanding of a driving power, as we most certainly were in the reading of "Chambers." These things are not funny: all of these tones of writing are significant of the popular psychology. We must make a very clear distinction between writing which definitely shapes the reader, or tries to shape him, and writing intended only as a drug.

Note that the cheap tired mind, picking up its paper, apparently likes a couple of dozen of these pert paragraphs, snippets. The aperitif before supper.

Interspersed with these snaps are five longer paragraphs and a poem (more or less Kippled). The paragraphs deal with anthrax imported from China, the price of palaces, value of man-power, and wisdom of having children grow up strong. "As a nation, we need to see vividly, to appreciate vitally, to understand fundamentally, that when a child has reached the age of fourteen the chief opportunity of life is past." If these years are rightly utilised the rest of the life "can be trusted, as a general rule, to look after itself." "American baseball players will make good bomb-throwers." The most interesting paragraph is, however, at the foot of the first column. It concerns "Chlorophyll green." It is a brief lesson in botanic chemistry; three inches of science. Near the end of it we find the sentence: "If the chlorophyll contained in the plants were to perish with the 'fall of the leaf,' there would be an end to the vegetable kingdom, and 'man the biped' would also disappear."

This statement may, for all I know, be perfectly true. Its truth is not the interesting thing at the moment. The thing for us to observe, as anthropologists, is that it is the same thing, the same teleological wheeze that Mr. Bart Kennedy gave us at the end of his prose rhapsody about water. ("Chambers' Journal," September 1, 1917, page 592) sic: "A time will come to pass when the wine of the earth will have gone. And when it has gone, gone will be man and his works. Gone will be the trees and the grass and the flowers. Gone will be the beings who lived with man." ("Chambers" costs 9d. Mr. Kennedy can afford to be richer and fruitier than "Answers," 1d.) "The earth will be but a vast desert . . . . , etc. Man and his works, etc. , . . . nothing gone nowhere. And the earth will roll a thing of desolation,

When gone is the earth wine."

As a matter of material science, putting both statements together, we deduce that both water and chlorophyll green are necessary to our preservation and comfort. As a matter of psychology we have hit on one of the simple devices of people who wish to stir the lay mind or wring the appreciative "Bah Goom!" from the yokel. It is the old question, "Where'd ye be if you wasn't?" The theologians have used it for ages; it is in the grip-sack of the popular exhortationists. With this one little implement in your possession you may sit upon any turnstile in the attitude of Rodin's "Penseur."

As the paradisiacal promise, such as that concerning the corsets, has always been used as a lure, so this wheeze about the horror of nothingness, the end of the world, the day of judgment, etc., has been used as a shake-up, as an hysteria-producer to weaken the will, and it has even masqueraded as an argument for believing or accepting or tolerating all sorts and conditions of doctrines.

There is, incidentally, nothing easier than this leap from an actuality into chaos. The shortest exact progress from known facts to a working conclusion, or to a workable theory, is infinitely more hard to attain. These swoops are probably primitive. Children think about the end of the world. They ask what will become of favourite toys after they are dead. One gropes in the void of the popular mind. What number of general concepts, or even what basis of "common sense," can we expect to find in the general mind, or in the minds of the average or majority?

They tell me that Maxim Gorky's mother spent a great part of her life saying to her neighbours, "You should wash more. If you would wash more you would not have so many lice." We smile from the heights of our superior Hesperian cleanliness. Yet to judge from our periodicals the vast majority of our neighbours do not know enough science to keep their bowels open. I think there is not one paper of all those I have looked at which does not proclaim some cathartic. If any number of Hindoos practise the hygiene some few among them profess, travelling Asiatics must spend their occidental life in one large grin at this widespread ignorance among Europeans. The difference between a great man and a failure, pages on pages of reading matter, columns of auroral language poured out for decades to teach Europe this one simple fact. Any cathartic, at least almost any cathartic, would serve just as any soap or almost any soap is more or less effective against vermin (under non-war conditions). It is all very well for Mazzini to say "Educate!" It is all very well for social theorists to explain systems for the distribution of wealth, etc . . .

We most of us believe, more or less, in democracy . . . But if man emerges from parental control at, let us say, fifteen, and if it takes him on an average of, say, ten years to learn this simple principle of hygiene and happiness, how long, etc., will it take him to learn to wield a vote, and decide on the most expeditious way towards the happiness of the race, the happiness of a multitude of various people?

AND what period will be required among a people so reticent, a people so bound by delicate periphrases of speech that the child of fifteen will not have been clearly instructed in these matters, but will, in most cases, be left to make the momentous discovery for himself with the aid of cathartic advertisements?

The other key paragraph on the first page of "Answers" is that about man-power, already referred to: "But sound men grow from sound children just as trees grow from good, straight saplings, etc. . . . horses from . . . foals . . . healthy vegetables from a well-tended, well-manured, rich-soiled, well-watered, sunny market-garden . . . we let our children grow like weeds . . . blown by winds of circumstance . . . conditions predestined to produce poor results. . . . Yet they are the nation's chief wealth —the wealth which will best repay preserving."

This is interesting. We had the Countess of Warwick anti-Malthusing in the "Hibbert," and even applying the argument emotioné, the pleasures of motherhood, in a tone not unlike that of Mr. Bart Kennedy proclaiming his orgy of water in "Chambers' Journal." We had "Chambers" bucking up the adolescent lower deck and instructing the young how best to become superior cannon-meat, how to bite through a three-inch board, and be stout defenders; we had the middle-aged mother, and some writer in, I think, "The Edinburgh," beseeching us to breed and overflow into the colonies.

The international view point is apparently not the same as that of the author, who beseeches us to produce wealth from our loins; no owner of slaves could, indeed, be more fervent, personal and explicit. The worst type of Socialist may have exhorted us to cooperate with the State to the point of self-annihilation, but this specific statement that the child is the property of the State (even after a recent judicial pronouncement that a man has no property in his wife) is interesting *as a symptom*. The garden will doubtless be manured.

Personally, I do not desire a revolution with violence, and idiocies of this sort therefore annoy me, even though they be only slips of the pens.

Children, for the first part of their life at any rate, should be consumers, not property; it is a dog's trick, this bringing them to tables ill-furnished. Still, the Countess was very much shocked when she found a working woman in the North of England who declared herself unwilling to do so. If, however, human beings are "wealth," a form of superior live stock, their owners should attentively listen to "Answers" and the advice about human conservatism, and his fattening of the child for the market.

11 [12]. Hash and Rehash
NOVEMBER 8, 1917

A THING that strikes one in this descent from "Shaw and Nietzsche"; in this descent from the authors who write for "us" to the authors who write for the people Wells and Bennett aim at and miss, is the "fine-cut" or hash system of presentation. I have not yet reached the nadir, the mediaeval basis of stupidity and superstition upon which "the Empire rests"; I am but half-way toward the reader whose food is "Old Moore" almost exclusively, and who does *not* "read the papers." But as I submerse myself lower and lower I note that the "article" diminishes; that the amount of any given subject exposed to the single lectorial contact is slowly but surely diminished.

This diminution is not measurable by simple space; the real diminution is much less than the diminution in the actual number of words devoted to any particular topic. Or, baldly: the "Spectator" would take a great deal longer to make any given statement than would "Answers" or the "Family Herald." The populace, the *popolaccio,* is in some ways much better served than the ex-intelligentsia.

Despite its almost incredible mendacity and its falsification-by-distortion, the Daily Press is a great educational force. In this series, however, I am avoiding the daily Press, I am deliberately avoiding any discussion which would involve the question of "news" or news-getting, or the value of news, or any question or paper in any way involved or complicated by a news-value. (The only points at which I can be said even to have grazed such an issue have been in the timeliness of the "Family Herald's" informative page *re* German municipal government, and in the possible news-value of the "Edinburgh's" reports of foreign authors relatively antecedent to their demises.) Our study is a study of contemporary psychological states and of the psychological aptitudes of various masses. Among these we find the necessity for the fine-cut.

The fine-cut is a dope. It is hedonistic. It is often sham-utilitarian; that is, it possesses all the vulgarity of the utilitarian tone; it professes to give "practical" information; and it is a sop to the tired or ineffectual mind, to the vagrant attention or inattention, and is fundamentally useless.

You may study enough of a subject to become a specialist, or little enough to become a first-aider, or to fit you to do your own plumbing, or you may imbibe too little even to enable yourself to ask intelligent questions. It goes back even to schooldays, when a boy may study a language, which, if he learn it, will be all his life an almost extra sense, an open avenue for sensation and knowledge; or he may read through a classic which will be a life-long possession; or he may take a year's physics or chemistry, which unless he continue the study, unless he make one of these sciences his profession, will be out of date before he is twenty-five. (He may also receive so dead, pedantic and incomplete an impression of a Greek or Latin author that the said author will *not* be a "possession.")

Even some of our least commendable but prominent writers have been taught by their forebears the value of a "subject." The *basso popolo* never learns the value of a subject; they accept fine-cut, and as long as they insist on, or take, fine-cut, just so long will they remain of the *basso popolo,* impotent, mastered. Believers in imperia will say: "let them be mastered," but unfortunately they serve to no purpose. The dominator but floats like Jules Romains' "drop of oil." And we have heard of the member of a mystical order who spent his whole life intriguing for the leadership of twenty second-rate souls.

There is a social determinism, and it is indicated when the Italian immigrant mother in America comes to school to say, "Jenny not study any more. Jenny not read book. She read book, it makes her sick." (Note: "sick" in American is used of other ailments beside simple nausea.)

Keeping this simile, we may say that a man's social ascent or descent is determined largely not only by how much he can "digest," but by how much he can "take in" or "hold" at one time. The number of people who can read Doughty's "Arabia Deserta" is decently and respectfully limited; so much so that the readers of that work tend to form an almost secret society, a cellule, at least, of an actual, if almost imperceptible aristocracy.

I see no reason why the perusers of "Answers" should be held inside any limit. There is no mind so flabby that it need quail before "A Ducal Farmer," "Hindenburg British Subject," "Princess as Typist," done at three or four to the ten-inch column. In the same column we learn that "Miss Brayton's 'dressing-room library' also contains some books on golf," "works on gardening and old china, in both of which subjects she takes a keen interest. She says that nothing soothes her nerves better than to read a book on one or other of these topics before going on the stage." This paragraph is headed: MISS BRAYTON'S LIBRARY. It contains a masterly phrase, or at least an implication, as valuable as that of the Admiral who suggested that the Navy was just the least shade photographic. The paragraphist who dealt with Miss Brayton has illuminated for us the distinction between a "subject" and a "topic." Between them there is an exceeding great gulf.

A "contributor" in the next col. of "Answers" "SUGGESTS THAT BROKEN HEARTS CANNOT BE MENDED WITH CASH." This subject appears to supply the whole column, but on closer examination we find the column divided into four sub-headed paragraphs. It contains an expression of opinion from Mr. Justice Low, one from Miss Lind-af-Hageby, and one from Lord Herschell in 1879; it touches on male and female breach of promise, and ends with a touch of the "new" optimism, sic: *"but perhaps after the war* our legislators may be prevailed upon to enact a law abolishing breach of promise cases altogether."

The next salient feature (for the topics in "Answers" are cut so fine we must confine ourselves to salient features) is called, I believe, on the American vaudeville stage, "the reel genn-u-ine sob-stuff." It is all about the "dark-haired soprano, and the men who softly join in the haunting refrain." It is, in part, anapaestic tetrameter. We are promised the next instalment in a single line at the foot of p. 279, sic: "A Pathetic Description of Our Graves in France, by Miss Hilda M. Love, next week." Miss Hilda is their special woman war correspondent.

As in a village one is surrounded by individuals, so in the metropolis we are surrounded by these agglomerate personalities. Only in cities, perhaps, do they become articulate and distinguishable . . . even though the outline be indistinct. One need not put oneself down as "unanimist" to be increasingly aware of their imminence, of their power, of their impotence. One may shut one's door in a village; one may shut one's letter-box in a city, and refrain from reading the papers, or from reading current publications of any sort; but one cannot wholly shut out the consciousness of other existences in one's neighbourhood.

Besides, even the attempt at anything like complete isolation is over-

misanthropic, it is a mental and social constriction no more to be com-
mended than the spiritual cowardice of the "Spectator." The modern
Ulysses will recognise Miss Hilda as a very extensive agglomerality. Miss
Hilda can "put over" "the sob-stuff." Her editor says in his little black-
letter heading, "In her inimitable way she shows Tommy exchanging
fighting for fun for a brief spell. No greater war work is being done than
that by those clever people who enable our troops to forget the grim business of war by organising entertainments." "Sentiment and Humour" is
the label upon her first sub-section. "Blue-eyed, with a mass of shining
fair hair, a typical daughter of Britain is singing." "The sweet notes," "a
thousand clear voices," "an audience such as only a war of this magnitude could produce." Miss Hilda's inimitability consists to some extent
in the omission of certain verbs, and in a lavish use of the present tense
in such verbs as she permits herself to retain.

In "Answers" next salient, "Taffy—Fighting Man," we are hallowed
with the black-type heading: "The Welshman butts into battle like his native goat. He goes for the enemy at sight, and asks no questions. In this,
the final article of the brilliant series on British nationalities, the Welshman is dealt with as faithfully as the writer has dealt with his brothers,
John, Sandy, and Pat." This statement is comparative, and I have no
doubt the comparison is most just. I have at my elbow no reference book
which will reveal to me the precise meaning of "argumentum ad hominem," but I suspect that this statement concerning "his native goat" is
"the argumentum ad hominem."

I have two other examples in my file: (a) The advertisement which
says, "There won't be much the matter with the young chap who takes a
good dob of X's mustard with every meal["]; (b) an incident by me observed, and as follows: The bard, once mentioned for laureate honours,
had been with difficulty induced to read from his works. "Induced" is
perhaps the wrong word. He had absolutely refused, but younger authors
arising and reading, he seized upon the only method of keeping them
quiet. He read from "The Purple East" with the emphasis and sweep of
a Melancthon; he was very impressive. When he had finished his thun-
ders, there arose the female sculling champion of the Orinoco, or some
such river. She was what "Answers" would call "blue-eyed, with a mass
of shining, fair hair, typical daughter of Britain." She had the *allures* of a

prize-fighter, and approaching our un-Herculanean host, she demanded
in a hoarse whisper (in what "Answers" might term the "throbing notes
of the contralto"): "Who'z that man talkin' against our country?" The
host with greater deliberation responded (in tones such as are usually
reserved for "Lift up your heads, O ye gates, and be lifted," etc.), "That!
. . . . is Mr. William . . . . Watson."

"Well, you tell Mr. Watson if he wants to-settle-this-thing-he-can-
step-right-out-into-the-hall, an'-right-NOW."

Even long residence out of Albion had not altered her intrepidity.

My difficulty with the sentence about the Welshman and his native goat is that there are, metaphorically, native goats elsewhere. I am
unable to see the statement as definition—the particular statement about
the goat and other statements in the two columns following. It is not always clear that these statements apply, or are intended to apply, to all
Welshmen, or to Welshmen exclusively; and if they do not apply to all
Welshmen and to Welshmen and Welsh goats exclusively, their definitive value is open to objection; is, if we may so phrase it, inoperative, in-
efficient.

In fairness to the editor of "Answers," we must state that the editor does not claim for the article definitive or absolute value. He merely
says that it is brilliant, and that the anonymous author has "dealt with"
the Welshman quite as well as he had done with his brothers.

He goes on to a £500 prize, and thence to "Our Kiddies' Zoo." This
consists in a small black and white picture of an animal not unlike a po-
tato. Beneath it are the following lines:—

"The Spotted Ponk sits on the hill
    While morning dew is wet,
And stays there patiently until
    The evening sun has set."

12 [13]. The Emblematic
NOVEMBER 15, 1917

I HAVE been accused of living too exclusively among artists, among "my
own generation," among unpleasing people engaged in altering the gen-

eral state of affairs, or at least in tampering and making attempts. Desirous of getting not only out of myself, but out also of "a circle of art
interests," out of "my world," my "generation," I said to my butcher: "What
papers does your mother-in-law read—I mean what weeklies and
monthlies?"

My butcher (pronounced "beutcher") is a man from Unst, or some
such island. He hates the Scotch. His mother-in-law must be about sixty.
She cannot be called of my generation. He said he did not know, but
would ask her. He informed me in due time that the old lady liked "The
Christian Herald," "The Sunday Companion," and the "People's Friend,"
but "*not* the 'British Weekly'—THAT's Robertson Nicoll." He particularly cautioned me against this latter organ and its editor.

I set out in search of these weeklies. The first "news-lady" was firmly
negative. I noticed the "Catholic Suffragist" on her counter. The next
newsagent was without them. He had heard of them. I suggested that I
was on a wild-goose chase. He informed me that the likeliest place would
be the shop at the corner by Notting Hill Gate, wheretoward I proceeded,
stopping in two shops by the way.

The female in the first treated the matter as a joke, she grinned, to
the peril of her splendidly furbished complexion. (This shop also provides "minerals.") The next shop, also for the vendage of "minerals" was
almost derisive. I purchased the "Union Jack," the "Penny Popular" and
"The Marvel" to reinstate myself in their graces.

At the next corner a cleric was exhorting his auditors to beware of
the wrath to come, of the last days; and beseeching them to get right with
God, for "many terrible things are still to happen." His voice was rather
apoplectic; the audience was perfumed with liquor.

At the Notting Hill Gate shop I found "The Sunday Companion,"
"The Christian Herald," "Ideas," and "Forget Me Not." Mackensen
claimed 60,000 and 450 guns. I asked for the "People's Friend." No! Didn't
stock it. I asked what it was like: "Just like these?" "Uumhn, nah! more
like 'Tit-Bits' and 'Answers'; got no call for it."

On returning, I found the cleric had ended his rhapsody. A white-
headed layman was saying, in a tired, trainy, and sympathetic voice, that
the "blood of his blessed Saviour had taken them all away."

"The Christian Herald and Signs of our Times." "Attractive Autumn Number Next Week—New Serial Story." "This paper is an insurance policy of £1,000." "Largest circulation of any unsectarian religious paper."

It bears upon its smear-grey cover the representation of a young woman at a piano, a young man seated with child aged about two years on his knee, one aged about 3½ years perched in or on chair by his shoulder; further children, one male and one female, in right-hand corner. One and one-third of male adult's trouser-legs are pale grey, the remaining two-thirds being of the same colour as his coat. The mouths of female adult and of the four children are open. There is a potted and feathery palm plant in upper right-hand corner, and beneath the whole this inscription: "A NAVAL OFFICER HOME ON LEAVE: A Restful Sunday Evening with His Family."

Reader, pause! We are about to take a jump out of sanity and into the thick of a peculiar, a very peculiar, milieu.

Old Moore advertising a "Splendid Principal Hieroglyphic," to say nothing of minor displays, heads his March, 1918, page with a little lead-block portraying a kangaroo harnessed to an ordinary four-wheeler; a nude leg projects from the window of said four-wheeler; a notched sign-post, with no inscription, stretches above it; and behind it follow six apes bearing each on his, her, or its back an apelet. In the background a forest; at the extreme right edge of the picture the carcass of a pig is suspended by its hind feet. Old Moore says that the kangaroo, harnessed to the cab, "represents marvellous advance, not only in trade, but improvement all round, including art, literature and music. The mob of hairy monsters is emblematic of the undesirable section of the colony."

For July, Old Moore shows a ballet-dancer standing on a swift motorcycle, pursued by cowboys. He says: "The spirited picture selected by the Prophet for the month of July shows us that the eternal feminine will be in great demand, especially in our colonies." (Note: We have heard about this colony matter before: "Hibbert" and "Quiver.") Moore continues: "The ragged tramp leading the lusty goat is by no means a good omen."

For February he shows . . . but why say what he shows? when he says that "The heading chosen by the Prophet for the month of February needs little or no explanation." Neither, in one sense, does it. We all understand the prophetic significance of a policeman watching a monk sharpen a carving knife; of a cat gazing on a stubby man with a feather in his bowler, drawing a skeleton on a black-board. The nude leg in the four-wheeler was, doubtless, Old Moore's conception of art, and, perhaps, also that of his readers.

The "Christian Herald's" "Sidelights on the War" tells us that "the Book of Revelation deals with the Protestant Reformation, not with the Mahomedan system at all, but with the Western Anti-Christ, the Papacy." (Note, this is unfair to the Papacy. The Kaiser has some claim, and I shall perhaps put in one of my own. And (sotto voce): What price the late "Boney" or N. Buonaparte?)

Return to the "Christian Herald" and remember the butcher's mamma-in-law: "And it will be remembered that when we were dealing with the seventh chapter of Daniel, we there met with the period of 'a time, times and a half,' and I pointed out that it referred to

The Western Anti-Christ,

and, hence, must be reckoned in solar years, because it is the habit of Western people to reckon by solar, and not lunar chronology. I noted that the Papacy reached the climax of its greatness in the year 663, because the Pope in that year enjoined that all the services should be in Latin."

(Note: Italian and braw Scots not being current).

"That year, therefore, is looked upon by competent historians as marking the full development of Latin Christianity."

(Note: What price Thomas Aquinas?)

"If we reckon 1,260 years from then, we are brought to the year 1923; so that it seems likely that these years 1917 to 1923 will be most remarkable and momentous years in the history and decline both of the Papacy and of Mahomedanism."

("'Le Pape est boche,' dit M. Croquant").

"To return again to the tenth chapter of Revelation."

(Note: The "Christian Herald" has already told us that Daniel is an introduction to "Rev.").

"Angel swearing that time shall be no longer, and that the mystery of God is to be finished."

(Pauvre Père Eternel! He won't last out our grandchildren).

"Now a 'time' in symbolic prophecy always means a year of 360 days."

(Possibly a five days' reduction for good behaviour. "Time" and "a time" are subject to divergent interpretations).

Continues the heraldist! "Always means a year of 360 days. So that a year of 360 days symbolises a period of 360 years."

(Note: "A four-wheeler drawn by a kangaroo" = marvellous progress not only in trade, but with art, literature, etc., into the bargain).

"A period of 360 years. This is reckoned from the beginning of the sounding of the voice of the seventh angel."

(Clear as a bell!)

"Now, when did the seventh trumpet begin to sound?"

(Answer in next week's "Christian Herald." Leading prize winners £5, and three consolation prizes, in event of two correspondents giving same answer . . . ????? Not a bit of it!)

The author tells us that "the seventh trumpet begins to sound immediately after the Reformation."

(All clear!)

"Immediately after the Reformation. The question, then, is, When did the Reformation end?" Add 360 to 1563, and you get 1923.

(Note: 4—11—44, 23 skiddoo).

Heraldist continues: "Many people have added two and two together, only to be disappointed. But this we know: the nearer we come to the end, the more light we shall get. . . . The Lord comes as a thief in the night."

(Note: Most Bohemian of Him).

"But only to the world does He come as a thief; not to those who understand and wait for Him."

(In the latter case he rings the bell, and politely inquires of the butler?)

"Blessed are we who wait and come to the thousand three hundred and five-and-thirty days. If those years do not witness His longed-for-coming, they will at least prepare the way."

Let us go back in quiet to Mr. Moore and his almanac, to its little pictures of diminutive boys upon stilts stalking among huge exotic roosters; to coffin caskets with a whirl like a pin-wheel in front of them; to the man in a swallow-tail coat holding a clock while a fireman turns his hose on a blackamoor. Let us note that for twelve pages of "text" and some further pages thereof scattered through the ads., Old Moore carries twenty-four pages of ads. Sic: Nerve force, free to the ruptured, asthma, drunkard saved (18 pictures showing swing of the pendulum), rupture, magnetic girl, whooping-cough, fits, why be fat, pine-forest in every home, children's powders, message to mothers, don't wear a truss, life-pills, test horoscope, no more grey hair, grey hairs, gold watch free, eye ointment, drink habit conquered, neuraliga, free offer superior to steel and pennyroyal, ditto, infinitely superior to bitter apple, pills for women, kidney, renal pills, given away: information to the married, pills, pills, £5 notes for correct answer and stamp, free gift, without medicine, gold watch free, surgical appliance, lung tonic, Eno's.

And some ass has said that the age of Faith is dead!

13 [14]. The Celestial
NOVEMBER 22, 1917

"Ezra's next move was to make the priests responsible for the valuables, the silver,

the gold, and the vessels which had been offered for the temple."

—MRS. M. BAXTER in the "Christian Herald and Signs of our Times"

for October 25, 1917.

THE "move" narrated by Mrs. M. Baxter was, doubtless, most laudable; it is even quite credible that my august, more or less mythical namesake may have passed some such legislation, credible even that a flattering biographer might have claimed for it some degree of success. One permits oneself, however, to doubt whether the move or any such move, ever was or is wholly successful; and Mrs. Baxter may be accused of undue optimism when she heads the paragraph containing her statement with the heavy italics *"We May Do Likewise."*

Adam Smith wrote some time ago: "People of the same trade seldom meet together, even for merriment and diversion, but the conversation ends in a conspiracy against the public, or in some contrivance to raise prices." The priest, or his modern Levite, the man whose livelihood depends on religion, be he secretary to a more or less religiose organisation, be he a writer for religiose journals—is of a peculiar and segregated employment. As we saw in "Old Moore's Almanac," vendors of the future flock together. Heaven or freedom from "bad legs" are both commodities immaterial and quite vendable. They depend upon supply and demand, and the demand depends upon the supply of credulity. Let us observe "COMING IN THE CLOUDS, a sermon by Rev. C. H. Spurgeon":

"'NEVERTHELESS, hereafter.'" I like the sound of those two bells together; let us ring them again. "Nevertheless, hereafter." The "Hereafter" seems in brief to say to me that the main glory of Christ lies in the future. Not to-day, perhaps, nor to-morrow, will the issue be seen. Have patience! Wait a while. "Your strength is to sit still." God has great leisure, for He is the Eternal. Let us partake of His restfulness while we sing, "Nevertheless, hereafter." O for the Holy Spirit's power at this moment; for it is written, "He will show you things to come."

"Hereafter!" "Hereafter!" ["]Oh, when that hereafter comes, how overwhelming it will be to Jesus' foes! Now, where is Caiaphas? Will he now adjure the Lord to speak? Now, ye priests, lift up your haughty heads! Utter a sentence against Him now!

There Sits Your Victim

upon the clouds of Heaven. Say now that he blasphemes, and hold up your rent rags, and condemn him again. But where is Caiaphas?"

The repetition of this question naturally stumps the yokel. He looks under the seat, he looks under his neighbour's pew, and no Caiaphas! The simple answer is that Caiaphas is with the snows of yester year; that he as well as another; that he along with Caesar and the golden lads might stop a hole to keep the wind away; that, in any case, he to no such aureate earth is turned that we wish him dug up again. But this simple answer does not occur to the yokel. He is stumped by the inquiry. He is beaten. Mr. Spurgeon leaps upon his bewilderment: "But where is Caiaphas? He hides his guilty head; he is utterly confounded, and begs the mountains to fall upon him. And, oh, ye men of the Sanhedrim . . . etc."

Now, gentlemen, under which thimble is the pea? The yokel is utterly confounded. Where is Caiaphas? There is Caiaphas. The yokel being unable to state Caiaphas' whereabouts, or to perceive Caiaphas when said Caiaphas is postulated to be present, sinks into a state of coma (as desired).

Mr. Spurgeon goes on to Antichrist, and then turns up Julian the apostate, sic:

"Julian, as He Died, Said:
'The Nazarene has overcome me'";
Mr. Spurgeon overlooks the fact that Julian had had a difficult life, and that his nerves might have been undermined; he overlooks the fact that Julian died a long time ago, and that since that date of demise, numerous quiet gentlemen have died with no such confession of defeat on their lips. Mr. Spurgeon "would fain whisper in the ear of the sinner, fascinated by his pleasures,
Hereafter, Hereafter!"
These black italic headings set current in the text are a feature of the "Xtn. Herald."

While scarcely including myself in the category of "sinners fascinated by pleasure," Mr. Spurgeon might pause to consider my reasons for not proclaiming myself to be Antichrist.

First, if I found myself entertaining the idea with any seriousness I should suspect megalomania; I should try to tone the thing down; I should not wish to be the victim of megalomania, of obsession, of an idée fixe, however decorative or delightful.

Second, I should feel that I was abrogating my integrity as an artist; that I was degenerating into a religious teacher or founder; that I was becoming a fumiste; that I was swinging too large a megaphone.

Third, it is too old a game; there are too many candidates— Leonardo, Napoleon, the Kaiser, our old friend the Papacy. *On s'encanaille.* One does not wish to be confused with Mrs. Besant's little black gentlemen.

But if I overcame these objections and proclaimed myself Antichrist, I should not expect the fortnight or the aeon after my death to be one jot more uncomfortable. Being Antichrist is an employment like another, like taking the City Temple, or exhibiting at the Leicester Gallery, or getting elected to Parliament. It would be less difficult than painting a really good picture, or writing a masterly novel.

A few weeks ago, someone was clamouring for the new revelation or new religion. As Antichrist one's doctrine would be simple:
CREED OF ANTICHRIST.
Intellectual Honesty, the Abolition of Violence, the Fraternal Deference of Confucius, and Internationalism.

A man calling himself, to-day, Antichrist, and proclaiming this doctrine in four parts, might well be stoned to death by a Chauvinistic mob, or by a mob of Christian fanatics. This creed has all requirements of religion; the first clause has the difficulty, it is the via ardua et exigua; the second and fourth clauses have the requisite present impracticality; and the third contains all that is sound in the teachings of St. Francis of Assisi. Without wishing to assume any undue celebrity, without robing myself in the mantle of Antichrist, I do not hesitate to proclaim this religion (to the abolition of Spurgeons, Talmages, Benedettoes). I do not ask a yearly "screw" for proclaiming it. I do not offer bribes to believers.

Let us examine the tone of the "Xtn. Herald":

"'He died trusting in his Saviour and mine. Mona, he left you in my care. Will you give me the right to love and cherish you?'

And Mona did not answer him in words. She just raised her face to his, and gave him her lips."

We have here the bacillus of contemporary religiose fiction. Marriage in this life and heaven after demise. Mahomet offered houris in the future. Protestantism will "have nothing of that sort" in its heaven. The Rev. Geo. Twentyman of the Christian Police Association will be there to prevent it. Mahomet has in the interim gobbled the more torrid districts of the planet.

The "Christian Herald" for the present goes on maintaining the mental attitudes of credulity. One picture shows a man waving his arms at a lion, the letterpress stating that he scared off the lion by yelling at it. Another picture shows "A converted African and His Bible"; another picture is labelled, "A Romance of the Battlefield" (a driver, R.F.A., picked up a photograph . . . married quite recently). Beneath this begins: "Mud and Marble, New Chapters from the life story of Joe Wentworth, the Summerton Humorist." The same page displays, "I cure Skin Disease," "War—Worry—Headache," "Instant toothache cure." We turn to the reverse of the sheet: "War—Consumption," "Dandruff," "A child doesn't laugh and play if constipated"; and still further proceeding: "Why wear a truss, Free book of amazing bargains, Let me build up your normal weight, cough elixir, three children with ringworm, girl of fourteen as church organist, hair-grower, pimples, freckles, blackheads, eruptions, £1 a week all the year round at home, fits, epilepsy, pomade, Heart and

nerves, Box Free five days' supply, varicose, ladies who value their health."
There is nothing about bitter apple.

XIIIA.

One should perhaps devote a whole chapter to the Rev. Joseph
Hocking. "The Pomp of Yesterday, A story of the present World-Crisis"
is, we are informed, "A Famous Author's Great Story of the War."

No words of mine; nothing, in fact, but the reader's own power of
computing the infinite, of holding the inexpressible in his grasp, of presenting to the eye of his own imagination the unseeable and unimagin-
able, can possibly convey to the reader the exact shade of inevitability,
the exact weight of overwhelming fatality with which it is fatal and inevitable that the Rev. Jo. Hocking should in this given number of the
"Xtn. Herald" be writing of "The Present World Crisis." Nor is the conspiracy of the Three Parcae, of Predestination (Hebrew), or Foreordained-
ness (Protestant), less apparent in this story in the "Xtn. Herald" being
a "great story" from the pen of a "famous author." The realm where literary values are subject to disputation, the realm wherein the critic is dif-
fident, wherein he balances the merit of one author against the merits of
other authors is far, afar from us. It is as far, afar from us as the realm
wherein subjects can by force avoid being topical. It is, let us say, briefly,
fatal and natural and inevitable that the Rev. Hocking should be writing
a "great" tale of the War.

The first col. of this final instalment begins with black letter as follows:—

"'She'll be Mine Some Time'—When the War will End—A
Tremendous Change—The Pomp of the Kaiser—Alone with Lorna—
The Sealed Letter—'I Knew he was a Bad Man'—The Victim of a Plot
—An Unexpected Interruption—A Long Walk and Its Result."

This little black-letter summary is possibly presented to us lest we
should remain too long in doubt as to the contents of the ensuing five
columns—which are broken and diminished by a lead block labelled,
"THE QUEEN PAID A SURPRISE VISIT to the men of the Coldstream Guards
at a Y.M.C.A. hut at Windsor while the men were engaged in writing
letters, playing billiards, and reading. Not long since her Majesty had presented a gramophone to the hut, and the men were anxious that she
should hear it. Two records were, therefore, given before the Queen left."

Picture shows Queen, Chaplain and Officer standing at attention, man at gramophone, billiard table, etc. It is in no way connected with the story by the Rev. Hocking.

The next interruption to his five cols. is:—

"......................................Please cut across here...................................... NATIONAL MOVEMENT FOR A GREAT SPIRITUAL REVIVAL Believing that Jehovah. . . . . etc. PLEASE ENROL ME AS A MEMBER OF THE NATIONAL FAMILY PRAYER LEAGUE;" blank space for signatures and addresses, also instruction to paste the printed heading at top of sheet of foolscap, and "get all your friends to sign."

To cut out this piece of "Xtn. Herald" would irrevocably damage the text by Rev. Hocking on reverse of the sheet. It is, perhaps, for this reason that the summary of his contents is given at the head of his chapter, which summary is, we may say, not printed on the reverse of anything to be "cut out."

His five cols. are again diminished by picture of "Jack Barmouth leaped over a stile into the lane where we were walking." Rev. Hocking's text is also enlivened or reinforced by having certain phrases, fourteen, to be exact, printed in heavy italics, and set out to look like sub-headings. I do not know whether this idea originates with Rev. Hocking, or whether it is imposed upon him by his editors, desirous of having his pages uniform with the other pages of their paper. His text appears somewhat as follows:—

"'To-morrow? I say, old chap, has—has she written to you?' I nodded. 'No, her letter contained nothing that would interest you,' I continued, as I noted the look of inquiry in his eyes. 'Why don't you go with me? It would seem quite natural, seeing you are off to the Front so soon,'

He Hesitated a Second

and then shook his head. 'No, old man,' he said; 'she'll send for me if she wants me.'

"'That's not the way to win a girl. How can she send for you?' 'I seem to have lost confidence since my memory came back,' he replied. 'When I told her I loved her, although I didn't seem to have the ghost of a chance, I felt confident, serene. Now, I'm sure of nothing.' 'Nothing?' I queried. 'Do you mean to say that—that your faith in God is gone?'"

Let us glance at the other heavy headings. Sic:—

"You said we were not fit for victory.

What are your Views Now?

. . . .

"Just so long as England remains in a state of Religious indifference, just so long will the war continue."

"*I Don't Understand,*" *I said.* "*Empty-Headed Society Dudes.*" "*Russia Becoming a Republic?*" "*Talking with Her Alone.*" "*You Must Know the Truth.*" "*Oh, I have been Mad.*" "*You Must Trust Me,*" *I replied.* "*You Love Each Other.*" "*He Made Me Believe It.*" "*You Followed Us,*" *I interjected. She Looked at Me Shyly.*

The final words of the story are: "I'm going to beard the lion in his den. I'm going to have a serious talk with Sir Thomas. Will you look after Lorna till I return?"

Rev. Hocking tells a marvellous lot in five columns. (46 inches of 3 inch.)

14 [15]. Progress, Social and Christian
NOVEMBER 29, 1917

"Bugges with hundred heades." Phaer's "Aeneid."

IBSEN has made at least one pertinent remark about the phantoms of one's own subjectivity. Choice samples are spread before us; the "Family Herald" has trotted out the Papacy-Antichrist, along with its abracadabra from the sacred and prophetic book of Daniel, than which no modern psychological novelist is so muzzy-headed as not to write better. I do not in the least wish to diminish the historic horrors of the Papacy, its history of intellectual suppression, preceding and following its periods of intellectual enlightenment as under Nicholas V. or Leo X. Nor would I have anyone forget for half an hour that the inquisition was reestablished in 1824; and that burning for heresy occurred so late as 1751. The degradation of French intellect at the hands and pens of the Claudelo-catholico present movement is but a re-irritation to brandish these facts with new vigour.

Let us remember, then, that there are co-inhabitants of this planet, still living, and even in command of sufficient education to write complete sentences, who still believe in Antichrist and the application of Hebrew almanacists to the current affairs of Christian internecine sectaries. I myself know one rather fine old relic who believes literally that the "Church of Rrrome" is the "Scarrlet Woman of RRevelation." I am not saying that the Church is one scrap better or worse than the fictitious lady in question, or that she is any safer or more trustworthy a companion for the "Allies"; in fact I am not trespassing on questions of the moment. I am simply stating that human beings can be found (and in no scant number) who still identify the creation of one Hocus pocus, with the continuing creatrix of a great deal more Hocus pocus, i.e., the "Church" and "The Scarlet Woman," and that this identification is deplorable in a literate country. Even granting that the Roman Church is so perpetually perilous as to need more than an intellectual barrier to keep it out, any barrier would be almost preferable to this barrier of blind stupid bigotry, and more efficient.

"Old Moore" has his bugaboo also. The following are headed "Predictions":

"The ubiquitous constable seems to be making careful inspection of the busy tinker. This small group means that extra special care will have to be exercised throughout the land to cope with and stamp out any signs of rebellious conduct on the part of the Socialists."

"We may expect some strange, not to say disturbing, news reaching us toward the end of the month from Petrograd."

"Death of noble duke . . . beloved of all classes."

"We shall enjoy during the most wonderful year 1918" (refer back to the "Christian Herald" on annos mirabiles) "a feeling of security and satisfaction which can only be built up by true religion and brotherly love. OLD MOORE can see with certainty permanent changes—changes for the betterment of us all. The so-called upper classes will remain and mix with their least fortunate fellows who are styled the poor people. The upper middle folk will become a thing of the past."

(Ah, ah, that's where the wind blows! Duchess marries a chimney-sweep, trading classes annihilated.)

In the same mad month as the last citation

"OLD MOORE can trace in secret meetings, which will be held in several cities at once, the black hand of the bloodthirsty Teuton."

(Brotherly love, sense of security, Guy Fawkes and Co. all on the old vaudeville!)

"Outbreak of influenza . . . John Chinaman is no fool."

Let us move on past May day:

"It is more than probable that towards the end of the month a raid will be made by the police upon the premises of what was thought by the public to be a social club, but which proved to be the meeting-place of many desperate and hot-blooded Socialists. Much literature will be impounded, and several arrests made, bail being refused."

(So our friends in Tothill Street should beware of the weeks following the ides of May in 1918.)

Old Moore also in his calendar calls to our attention the anniversaries of the births of Trollope, of the Princess Royal, of Alfred Austin, George Washington, Lord Haldane, Tho. Hood, of the death of Hugh Conway, of the birth of Sir A. Sullivan, of "Spenser Perceval assass., 1812.["] He says: "Trade will be good and cash plentiful" in December, all England shocked by terrible crime, alarming news from Ireland, "outbreaks and riotous conduct among a dangerous and reckless body of the Commonwealth," and, I think, the birth of an heir in some noble family, but I cannot stop to verify this citation.

On my own and unaided initiative I do not hesitate to predict the births of heirs in *at least three* families of title; and I venture to predict that at least two tiara'd mothers will have photos by Swaine reproduced in one of the leading Illustrated Weeklies, and I predict that several noted politicians will be discontented with the Government, and that several new appointments will be made, and that there will be religious protests against sanity in divorce laws, and that grey hairs will appear on the occiputs of more than one well-known politician, and that rain will fall in the London district during the month of April, and that the sun will rise more or less in the East.

The British Weekly.

I was, as the more slavishly attentive among my readers may recall, warned against the "British Weekly" by my butcher. I wish I had heeded the warning. The rag is twice the size of the "Sunday Herald." It contains more Joseph Hocking. And, moreover, my butcher was kind enough to tip me the wink in that all-embracing phrase: "*That's* Nicoll, that's Robertson Nicoll."

I know nothing personally of this Sir, Dr., or whatever he may be, Nicoll, save that he was once seen talking with Mr. Shorter in the hall-way of the Royal Societies Club. I have heard no other rumour of his living and fleshly presence. Of his spiritual presence, I am told "The Bookman" is a constant and eloquent witness. In a more enlightened community such a statement might be considered as libellous. I do not, however, find his name in the "British Weekly," and have no better as-surance for connecting him with it than the stalwart speech of my butcher, and a few lines in a reference book. I do, however, find a name praeclarus and well accustomed—it is the name of Claudius Clear.

On coming to England I heard this name somewhere, and supposed the owner was some connection or other of Smiles. However, the "British Weekly" has still got him. And, what is more, I find him reviewing some sort of book or criticising some sort of Victorian Essayist, of doubtless irreproachable morals.

In the cols. next him, someone signing himself, "A Man of Kent," says that Conan Doyle's "His Last Bow" appears to him "one of the most agreeable and entertaining of all the inimitable Sherlock Holmes series." It is always nice to find these people criticising something one has read. The gentle peruser may turn back to No. V of this series for an analysis of the title story of this Conan Doyle volume. He will then get the full idiomatic savour of the words "agreeable," "entertaining," and "inim-itable," as current in Sir R. Nicholl and his publications.

This is as brief a summary of contemporary journalistic criticism of contemporary books as I am able to offer. The "British Weekly" is "A Journal of Social and Christian Progress"; at least, so we are told on its cover. The subscribers are told where to subscribe: the advertisers, that "the 'British Weekly' has by far the largest circulation of any religious newspaper published in this country—Church or Nonconformist."

And I by my choice of subject have got myself into a position where I am morally and socially bound to read or read at the sheets of the issue before me, numbered 89 to 108, and measuring 13 by 19 inches.

The Rev. Principal Alex. Whyte, D.D., had a reverie on a raid night (alliterative). He wrote: "With the instruments of death hurtling over my head, I said to myself—let me now lay hold of the right handles, and thus work out my salvation, even in the moment of death; if that moment should come to me during this midnight." The fine old Anglo-Saxon alliterative measure seems coming back to its own, the exact position of the "handles" must remain metaphorical.

On the next page we learn that ten prizes of ten shillings each are offered for the best paper on "MY FAMILY BUDGET" sent in by a minister's wife or housekeeper.

Hocking is here, as we noted. "Synopsis: Captain John Penrose, D.S.O., is staying at the home of his friend Teddy Onslow, in Hertfordshire, when a telegram arrives from Athens to say: 'Athene mysteriously disappeared. No trace. Fear foul play, etc.'" etc., and as usual. It is quite clear wheretoward Xtn. and Soc. Progress is progging.

Three generals talk about God. The Sayings of the week are full of pep. sic: from the "Xtn. World." "If shortly after twenty years of age a human face has not acquired certain mental and spiritual qualities, its very beauty becomes a defect." "Church Times": "It has come to this, that nothing the clergy do, or leave undone, is right."

The "B.W." in the rest of its vast and gloomy extent seems Christianly to have progressed to about the same status as the other Sunday weeklies we have inspected. The Ladies' Column addresses "Dinah" in these words: "I cannot tell you the reason of your hair falling out, etc." "Inquirer" receives the following: "Since your letter has reached me, I have been making inquiries, but cannot learn of anyone suitable."

Their one distinguishing feature, apart from the illustration of "Ficolax" is the "WHAT TO DO, Problems of Conduct" column.

670. Young man on leave marries in haste (I condense their phraseology à la synopsis of Hocking), he returns to front, lady unsatisfactory, declines to work now she is married, overdraws his bank account: What shall he do? "A copy of 'In the Northern Mists,' by a Grand Fleet chaplain," will reward, comfort, and enlighten the well-constellated emitter of the successful solution.

Let me close with a citation from the International Lesson:

"When he heard the tidings, he had sat down and wept, and had mourned for several days."

Il ne manquait que ça. "With Sorrow in his heart it was difficult for Nehemiah" to foresee the day when he should be copyrighted at so much per col. "to the north under Sanballat and the Ammonites to the east under Tobiah"

"to Jerusalem and a grant of material for the work."
"And he also provided him with a military escort"
Sermon on the Mount lately patented and issued with each pair of boots.

15 [16]. A Nice Paper
DECEMBER 13, 1917

THESE dreary and smeary penny weeklies seem innumerable; they stretch about the inquirer as the dismal grey-yellow brick of the dingy houses one sees in S.E. London coming in on the Dover train. The statistician will explain to you that the multitude of these papers is not infinite; but for the purposes of psychology they are infinite, and the mentality they feed is unknowable. It is translatable in colour effects, like the quasi-volcanic appearance of Islington, *morne,* desolate; the grey soot-covered mud appears to have pushed itself up into rectangularish hummocks of houses; the grey soot-covered hummocks seem to have spawned into grey sootish animalculae, and for this grey sootish compost, grey sootish periodicals are provided, and hope is deferred till post-mortem, and the landed classes plead that religion be left as a comfort, and that contentment is advisable.

Heaven has been moved off Olympus, and as astronomy pushes it further and yet further from us, it is natural that new and more tangibly formed, sensuous heavens should arise in place of Milton's loathsome conception for the perpetual boredom of the blest. The non-conformist has so denuded his paradise, he has so stripped the deity of all charm, that some substitute has to be provided for the pagan, catholic, and Mohammedan temperaments. The early heavens of mankind are only their novels of luxury, the "Forget-Me-Nots" of their day.

For "Forget-Me-Not" I have little but praise. Any intelligent person would probably prefer to move among well-natured, well-mannered people, in surroundings of comfort, than to envisage eternity set down opposite Dr. Talmage or Moses. Even the perpetuity of the antediluvian heaven has ceased to be an attraction; and no area spatial, temporal, conditional, or infinite even, can seem so commodious as to make one wish to be boxed up in it for ever with nothing but Christians. The harp, the crown, and the other properties of the Hen. Irving period are wholly inadequate. We can do better at the Ritz.

The gleam of sense in the populace has shown itself in the semiconscious perception that it could do itself better at the Ritz; that nice-natured people with relatively considerate manners are a far more paradisaical periphery than harsh-voiced, wheezing fanatics, brandishing remnants of disguised fire-worship, reminiscent of people who sat over smoking oil-wells and thought the earth was on fire for their special post-mortem envelopment. Olympus and the sylvan imagination befit a more temperate climate; it is natural that a Northern people should imagine a heaven, if not indoors, at least with houses one can get into during the inclement weather. The novel of luxury is the natural celestial creation or fairy tale, or perhaps we should say "terrestrial paradise" of the English, as was Olympus a natural and terrestrial paradise of the Greeks, just a wee bit out of reach in both cases. A people must have been to their heaven, or seen it, or know someone who knows someone who . . . The saints once supplied this gradation and the well-dressed intellectual wittol is still rumbling on in the Sunday papers, debating this after-death business. The populace, or its sincerer and more practical sections, desire gods that appear, at least now and then, and with an exciting infrequency—even if only in "The Sketch."

Old Moore is going to get rid of the intervening stratum, and have only people and gods. The young men from Oxford are sceptical concerning the reality of the divinities. Current Church of England theology, ever trimming, has, as I wrote before, gone in for the democratisation of heaven.

Note that in the theoretic heaven and in the theoretic earth there is apparently no choice between some sort of Kaiser, and some sort of glorified House of Commons. And despite this, people go on making luxurious heavens, from Olympus to the Carlton as imagined, and peopling

them with Gods, and with saints and protectors who have a kindliness
for all sorts of peccadilloes, as, for example, a god or a saint to help thieves.
It is pleasant among smeary grease-printed papers to take up "Forget-
Me-Not," the pleasure is sensuous, not intellectual, it reaches one through
one's finger-tips. The paper is printed for people who prefer keeping their
hands clean. It is religious and moral, i.e., it is religious in providing a
paradise, sic: a country house, a picture gallery, etc.; it is moral in that
virtue is rewarded. It has even some literary merit, I mean solely that part
of the complete novelette which forms the number before me must be
well told, even though it is not well written.

I feel that I am cruel and captious to point out in this tale certain
wens. I feel about these dainty little romances very much as the landed
class feel about religion: "Why destroy it, why attack it, what are you going
to put in its place? It keeps so many people contented." This feeling is,
of course, in the present case, sheer sentimentality. The reader would be
neither more nor less happy if the flaws were removed.

Chap. I throws in gratis a *whole* ex post facto detective story. Cf. the
construction of the "Iliad."

"The girl was tall and most divinely fair."

"Broken in health, but with his name and honour stainless, Mr. Or-
pengray had been released."

His son, however, refuses to appear under his own name, lest the
widow of the ruiner of his father, should feel under an obligation to him.
He is also wholly indifferent to £20,000.

Chap. II. "Tall and most divinely fair," thought Mr. N. O. "The
girl was dressed in black, and carried a bunch of scarlet roses. She moved
quickly but gracefully, pausing to pin one of the roses in her blouse. She
glanced over her shoulder, and laughed again. . . ."

"Her hand was on the electric-bell. The summons brought the butler." (cf. Aladdin and his lamp. Butler very withered and wrinkled.)

"Miss Garton spoke to him with an air of quiet authority in the most
musical of quiet voices."

(Note this when addressing the butler.)

"She glanced at Mr. Neil Grant. She had eyes, pure and clear."

(Note this when glancing at Don Fulano.)

"Neil bowed and followed the butler. He knew, having consulted the will at Somerset House, that Mrs. Ricksdale was a woman of wealth."

(Note this when bowing and following.)

He has just reached his room, noted the pleasant quarters, wondered how he stood, when:

"A subdued knock called him to the door. It was Miss Garton."

Next, villainess is brought on, looking less than her age. Hero decides that he does not like her; nor her slick son. Heroine tells him (heroine being naturally person of delicate feelings, employed as old lady's companion) that he need not dress for dinner.

"Evidently they did dress, etc. . . . Luckily Neil had brought a suit of dress clothes, though he had come to despise such garments."

Note that it is not "*his*" evening clothes. It is "a" suit. I don't know that this matters. One must consider very carefully the ratio between his real position, his despisal of evening clothes, and the number of evening suits at his disposal; also the number usually "brought" by curators of private collections.

Possession of supposedly several of these adornments has not, however, trained him to get into one with great ease. The butler assists him with his tie.

Hero "seldom drank intoxicants."

Note that villainess has violet eyes, and heroine (old lady's companion) enters "still in black, with a string of small pearls clasped round her throat and a solitary rose pinned to her breast."

("Great elegance," as Li Po has remarked. The exact size of the pearls is left to the reader's imagination. Value at moderate estimate £800? They were possibly a treasured heirloom from some noble ancestor. Passons!)

Hero says: "One seldom puts on too much weight in the army. . . . I can speak from experience."

Eventually, the villainess sews her diamond bracelet into the kimono of the heroine (or has it sewn in by her (villainess's) maid), kimono is locked in drawer of heroine's wardrobe—key hidden under carpet, where police find it. Note: This is a bit daring, as it is part of notorious swag villainess has lifted elsewhere. This point does not seem to have presented itself to the author.

Religious feeling shown in depiction of police (cf. guardians of the law, divine messengers, angels with flaming swords in earlier and more cumbrous religions).

Police never for a moment suspect innocent heroine. Hero thinks that villainess shook hands with him graciously *just* before bracelet disappeared in order to make him a witness to the fact that she had the bracelet up to the last possible moment before its disappearance, but he omits to mention this detail to the police. Author does not note this omission by a word of his pen, even though police bring recovered bracelet into hero's room to be photographed. The real celestiality of the police is, however, displayed to our inner gaze when the chief cop, some days after the death of the victim and the departure of the villainess, is seen riding up the "carriage-drive in the teeth of the rain." He had sent the photos to London, and says, "Very likely you remember the big jewel robbery at the Drexington Hotel just before the war, perhaps."

The chief cop was certain he had read a description of that there particular bracelet. And the London cops were now looking for Mrs. Fullbridge-Hart.

The other characters then remember that there had been a robbery in the hotel where Mrs. F.-H. had stayed with the victim. Let us pass over the super-luminous intellect of the local cop. The reader may have met local cops before, both in the flesh and in fiction. "Mr. Brigsand" is a man of big possibilities. I dare say the subscribers to "F.M.N." will hear of him in the future.

"And you'll come and tell me? I shall be in the rose-garden."

(Beside the Shalimar, shaded lights, and low music.)

"He was desperately anxious."

"Dear boy of mine, I'll try hard never to disillusion you."

"Amber depths," "first kiss," "nestled"; the tender words fly and flutter about one in a very aurora, beating upon the heart of the peruser.

("Beside the Shalimar, shaded light, and low music.")

16 [17]. Aphrodite Popularis
DECEMBER 20, 1917

WE have, in this series, observed the affairs of the spirit; we have noted the tendency to make other-worlds, paradisaical retreats from reality: the unattainable, or the with difficulty attainable Ritz glitters as a new Jerusalem before the truly spiritual mind which will have no earthly content in the Regent's Palace. For the genii in contemporary faith we find Sherlock Holmes or (in "Forget-Me-Not") the policeman, half genii, half angel-guardian.

The captious praiser of acted time may complain that the religions of antiquity gave us a mythology with emotional values: as in the tale of Pyramus or that of the daughters of Mineus; while the contemporary mythology is lacking in these notable values. Compare the emotional value of Cardinus with the emotional value of Sherlock, who has as much moral force as you please.

In contrast to paradises and mythology, which are the decorations of a religion, we find the prophets (and the interpreters of Sibylline books).

Mr. Zadkiel's "Almanac and Ephemeris for 1918" (a much more serious work than Moore's "Vox Stellarum Almanac") bears on p. 67, these lines of footnote "See page 77 of Z.A. for 1917. Unfortunately, the last figure of 1918 was printed as 7. As one degree measures to one year of life the arc 53° 2', etc."

Mr. Zadkiel in his 1917 number was forecasting that "British and Allied forces will achieve a great victory and dictate terms of peace before Midsummer Day (1917)."

The readers will agree that this misprint of a 7 for an 8 as the last digit of the date was most regrettable. He will also sympathise with Mr. Zadkiel whose almanac appears only once a year. Mr. Bottomley with his more felicitous frequency of appearance is able to attend to such little errors with much greater promptitude.

The mathematic detail, the stellar paraphernalia and terminology of Mr. Zadkiel compare as favourably with the mumbo-jumbo symbology of Moore as does the hard commonsense tone of Mr. Bottomley with the utter silliness of various other weeklies.

Mr. Bottomley's hard commonsense fairly bulges out of his paper. In the one number I have read minutely, I found only one slight slip, so tiny that it would be mere pedantry to take note of it. He is as self-consistent as the theology of Aquinas, and about as much use.

It is perhaps beyond the scope of this series to assail all the Church Fathers at once; dogmatic theologico-philosophy is so imposing an edifice. Still the printer may amuse himself by copying the following figures:

$$O \times \frac{996}{423} \div \frac{\sqrt{777}}{463} \times \frac{441}{663} \div \frac{1077}{9} =$$

If I pick up that line of figures somewhere in the middle I can get a substantial answer. I can obey all the laws of mathematics. I might even add three to the end or beginning of that little strip of figures. My results, if I take all of my first line of figures, will be either zero or the three I have added.

But supposing I do this in the presence of a yokel I can both bewilder him by taking up the final terms of my equation, and by the accuracy wherewith I divide, let us say,

$$\frac{441}{663} \text{ by } \frac{1077}{9}$$

; I can assure him that this accuracy is science and dialectic, and that he is foolish to combat it with ignorance, and that he had better leave such transcendental questions to the scientific mathematician. I can even surprise him by the swiftness with which I get an answer whenever I add or subtract a simple number to or from my first complicated array of fractions; but the value of my first line of fractions remains the zero it started. If I substitute infinity for my first zero, the answer for my whole line of figures will not be a computable number. Neither from an unknowable god can we deduce a precise code of morals; or a precisely known "will of God."

I do not imagine this will greatly disturb the editors of the "Tablet" (a most mathematical organ) or of the so polite and kindly "Stella Maris," or the "Messenger of the Sacred Heart."

These people are a constant and unheeded lesson to the "Church" and Nonconformist papers, both in their tone and their internal coherence. The two latter do not advertise hair-restorers or "bitter-apple." (I dare say the "Tablet" doesn't either. I haven't time to procure a copy at the present moment of writing.)

When it comes to manners in contemporary press-work I am inclined to think the Catholics the least objectionable of all Christians. In fact, all their surface is preferable to that of their opposed and contentious off-shoots. All denials of them in detail is, I believe, purely useless. If one cannot land on the initial zero or infinity, and land with a reasonably heavy shell of knowledge, historic and otherwise, one had better keep off the question. Their dialectic survives from a period of worthy robustness, and the smear of contemporary "Church" theology and modern impression-ist thought comes off very badly in any incidental combat.

This gets out of hand. I must return to the flesh, i.e., to "Nash's." (En passant let us deny that anybody knows anything about "heaven" in the Christian sense of that term; let us deny the authenticity of any despatches from any post-mortem Petrograds, flaming or otherwise).

I shall not settle the Roman Church in five minutes, though I re-call a modern "Church" (of England) writer who actually seemed to think he had added to our knowledge of The Trinity by six pages of writing, the logical deduction from which was (for anyone save himself) that the Trinity was shaped like a plover's egg. Let Catholicism stand for theoretic theology; for the mediaeval mind still persisting. The contemporary re-ligion "of the people" we have touched on in our observation of its last-ing predilection for genii, paradises and prophets. I want to leave these spiritual matters and complete my survey of contemporary mentality. Farewell, spirit, for the page! Let us turn our attention to "Nash's" (which must stand here for the "Flesh"). [See plate 8.]

This sensuous and carnal production greets us with a paradisaical cover (Venusburg, Tannhauser, etc.). It is the November number, but the scene is from some summer far away, or from some happier clime. Against a verdurous background we see the head and shoulders of the Young Apollo type. Below his roseate features leans the head of a damsel with coral lips; and with crow-black hair. Her head and forearms are bare, the bosom covered by white linen (or some such fabric), as is that of the youth. She lies, as much of her as is portrayed, in a hammock, upon a cushion covered in cretonne. The youth holds in his right hand a green sprig of forky grass, and with this he tickles, or appears about to tickle, the aforesaid coral lips of the young lady, whose eyes are closed in sleep either actual or pretended. (The face shows none of the contractions which occasionally occur in sleep; the mouth has not sagged open. If she sleeps she sleeps delicately.) The susceptible beholder will almost feel the light pressure, the diaphanous titillation of the grass tip brushing his (or her) own surrisent lips. Across the foot of the enticing portrayal we read, "New Serial, by MARIE CORELLI."

In this life we find certain perfect adjustments.

Who, for example, could have dreamed of finding a poem by E. W. Wilcox, a serial by Miss Corelli, a poem by Chas. Hanson Towne, a tale by Gouverneur Morris, another by Robt. W. Chambers, another by Stephen Leacock, and "Beyond" by John Galsworthy, together with sundry actresses' limbs, *all, all* assembled in the one set of covers, all surrendered to one for 8d.?

Christian and Social Progress has found no more happy equation; for what, in Zeus' name, could be more Christian than Miss Marie Corelli, or more social than Mr. John Galsworthy? And how united the tone, how beautifully, how almost transcendentally all these people "belong"; what utter and super-trinitarian unity thus binds them together in Nash's! The face on the cover almost recalls another celebrity.

Even the actresses are united; without altercation their heads, backs, legs, ruffles are potpourri'd on to the pages. The head of one projects from the hip of another, the fingers of the lady with the hair-brush jut from the upper arm of a third, the sleepy head of a fifth reposes on the bosom of the sixth who appears colossally larger. A ninth with one luxurious arm has her little oval in a corner.

One is fairly bewildered by the opulent charms of this magazine. The chronicler knows not where to begin. Shall we, O Quirites, dwell first upon the portrait of Miss Corelli, taken from a photograph, presumably of some vintage, that hath been cooled a long age (from 1878 at least) in the deep-delved cubby-holes of the editor? Shall we turn first to the metrical triumphs of Ella Wheeler whose protagonist exclaims:

"My sins and derelictions cry aloud. . . . ." "The world loves to believe in Man's depravity and Woman's worth; But I am one of many men upon the earth Whose loud, resounding fall Is like the crashing of some well-built wall, Which those who seek can trace To the slow work of insects at its base.

Be not afraid, The alimony will be promptly paid."

(It has become so much the custom to reprint vers libre as if the original were written as prose, that I have done a similar violence to Mrs. Wilcox's publication, preserving however the capital letters with which the lines of the original commence; thus the reader may reconstruct the metric if he chooses).

The actual works of Corelli, Chambers, Galsworthy and Co. are perhaps too familiar, and are certainly too voluminous to be discussed in this place. (If the energy remains with me I may elsewhere set out upon an exploration of these individual writers who so miraculously mirror their time. For who is there among "us" who has not read something by at least one of these authors?)

We judge from the ads. that *charm* is what these people (writers, publishers, entrepreneurs of Nash's, etc.) "go in for"; they are neither malthusian, nor yet fanatically set on the fecundity plus overflow into the colonies propaganda. We find maternity gowns, and everything for mother and baby filling hardly more than one quarter page; the prevailing tone is: Your hair; Macassar Oil; Eyes Men Idolize; The Kind of beauty that men admire; Add a pleasure to life; Protective Knickers; Author's Manuscripts; Somebody's Darling; A sweet little set, beautifully handmade and picot edged; Irresistible; What does your brain earn; Good Pianist; Asthma; Daisy; don't let pain spoil your good looks; Why People Marry; King of Hearts; Autumn Beauty; Neptune's Daughter; Beauty pictures; Soap; Safety-filler; the cure of self-consciousness; Lovely Eyelashes; Add to your income; Power: scientific concentration; Height increased; Healthy Women; Esperanto; Makes straight hair wavy and lustrous; YOU can PLAY the PIANO. In the smaller paragraphs we learn that "'LOVE AND LOVERS' is a wonderful book of 'Hints to both Sexes,' profusely illustrated"; also that "handsome men are slightly sunburnt."

17 [18]. The Slightly Shopworn
DECEMBER 27, 1917

"Do them, they'll only feel hurt if you don't." In response to this friendly advice, I can answer but "*Quare*? For what cause, and to what effect?" The "Saturday Review," "The Athenaeum," "The Nation," the etc., are in about the same format. What, under heaven, should I find there worth my sixpence? Concerning these papers I have already an impression—

and not the least curiosity. My impression is that no one of the least con-
sequence has written in these papers during the last ten years; that no
active ideation has celebrated itself in their columns; that no critic whose
mind is of the least interest has therein expressed himself in regard to
literature or the arts. Books have in them been reviewed, and essays (by
courtesy) printed, and these have, I think, been fashioned in accord with
some half-forgotten editorial policy formed by the editor before the editor before last. Not one of their writers has looked upon literature, or
painting, or even politics, for himself; they are a limbo of marcescent
ideas: ideas that, when they are too worn out even for "The Athenaeum,"
are passed on to Messrs. Hodder and Stoughton and their clerks to be re-
sentimentalised, to be fitted a little more snugly into glucose christi-
inanity, and later to appear in the "Bookman," that treacle and margarine
composite. Life is too short to wade through the pages of these periodicals to see if my statement does any slight injustice. If the editors of any
of them can remember the work of any man of distinction which they
have printed, they may reply and point out my possible error. (N.B.—I
know there was once a man named Henley, and that Symons wrote his
"Spiritual Adventures," and contributed to the "Saturday Review," before the present administration had been weaned. I am concerned with
the twentieth century.)

We find also the type of author who is printed in Bangor, Maine,
U.S.A., on japanese vellum. A few excerpts from a recent article of criticism by him of a sober contemporary will perhaps throw light on his
darkness. He says:—

"'This poet,' says Miss Sinclair, 'hath a devil.' I go further. He is a
devil."

Let us adore this theological vigour.

Continue:—

"He is more calmly horrible than Tchekov or Reinhardt, or any of
the slimy reptiles that used to shimmer in the Russian Ballet."

"There you have the cold pride of the devil—the utterly inhuman
pride."

"Devilish, most devilish! Let us be thankful that we are not devil-
worshippers. We prefer the jungle."

After three-quarters of a col. of this sort of thing, the reader can only wish that Mr. James Douglas *would* retire to the suitable habitat which he mentions, therein to heave cocoanuts with his hind paws rather than remain here to push a pen with his front ones. Concerning De Bosschère's style, De Bosschère's sense of the human tragedy, he has said nothing at all. The author whom he "criticises" has committed the satanic sin of seeing some things for himself. He even describes how a man going on a long journey lent his house to a friend, and, on return, found the house no longer his own:—

"Pierre a pris le coeur de ma maison."

However, I must not turn aside to a question of literary taste. I only wish the reader to note the theological tone of Mr. Douglas' denunciation. We find him at the old jig about kind hearts being more than coronets, a contention long since granted, but not relevant to the question of M. De Bosschère's literary attainment.

In fact, this old jig about the kind heart and the coronet is the sum total of all the literary (alleged) criticism that has appeared in England for a decade, in "Punch," in the "Bookman," in whatever of these old puddings you will. It is all they have had to say about the novel, or about poetry, or the drama. They say such-and-such a character . . . etc. . . . but we all know what they say and what they do not say. Passons.

They have even tolerated the exuberance of the Russian novel, because someone was crafty enough to whisper that Dostoievsky was kindhearted.

There has been the critical kind heart, as well, or perhaps we should say the kind stomach, the "of-course-I-can't-slate-him, you-know-he-once-asked-me-to-dinner, and-I'm-no-longer-young" attitude. But this is common to all ages and eras, and no needful part of our subject. Still, it *is* time that English criticism shook off the hand of Polonius.

Even mixed staffs like that of the "Times" might drop all men over sixty and all women over forty, with no great detriment to themselves, and all English weeklies, monthlies and quarterlies more than twenty years old might cease this morning, and the world of thought be no poorer.

I am not saying this in any contempt for old age, and I have, I think, not been tardy in expressing my respect for old men when they were worth it, or while the great ones were still among us. Even so the aged have never, I think, been acute critics of what came after them. The great critics have usually contented themselves with an analysis of their predecessors, or at most, their contemporaries. It has been the rarest thing in the world for an old man to know good from bad in the work of succeeding decades.

The creative faculty may, and often does, outlast the critical. On the whole, about all an old critic can do, if he is to stay in the ring, is to use himself and his position as a megaphone for some younger man's ideas, a course where his conceit usually prevents and forestals him.

A few doddards should, of course, be preserved, to run wode when the wind blows; to act as a sort of barometer for the energy of new work. People like Waugh, Dalton, James Douglas might be collected in one place and used as a sort of composite instrument. They have at least the virtue of *animus* which is lacking in the hee-haw and smart-Elic varieties (Douglas can belong to this last also, on opportunity). Still, I would separate these people from Austin Harrison, and G. K. Chesterton, and the writers in the "Bookman," for whom there is, so far as I can see, no extenuation whatever. They are not even daft seismographs. C. E. Lawrence is, perhaps, even lower in the scale, not being even offensive.

I know that I differ violently from the Editor of THE NEW AGE, in believing that Mr. G. K. Chesterton has definitely done considerable harm to contemporary letters. I give him the credit for having been sufficiently effective to do harm.

Harrison's insult to literature and the harm he has done has been purely negative, and has consisted in getting hold of the "English Review," and expressing his mentality in it after it had been edited by an abler man who honestly cared for good writing, and was usually able to detect it. The difference between that "Review" before and after his advent is a matter of history, and anyone who cares to do so may verify my statement by reference to the files in the British Museum. The act was, of course, shared by abettors and sponsors. There is no reason to forget this, or to condone it.

Let us turn our attention to Christians.

THE CHURCH TIMES in its address to prospective advertisers claims to have "the Largest Circulation of All Church of England newspapers." On page 483 current the following people protest against a reform of the present English marriage laws, against the tempering of this at present mediaeval institution (as contrasted with the forms of matrimony practised with great comfort and convenience under the so orderly and comparatively civilised Roman Empire).

Randall Cantaur: Parmoor.
Cosmo Ebor: W. H. Dickinson.
A. F. London: Laurence Hardy.
Handley Dunelm. Walter Runciman.
Edw. Winton: Edmund Talbot.
Francis Cardinal Bourne. W. K. Robertson, General
W. B. Selbie. Thomas Barlow.
J. Scott Lidgett. Alfred Pearce Gould.
F. B. Meyer. Mary Scharlieb.
J. H. Shakespeare. Margaret Ampthill.
R. S. Gillie. Adeline M. Bedford.
Northumberland. Louise Creighton.
Salisbury. May Ogilvie Gordon.
Beauchamp. Constance Smith.
Selborne. Emily Wilberforce.

As it was, so to speak, a streak of luck that I should hit on the very number of "Nash's" which had "all of them in it," all the gang of wash-fictioneers, so also I count it a stroke of luck that I should find the plumb centres of British bigotry so neatly and beautifully in tabulation.

When you consider that the only force sufficiently powerful to combat this set of log-heads, is a gang of people who desire to repopulate the Empire to a repletion such as will keep a vast number of people within the borders and purlieus of if not slavery, at least something near it; you may judge the misfortunes of England.

It has been said that all our real liberties are surreptitious. Surely good customs and enlightenment must also be surreptitious.

When you consider that England is, on the whole, of all countries, the most comfortable, and the one wherein there is, or has been, the most individual freedom; that America is now boasting of the efficiency of her secret police, and the facility wherewith she can suppress publications, you may, in some measure, gauge the misfortune of the world; you may consider what terrible cunning is required for any man to exist with intelligence.

One is driven back upon Remy de Gourmont's half ironical questioning:—

"Demain on fera la chasse aux idées": "Nul libraire ne sera à l'abri d'une haine confraternelle." And as for remedy there is presumably only the slow remedy as Mazzini perceived it: Education. But by what, and through what? Through the schools? Through the weekly or daily Press? Through the Universities of England? which have had several centuries start; through the universities of America which, according to newspaper account are now waking, out of Chauvinism, to the evils of Teutonisation, which no amount of intellectual perception unaided by a world-war, would have roused them to looking into?

"Renan avait bien raison: la bêtise humaine est la seule chose qui donne une idée de l'infini." And it is perhaps well that we should have some idea of "The Infinite."

FOOTNOTE.—E pur si muove? So far as I can make out from the florid columns before me, the association of American professors who have set out for "un-Germanisation" has not yet got to the evil bacillus of philology; they have only done a day's flag-waving. I have several times in these columns dwelt on the effects of this bacillus, and ten years ago I made myself very much persona non grata by perceiving it in my own university. The particular college president who is "talking for the Press" in the example before me has not apparently gone into the nature of "germanisation"; he treats the matter not on intellectual but wholly on national lines. God help the lot of 'em!

18 [19]. Nubians
JANUARY 3, 1918

I PERCEIVE that there will be omissions from this series. I have not read "Butterfly," nor "The Paper that Cheers up the Boys" ("Visage en profile avec une oeil qui lui regardait en face," as Anatole has it). I have not read the "Contemporary," nor "The Nineteenth Century *and After,*" nor "Harrison's Girls' Paper," nor "The New Witness," nor "Land and Water," nor

"The Bystander," nor the "Union Jack," nor "Everywoman," nor "Every-man," though I suspect it of needing a more severe drubbing than has been required by most of the gloomy rags I have gone though, Charles Sarolea in especial. Nor have I read the "Marvel" (cover displays boys of disordinate sizes, one of them throwing an ink-pot or some vessel once full of liquid); nor the "Penny Popular"; nor "Ideas," in which I observe a column headed "GILT AND GLOSS, The Feminine Passion for Rich Clothes and Gay Living," and another col. headed "BITS OF FLUFF, The Girls Who Really Care Are The Girls That Matter," and also a page headed "THE HIDDEN HAND IN ENGLAND." This last ends with the "idea" that: "We must always be gentlemen, but don't let us always be fools." It contains also "The Girl from 'Frisco, The Great Kalem Film Series, Episode X." It advertises "Tatooing," "Free—Pocket rubber stamp of your name and address," "Psoriasis," and "Handsome Men are, etc." It also wonders "Who is the Scottish peer who paid, etc. . . ."

Some of these features are to be discovered in older and better known papers: Both the hidden hand and the peer.

The "People's Friend" produces crocheting and Annie S. Swan. The editor personally addresses his supporters in the following vignette:—

A WORD OF CHEER.

I HOPE you are all keeping duly cheerful in these somewhat uncheerful times. We are walking through the dark at present, but our faces are towards the dawn, to which every fearful step brings us nearer; the perils and discomforts of the way will soon be over. So let us keep our faces bright to meet the brightness that will shortly shine upon them. That is the message the "Friend" would bring you and all we who help to write and turn out your welcome weekly visitor seek to do our best to brighten your homes every time we come. I trust that the "Friend" enters every home it goes to like a ray of sunshine. That is what we all want it to do.

YOUR EDITOR AND FRIEND.

And I dare say it does, you know—along with the "Astrological pronouncements. . . . Advice on Health, Business, Marriage." This paper, at a superficial glance, does not appear to be one of the most benighted. One must not forget the distinction between papers for "harmless" amusement of the poor: cheap sweets, barley sugar; and papers definitely malignant, definitely run to maintain certain superstitions, oppressions, monopolies.

Against this one must set the positive achievement of publishers like Mr. John Dent (yes, despite his publication of "Everyman" (the periodical)[)], for his production of classic books in cheap format. I remember that twenty years ago there was even an edition of standard fiction at a penny. I do not know how far it got beyond Scott and Dumas (j'avais alors douze ans) but its disappearance is regrettable.

"Home Chat" shows on its cover a young lady in red, seated upon an ebony piano-stool in what appears to be a bath-room; at least, I have never seen just this peculiar blue and white tiling used in any other architectural feature.

"The Church Times" . . . but why go on with this camouflage? Christ Himself, His brilliant remarks, His attractive personality, His profound intuitions, being now scarcely more than a bit of camouflage draped over a corporate body, or, rather, several corporate bodies styling itself and themselves, "His Church." These corporations are useful to various people and participants; so effective is the camouflage that only now has someone in America let out the egregious cat that Lincoln once consorted with free thinkers, read Payne and Voltaire, wrote an essay in accord with their beliefs, *and that this did not ruin his character.*

For the rest of the camouflage—the part that is not religious—I think there lies this much under it. Labour and Capital are in a race towards internationalism. In this race Capital will almost indubitably arrive first. It would be, after all, so infinitely easier for Capital to arrive; she has crossed so many boundary lines, as I write this.

If after the war we see sporadic outbreaks of "nationalism," they will be all so much time gained for Capital, so much time lost to the internationalisation of Labour; they will allow Capital just so many more months or years in which to perfect its organisation.

From my personal point of view, as an artist, it is infinitely preferable that there should be Internationalism *of any sort* than that there should be nationalism. Civilisation has everything to gain by internationalism, by tunnels, by aerial posts. Even Labour has everything to gain by an internationalisation of Capital in so much as it will, when realised, bring the economic question into more clear definition.

I think I write this with as much detachment as any man can write anything. It seems to me that every poor man who joins a national movement of any sort acts against his own interest.

The sooner we are international, the sooner shall we escape the tyranny of uniform laws for great areas. I do not mean this as paradox. The thing will be too big for this form of stupidity, au fond, a bigotry of demanding uniform moral codes for different races and climates.

Au fond, I think this war has come either because Germany is not governed by capitalists, or because those capitalists were shut out of some larger ring.

As a sub-heading under that last sentence I can but quote and re-quote the answer I got from a maker of war materials, in, I think, 1912. Never having met a man of his profession before, I asked his views on universal peace. He said, "You will never get universal peace as long as you have 2,000,000,000 dollars invested in the making of war machinery."

THIRDLY: International Capital is under the present state of things, very nearly irresponsible. I am by no means sure that during the period when Capital shall be internationalised and before Labour has been so internationalised, international capital might not very well focus the force of the world's arms upon any section of the planet which too daringly attempted to interfere with, tax, or restrict the action of Capital.

FOURTHLY, these are the thoughts of an amateur in these matters, of one who has turned from the, to him, far more serious matter, that of making poetry, of considering the nature of individual man retired within the recesses of his own subjectivity, within what Swedenborg would have called "his interiors."

On the other side of the question: I believe that no people will be troublesome to their rulers if allowed a sufficiency of orgies and fiestas. The pagan world has much to teach our present parvenu rulers.

Let us leave these matters and note the tone of the "Church Times." The existing marriage and divorce laws are so iniquitous that one's moral contempt for them is inexpressible. It is proposed to amend them. Cosmo Ebor: Walter Runciman and their gallery burst out with "we regard them (the ameliorations) as running counter to the consistent teachings of Christ." They are backed up by an unsigned editorial: "And since our

Christian rule, based by our Lord on the natural law from the beginning, requires monogamy. . . ."

King Solomon is our witness.

"neither of them (parties in marriage) is free to contract a new marriage while the other party lives."

Then follow a few citations of liberties permitted by early bishops (ref. Origen) to prevent worse evils; also opinion of Theodore of Canterbury, but

"Nothing of the kind, however, has been allowed by the Western Church for many centuries."

By all means take the Middle Ages for a model. "Church Times" continues that second marriages while wife or husband is alive may be legal, as being granted by the State, not really dissolving the first marriage, but permitting a mild form of polygamy. "But no member of the Church can rightly avail himself of this liberty without the express permission of the spiritual authority. Such permission is not granted in the English Church."

The "Church Times" says it is right to oppose extension of such permission given by the civil power, and ends up with: "The State of South Carolina" (well known as the apex of contemporary intelligence) "did in the year 1877 wisely abolish the practice."

There are, the astronomers tell us, several millions of suns, with an equal number of solar systems attached, but these Christian matoids still go on believing that they have had a private wireless from the boss of the conglomeration, and that to them alone has been revealed the particular set of taboos that most puts His godly back up. There is also the State of S. Carolina. I grant them, at least, originality in dragging up this black and tan community as a model for enlightened nations.

(A Bill was also introduced into one of the "black and tan" by-elections for the annulment of all marriages between whites. This was in one or other of the Carolinas.)

The "Church Times" correspondence col. tells one party that "the consent of the vicar must be obtained"; another that "We know of one case in which a woman acts as 'scout-master,' but we do not know if the arrangement is officially recognised."

(The woman probably goes covered "because of the angels," otherwise we see no objection.)

Further: "The Roman Church forbids any person to demand cremation for his own body or for that of another." J. L. M. is told "No, the unbaptized are incapable of receiving the grace." Zeta is told re/ some question apparently about souls of some sort or other. 1. "They are taken to be in enjoyment of the beatific vision. 2. Mr, Chesterton's 'Short History' could not be used as a text book." Another is told that the first council of Toledo forbade priests to bear arms, forbade even the ordination of those who had served in the army. (So there now!)

Some of these people are as quaint as any Fraser has enumerated in his discussion of Africa. Macassar Oil; Nervine; Fits, "Epilepsy"; vie with the ads. of religious books printed by Skeffington, by Macmillan; vestments and governesses strive to get from one place to another. "A priest wanted"; "Irish Incumbent," "Head, Hands, Heart of Girls 8–18 Trained at . . . . Many successes in music examinations." Resident master in holy orders wanted. "Lady (by birth) young, well educated, etc. . . ." "Gentleman, middle-aged, refined, alone, requires situation, COMPANION to an elderly gentleman who needs care and attention. No gardening. Steady, cheerful, etc."

"Required two gentlewomen, sisters or friends, as COOK and HOUSE-PARLOURMAID."

(Possibly would suit a knight's widow or indigent baroness.)

"Artificial teeth bought," jig-saw puzzles, Diabetes, "Safety from raids—clergyman's wife takes P.G.'s," "Magazine for localisation," "Girls' Friendly," "The Gospel Stamps," "Church Literature," ad infinitum.

(*To be concluded.*)

19 [20]. ? Versus Camouflage
JANUARY 10, 1918

"Je n'aurais jamais fait."—BRANTÔME.

THE market value of man per head depends somewhat upon the supply. It is to the advantage of the purchasers to keep this value fairly low. The populace, as the only producer of more populace, has a monopoly of the production. This monopoly has never, so far as we know, been gripped and used by the populace to its own special advantage.

Mr. W. H. Hudson in "The Purple Land that England Lost" describes a country where men were too scarce. Too high a value per head per labouring human may endanger the civilisation of any given area, i.e., we may arrive at a condition of primitiveness, a state of affairs when no one will do anything for, or even in co-operation with, anyone else; as, per example, the flat, dull and nearly useless condition of much of rural New England to-day. The danger of this sort of set-back, this relapse into pastoral inanity, is, however, only operative when the relatively high value of labour is accompanied by an inability or an unwillingness to co-operate; by a lack of interest in diversity, by a lack of impetus in dividing and diversifying the modes of expending energy.

The repopulationists, in yelling for more and more populace, forget or conceal the fact that a few brains are of more use in defending a country than a large lot of human bodies. A few more skilful professors of chemistry would be worth a number of regiments, and, in the end, cheaper to produce and maintain.

It is not only conceivable but highly probable that early civilisations disappeared when, either by invasions of barbarians or by uprisings of the lower inhabitants, the skilled men, the scholars, the intellectuals of the country, were exterminated. (The art of trepanning was known in South America ages ago and for as many ages forgotten. We now know this by the discovery of skulls mended with silver plates around which the bone has re-grown.)

The danger to civilisation lies not so much in destroying a score or so million human beings, as in destroying perhaps half a million of the intelligent. The restrengthening of any nation or party depends far more upon gathering to it the intelligent, and in enlightening such populations as it has, than in a senseless multiplication.

Notwithstanding these facts, which it is decidedly unpleasant of me, and decidedly bad form for me, to mention, we find the publications to which I have drawn the reader's attention busied almost if not all of them in the construction of camouflage, in a diverse-appearing but fundamentally unified endeavour to prevent thought, or at least to deaden it, to damp it down, to prevent, if not thought, at least any vigour, any explorativeness, but, *above all, any accuracy,* in popular thinking.

Whether it be the timorous treading of the "Spectator," and that sort of press, deploring the unusual *in all its forms;* whether it be the grab-the-Earth tone of "Chambers," or the suet-pudding roll of Mr. Bart Kennedy's phrases, or the silliness of the illustrated weeklies and fashion papers, or the commonsense exterior of Mr. Bottomley, or the sweet-reasonableness of the papists, or the unspeakable stupidity of the "Church," or the epilepsy of the chapel, or the plot full of lacunae from the pen of the cheap fictioneer, it all goes into camouflage.

Is all this necessary? Is the stuff under the camouflage worth all this painting?

Roughly, this canvas and cording seem to be spread over a few very simple matters: one, that Christianity is no longer believed in by a number of enlightened people. Some humane principle, as, for example, the "fraternal deference" of Confucius would, if introduced, finish off Christianity. The German, seeing that Christianity was ready for extinction, took, in his usual blunt-headedness, the wrong end of the stick. He tried to substitute the ethics of the alligator. This is what Mr. Yeats would call attempting to "restore an irrevocable past."

The principles of Confucius will do quite as well, probably better than those of the Gospels; any humane ethics would probably serve; at least they would free us from the plague of vendors of taboos, and practitioners of sacerdotal monopolies; from bigots who will pretend to a right, a sort of droit du seigneur, to interfere in other men's private lives. This defines the camouflage of the religious and semi-religious publications, put up mostly, but not entirely, by people with a definite material interest in Christianity.

The other papers are camouflage over the "economic situation." Is this necessary? Do we not all know that there is a tension between capital and labour? Will this great cat and its infinite progeny stay forever in its various and commodious bags?

Since presumably "Capital" in the abstract desires the enslavement of "labour" in the abstract, the docile, ductile enslavement; since "Labour" in the abstract desires the annihilation of capitalists; is there any reason why the intellectual, if he exists, should not discuss the two forces cleanly and clearly, seeing presumably nothing but his own destruction in the uncontrolled reign either of capital or of labour-with-its-present-mentality?

The capitalist (perhaps one per cent. of him) might keep a few intellectuals in his scullery. I am inclined to think one per cent. a rather excessive estimate.

Labour? I doubt if the intellectual life is much led in Petrograd as managed by Trotsky-Lenin. My domicile has three rooms, one of them exceeding small. I feel that a lodger, chosen at his own instigation, would be an incursion and, more or less, an interruption. I prefer some more temperate treatment of financial inequality. Tsarist Russia has got what she played for. Any aristocracy or ruling class that does not work and sweat to educate the people under it is bound to go down in blood, and I am inclined to think it deserves to. The German ruling caste is probably more firmly fixed than any other in Europe or America. I have already, in these columns, said my say of the German educational system, the philosophy underlying it, and my reasons for condemning it fundamentally; but the German class is seated firmly because it has worked to educate its populace *in certain directions.* It has had perhaps only one blind spot, or has offered its people facilities for vision along every other line, if only they will bow down to the particular national fetich.

It has been the brag of English and American commerce for at least two decades that "Brains are cheap." For the folly of that hucksters' slughorn England and America are now paying.

It seems to me desirable that no future bills, or at least fewer future bills of this sort should be "run up." Or conversely, it seems advisable to do away with a good deal of the "current magazine, and periodical" camouflage.

I have endeavoured in this little series of articles to indicate certain phases of "current magazine and periodical" activities or declivities or whatever the just term may be. Their aim, as stated, would seem to be a clogging rather than an aiding of the nation's mental activities.

There remains, in Mazzini's terms, "education." I think he spoke both of that of the press and that of the schools. It might be not inadvisable to do away with the parson altogether, and apply the Church endowments to a betterment of the local schools.

It is undoubtedly a good thing for the people of scattered communities to meet once a week. Too great a seclusion may breed a sort of barbarous dullness. This excuse is often given for the continuing of church services after a religious belief is extinct. The same purpose would be served if a rather better village schoolmaster were provided, and if on the Sabbath he should discourse on some literary or scientific subject, (it might be well to avoid politics and economics, leaving the "Lord's Day" a day of peace, and preventing the informative flow of words from dropping into argument). By providing, not a clerk in orders, but a free man with a university education, the ground would be cut away from those good Tories who argue that the Church should be kept up because "at least it keeps a gentleman" (or something more or less like one) in every parish.

Of the two chief branches of camouflage, the religious is the less real. I mean that enlightened people are practically through with it. It is a moribund issue. It has been burbling along for two thousand years. It is really much more easy to settle, or dispose of.

The economic reality is not only "under discussion," but the discussion is new; it is full of new and constantly renewed complications. Intelligent people are by no means of one mind. All one can pray for is more honesty and less camouflage. The thing is so tremendously difficult that we need every scrap of honesty and every scrap of intelligence that can be focussed on it. Only German Emperors and Bolsheviks see the thing as a quite simple matter.

Here is the future struggle. In the affairs of culture the peace terms are much more easy to settle: we should by all means keep Shakespeare. Let the Kaiser take Jahweh (preferably to the island of Elba). The monotheistic temperament has been the curse of our time.

Works Cited and Consulted

Digital editions of periodicals cited in this book may be found at www.modjourn.org. They have not been listed separately below.

Arnold, Matthew. "The Scholar Gypsy." *The Poetical Works of Matthew Arnold.* London: Oxford University Press, 1945.

Ashley, Mike. *The Age of the Storytellers: British Popular Fiction Magazines, 1880–1950.* London: British Library, 2006.

Baron, Wendy. *Perfect Moderns: A History of the Camden Town Group.* Aldershot, England: Ashgate, 2000.

Baudelaire, Charles-Pierre. *Selected Writings on Art and Literature.* New York: Penguin Classics, 2006.

Berger, John. *Ways of Seeing.* London: British Broadcasting Corporation, 1972.

Bernier, Georges. *"La Revue blanche": Paris in the Days of Post-Impressionism and Symbolism.* New York: Wildenstein, 1983.

Blizard, Dawn. "Authentic Modernism: Literature, Painting and the Revaluation of Art in the Early Twentieth Century." Ph.D. diss., Brown University, 2009.

Borges, Jorge Luis. *Other Inquisitions, 1937–1952.* Trans. Ruth L. C. Simms. New York: Simon and Schuster, 1965.

Bornstein, George. *Material Modernism: The Politics of the Page.* Cambridge: Cambridge University Press, 2001.

Brooker, Peter. *Bohemia in London: The Social Scene of Early Modernism.* Houndmills, England: Palgrave Macmillan, 2004.

Carswell, John. *Lives and Letters: A. R. Orage, Beatrice Hastings, Katherine Mans-*

field, John Middleton Murry, S. S. Koteliansky, 1906–1957. London: Faber and Faber, 1978.

Chielens, Edward E. *American Literary Magazines: The Eighteenth and Nineteenth Centuries.* New York: Greenwood, 1986.

———. *American Literary Magazines: The Twentieth Century.* New York: Greenwood, 1992.

Churchill, Suzanne W., and Adam McKible, eds. *Little Magazines and Modernism: New Approaches.* Aldershot: Ashgate, 2007.

Clair, Colin. *A History of Printing in Britain.* New York: Oxford University Press, 1966.

Clarke, Bruce. "Dora Marsden and Ezra Pound: *The New Freewoman* and 'The Serious Artist.'" *Contemporary Literature* 33 (1992): 91–112.

Clifford, Lucy Lane. *The Dominant Note.* New York: Dodd, Mead, 1897.

Dujardin, Édouard. *De Stéphane Mallarmé au prophète Ezéchiel, et essai d'une théorie de réalisme symbolique.* Paris: Mercure de France, 1919.

Ellmann, Richard. *James Joyce.* New York: Oxford University Press, 1959.

Ensor, R. C. K. *England, 1870–1914.* Oxford: Clarendon, 1936.

Esenwein, J. Berg, and Mary Elanor Roberts. *The Art of Versification.* Springfield, Mass.: Home Correspondence School, 1920.

Faxon, Frederick Winthrop. *"Ephemeral Bibelots": A Bibliography of Modern Chap-Books.* Boston: Boston Book, 1903.

Finkelstein, David, ed. *Print Culture and the Blackwood Tradition, 1805–1930.* Toronto: University of Toronto Press, 2006.

Fitzgerald, F. Scott. *The Great Gatsby.* New York: Scribner's, 1925.

Gallup, Donald. *Ezra Pound: A Bibliography.* Charlottesville: University Press of Virginia, 1983.

Garvey, Ellen Gruber. *The Adman in the Parlor: Magazines and the Gendering of Consumer Culture, 1880s to 1910s.* New York: Oxford University Press, 1996.

———. "What Happened to the Ads in Turn-of-the-Century Bound Magazines, and Why." *Serials Librarian* 37, no. 1 (1999): 83–91.

Gold, Arthur, and Robert Fizdale. *Misia.* New York: Knopf, 1980.

Gray, Stephen. *Beatrice Hastings: A Literary Life.* Johannesburg: Penguin, 2004.

Hamnett, Nina. *Laughing Torso.* London: Virago, 1984.

Hartley, L. P. *The Go-Between.* London: Penguin, 1985.

Hastings, Beatrice. *The Maids' Comedy: A Chivalric Romance in Thirteen Chapters.* London: Stephen Swift, 1911 (also serialized in *The New Age*).

Hoffman, Frederick J., Charles Allen, and Carolyn F. Ulrich. *The Little Magazine: A History and a Bibliography.* 2nd ed. Princeton: Princeton University Press, 1947.

Huneker, James. *Egoists: A Book of Supermen.* New York: Scribner's, 1909.

Jackson, A. B. *"La Revue blanche" (1889–1903): Origine, influence, bibliographie.* Paris: Minard, 1960.

Jensen, Robert. *Marketing Modernism in Fin-de-Siècle Europe.* Princeton: Princeton University Press, 1996.

Joyce, James. *Ulysses.* New York: Modern Library, 1961.

Martin, Wallace. *"The New Age" Under Orage: Chapters in English Cultural History.* Manchester: Manchester University Press, 1967. Available at www.mod journ.org.

Meyer, Susan E. *America's Great Illustrators.* New York: Galahad, 1989.

Mill, John Stuart. *On Bentham and Coleridge.* New York: Harper, 1962.

Mitch, David. *The Rise of Popular Literacy in Victorian England.* Philadelphia: University of Pennsylvania Press, 1992.

Monroe, Harriet. *A Poet's Life: Seventy Years in a Changing World.* New York: Macmillan, 1938.

Moody, A. David. *Ezra Pound: Poet, a Portrait of the Man and His Work.* Vol. 1, *The Young Genius, 1885–1920.* Oxford: Oxford University Press, 2007.

Mott, Frank Luther. *A History of American Magazines.* 5 vols. Cambridge: Harvard University Press, 1930–1968.

North, Michael. *Reading 1922: A Return to the Scene of the Modern.* Oxford: Oxford University Press, 1999.

Peterson, Theodore. *Magazines in the Twentieth Century.* 2nd ed. Urbana: University of Illinois Press, 1964. Digital version available at www.modjourn .org.

Pound, Ezra. *The Letters of Ezra Pound, 1907–1941.* Ed. D. D. Paige. New York: Harcourt, 1950.

———. *Make It New.* New Haven: Yale University Press, 1935.

———. *Pound/Joyce.* Ed. Forrest Read. New York: New Directions, 1967.

———. *Pound/Lewis.* Ed. Timothy Materer. New York: New Directions, 1985.

———. *The Selected Letters of Ezra Pound to John Quinn, 1915–1924.* Ed. Timothy Materer. Durham: Duke University Press, 1991.

———. "Small Magazines." *English Journal* 19 (1930): 689–704. Digital version available at www.modjourn.org.

Preface to *Some Imagist Poets, 1915.* Ed. Richard Aldington and H[ilda]. D[oolittle]. Boston: Houghton Mifflin, 1915.

Rainey, Lawrence. *Institutions of Modernism: Literary Elites and Public Culture.* New Haven: Yale University Press, 1999.

Reed, David. *The Popular Magazine in Britain and the United States, 1880–1960.* Toronto: University of Toronto Press, 1997.

Richards, I. A. *Principles of Literary Criticism.* New York: Harcourt, 1925.

Sader, Marion. *Comprehensive Index to English-Language Little Magazines, 1890–1970.* 8 vols. Milwood, N.Y.: Kraus-Thomson, 1976.

Scott, Thomas L., and Melvin J. Friedman, eds., with the assistance of Jackson R. Bryher. *Pound/"The Little Review,"* New York: New Directions, 1988.

Stansky, Peter. *On or About December 1910: Early Bloomsbury and Its Intimate World.* Cambridge: Harvard University Press, 1997.

Steele, Tom. *Alfred Orage and the Leeds Art Club, 1893–1923.* Worcester: Scolar, 1990.

Stirner, Max. *The Ego and His Own.* Trans. Steven T. Byington. New York: Benjamin R. Tucker, 1907.

Stokes, Roy. *Michael Sadleir, 1888–1957.* Metuchen, N.J.: Scarecrow, 1980.

Sullivan, Alvin, ed. *British Literary Magazines.* 4 vols. Westport, Conn.: Greenwood, 1984–1986.

Synge, John Millington. *Poems and Translations.* Churchtown: Cuala, 1909.

Taupin, René. *L'Influence du symbolism français sur la poésie américaine (de 1910 à 1920).* Paris: Honoré Champion, 1929.

Washington, Booker T. *My Larger Education: Being Chapters from My Experience.* Garden City, N.Y.: Doubleday, 1911.

Wilde, Oscar. *The Writings of Oscar Wilde.* Vol. 3, *The Happy Prince and Other Fairy Tales.* London: A. R. Keller, 1907.

Williams, Raymond. *Culture and Society, 1780–1950.* New York: Columbia University Press, 1983.

Wilson, Edmund. *Axel's Castle: A Study of the Imaginative Literature of 1870–1930.* New York: Scribner's, 1931.

Woolf, Virginia. *The Captain's Death Bed and Other Essays.* London: Hogarth, 1950.

———. *Jacob's Room.* Richmond, U.K.: Hogarth, 1922.

———. *Letters of Virginia Woolf.* Vol. 1. Ed. Nigel Nicholson and Joanne Trautmann. New York: Harcourt, Brace, 1975.

———. *Mr. Bennett and Mrs. Brown.* Richmond, U.K.: Hogarth, 1928.

———. *Mrs. Dalloway.* Richmond, U.K.: Hogarth, 1925.

Zuilen, A. J. van. *The Life Cycle of Magazines.* Uithoorn, the Netherlands: Graduate, 1977.

Index

Page numbers in **bold face** refer to illustrations and tables. The Appendix is not included in this index; see www.modjourn.org for the searchable file.

abstraction, 35
Academy, The, 12
Adams, Samuel Hopkins, 120, 121, 127
advertising, 20–24, 29–31, 42–43, 47, 51, 52, 54, 55, 59, 60, 112–117, 118–142, 145, 169, 189, 202, 205, 210; American vs. British, 181–184; circulation and, 31, 127; data, 66, 71, 72; *Family Herald,* 20, **21**; library copies bound without, 140, 169, 197, 206; *Midland,* 38–39, **39**, 40; modernist magazine, 29–31, 35–43, 112–117, 118–142; *The New Age,* 85, 119, 153–154, **155**, 171; *Poetry,* 36–37, **37**, 38, 122–124, **124**, 125–126, 128; relationship between readers and, 126–127; *La Revue blanche,* 81, 83; *Rhythm,* 112–115, **115**, 116, **116**, 117; *Scribner's,* 128–129, **130**, 131, **132**, 133, **134**, 135–136, **136**, 137, **138**, **139**, 140–142; *World's Work,* 172, 181, **182–182**, 183–184, **185**, 186–187; World War I and, 136–141
Africa, 192–193
Aldington, Richard, 11, 34
Allied Artists Association, 105

American Magazine, 120
Anderson, Margaret, 3, 7, 12, 13
annotation, 214–216
annuals, 48
Answers, 15
Antidote, The, 36, 56
Apple (of Beauty and Discord), The, xii, 57
archive, 42–43, 140, 169; digitization and, 198–222; hole in the, 140, 169, 196–222
Art moderne, L', poster for, 80, **80**
art nouveau, 80, **80**
Art of Versification, The (ad in *Poetry*), 36–37, **37**
Ashley, Mike, *Age of the Storytellers: British Popular Fiction Magazines, 1880–1950,* 62–63
Athenaeum, The, 7, 8, 14, 48
Atlantic Monthly, The, 127, 131, 190–191, 193
audience, 44, 48, 52, 54, 145, 146–147, 153, 165, 181

Baker, Ray Stannard, "Negro Suffrage in a Democracy," 191

Banks, Dorothy "Georges," 96, 110, 111; *Katherine Mansfield,* from *Rhythm,* **107**, 110; *The New Spirit in Art and Drama,* from *Rhythm,* **107**, 110
Baron, Wendy, *Perfect Moderns,* 103
Baudelaire, Charles, 11, 27, 32
Bell, Vanessa, 104
Belloc, Hilaire, 12
Benjamin, Judah, 167
Benjamin, Walter, 75
Bennett, Arnold, 50, 152, 153, 161, 168
Berger, John, *Ways of Seeing,* 76
Bergson, Henri, 88–90
Berlin, 78, 83–84
Bernier, Georges, 79
Bibelot, The, 4, 41
bibelots, 41, 60, 211
binding, 42
Binckes, Faith, 91
Binyon, Laurence, 90–91
biweeklies, 48
Blackwood's, 8, 50–51, 143–144
Blaker, Hugh, 165
Blast, 7, 12, 14, 51, 52, 91, 96, 100, 102, 104, 105, 106, 111, 145, 214
Blizard, Dawn, 77, 87
Bloomsbury, 103–105
Blue Review, The, 75
bohemia, 103–105
Bookman, The, 15, 69
Book News Monthly, 4
Bornstein, George, 76; *Material Modernism,* 75
Brieux, Eugène, 162
Brigham, Johnson, 40
British Weekly, The, 15
broadsheet (term), 46
Bronner, Milton, 11
Brooker, Peter, *Bohemia in London,* 102–103, 106
Brown University, 205, 206; Library, 42
Brzeska, Sophie, 95, 103
Byington, Steven, 11

Calderon, George, 163–165, 167
Camden Town, 103–105

Carnegie, Dale, 36; *How to Win Friends and Influence People,* 36
Carswell, John, *Lives and Letters,* 94
Carter, Huntly, 85–87, 88–94, 152, 153, 162–163
cataloging, 212–213, 221
categorization, magazine, 16–18, 44–72; audience, 44, 48, 52, 54, 145, 146–147, 149, 153, 165, 181; circulation, 47, 52, 59, 62, 63, 71, 72, 145, 146, 147, 165, 171, 172, 189, 196; content, 48, 53–55, 59, 63–66, 71, 72, 147, 150–153, 154–167, 187, 197; data and, 66–73, 147–149; dates, 47, 48, 54; duration, 48, 51, 54, 59; editors and publishers, 47, 52–53, 54, 148, 165, 167, 208; information provided in studies of magazines, 47, **47**, 48; language, 48, 54, 67, 70–71; little magazines, 55–60; mass magazines, 60–62; periodicity, 16, 47, 48–49, 54; places, 54; Pound on, 16–18, 44; price, 48–51, 54; size and format, 48, 51–52, 54, 148, 165–66, 171; terminology and, 45–47, 50–51, 61; title, 47; volume and issue data, 47
Cather, Willa, 60, 61
Cavalier, The, 36
celebrity culture, 180
Century Illustrated, 66, 131
Cézanne, Paul, 76, 81
Chambers, Robert W., 188
Chambers' Journal, 15
Chap-Book, 31
chapbooks, 31, 60
Chekhov, Anton, 81, 162, 213
Chester, George Randolph, 188, 189
Chicago, 8, 9, 10, 13, 51, 122
Chielens, Edward E., 47; *American Literary Magazines,* 47
Christian Herald, The, 15
Christianity, 16, 17–18
Churchill, Suzanne, *Little Magazines and Modernism: New Approaches,* 58–59
Church Review, 15
Church Times, The, 15
cigarette ads, 135–36, **136**
cinema, 27, 172–73, 174–75, **176**, 187

circulation, 47, 52, 59, 62, 63, 71, 72, 127, 127, 145–147, 165, 171, 189, 196

cities, 27–29; modernity as urban condition, 27–29, 40

Civil War, 190, 191

Clarke, Bruce, 10

Clifford, Lucy Lane, 49

College English, 24

Colliers, 63, 120, 146

commerce, 27–31. *See also* advertising

concordances, 68

Conference of Eastern College Librarians (1935), 43

Conrad, Joseph, 65, 143, *Heart of Darkness,* 144, 192

consumerism, 27, 29–30

content, 48, 53–55, 59, 63–66, 71, 72, 147, 150–167, 187, 197; *The New Age,* 147, 150–167, 170–171

Cook, E. Wake, 165

Cooke, M. L., 179

copying, 198

copyright, 209, 211, 219–220

Cosmopolitan, 63, 65–66, 188–189, 193

Country Life in America (ad in *Midland*), 38–39, **39**

Cover-to-Cover Initiative, 206

Craig, Cordon, 59

Crane, Stephen, 61, 65

crank papers, 16–17

Crisis: A Record of the Darker Races, The, 56, 192

critical magazines, 55, 56, 64, 65

Cubism, 12, 92

da Costa, John, 133, 135

Dana, 74

data, 44, 47, 54, 66–72, 147–149; advertising, 66, 71, 72; collection of, 66–72; digitization, 198–222; metadata, 205, 212–214, 221

database, 70–72, 202, 212–214, 219

dates, 47, 48, 54

Davis, Charles Belmont, 188, 189

Degas, Edgar, 87

Denis, Maurice, 81

Derain, André, 100; *Creation,* from *Rhythm,* 100, **101**

Dial, The, 7, 13–14, 55, 58, 75; Pound and, 13–14

Dickinson, Emily, 10, 34

digitization, 41, 66, 70–72, 119–120, 127, 140, 142, 149, 150, 154, 169, 198–222; annotation, 214–216; cataloging, 212–213, 221; distinction between transcription and simulation in, 199–204; imaging, 212; metadata representation, 213–214; OCR programs, 199, 200, 202–206, 217; reproduction, 217; retrieval, 218–219; rights management, 219–220; selection of magazines for, 207–211; storage, 216–217

Dismorr, Jessie, 96, 99, 106; *Izidora,* from *Rhythm,* **106,** 107

Doolittle, Hilda (H.D.), 3, 9, 34

Doubleday and Company, 38, 172

Douglas, Lord Alfred, 36, 56

Doyle, Arthur Conan, 22–23, 38, 61

Dreiser, Theodore, 38, 105; "Ellen Adams Wrynn," 105

Dresden, 89, 90, 92

Du Bois, W.E.B., 56, 192

Dujardin, Édouard, 33–34; *Les Lauriers sont coupés,* 33–34; *De Stéphane Mallarmé au prophète Ezéchiel,* 34

Dukes, Ashley, 152, 153, 162, 163

duration, 48, 51, 54, 59

Dyson, Will, 111; *Progress,* from *The New Age,* 111, **114**

eclectic magazines, 55, 56

Edinburgh Review, 15, 46

Edison, Thomas A., 172

editorship, 52–53, 54, 148, 165, 167, 208; Pound and, 6–7, **7,** 8–14, 53, 144. *See also specific magazines and editors*

education, 30, 187; college teaching, 179; public, 27, 29, 177–179

egoism, 11

Egoist, The, 6, 7, 10, 11, 14, 35, 53, 74, 88, 104, 119; Pound and, 11

elder magazines, 119, 126, 127, 128; advertising, 128–142

Eliot, T. S., 2, 9, 11, 12, 13, 79, 103, 143;
  "The Love Song of J. Alfred Prufrock,"
  9; Pound and, 2, 9, 11; *The Waste Land,*
  2, 13, 35
Ellmann, Richard, 2–3
Enemy, The, 145
English Journal, The, 24, 119
English Review, The, 4, 7, 8, 15, 46, 50, 53,
  58, 83, 84, 194, 208; digitization, 207;
  Pound and, 7
Ensor, R.C.K., *England, 1870–1914,* 49
"ephemeral bibelots," 31–32, 211
Epstein, Jacob, 50, 87, 104; *Rock Drill,* 87–
  88
Esenwein, J. Berg, 36–37; *The Art of Public Speaking,* 36; *Writing the Photoplay,*
  36–37
eugenics, 152, 161–62, 170
Everybody's Magazine, 38
Exile, The, 12
experimentalism, 35–36, 55
extensible markup language (XML), 205,
  213–214, **215**

Family Herald, The, 15, 20; advertising,
  20, **21**
Fantaisistes, 96
fascism, 143
Fauvism, 88, 96–100; from *Rhythm,* 97, **97**
Faxon, Frederick Winthrop, "Ephemeral
  Bibelots," 31–32, 52
Fergusson, John Duncan, 96–102, 105,
  106, 110; *Head of a Woman,* from
  Rhythm, **108**, 110; *Seated Woman,* from
  Rhythm, **108**, 110
fiction, 64, 65, 187–189
Fifth Avenue Section, from *Scribner's,*
  129, **130**, 131
Fitzgerald, F. Scott, 38
Flaubert, Gustave, 11, 33; *Bouvard et
  Pécuchet,* 2
Fletcher, John Gould, 10, 14
Ford, Ford Madox, 3, 4, 7, 12, 53, 104, 207,
  208; Pound and, 7, 8, 9, 10
Forget-Me-Not, 15, 23
Forum, The, 193

France, 12; Impressionism, 78; magazines,
  78–83; symbolism, 33–34, 79–80
Frederick, John T., 38–40
Friesz, Othon, *Study,* from *Rhythm,* 99,
  99, 100
Frost, Robert, 9
Fry, Roger, 77, 81, 86, 87, 103, 105
Fry's Magazine, 191
Futurism, 12, 133

Gallup, Donald, *Ezra Pound: A Bibliography,* 3, 4, 5
Garver, Lee, 154
Garvey, Ellen Gruber, 29
Gaudier-Breska, Henri, 3, 50, 95, 103,
  104, 110, 111; *Dancer,* from *The New
  Age,* 88, 110, **110**; *Head of a Man,*
  from *Rhythm,* **109**, 110; *Head of a
  Woman,* from *Rhythm,* **109**, 110;
  Whitechapel Jew, from *Rhythm,* 110,
  110
genres, magazine, 16–18, 44–66, 69, 190,
  208; categorization and, 16–18, 44–72;
  little magazines, 55–60; Pound on, 16–
  18, 44. *See also specific genres*
Gentleman's Magazine, 45–46
George, W. L., 151, 153, 157–158
Géricault, Théodore, *Raft of the Medusa,*
  75–76
Germany, 11, 78, 100, 136–138; magazines,
  78, 81, 83–84
Gibson Girl, 188
Gide, André, 81
Ginner, Charles, 87, 103; *Leicester Square,*
  from *The New Age,* 111, **112**
Good Housekeeping, 193
Google Books, 217
Grant, Duncan, 104
Gray, Stephen, *Beatrice Hastings: A Liter-
  ary Life,* 94
Great Britain, 6, 7, 29, 78, 168–169, 174;
  London bohemia, 102–105; maga-
  zines, 6, 7, 10, 12, 16–25, 32, 38, 42, 45,
  50, 78, 84–117, 144–167, 169, 170–171; Pre-
  Raphaelism, 77–78; public education, 29
Guys, Constantin, 32

Haggard, H. Rider, 65
Hamnett, Nina, 103, 104, 105
Hanfstaengl ad, from *Rhythm*, 115, **116**
Harper's, 36, 131, 193
Harper's Bazar, 125, 126
Harrison, Austin, 207, 208
Hastings, Beatrice, 8, 92, 94–96, 103, 104, 152, 153, 161; *The Maid's Comedy*, 161, 166
Heal and Son ad, from *Rhythm*, 115, **115**
Heap, Jane, 13
Hemingway, Ernest, 3
Henderson, Alice Corbin, 3, 9, 125–126
Henry, O., 38
Hoffman, F. H., 4, 6, 8, 44, 55; *The Little Magazine*, 6, 55–59
Homer, Winslow, 172, 175, 187, 190
Hornung, E. W., 38
Hulme, T. E., 12, 87, 88, 100, 102, 104, 111
Huneker, James, 105; *Egoists: A Book of Supermen*, 11
Hunt, Violet, 10
Ibsen, Henrik, 81, 162

ideology, 17–18, 44
imaging, 212
Imagism, 12, 34, 120
Impressionism, 78, 141
indexes, 68–69, 194
industrialization, 28–29
Irish Homestead, The, 74

Jackson, Holbrook, 84, 96, 105
Jensen, Robert, *Marketing Modernism in Fin-de-Siècle Europe*, 35
Jerome, Jerome K., 105
John, Auguste, 104
Johnson, Jack, 191–192
journal (term), 45, 46
Joyce, James, 2–3, 7, 9–10, 11, 33, 34, 53, 79; *Dubliners*, 7; "epiphanies," 33; *Finnegan's Wake*, 74; *Portrait of the Artist as a Young Man*, 11, 74; Pound and, 2, 7, 9–10, 11; *Ulysses*, 13, 14, 30, 33, 34, 35, 36, 74
Juvenal, 152, 160–161

Kandinsky, Wassily, 100–102; *On the spiritual in Art*, 100
Kennedy, J. M., 151, 153, 156, 166
Kipling, Rudyard, 38, 60, 65, 81
Kodak ad, from *Scribner's*, 136–137, **138**, **139**
Kokoschka, Oskar, 83, 84

Ladies' Home Journal, The, 61
language, 48, 54, 67, 70–71
Lasker-Schüler, Elsa, 83
Laughlin, James, 3
Leblanc, Maurice, 188
Leclerq, Charles, 78, 79
Leeds Art Club, 84–85
leftist magazines, 55
Lessing, Bruno, 188–189
Lewis, Wyndham, 2, 3, 7, 11, 12, 57, 100, 103, 104, 106, 111, 145; as *Blast* editor, 12; drawing of Ezra Pound, *xii*; Pound and, 11, 12, 14
libraries, 196, 207, 221; bound periodicals without advertising, 140, 169, 197, 206; digital technology and, 196–198, 207–222; hole in the archive, 140, 169, 196–222
Library of Congress, 203, 213, 221
Lincoln, Abraham, 180, 187, 191
linotype, 28–29
lists, 68–69
literacy, 29, 30, 68
literary magazines, 55, 60–61
literature, 64, 65, 75
little magazines, 6, 8–10, 24, 25, 36–41, 45, 46, 52, 55–60, 65, 74, 119, 127, 208; advertising, 36–40, 85, 112–117, 119–126, 128; categorization, 55–60; study of, 144–167; terminology, 46–47, 61; visual art and, 73–117. *See also specific magazines*
Little Review, The, 6, 7, 8, 12, 13–14, 34, 35, 41, 51, 53, 55, 60, 74, 144; Pound and, 13–14
Lloyd George, David, 151, 156, 157
LOCKSS, 216
London, 6, 28, 38, 42, 78, 84, 90, 96, 100; bohemian, 102–105; population growth, 28; Pound in, 6, 12

London, Jack, 38, 60, 188
London Mercury, The, 58
Lowell, Amy, 38, 128, 133
Ludovici, Anthony, 94

magazine (term), 45–47, 50–51
Mahogany Tree, The, 32
Malatesta, Sigismondo, 11
Mallarmé, Stéphane, 34, 79, 81
Manet, Edouard, 38, 163, 167
Mansfield, Katherine, 50, 75, 94–96, 103, 104, 110; *In a German Pension*, 95
Marsden, Dora, 7, 10–11
Martin, Wallace, *The New Age Under Orage*, 53, 208
Marx, Karl, *The Communist Manifesto*, 186
Mask, The, 58, 59, 193
Masses, The, 55
mass magazines, 27–31, 38, 40, 41, 45, 47, 60–62, 127, 208; advertising, 127–142; categorization, 60–62. *See also specific magazines*
Matisse, Henri, 38
Maupassant, Guy de, 33
McAndrew, William, "How to Choose a Public-School Teacher," 177–179, 287
McCall's, 36, 61–62
McClure's, 60–61, 127, 191, 208
McGee, W. K. (John Eglington), 74
McIntosh, Hugh D., "My Reminiscences, and the Search for a White Champion," 191–192
McKible, Adam, 58
Medici, 9
Mencken, H. L., 7, 42, 105
Mercure de France, 12
metadata, 205, 212–214, 220–221; descriptive, 205; representation, 213–214; structural, 205
Metadata Object Description Schema (MODS), 214, **215**, 221
Midland, The, 38–40, 55; advertising, 38–39, **39**, 40
Mill, John Stuart, 140, 141
Millay, Edna St. Vincent, 59
modernism, 12, 20, 25, 26–43; advertising and, 29–31, 35–43, 118–142; data and, 66–73; definition of, 26, 74, 77; egoism and, 11; "high," 74; 1922 and, 209; rise of, 26–43; start of, 168–169; symbolism and, 33–35, 79–80; urbanization and, 27–29, 40; visual art, 35–38, 73–117
Modernist Journals Project (MJP), 3, 42, 169, 192, 203–206
modernist magazines: advertising and, 29–31, 35–43, 112–117, 118–142; December 1910 timing and, 168–195; digitization of, 198–222; genres and categorization, 16–18, 44–72; hole in the archive, 140, 169, 196–222; Pound's involvement with, 2–5, **5**, 6–25, 144; study of, 143–167; visual art in, 73–117. *See also specific magazines*
Modernist Studies Association, 41
modernity, 20, 25, 26–43; advertising and, 29–31, 35–43, 118–142; definition of, 26; printing process and, 28–29; rise of modernism and, 26–43; as urban condition, 27–29, 40
Modigliani, Amedeo, 104
Monroe, Harriet, 3, 7, 8–10, 34, 37–38, 59, 122–126; Ad for, from *Poetry*, 123, **124**; Pound and, 8–10, 13, 41
monthlies, 48, 50–51, 144
Moody, A. David, *Ezra Pound: Poet*, 3, 4, 6, 33
Moore, Marianne, 3
Morris, William, 163
Mosher, Thomas, 41
Mott, Frank Luther, 45–48; *History of American Magazines*, 45
"The Moving-Picture Show" (article), 172–173, 174–175, **176**
Munsey, Frank A., 30–31
Munsey's Magazine, 4, 30–31, 41, 54, 127
Murry, John Middleton, 7, 74, 88–96, 97, 103, 111, 117
music, 6; Pound on, 6, 8

Nabis, 96
Nansen, Fridtjof, 38
Nash's Magazine, 21–22

Natanson, Misia, 81, 83
Natanson, Thadée, 79, 80, 81
Nation, The, 48, 146
National Council of Teachers of English, 6, 119
National Geographic, The, 193
naturalism, 33
Nazism, 162
Neue Rundschau, Der, 81
New Age, The, 2, 4, 6, 7, 8, 13, 14–25, 48, 49, 50, 52, 53, 62, 75, 78, 79, 80–81, 84–94, 95, 96, 103, 104, 105, 144–167, 187, 194; advertising, 85, 119, 153–154, **155,** 171; art, 84–93, **93,** 94, 100, **110,** 111, **112–114;** audience, 146–147, 149, 153, 165, 171; circulation, 146, 147, 165; content, 147, 150, **150,** 151–153, 154–167, 170–171; of December 1, 1910, 149–167, 170; digitization, 203–207; editor, 148, 165, 167; format, 148, 165–166; history, 148, 166; Pound and, 2, 6, 14–25; regular contributors, 147, 165, 166; *-Rhythm* dispute, 88–96; "Studies in Contemporary Mentality," 2, 6, 14, **15,** 16–25, 119, 126, 143, 144, 160, 170, 197; study of, 144–167
New Age Project, 203–204
New Freewoman, The, 7, 14, 88, 104; Pound and, 10–11; title changes to *The Egoist,* 11
New Republic, The, 146
newspapers, 27, 29, 144; terminology, 46
New Statesman, The, 48, 49
New York, 13, 28, 38, 43, 51, 129–131; population growth, 28
New Yorker, The, 119, 127, 209
New York Times, The, 119, 122, 127, 144
Nietzsche, Friedrich Wilhelm, 11, 19, 159–160
Norris, Frank, 38
North American Review, 193
Nouvelle Revue française, La, 83

Old Moore's Almanac, 15
Ollivant, Alfred, 151, 153, 155, 157
Omega Workshops, 103, 104, 105

optical character recognition (OCR), 199, 200, 202–206, 217
Orage, A. R., 7, 8, 13–14, 52, 62, 79, 84, 85, 94–96, 103, 151, 153, 155, 160, 162, 167, 203, 206, 208
Orczy, Baroness, 38
Orwell, George, *1984,* 174

Page, Arthur W., "What is 'Scientific Management'?" 173–174, 184, 187
Page, Walter Hines, 172, 173, 179
paper (term), 45, 46
Paris, 12, 27, 51, 60, 75, 78, 81, 83, 88, 96, 102; bohemian, 104, 105; Salon, 35
People, Samuel John, 96, 99
periodicals, 45, 78; categorization of, 45–72; terminology, 45–47
periodicity, 16, 47, 48–49, 54
Peterson, Thomas, 30–31; *Magazines of the Twentieth Century,* 47
photogravure, 29
Picasso, Pablo, 38, 86, 91, 99; *Study,* 91–93
Poetry, 6, 7, 8–10, 14, 34, 35, 41, 53, 55, 61–62, 74, 119, 145, 198; advertising, 36–37, **37,** 38, 122–124, **124,** 125–126, 128; Pound and, 8–10, 11, 13, 36
poetry magazines, 55, 61, 64, 65
Pointillism, 98
Pollak, Felix, 57–58, 59, 60
popular magazines, 63–66
population growth, 28
posters, 81; *L'Art moderne,* 80, **80;** *La Revue blanche,* 80, **80,** 81; *Der Sturm* collage, 84, 85
Post-Impressionism, 86, 87, 97, 105, 163, 167, 170
Pound, Ezra, 1–25, 30, 33, 42, 43, 51, 57, 59, 67, 72, 91, 95, 96, 103, 105, 111, 127, 128, 141, 144, 210; "Alba," 41; anti-Semitism of, 143; art criticism of, 6, 8; on categorizing magazine genres, 16–18, 44; *Catholic Anthology,* 9; contributions to magazines, 2, 5, **5,** 6–25; critical writings of, 6, 8, 10, 14–25, 144; "Dawn Song," 41; *The Dial* and, 13–14; as drama critic, 8; drawing of, by Wynd-

Pound,Ezra (*continued*)
ham Lewis, *xii;* editorial involvement
in magazines, 6–7, **7**, 8–14, 53, 144;
Eliot and, 2 9, 11; as founder of modern periodical studies, 1–25; "I Gather
the Limbs of Osiris," 4; "In a Station
of the Metro," 198; Joyce and, 2, 7, 9–
10, 11; *The Little Review* and, 13–14;
Make It New, 1, 2, 17, 26; misogyny of,
11–12; as music critic, 6, 8; *The New
Age* and, 2, 6, 14–25; *The New Freewoman* and, 9–10; pen names of, 6, 8;
Poetry and, 8–10, 11, 13, 36; poetry of,
6, 10, 41, 120, 143, 198, 214; *Pound/Joyce,*
1; "The Serious Artist," 10; "Small
Magazines," 6, 24, 25, 35, 56, 119, 127;
"Studies in Contemporary Mentality,"
2, 6, 14, **15**, 16–25, 119, 126, 143, 144, 160,
170, 197
Pound, Reginald, *Mirror of the Century,*
118
Pre-Raphaelitism, 77–78
price, 48–51, 54
Princeton University, 205
printing, 27, 28–29; linotype, 28–29; rotary press, 28
Proust, Marcel, 79, 81
publications, 45
public education, 27, 29, 177–179
Punch, 15, 20

Quality Magazines ad, for *Scribner's,* 131,
132, 133
quarterlies, 16, 48, 145
Quarterly Review, 15
Quinn, John, 3, 11, 12–13, 14
Quiver, The, 15, 18

race and racism, 161–162, 175–179, 187,
190–193
radio, 27
Rameses cigarettes ad, from *Scribner's,*
135–136, **136**
Randall, Alfred E., 152, 153, 161–162
Rankin's Head Ointment ad, from *Family Herald,* 20, **21**
Read, Forrest, 2

regional magazines, 38, 55
Reed, David, *The Popular Magazine in
Britain and the United States, 1880–
1960,* **63–64**, 64, 65–66, 189
Reeve, Arthur B., 188, 189
religion, 16–17, 18, 23–24
religious periodicals, 16–18, 23
Renaissance, 9, 78
review (term), 45, 46, 50–51
Review of Reviews, The, 193
Revue blanche, La, 78–83, 84, 96; art, 78–
80, **80**, 81–83; back inside cover, 81, **82**
Revue Wagnérienne, 34
Rhythm, 73, 74, 75, 78, 88–94; advertising,
112–115, **115**, 116, **116**, 117; art, 88–94, **94**,
95–97, **97**, 98, **98**, 99, **99**, 100–101, **101**,
102–106, **106–110**, 110–115, **115**, 116, **116**,
117, **117**; and *New Age,* dispute, 88–96
Rhythmism, 90, 92, 95, 97–98, 104, 106–
117
Rice, Anne Estelle, 96, 97–100, 105, 106;
Russian Ballet, from *Rhythm,* 116, **117**;
Schehérazade, from *Rhythm,* 98, **98**, 99,
100, 106
Richards, I. A., 140, 141
Roberts, Mary Eleanor, 36
Roberts, William, 106
Robinson, E. A., 38
Romain, Jules, 34
Roosevelt, Theodore, 38, 176–177
rotary press, 28
Royal Magazine, 38
Royce, Josiah, "Provincialism," 40
Ruskin, John, 78
Russell, George (AE), 74
Rutter, Frank, 105

Sabatini, Rafael, 38, 65
Sackville-West, Vita, 104
Sader, Marion, 4; *Comprehensive Index to
English-Language Little Magazines,
1890–1970,* 57–58, 194
Sadleir, Michael, 96–97, 105; "After Gau-
guin," 100
Sanatogen ad, from *The World's Work,*
184, **185**, 186, 187, 210
Saturday Evening Post, The, 66, 146

Scholes, Robert, *Paradoxy of Modernism,* 61, 87, 128
Schwitters, Kurt, 84
scientific management, 173–174, 184, 187
Scribner Archive, 205–206
Scribner's, 4, 31, 38, 42, 63, 64, 66, 127, 128, 194; advertising, 128–129, **130**, 131, **132**, 133, **134**, 135–136, **136**, 137, **138**, **139**, 140–142; digitization, 205–206
Segonzac, André Dunoyer de: *Les Boxeurs,* from *The New Age,* 92–93, **93**, 94; *Les Boxeurs,* from *Rhythm,* **94**, 94
Seven Arts, The, 55
Shaw, George Bernard, 19, 84, 160, 162; *Man and Superman,* 160; *Pygmalion,* 38
shilling magazines, 51
Sickert, Arnold, 50
Sickert, Walter, 86–87, 92, 103, 111; "Encouragement for Art," 86–87; "Exhibititis," 87
Signac, Paul, 81
simulation, 198–199; distinction between transcription and, 199–204
Sinclair, Upton, 38
sixpenny weeklies, 48–50
size and format, 48, 51–52, 54, 148, 165–166, 171
Smart Set, The, 4, 7, 41, 55, 58, 193; Pound and, 7, 8, 41–42
Spectator, 30, 42, 48, 154, 197
Stein, Gertrude, 79
Stendhal, 11
Stephen, Leslie, 103
Stevens, Wallace, 10, 59
Stevenson, Robert Louis, 38, 65, 81
Stirner, Max, 11; *The Ego and His Own,* 11
Strand, 22, 118, 198
Sturm, Der, 78, 83–84; art, 83, **83**, 84, **85**
suffrage, 191, 193
Sullivan, Alvin, 47; *British Literary Magazines,* 47
Swift's Bacon ad, from *Scribner's,* 133, **134**, 135
Swinburne, Algernon, 33
symbolic realism, 34, 35–36
symbolism, 33, 79–80, 96; modernism and, 33–35, 79–80

synchronic reading, 170, 194–195
Synge, J. M., *Poems and Translations,* 74

Tarkington, Booth, 38
Tatler, 30, 154
Taupin, René, *L'Influence du symbolisme français sur la poésie américaine,* 33
Taylor, Frederick W., 173–174
Teasdale, Sara, 38, 59
technology, 27, 183; digital, 41, 66, 70–72, 119–120, 127, 140, 142, 149, 150, 154, 169, 198–222
Teillard, Dorothy Lamon, "Lincoln in Myth and Fact," 180, 187
television, 27, 146
Thayer, Scofield, 7, 13, 14
Titt, Tom, 111; *New Oxford Street,* from *The New Age,* 111, **113**
To-Day, 105
Tolstoy, Leo, 81
Toulouse-Lautrec, Henrí, 83
trade journals, 16
transcription and simulation, distinction between, 199–204
transportation, 27
Turkey, 135, 137, 170
Turner, J.M.W., 78
Twain, Mark, 81
Tyro, The, 12, 106, 145

Ulrich, Carolyn, 4, 6, 8, 44, 55; *The Little Magazine,* 6, 55–59
Unanimistes, 34
United States, 7, 28, 55; magazines, 7, 9–11, 13, 32, 46, 51, 128–142, 169, 170, 171–195; population growth and urbanization, 28
Upward, Allen, 151, 153, 157
urbanization, 27–29, 40

Valéry, Paul, 79
Vallotton, Félix, 81
Van Dine, S. S., 42
Van Dongen, Kees, 81
van Zuilen, A. J., *The Life Cycle of Magazines,* 145–146
Verdad, S., 151, 153, 156, 166

visual art, 35–38, 73–117, 170, 206; criticism, 6, 8, 74; marketing of, 35–36; modernism, 35–38, 73–117; in modernist magazines, 73–117; in *The New Age,* 84–93, **93,** 94, 100, **110,** 111, **112–114;** original vs. reproduction, 76–77; Pound on, 6, 8; in *La Revue blanche,* 78–80, **80,** 81, **82,** 83; in *Rhythm,* 83–94, **94,** 95–97, **97,** 98, **98,** 99, **99,** 100–101, **101,** 102–106, **106–110,** 110–115, **115,** 116, **116,** 117, **117;** in *Der Sturm,* 83, **83,** 84, **85.** *See also specific art movements and artists*

Vorticism, 8, 12, 195, 100, 102, 104, 106, 111, 133

Vuillard, Édouard, 81

Wadsworth, Edward, 100

Walden, Herwarth, 83–84

Walden, Nell, 84

Washington, Booker T., *My Large Education, Being Chapters from My Experience,* 176–177, 187, 190

Weaver, Harriet Shaw, 7, 11

Webb, Beatrice and Sidney, 49

weeklies, 29, 47, 48–50, 144, 149–150

weekly review (term), 47

Wells, H. G., 65

Wescott, Glenway, 10

West, Paul, 188, 189

West, Rebecca, 10, 11, 12, 104

Wharton, Edith, 38

Whibley, Charles, 143–144

Whistler, James Abbott McNeill, 78

Whitman, Walt, 9, 123

Wilde, Oscar, 81, 104; *The Importance of Being Earnest,* 24

Wilkins, Mary E., 38

Williams, William Carlos, 10

Wilson, Edmund, *Axel's Castle,* 33, 79

Winters, Yvor, 10

women, 18–19

Woolf, Leonard, 48

Woolf, Virginia, 27, 56, 71, 72, 77, 103, 104, 105, 168–169, 180–181, 184, 210, 211; *Jacob's Room,* 35, 48–49, 168; *Mr. Bennett and Mrs. Brown,* 168; *Mrs. Dalloway,* 35; "Walter Sickert," 105

Wordsworth, William, 69

World's Work, The, 171–188; advertising, 172, 181, **182–183,** 183–184, **185, 186–187;** audience, 181; circulation, 171; content, 172–180, 187, 190; of February 1911, 171–176, **176,** 177–188; Photo from, 175, **176;** size and format, 171

World War I, 12, 61, 128, 136–139, 141, 145, 171, 188

World Wide Web, 204, 216, 219

Worringer, Wilhelm, *Abstraction and Empathy,* 111

Wright, Willard Hunting, 7, 41–42

Wyeth, N. C., 38, 206

Yeats, William Butler, 3, 41, 61, 79, 210

Yellow Book, The, 96

Zamyatin, Yevgeny, *We,* 174